THE LOEB CLASSICAL LIBRARY

EDITED BY

E. CAPPS, PH.D., LL.D.   T. E. PAGE, LITT.D.

W. H. D. ROUSE, LITT.D.

LIVY

III

BOOKS V, VI AND VII

LIVY

WITH AN ENGLISH TRANSLATION BY
B. O. FOSTER, Ph.D.
OF STANFORD UNIVERSITY

IN THIRTEEN VOLUMES
III

BOOKS V, VI AND VII

LONDON : WILLIAM HEINEMANN
NEW YORK : G. P. PUTNAM'S SONS
MCMXXIV

Printed in Great Britain

TRANSLATOR'S PREFACE

THE Latin text of Vols. II. to IV. (comprising
Books III.–X.) has been set up, like that of Vol. I.,
from the latest revisions of the Weissenborn-Mueller
edition with German notes, except that the *Periochae*
have been reprinted from the text of Rossbach
(1910). But the spelling is that adopted by Pro-
fessors Conway and Walters in their critical edition
of Books I.–V. and Books VI.–X. (Oxford, 1914 and
1919), which is the source also of most of the rather
numerous readings which differ from those of the
Weissenborn-Mueller text, and has furnished besides
the materials from which the textual notes have
been drawn up. I have aimed to record every
instance where the reading printed does not rest on
the authority of one or more of the good MSS., and
to indicate the provenience of the emendation. In
addition to the symbols used by the Oxford editors,
I have employed Ω to designate such of the good
MSS. as are not cited specifically for some other
reading, and ς to designate one or more of the late
MSS. or early printed texts.

Besides the translations mentioned in the preface
to Vol. I. (those of Philemon Holland, George

Baker, and Canon Roberts) I have had by me the anonymous version printed in London in 1686, in folio, "for Awnsham Churchill at the Black Swan in Ave-Mary Lane, near Paternoster Row."

I am also indebted to the following editions of parts of Livy: Book III. by P. Thoresby Jones, Oxford, 1914; IV. by H. M. Stephenson, Cambridge, 1890; V. by Leonard Whibley, Cambridge, 1910; V.–VII. by Cluer and Matheson, Oxford, 1904; VI. by F. H. Marshall, Cambridge, 1908; IX. by W. B. Anderson, Cambridge, 1909, and by T. Nicklin, Oxford, 1910. The commentaries of Weissenborn-Mueller and Luterbacher have, of course, been constantly consulted.

The maps illustrating the campaign of the Allia have been adapted from Kromayer and Veith, Schlachten-Atlas zur antiken Kriegsgeschichte, published by Wagner and Debes, Leipzig.

B. O. F.

CONTENTS

CONTENTS

THE MANUSCRIPTS

V = Veronensis, 4th century.
F = Floriacensis, 9th century.
P = Parisiensis, 10th century.
E = Einsiedlensis, 10th century.
H = Harleianus prior, 10th century.
T = Thuaneus, 10th century.
t = the 1st and 2nd leaves of T, by another scribe.
B = Bambergensis, 10th or 11th century.
M = Mediceus, 10th or 11th century.
Vorm. = Vormatiensis (as reported by Rhenanus).
R = Romanus, 11th century.
U = Upsaliensis, 11th century.
D = Dominicanus, 11th or 12th century.
L = Leidensis, 12th century.
A = Aginnensis, 13th century.
a = later part of A, 14th century.
Frag. Haverk = Fragmentum Havercampianum (cf. Conway and Walters, vol. i., Praef, p. ix [1]).
M^1, M^2, etc., denote corrections made by the original scribe or a later corrector. When it is impossible to identify the corrector M^x is employed.
Ω = such of the above MSS. as contain the passage in question and are not otherwise reported.
ς = one or more of the late MSS. or early printed texts.

ABBREVIATIONS

Ald. (or ed. Ald.) = the Aldine edition, Venice, 1518

Cassiod. = Cassiodorius.

Class. Quart. = *The Classical Quarterly,* London, 1907 ff.

C.I.L. = *Corpus Inscriptionum Latinarum,* vol. i.²
   Berlin, 1893–5.

Diod. = Diodorus Siculus.

Dion. Hal. = Dionysius of Halicarnassus.

LIVY

FROM THE FOUNDING OF THE CITY

BOOK V

T. LIVI

AB URBE CONDITA

LIBER V

A.U.C.
351

I. Pace alibi parta Romani Veiique in armis erant
tanta ira odioque, ut victis finem adesse appareret.
Comitia utriusque populi longe diversa ratione facta
2 sunt.   Romani auxere tribunorum militum consulari
potestate numerum ; octo, quot nunquam antea,
creati, M.'[1] Aemilius Mamercus iterum L. Valerius
Potitus tertium Ap. Claudius Crassus M. Quinctilius
Varus L. Iulius Iulus[2] M. Postumius M. Furius Camil-
3 lus M. Postumius Albinus.   Veientes contra taedio
annuae ambitionis, quae interdum discordiarum causa
erat, regem creavere.   Offendit ea res populorum
Etruriae animos, non maiore odio regni quam ipsius
4 regis.   Gravis iam is antea genti fuerat opibus superbiaque, quia sollemnia ludorum, quos intermitti nefas

---

[1] M.' *Sigonius* (*cf.* IV. lxi. 1) : m̄ (*or* m) Ω.
[2] L. Iulius Iulus ç (*C.I.L.* i[2], *p.* 116) : m̄. iulius rullus
Ω : m̄. iulius tullus *a* : m iulius publius *L* : m̄ uilius
publius *D.*

---

[1] Livy seems to have erred through including the names of
the censors, Camillus and Albinus, in his list of tribunes,

2

LIVY

FROM THE FOUNDING OF THE CITY

BOOK V

I. PEACE was now established elsewhere, but B.C. 403
Romans and Veientes were at war, and their rage
and animosity were such that the end was clearly
at hand for those that should be vanquished. Each
people held an election very different from that of
the other. The Romans enlarged the number of
their military tribunes with consular authority, and
elected eight,[1] a greater number than ever before,
to wit, Manius Aemilius Mamercus (for the second
time), Lucius Valerius Potitus (for the third), Appius
Claudius Crassus, Marcus Quinctilius Varus, Lucius
Julius Iulus, Marcus Postumius, Marcus Furius
Camillus, Marcus Postumius Albinus. But the
Veientes, weary of annual canvassing, which was
sometimes the cause of brawls, chose a king. This
gave offence to the feelings of the Etruscan peoples,
who loathed not more the institution of kings than
the King himself. He had for some time been
hateful to the nation by reason of his wealth and
arrogance, since he had violently broken up a solemn

of whom there were at this time but six. See chap. x. § 1
and chap. xiv. § 5 and notes there.

3

A.U.C
351

5 est, violenter diremisset, cum ob iram repulsae, quod
suffragio duodecim populorum alius sacerdos ei prae-
latus esset, artifices, quorum magna pars ipsius servi
6 erant, ex medio ludicro repente abduxit. Gens
itaque ante omnes alias eo magis dedita religionibus,
quod excelleret arte colendi eas, auxilium Veientibus
7 negandum donec sub rege essent decrevit; cuius
decreti suppressa fama est Veiis propter metum
regis, qui a quo tale quid dictum referretur, pro
seditionis eum principe, non vani sermonis auctore [1]
8 habebat. Romanis etsi quietae res ex Etruria nun-
tiabantur, tamen quia omnibus conciliis eam rem
9 agitari adferebatur, ita muniebant ut ancipitia munimenta essent : alia in urbem et contra oppidanorum
eruptiones versa, aliis frons in Etruriam spectans,
auxiliis si qua forte inde venirent obstruebatur.

II. Cum spes maior imperatoribus Romanis in
obsidione quam in oppugnatione esset, hibernacula
etiam, res nova militi Romano, aedificari coepta,
consiliumque erat hiemando continuare bellum.
2 Quod postquam tribunis plebis, iam diu nullam
novandi res causam invenientibus, Romam est allatum, in contionem prosiliunt, sollicitant plebis
3 animos, hoc illud esse dictitantes quod aera militibus
sint constituta; nec se fefellisse id donum inimi-
4 corum veneno inlitum fore. Venisse libertatem

---

[1] auctore *MP'FUBD*[4]: auctorem *Vorm.?* *M*[2] (*or* *M*[1])
POEHDLα.

4

festival, which it is impious to interrupt, in his resentment of a political rebuff; and because the
suffrages of the Twelve Peoples had returned another
man as priest in preference to him, he had suddenly
carried off the actors, most of whom were his own
slaves, in the middle of the games. And so the
nation which was devoted beyond all others to
religious rites (and all the more because it excelled
in the art of observing them) voted to refuse its help
to the men of Veii, so long as they should obey a
king. This vote the Veientes would not suffer to
be mentioned, in their fear of the King, who had
a way of treating the man by whom any such saying
was reported as a leader in sedition, not as the bearer
of an idle tale. Although the Romans got word that
things were quiet in Etruria, still, because they heard
that this question came up at all their meetings,
they so constructed their works as to have a double
fortification, one facing Veii, to oppose the sallies of
the townsfolk, the other confronting Etruria, to shut
off any assistance that might come from thence.

II. As the Roman generals hoped more from a
siege than from an assault, they even began the
erection of winter quarters—a new thing to the
Roman soldier—and planned to carry the campaign
on, straight through the winter. When news of
this came to Rome, to the plebeian tribunes, who
had now for a long time been unable to hit upon
any pretext for agitation, they hurried before the
assembly and set to work upon the passions of the
commons: So this was the reason that the soldiers
had been granted pay! They had not been mistaken in thinking that this gift of their opponents
would be smeared with poison. The liberty of the

5

plebis; remotam in perpetuum et ablegatum ab urbe
et ab re publica iuventutem iam ne hiemi quidem
aut tempori anni cedere ac domos ac res invisere
5 suas. Quam putarent continuatae militiae causam
esse? Nullam profecto aliam inventuros quam ne
quid per frequentiam iuvenum eorum in quibus vires
omnes plebis essent agi de commodis eorum posset.
6 Vexari praeterea et subigi multo acrius quam
Veientes; quippe illos hiemem sub tectis suis agere,
7 egregiis muris situque naturali urbem tutantes, militem Romanum in opere ac labore nivibus pruinisque
obrutum sub pellibus durare ne hiemis quidem spatio,
quae omnium bellorum terra marique sit quies, arma
8 deponentem. Hoc neque reges neque ante tribuniciam potestatem creatam superbos illos consules
neque triste dictatoris imperium neque importunos decemviros iniunxisse servitutis, ut perennem militiam
9 facerent.[1] Quidnam illi consules dictatoresve facturi
essent, qui consularem[2] imaginem tam saevam ac
trucem fecerint? Sed id accidere haud immerito.
Non fuisse ne in octo quidem tribunis militum locum
10 ulli plebeio. Antea trina loca cum contentione
summa patricios explere solitos: nunc iam octoiuges
ad imperia obtinenda ire, et ne in turba quidem
11 haerere plebeium quemquam qui, si nihil aliud,

---

[1] *After* facerent *the MSS. have*: quod tribuni militum in
plebe Romana regnum exercerent. *Conway and Walters
bracket these words*; *cf. Class. Quart.* V. (1911) *p.* 10.
[2] consularem *Conway and Walters in their note*: pro-
consularem Ω.

commons had been sold; the young men, having B.C. 403
been permanently removed and banished from the
City and from the state, were no longer free, even
in winter and the stormy season, to see to their
homes and their affairs. What, they asked, did
their hearers suppose to be the reason for making
the service continuous? They would assuredly find
no other motive than this: lest, through the presence
in large numbers of the young men in whom lay all
the vigour of the commons, something might be
accomplished for the people's good. Moreover, they
were far more ruthlessly abused and trodden down
than were the Veientes, who, for their part, spent
the winter in their houses, safeguarding their city
by means of strong walls and natural defences,
whilst the Roman soldiers were enduring toil and
danger, overwhelmed with snows and frosts, in tents,
not even laying aside their weapons in the winter
time, a season of respite from all wars both by land
and by sea. Such slavery as this neither kings, nor the
proud consuls who came before the establishment of
the tribunician power, nor the stern authority of a
dictator, nor harsh decemvirs, had laid upon them,—
that they should wage perennial war. Pray what
would those men do if they should become consuls
or dictators, who had made the semblance of consular
authority so savage and truculent? But the commons were only getting their deserts. There had
been no room even amongst eight military tribunes
for a single plebeian. Heretofore the patricians had
been wont with the utmost exertion to fill three
places in a year: now they were advancing eight
abreast to make good their authority, and there was
never a commoner hanging on to the crowd, were it

A.U.C.
351
admoneat collegas liberos et cives eorum, non servos,
militare, quos hieme saltem in domos ac tecta re-
12 duci oporteat et aliquo tempore anni parentes liberosque ac coniuges invisere et usurpare libertatem et
creare magistratus.

13 Haec taliaque vociferantes adversarium haud im-
parem nacti sunt Ap. Claudium, relictum a collegis
ad tribunicias seditiones comprimendas, virum im-
14 butum iam ab iuventa certaminibus plebeiis, quem
auctorem aliquot annis ante fuisse memoratum est
per collegarum intercessionem tribuniciae potestatis
dissolvendae.

III. Is tum iam non promptus ingenio tantum
sed usu etiam exercitatus, talem orationem habuit:
2 "Si unquam dubitatum est, Quirites,[1] utrum tribuni
plebis vestra an sua causa seditionum semper auctores
fuerint, id ego hoc anno desisse dubitari certum
3 habeo; et cum laetor tandem longi erroris vobis
finem factum esse, tum, quod secundis potissimum
vestris rebus hic error est sublatus, et vobis et propter
4 vos rei publicae gratulor. An est quisquam qui
dubitet nullis iniuriis vestris, si quae forte aliquando
fuerunt, unquam aeque quam munere patrum in
plebem, cum aera militantibus constituta sunt, tri-
5 bunos plebis offensos ac concitatos esse? Quid illos

---

[1] Quirites D^4a: quiī OE^1D?: qur H: qui in PD?: quin
F^2F? UBE: quis L: qui V: *omitted by M.*

---

[1] See Book IV, chap. xlviii. The Appius Claudius here
mentioned was a grandson of the decemvir.

only to remind his colleagues that their soldiers were B.C. 403 not slaves but freemen and fellow citizens; whom, at least in winter, they were bound to bring back to the shelter of their houses, and to leave them some portion of the year to look after their parents, their children, and their wives, and to use their liberty and elect magistrates.

As they shouted forth these and suchlike arguments, they found an opponent not unequal to them in Appius Claudius, whom his colleagues had left behind to repress sedition on the part of the tribunes. He was a man experienced from his youth up in contentions with the plebs, and I have related how, some years before, he had advised that the intervention of their colleagues be used to break the power of the tribunes.[1]

III. The man not only had a nimble wit but was already a practised orator, and he delivered on this occasion a speech to the following effect : " If it has ever been a question, Quirites, whether it was for your sake or their own that the tribunes of the commons have always encouraged sedition, I am certain that the doubt has this year been resolved ; and not only do I rejoice that you have at length cleared up a long misunderstanding, but I congratulate both you, and on your account the state as well, that it has happened at a time, of all others, when your affairs are prospering. Or is there anyone who doubts that no wrongs which you have suffered, if haply such there have sometimes been, have ever so offended and stirred up the plebeian tribunes as has the boon which the Fathers bestowed upon the commons, when they granted pay for military service? What else do you believe they

9

aliud aut tum timuisse creditis aut hodie turbare
velle nisi concordiam ordinum, quam dissolvendae
6 maxime tribuniciae potestatis rentur esse? Sic
hercule tamquam artifices improbi opus quaerunt;
quippe [1] semper aegri aliquid esse in re publica
volunt, ut sit ad cuius curationem a vobis adhibean-
7 tur. Utrum enim defenditis an impugnatis plebem?
Utrum militantium adversarii estis an causam agitis?
Nisi forte hoc dicitis: 'Quidquid patres faciunt dis-
plicet, sive illud pro plebe sive contra plebem est,'
8 et quemadmodum servis [2] suis vetant domini quicquam rei cum alienis hominibus esse pariterque in iis
beneficio ac maleficio abstineri aequum censent, sic
vos interdicitis patribus commercio plebis, ne nos
comitate ac munificentia nostra provocemus plebem
nec plebs nobis dicto audiens atque oboediens sit.
9 Quanto tandem, si quicquam in vobis, non dico civilis,
sed humani esset, favere vos magis et quantum in
vobis esset indulgere potius comitati patrum atque
10 obsequio plebis oportuit? Quae si perpetua concordia sit, quis non spondere ausit maximum hoc
imperium inter finitimos brevi futurum esse?

IV. "Atqui [3] ego, quam hoc consilium collegarum
meorum, quo [4] abducere infecta re a Veiis exercitum
noluerunt, non utile solum sed etiam necessarium
fuerit, postea disseram: nunc de ipsa condicione
2 dicere militantium libet; quam orationem non apud
vos solum sed etiam in castris si habeatur, ipso

---

[1] quippe *Büttner*: qui et Ω: *wanting in V*: et *Muretus*:
qui *Conway*.
[2] servis *Ald.*: cum (tum *L*) seruis Ω.
[3] Atqui *OEH*: atque Ω.
[4] quo Ω: quod *VB*.

were afraid of then, or are seeking now to shatter, B.C. 403
but the harmony of the orders, which they regard
as very apt to overthrow the tribunician authority?
Indeed they are like quack-salvers seeking employment, since they desire that there should always be
some disease in the body politic, that there may be
something which you may call them in to cure.
Pray, are you tribunes defending the commons, or
attacking them? Are you adversaries of the soldiers,
or their advocates? Or perhaps this is your plea:
'Whatever the Fathers do displeases us, be it in
behalf of the commons or against them'; and just
as masters forbid outsiders to have aught to do with
their slaves, and think it right that they should
abstain alike from benefiting and from harming
them, so you deny the Fathers intercourse with the
commons, lest we by our friendliness and liberality
encourage them, or they become dutiful and obedient
to us. How much more, if you had in you the
slightest—I say not patriotism, but—humanity,
ought you rather to have favoured, and, so far as in
you lay, to have encouraged the kindly spirit of the
Fathers and the complaisance of the plebs? And if
this harmony should last, who would not make bold
to warrant that our empire would soon be the
greatest among the neighbouring peoples?

IV. "I shall presently explain, in regard to this
plan of my colleagues, who have not been willing to
withdraw the army from Veii with its task unaccom-
plished,—how not merely profitable but even
necessary it was. But first I wish to speak about
the actual condition of the soldiers; and I think
that if I should express my meaning not in your
presence only but also in the camp, the army itself

A.U.C.
351

exercitu disceptante aequam arbitror videri posse.
In qua si mihi ipsi nihil quod dicerem in mentem
venire posset, adversariorum certe orationibus con-
3 tentus essem. Negabant nuper danda esse aera
militibus, quia nunquam data essent. Quonam
modo igitur nunc indignari possunt, quibus aliquid
novi adiectum commodi sit, eis laborem etiam novum
4 pro portione iniungi? Nusquam nec opera sine
emolumento nec emolumentum ferme sine impensa
opera est. Labor voluptasque, dissimillima natura,
societate quadam inter se naturali sunt iuncta.
5 Moleste antea ferebat miles se suo sumptu operam
rei publicae praebere ; gaudebat idem partem anni
se agrum suum colere, quaerere unde domi militiae-
6 que se ac suos tueri posset : gaudet nunc fructui sibi
rem publicam esse et laetus stipendium accipit ;
aequo igitur animo patiatur se ab domo ac re familiari, cui gravis impensa non est, paulo diutius abesse.
7 An si ad calculos eum res publica vocet, non merito
dicat : 'annua aera habes, annuam operam ede ; an
tu aequum censes militia semestri solidum te sti-
8 pendium accipere ?' Invitus in hac parte orationis,
Quirites, moror ; sic enim agere debent qui mercen-
nario milite utuntur ; nos tamquam cum civibus
agere volumus agique tamquam cum patria nobiscum
9 aequum censemus. Aut non suscipi bellum oportuit
aut geri pro dignitate populi Romani et perfici quam
10 primum oportet. Perficietur autem si urgemus obsessos, si non ante abscedimus quam spei nostrae

would judge it reasonable. Indeed, though I were B.C. 403
unable to think of anything to urge myself, I could
be quite content with the speeches of my opponents.
They were lately insisting that pay ought not to be
given to the men, because it never had been given.
How then can they object, if to those who have
gained some new advantage be allotted new labour
also, in proportion. Nowhere, as a rule, is service
given without recompense, nor recompense except
for service; toil and pleasure, most unlike in nature,
have been linked together in a sort of natural bond.
Formerly the soldier was vexed that he must serve
the state at his own cost; yet he was happy to be
able, for a half of the year, to till his own field and
gain the means of keeping himself and his family,
whether he were at home or with the army. Now
he is happy that the state affords him gain, and is
glad to receive his pay. Let him therefore be
resigned to remaining away a little longer from his
home and his property, on which he is now no heavy
charge. Why, if the commonwealth should call him
to a reckoning, would it not justly say, 'You have a
year's stipend, render a year's service; do you think
it right that for a campaign of six months you should
receive the pay of twelve?' I dislike to dwell upon
this point, Quirites; for it is thus that men who
employ mercenaries ought to argue; we would deal
as though with fellow citizens, and we think it only
right that you deal with us as with your native
country. Either we ought not to have undertaken
the war, or we ought to conduct it as befits the
Roman People, and end it as quickly as possible.
And we shall end it, if we press our beleaguered
foes, and quit them not till we have fulfilled our

A.U.C.
351 finem captis Veiis imposuerimus. Si hercules nulla
alia causa, ipsa indignitas perseverantiam imponere
11 debuit. Decem quondam annos urbs oppugnata est
ob unam mulierem ab universa Graecia, quam procul
12 ab domo? quot terras, quot maria distans? Nos
intra vicesimum lapidem in conspectu prope urbis
nostrae annuam oppugnationem perferre piget? Scilicet quia levis causa belli est nec satis quicquam
iusti doloris est quod nos ad perseverandum stimulet.
13 Septiens rebellarunt; in pace nunquam fida fuerunt;
agros nostros miliens depopulati sunt; Fidenates
deficere a nobis coegerunt; colonos nostros ibi inter-
14 fecerunt; auctores fuere contra ius caedis impiae
legatorum nostrorum; Etruriam omnem adversus
nos concitare voluerunt hodieque id moliuntur; res
repetentes legatos nostros haud procul afuit quin
violarent.

V. "Cum his molliter et per dilationes bellum geri
oportet? Si nos tam iustum odium nihil movet, ne
2 illa quidem, oro vos, movent? Operibus ingentibus
saepta urbs est, quibus intra muros coercetur hostis;
3 agrum non coluit, et culta evastata sunt bello; si
reducimus exercitum, quis est qui dubitet illos non
a cupiditate solum ulciscendi, sed etiam necessitate
imposita ex alieno praedandi, cum sua amiserint,
agrum nostrum invasuros? Non differimus igitur
bellum isto consilio, sed intra fines nostros accipimus.

hopes and captured Veii. Truly, if there were no
other reason, the very indignity of the thing should
compel us to persist! Did all Greece once, for one
woman's sake, war ten years against a city so far
from home, with all those lands and seas between?
And does it irk us, being less than twenty miles
away and almost within sight of Rome, to maintain
a siege for a single year? Doubtless our reason
for fighting is a trivial one, and we have no proper
and sufficient grievance to incite us to persevere!
Seven times have they renewed the war; never have
they kept faith in peace; our fields they have
pillaged a thousand times; they forced the Fidenates
to forsake us; our settlers there they put to death;
it was they who instigated, in violation of the law
of nations, the impious murder of our envoys; they
sought to raise up all Etruria against us, and they
are striving to this end to-day; when our ambassadors sought redress they well-nigh did them bodily
injury.

V. "With such enemies ought we to wage a faint-
hearted and dilatory war? If so just grounds of
resentment have no power to move us, pray have the
following considerations none? The city is hemmed
in with vast siege-works, which confine the enemy
within his walls; he has not cultivated his land, and
what was cultivated has been laid waste in the war;
if we bring our army back, who can doubt that not
only a desire for revenge, but also necessity, con-
straining them to plunder others since they have
lost their own possessions, will cause them to invade
our territory? So we are not postponing the war,
if we act on your advice, but are receiving it within
our own borders. And what of that matter which

A.U.C.
351

4 Quid? Illud quod proprie ad milites pertinet, quibus boni tribuni plebis tum stipendium [1] extorquere
voluerunt, nunc consultum repente volunt, quale est?
5 Vallum fossamque, ingentis utrumque [2] operis, per
tantum spatii duxerunt: castella primo pauca, postea
exercitu aucto creberrima fecerunt; munitiones non
in urbem modo sed in Etruriam etiam spectantes,[3] si
6 qua inde auxilia veniant, opposuere; quid turres,
quid vineas testudinesque et alium [4] oppugnandarum
urbium apparatum loquar? Cum tantum laboris
exhaustum sit et ad finem iam operis tandem per-
ventum, relinquendane haec censetis, ut ad aestatem
rursus novus de integro his instituendis exsudetur
7 labor? Quanto est minus operae [5] tueri facta et
instare ac perseverare defungique cura? Brevis
enim profecto res est, si uno tenore peragitur nec
ipsi per intermissiones has intervallaque lentiorem
8 spem nostram facimus. Loquor de operae et [6] de
temporis iactura. Quid? Periculi, quod differendo
bello adimus, num [7] oblivisci nos haec tam crebra
Etruriae concilia de mittendis Veios auxiliis patiun-
9 tur? Ut nunc res se habet, irati sunt, oderunt,
negant missuros; quantum in illis est, capere Veios
licet. Quis est qui spondeat eundem, si differtur
10 bellum, animum postea fore, cum si laxamentum
dederis, maior frequentiorque legatio itura sit, cum

---

[1] tum stipendium ς Madvig: cum stipendium Ω: olim
stipendium Heidenhain: stipendium V.

[2] utrumque Drakenborch: utramque rem V F²(or F³) a:
utrumque rem Ω.

[3] spectantes F³a: spec. antis V: expectantes Ω: ex
specstantes D?: exspectantes PE.

[4] et alium Dᵉa Rhenanus: et talium Ω (Vorm?): et talem
H: wanting in V.

[5] operae Hell: opera Ω.

16

specially concerns the soldiers, whom the worthy plebeian tribunes formerly wished to rob of their pay, but are now desirous of protecting? How does it stand with them? The rampart and the trench, each involving prodigious toil, they have carried all that distance; forts they erected only a few at first, but since then, with the growth of the army, they have built very many; they have thrown up earthworks, not only against the city, but also facing Etruria, if any aid should come from that side; what need to speak of towers, mantlets, penthouses, and the rest of the equipment for storming towns? When they have expended all this labour, and the end of their task is at last in sight, do you vote for abandoning these things, that when summer comes they may sweat and toil again to produce them afresh? How much less effort it requires to guard what is already made, and to press on and persevere and put an end to our anxiety! For surely it is a thing soon done, if we carry it through without stopping, and do not ourselves drag out our hopes with these interruptions and delays. I talk of the loss of time and labour; what of the danger that we run by putting off the war? Do the frequent debates in Etruria about the dispatch of succours to Veii allow us to forget it? Just now they are angry and resentful, and declare that they will send none; for all they care, we may capture Veii. But who is to guarantee that if we postpone the campaign they will hereafter feel the same: since if you slacken, a greater and more numerous embassy will set out,

---

⁶ operae et *Ussing* : opere et Ω : operis D^3 : operum D? : opera et *V*.

⁷ num 𝔰 : nunc Ω.

id quod nunc offendit Etruscos, rex creatus Veiis,
mutari spatio interposito possit vel consensu civitatis,
ut eo reconcilient Etruriae animos, vel ipsius voluntate regis, qui obstare regnum suum saluti civium
11 nolit? Videte quot res quam inutiles sequantur
illam viam consilii, iactura operum tanto labore fac-
torum, vastatio imminens finium nostrorum, Etrus-
12 cum bellum pro Veiente concitatum. Haec sunt,
tribuni, consilia vestra, non hercule dissimilia ac si
quis aegro qui curari se fortiter passus extemplo
convalescere possit, cibi gratia praesentis aut potionis
longinquum et forsitan insanabilem morbum efficiat.

VI. "Si mediusfidius, ad hoc bellum nihil perti-
neret, ad disciplinam certe militiae plurimum intererat
insuescere militem nostrum non solum parata[1] victoria
2 frui, sed, si etiam res lentior sit, pati taedium et
quamvis serae spei exitum exspectare et si non sit
aestate perfectum bellum, hiemem opperiri nec, sicut
aestivas aves, statim autumno tecta ac recessus[2]
3 circumspicere. Obsecro vos, venandi studium ac
voluptas homines per nives ac pruinas in montes
silvasque rapit: belli necessitatibus eam patientiam
non adhibebimus quam vel lusus[3] ac voluptas elicere
4 solet? Adeone effeminata corpora militum nostrorum esse putamus, adeo molles animos, ut hiemem

---

[1] parata $U\varsigma$: parta Ω: parua O.
[2] recessus V: recessum (recensum B) Ω.
[3] vel lusus *early edd.*: uel usus (lusus D) Ω.

and since what now offends the Etruscans—the setting up of a king at Veii—may be altered with the lapse of time or by agreement of the citizens, to the end that thereby they may regain the good-will of Etruria ; or with the consent of the King himself, who would not wish his sovereignty to hurt the safety of his people ? See how many undesirable consequences attend that line of policy : the loss of works constructed with such effort ; the imminent devastation of our fields ; the Etruscans, instead of the Veientes only, aroused to war with us. It is thus, tribunes, that you would manage matters, much as though in dealing with a sick man, who if he would undergo a strict regimen might begin at once to recover, you should protract his illness and perhaps render it incurable, by indulging his immediate desire for meat and drink.

VI. " If it were of no moment to this war, it was yet, I assure you, of the utmost importance for military discipline that our soldiers become accustomed not only to pluck a victory within their grasp, but if a campaign should be even more protracted, to put up with the tedium and await the outcome of their hopes, however long-deferred ; and if a war be not finished in a summer, to stay for winter, nor, like birds of passage, cast about at once, on the approach of autumn, for shelter and covert. Do the eagerness, pray, and delight that men have in hunting carry them through snow and frost into the mountains and the forests ; and shall not we use in the stress of war the same resolution which even sport and pleasure are wont to call out ? Do we think the bodies of our soldiers so effeminate, their hearts so faint, that they cannot endure to be one

19

unam durare in castris, abesse ab domo non possint?
Ut tamquam navale bellum tempestatibus captandis
et observando tempore anni gerant, non aestus, non
5 frigora pati possint? Erubescant profecto si quis eis
haec obiciat, contendantque et animis et corporibus
suis virilem patientiam inesse, et se iuxta hieme
atque aestate bella gerere posse nec se patrocinium
mollitiae inertiaeque mandasse tribunis, et meminisse
hanc ipsam potestatem non in umbra nec in tectis
maiores suos creasse.

6 "Haec virtute militum vestrorum, haec Romano
nomine sunt digna, non Veios tantum nec hoc bellum
intueri quod instat, sed famam et ad alia [1] bella et ad
7 ceteros populos in posterum quaerere. An mediocre
discrimen opinionis secuturum ex hac re putatis,
utrum tandem finitimi populum Romanum eum esse
putent cuius si qua urbs primum illum brevissimi
temporis sustinuerit impetum, nihil deinde timeat,
8 an hic sit terror nominis nostri ut exercitum Romanum
non taedium longinquae oppugnationis, non vis hiemis
ab urbe circumsessa semel amovere possit, nec finem
ullum alium belli quam victoriam noverit nec impetu
9 potius bella quam perseverantia gerat? Quae in
omni quidem genere militiae, maxime tamen in obsi-
dendis urbibus necessaria est, quarum plerasque
munitionibus ac naturali situ inexpugnabiles fame
10 sitique tempus ipsum vincit atque expugnat,—sicut

---

[1] et ad alia *early edd.* : et alia Ω: ad alia ⸢.

winter in camp, away from home; that like sailors _{B.C. 403} they must wage war with an eye on the weather, observing the seasons, incapable of withstanding heat or cold? They would certainly blush if any-one should charge them with this, and would main-tain that manly endurance was in their souls and bodies, and that they could campaign as well in winter as in summer; that they had given the tribunes no commission to protect softness and idleness; and that they were mindful that their grandsires had not founded the tribunician power in the shade or under roofs.

"It is due to the valour of your soldiers, it is due to the Roman name, that you should look not merely to Veii and this present war that is upon us, but should seek for the years to come a reputation that will serve you in other wars and amongst all other nations. Do you suppose there will be no great difference in men's opinion of us, whether our neighbours conclude the Roman People to be such, that if a city withstand the brunt of their first assault for a very brief time, it need thenceforward have no fears; or whether our name inspire such dread, that men believe that once a Roman army has sat down before a town, it will never budge, either from the weariness of a protracted siege or from the rigours of winter, that it knows no other end of war but victory, and relies in its campaigns not more on swiftness than on perseverance? For perseverance, needful in every kind of warfare, is especially so in besieging cities, since fortifications and natural advantages make most of them impregnable, and time itself subdues them, with hunger and thirst, and captures them, as it shall capture Veii, unless

21

A.U.C.
351

Veios expugnabit, nisi auxilio hostibus tribuni plebis fuerint, et Romae invenerint praesidia Veientes quae nequiquam in Etruria quaerunt.

11 "An est quicquam quod Veientibus optatum aeque contingere possit quam ut seditionibus primum urbs Romana, deinde velut ex contagione castra imple-

12 antur? At hercule apud hostes tanta modestia est ut non obsidionis taedio, non denique regni quicquam apud eos novatum sit, non negata auxilia ab Etruscis

13 inritaverint animos; morietur enim extemplo quicumque erit seditionis auctor, nec cuiquam dicere ea

14 licebit, quae apud vos impune dicuntur. Fustuarium meretur qui signa relinquit aut praesidio decedit: auctores signa relinquendi et deserendi castra non uni aut alteri militi, sed universis exercitibus palam

15 in contione audiuntur; adeo quidquid tribunus plebi loquitur, etsi prodendae patriae dissolvendaeque rei publicae est, adsuestis aequi[1] audire et dulcedine potestatis eius capti quaelibet sub ea scelera latere

16 sinitis. Reliquum est ut quae hic vociferantur, eadem in castris et apud milites agant et exercitus corrum-

17 pant ducibusque parere non patiantur, quoniam ea demum Romae libertas est, non senatum, non magistratus, non leges, non mores maiorum, non instituta patrum, non disciplinam vereri militiae."

VII. Par iam etiam in contionibus erat Appius tribunis plebis, cum subito, unde minime quis crederet, accepta calamitas apud Veios et superiorem Appium

---

[1] aequi *Rhenanus*: qui (*omitted by* UO: *space of not more than four letters in* V): ei E²: quidem D⁴: Quirites *Gulielmus*: quieti *Welz*.

---

[1] Livy implies that the speech which he has reported above was delivered in the Senate.

the plebeian tribunes help our enemies, and the B.C. 403 Veientes find in Rome those succours which they are seeking to no purpose in Etruria.

"Could anything happen which would so please the Veientes as that factions should spring up, first in the City of Rome, and then, as though by contagion, in the camp? But our enemies, by Heaven, are so well disciplined that no weariness of the blockade nor even of kingly rule has occasioned the smallest revolt among them; neither has the Etruscans' denial of help provoked their spirit; for whosoever prompts sedition shall forthwith die the death; nor shall any man there have licence to say what is said with impunity to you. Death by cudgelling is the wage of him who forsakes the standards or quits his post; but those who advise the men to abandon their standards and desert the camp gain a hearing, not with one or two soldiers, but with whole armies, openly, in public meetings; so accustomed are you to hear with complacency whatever a tribune says, even if it tends to betray the City and to undo the state; and captivated by the charm of that authority, you suffer any wickedness whatsoever to lurk beneath it. It only remains for them to utter in camp and in the presence of the soldiers the view which they noisily publish here, and to corrupt the armies and not to suffer them to obey their leaders. For in the upshot liberty has come to mean at Rome, that a man respect neither senate nor laws, nor ancestral customs, nor institutions of the fathers, nor military discipline."

VII. Appius was already holding his own with the tribunes of the plebs, even in public meetings,[1] when a sudden disaster, from a source which could

in causa et concordiam ordinum maiorem ardoremque
2 ad obsidendos pertinacius Veios fecit. Nam cum
agger promotus ad urbem vineaeque tantum non iam
iniunctae moenibus essent, dum opera interdiu fiunt
intentius quam nocte custodiuntur, patefacta repente
porta ingens multitudo facibus maxime armata ignes
3 coniecit, horaeque momento simul aggerem ac vineas,
tam longi temporis opus, incendium hausit; multique
ibi mortales nequiquam opem ferentes ferro ignique
4 absumpti sunt. Quod ubi Romam est nuntiatum,
maestitiam omnibus, senatui curam metumque iniecit,
ne tum vero sustineri nec in urbe seditio nec in
castris posset et tribuni plebis velut ab se victae
5 rei publicae insultarent, cum repente quibus census
equester erat, equi publici non erant adsignati, concilio prius inter sese habito senatum adeunt factaque
dicendi potestate equis se suis stipendia facturos
6 promittunt. Quibus cum amplissimis verbis gratiae
ab senatu actae essent famaque ea forum atque
urbem pervasisset, subito ad curiam concursus fit
7 plebis; pedestris ordinis aiunt nunc esse operam [1]
rei publicae extra ordinem polliceri, seu Veios seu
quo alio ducere velint; si Veios ducti sint, negant

---

[1] aiunt nunc esse operam *Cuper*: se aiunt nunc esse operamque Ω: seiciunt nunc esse operamque *B*.

24

least have been anticipated, befell the army before B.C. 403
Veii, giving Appius the advantage in the argument,
while it increased the mutual good-will of the orders
and their ardour for a more vigorous prosecution of
the siege. For when they had pushed forward the
terrace towards the town, and had all but brought
the mantlets into contact with the walls,—more
intent upon erecting their works by day than on
guarding them by night,—the gate was suddenly
flung open, and a vast horde, most of them armed
with torches, hurled fire on the works, and in an
hour's time terrace and mantlets, that had taken
so long to make, were consumed in the flames;
and many men perished by the sword or the fire, in
vain efforts to save them. When the news of this
came to Rome, it filled the City with sadness, the
senate with anxiety and apprehension, lest they
might now indeed be unable to check the disaffection,
either in the City or the camp, and the tribunes might
crow over the commonwealth as though they had overthrown it; when lo! those who were of equestrian
rating, but had not received horses from the state,
having first taken counsel together, came to the
senate, and being granted a hearing, volunteered to
serve on their own horses. These men had no
sooner received a vote of thanks from the senate, in
the most honourable terms, and the report of it had
spread to the Forum and the City, than the
plebeians suddenly ran together to the Curia, and
declared that it was now the turn of the foot-
soldiers to proffer extraordinary service to the state,
whether it would have them march to Veii, or anywhere else; if they should be led to Veii, they
promised that they would not quit their ground

25

se inde prius quam capta urbe hostium redituros
8 esse. Tum vero iam superfundenti se laetitiae vix
temperatum est; non enim, sicut equites, dato magi-
9 stratibus negotio laudari iussi, neque aut in curiam
vocati quibus responsum daretur, aut limine curiae
continebatur senatus; sed pro se quisque ex superiore
loco ad multitudinem in comitio stantem voce mani-
10 busque significare publicam laetitiam, beatam urbem
Romanam et invictam et aeternam illa concordia
dicere, laudare equites, laudare plebem, diem ipsum
laudibus ferre, victam esse fateri comitatem benig-
11 nitatemque senatus. Certatim patribus plebique
manare gaudio lacrimae, donec revocatis in curiam
patribus senatus consultum factum est ut tribuni
militares contione advocata peditibus equitibusque
12 gratias agerent, memorem pietatis eorum erga patriam
dicerent senatum fore; placere autem omnibus his
voluntariam extra ordinem professis militiam aera
procedere; et equiti certus numerus aeris est ad-
13 signatus. Tum primum equis suis merere equites
coeperunt. Voluntarius ductus exercitus Veios non
amissa modo restituit opera, sed nova etiam instituit.
Ab urbe commeatus intentiore quam antea subvehi
cura, ne quid tam bene merito exercitui ad usum
deesset.

VIII. Insequens annus tribunos militum consulari
potestate habuit C. Servilium Ahalam tertium Q.
Servilium L. Verginium Q. Sulpicium A. Manlium
2 iterum M.' Sergium[1] iterum. His tribunis, dum

---

[1] M.' Sergium *a Sigonius* (Sergium *C.I.L.* i², *p.* 116): m
sergium (*or* marcum sergium) Ω: martum sergium *F*: marcum seruium *DL*.

---

[1] *i. e.* from the steps that led down to the Comitium.

until they had taken the enemy's city. Then B.C. 403
indeed the senate could scarce control its already
overflowing joy; for they did not, as with the
knights, issue an order to the magistrates to thank
them, nor did they call them into the Curia to
receive an answer, neither did the senate keep
within the House; but each for himself cried out
from above,[1] to the multitude standing in the
Comitium, and by speech and gesture signified the
general joy. Rome was blest, they said, and in-
vincible and eternal, by reason of this noble harmony;
they praised the knights, they praised the plebeians,
they extolled the very day itself, and confessed that
the courtesy and good-will of the senate had been
surpassed. Fathers and commoners mingled their
tears of joy, till the Fathers were recalled into the
senate-house, and decreed that the military tribunes
should hold an assembly and thank the infantry and
the knights, and say to them that the senate would
remember their loyalty to their country, and that it
was voted that all who had volunteered to serve
out of their due order should receive pay. The
knights, too, were granted a definite money allowance.
Then for the first time cavalry-men began to serve
on their own horses. The volunteer army, having
marched to Veii, not only replaced the works that
had been lost, but added new ones. The city dispatched provisions with more than its former zeal,
that nothing might be lacking to an army that had
deserved so well.

VIII. The ensuing year had for consular tribunes B.C. 402
Gaius Servilius Ahala (for the third time), Quintus
Servilius, Lucius Verginius, Quintus Sulpicius, Aulus
Manlius (for the second time), and Manius Sergius

27

A.U.C.
352

cura omnium in Veiens bellum intenta est, neglectum
Anxuri [1] praesidium vacationibus militum et Volscos
mercatores volgo receptando proditis repente por-
3 tarum custodibus oppressum est.   Minus militum
periit, quia praeter aegros lixarum in modum omnes
4 per agros vicinasque urbes negotiabantur.   Nec Veiis
melius gesta res, quod tum caput omnium curarum
publicarum erat; nam et duces Romani plus inter
se irarum quam adversus hostes animi habuerunt, et
auctum est bellum adventu repentino Capenatium
5 atque Faliscorum.   Hi duo Etruriae populi, quia
proximi regione erant, devictis Veiis bello quoque
6 Romano se proximos fore credentes, Falisci propria
etiam causa infesti, quod Fidenati bello se iam antea
immiscuerant, per legatos ultro citroque missos iure
iurando inter se obligati, cum exercitibus necopinato
7 ad Veios accessere.   Forte ea regione qua [2] M.'
Sergius tribunus militum praeerat castra adorti sunt
ingentemque terrorem intulere, quia Etruriam omnem
excitam sedibus magna mole adesse Romani crediderant.   Eadem opinio Veientes in urbe concitavit.
8 Ita ancipiti proelio castra Romana oppugnabantur;
concursantesque cum huc atque illuc signa transferrent, nec Veientem satis cohibere intra munitiones
nec suis munimentis arcere vim ac tueri se ab ex-

[1] Anxuri *a*[2] *Bekker* : anxyri (*or* anexyri, *or* anxiri) Ω (*not
in V*).
[2] qua M.' Sergius *Sigonius* : qua m sergius *HDL* : quam
sergius *M*[1] *or M*[2] *PFBa* : qua sergius *MUOE*.

(for the second time). In their term of office, while B.C. 402
everyone was intent on the war with Veii, the
garrison at Anxur was neglected; soldiers were
given furlough, Volscian traders were admitted without discrimination, and, the sentinels at the gates
being suddenly overpowered, the town was taken.
Not many soldiers perished, because they were all,
except the sick, occupied, like sutlers, with trafficking
in the country-side and the towns near by. Nor
were things any better at Veii, which was at that
time the nation's chief concern; for the Roman
commanders showed more jealousy of one another
than spirit in dealing with the enemy, whose forces
moreover were enlarged by the unexpected accession
of the Capenates and the Faliscans. These two
Etruscan peoples, being nearest in situation, believed that if the Veientes were conquered it would
be their turn next to face a Roman invasion. The
Faliscans, besides, had incurred hostility on their
own account, because they had been mixed up before
in the war with Fidenae.[1] So they exchanged
embassies, bound themselves by an oath, and their
armies suddenly appeared before Veii. It happened
that they attacked the camp at that point where the
tribune Manius Sergius was in command, and great
was the terror they inspired, since the Romans
thought that all Etruria had risen and was come
with a mighty array against them. The same
belief roused up the Veientes in the town. Thus
a two-fold attack was directed against the camp.
The soldiers rallied into groups, facing now this way
and now that, yet were unable either quite to confine the Veientes within the siege-lines, or to ward
off the attack upon their own defences and protect

LIVY

9 teriore poterant hoste. Una spes erat si ex maioribus
castris subveniretur, ut diversae legiones aliae adversus Capenatem ac Faliscum, aliae contra erupti-
onem oppidanorum pugnarent; sed castris praeerat
10 Verginius, privatim Sergio invisus infestusque. Is,
cum pleraque castella oppugnata, superatas munitiones, utrimque invehi hostem nuntiaretur, in armis
milites tenuit, si opus foret auxilio collegam dictitans
11 ad se missurum. Huius adrogantiam pertinacia alterius aequabat, qui, ne quam opem ab inimico videretur petisse, vinci ab hoste quam vincere per civem
12 maluit. Diu in medio caesi milites; postremo de-
sertis munitionibus perpauci in maiora castra, pars
maxima atque ipse Sergius Romam pertenderunt.
Ubi cum omnem culpam in collegam inclinaret, acciri
Verginium ex castris, interea praeesse legatos placuit.
13 Acta deinde in senatu res est certatumque inter
collegas maledictis. Pauci rei publicae, plerique[1]
huic atque illi, ut quosque studium privatim aut
gratia occupaverat,[2] adsunt.

IX. Primores patrum, sive culpa sive infelicitate
imperatorum tam ignominiosa clades accepta esset,
censuere non exspectandum iustum tempus comitiorum, sed extemplo novos tribunos militum creandos

---

[1] plerique *inserted by Kiehl.*
[2] occupaverat ς: occupaverant *U*: occupauerunt Ω (*not
in V*).

themselves from the enemy outside. Their only
hope was if help should come from the larger camp,
so that the legions might face different ways, some of
them confronting the Capenates and Faliscans, and
others the sortie of the townsfolk. But that camp
was under the command of Verginius, who was
privately hated by Sergius and returned his enmity.
This man, though word was brought that many
bastions had been stormed and the ramparts scaled,
and that the enemy were attacking on both sides,
held his troops under arms, saying that if his
colleague needed help he would let him know.
His pride found a match in the other's obstinacy,
and Sergius, lest he should seem to have required
any aid of his rival, preferred defeat at the hands of
the enemy to victory gained through a fellow citizen.
For a long time the Romans were slaughtered
between the two attacking armies; finally they
abandoned their works, and a very few escaped into
the larger camp, while Sergius himself, with the
chief part of his men, kept on to Rome. It was
there decided, on his throwing all the blame upon
his colleague, to summon Verginius from camp, and
in the meanwhile put lieutenants in command of it.
The affair was then debated in the senate and the
colleagues heaped abuse on one another. There were
but few who spoke for the commonwealth : most of
them argued for one or the other disputant, according
as each was swayed by private interest or favour.

IX. The leading senators held, that whether the
fault or the misfortune of the commanders were the
cause of this shameful disaster, they ought not to
await the regular time for elections, but proceed
at once to choose new military tribunes, to begin

esse, qui kalendis Octobribus magistratum occipe-
2 rent. In quam sententiam cum pedibus iretur, ceteri
3 tribuni militum nihil contradicere; at enimvero
Sergius Verginiusque, propter quos paenitere magistratuum eius anni senatum apparebat, primo depre-
cari ignominiam, deinde intercedere senatus consulto,
negare se ante idus Decembres, sollemnem ineundis
4 magistratibus diem, honore abituros esse. Inter haec
tribuni plebis, cum in concordia hominum secundisque
rebus civitatis inviti silentium tenuissent, feroces
repente minari tribunis militum, nisi in auctoritate
senatus essent, se in vincla eos duci iussuros esse.
5 Tum C. Servilius Ahala tribunus militum: "Quod
ad vos attinet, tribuni plebis, minasque vestras, ne
ego libenter experirer quam non plus in iis iuris
6 quam in vobis animi esset; sed nefas est tendere
adversus auctoritatem senatus. Proinde et vos de-
sinite inter nostra certamina locum iniuriae quaerere,
et collegae aut facient quod censet senatus, aut, si
pertinacius tendent, dictatorem extemplo dicam qui
7 eos abire magistratu cogat." Cum omnium adsensu
comprobata oratio esset gauderentque patres sine
tribuniciae potestatis terriculis inventam esse aliam
8 vim maiorem ad coercendos magistratus, victi consensu omnium comitia tribunorum militum habuere
qui kalendis Octobribus magistratum occiperent,
seque ante eam diem magistratu abdicavere.

---

¹ The *senatus consultum* was no more than a 'resolution'
which the presiding magistrate might, if he chose, refuse to
carry out.

B.C. 402

their magistracy on the first of October. While the members were voting for this proposal, the other military tribunes raised no objection; but of all people Sergius and Virginius, the very men on account of whom it was evident that the senate was disgusted with the magistrates of that year, first begged to be spared the humiliation, then vetoed the senate's decree,[1] declaring that they would not resign their authority before the thirteenth of December, the accustomed day for entering upon office. Whereupon the tribunes of the plebs, who so long as harmony prevailed and the affairs of the City prospered, had reluctantly held their tongues, suddenly broke out and threatened the tribunes of the soldiers, that unless they submitted to the senate they would send them to prison. Then Gaius Servilius Ahala, a military tribune, said : " So far as concerns you, tribunes of the commons, and your menaces, I should indeed willingly put it to the proof how you have on your side as little legality as courage ; but it is impious to oppose the authority of the senate. Accordingly do you give over seeking in our quarrels occasion for working mischief, and my colleagues shall either do as the senate decrees, or if they persist in stubborn opposition, I will forthwith name a dictator, to compel them to lay down their authority." This speech was universally approved, and the Fathers rejoiced that they needed not the trumpery threats of the tribunician power, but had found another and a greater force to coerce the magistrates ; and the latter, overborne by the unanimity of feeling, held an election of military tribunes, to begin service on October the first, and before that date resigned their office.

33

X. L. Valerio Potito quartum M. Furio Camillo
iterum M.' Aemilio [1] Mamerco tertium Cn. Cornelio
Cosso iterum K. Fabio Ambusto L. Iulio Iulo [2] tribunis militum consulari potestate multa domi militi-
2 aeque gesta. Nam et bellum multiplex fuit eodem
tempore, ad Veios et ad Capenam et ad Falerios [3]
3 et in Volscis, ut Anxur ab hostibus reciperaretur,
et Romae simul dilectu simul tributo conferendo
laboratum est, et de tribunis plebi cooptandis contentio fuit, et haud parvum motum duo iudicia eorum
qui paulo ante consulari potestate fuerant excivere.
4 Omnium primum tribunis militum fuit dilectum habere, nec iuniores modo conscripti sed seniores etiam
coacti nomina dare ut urbis custodiam agerent.
5 Quantum autem augebatur militum numerus, tanto
maiore pecunia in stipendium opus erat, eaque tributo conficiebatur [4] invitis conferentibus qui domi
remanebant, quia tuentibus urbem opera quoque
militari laborandum serviendumque rei publicae erat.
6 Haec, per se gravia, indigniora [5] ut viderentur tribuni plebis seditiosis contionibus faciebant, ideo aera
militibus constituta esse arguendo, ut plebis partem
7 militia, partem tributo conficerent. Unum bellum
annum iam tertium trahi et consulto male geri ut
diutius gerant. In quattuor deinde bella uno dilectu

---

[1] M.' Aemilio *Sigon.* (*C.I.L.* i[2], *p.* 116): m̅ (*or* m *or* marco)
aemilio Ω (*cf. Diod.* xiv. xliv. 1).
[2] Iulio Iulo *Sigon.*: iulio tullo Ω: iulio tullii *HDL.*
[3] Falerios *D*[3] *a*[1] ⲋ: ualerios Ω.
[4] conficiebatur *Madvig*: conferebatur Ω.
[5] gravia indigniora *Vorm.?* ⲋ: grauia indignioraque Ω:
graui indignioraque *B.*

---

[1] Really the first term of Camillus. The error here and in
chap. i. § 2 (see note) is tacitly corrected in chap. xiv. § 5.
[2] Not the same man as mentioned in chap. i. § 2.

X. The consular tribuneship of Lucius Valerius B.C. 401
Potitus (for the fourth term), Marcus Furius Camillus
(for the second [1]), Manius Aemilius Mamercus (for
the third), Gnaeus Cornelius Cossus (for the second),
Caeso Fabius Ambustus, and Lucius Julius Iulus, [2]
was a time of great activity both at home and in
the field. For they made war at many points simultaneously, before Veii, at Capena, at Falerii, and in
the Volscian country—to recover Anxur from the
enemy;—and in Rome both the levy and the
payment of the war-tax occasioned difficulties, a
quarrel sprang up over the co-optation of plebeian
tribunes, and the trials of the two who had lately
exercised consular powers aroused no small commotion. The first concern of the military tribunes
was to levy troops, and they not only enrolled the
younger men, but also compelled the seniors to
enlist for service in guarding the City. But the
more they increased the number of the soldiers, the
more money they required for pay. This they tried
to collect by taxation; but those who remained at
home contributed with reluctance, because they had
also in defence of the City to perform the labour
of soldiers and serve the commonwealth. To make
this obligation, heavy in itself, seem yet more
grievous, the tribunes of the plebs delivered
seditious speeches, in which they alleged that the
senators had established pay for the troops for this
reason, that they might ruin one half of the plebs
with fighting and the other half with taxation.
They were now drawing out a single war into its
third year, and were purposely misconducting it,
that they might conduct it the longer. Again, with
one levy they had enrolled armies for four wars, and

35

exercitus scriptos et pueros quoque ac senes ex-
8 tractos. Iam non aestatis nec hiemis discrimen esse,
ne ulla quies unquam miserae plebi sit, quae nunc[1]
9 etiam vectigalis ad ultimum facta sit, ut cum con-
fecta labore volneribus postremo aetate corpora rettu-
lerint incultaque omnia diutino dominorum desiderio
domi invenerint, tributum ex adfecta re familiari
pendant aeraque militaria, velut fenore accepta,
multiplicia rei publicae reddant.

10   Inter dilectum tributumque et occupatos animos
maiorum rerum curis comitiis tribunorum plebis
11 numerus expleri nequiit.[2] Pugnatum inde in loca
vacua ut patricii cooptarentur. Postquam obtineri non
poterat, tamen labefactandae legis[3] causa effectum
est ut cooptarentur tribuni plebis C. Lacerius et
M. Acutius, haud dubie patriciorum opibus.

XI. Fors ita tulit ut eo anno tribunus plebis Cn.
Trebonius esset, qui nomini ac familiae debitum
2 praestare videretur Treboniae legis patrocinium.   Is
quod petissent patres quondam[4] primo incepto re-
pulsi, tandem[5] tribunos militum expugnasse ait[6]
vociferans legem Treboniam sublatam et cooptatos
tribunos plebis non suffragiis populi sed imperio

[1] quae nunc *Ald.*: quae ne Ω: quin *Vorm.* [2] *P²FUB.*
[2] nequiit ç: nequit (*or* nequid) Ω.
[3] legis *Madvig*: legis tribuniciae Ω.
[4] quondam *Haupt*: quidam (*omitted in a*) Ω.
[5] tandem *Weissenborn*: tamen Ω.
[6] expugnasse ait (expugnasse ç) *Luterbacher*: expugnas-
sent Ω.

[1] From the beginning no patrician might become a tribune
of the plebs (II. xxxiii. 1) and in 448 the Trebonian law
forbade co-optation to that office (III. lxv. 4).

had haled away even boys and old men. Now they B.C. 401
were confounding winter with summer, to allow no
rest ever to the unhappy commons, on whom finally
they had even imposed a tax; that when they should
drag home their bodies spent with toil, with wounds,
and at last with old age, and should then find all
things gone to waste in the long absence of the
owners, they might pay tribute out of their dimin-
ished property, and return to the state many times,
as it were with usury, the wages they had received
as soldiers.

What with the levy and the tax and the weightier
cares that preoccupied men's minds, they were unable on the day of election to return the full number
of plebeian tribunes. An effort was then made to
obtain the co-optation of patricians for the vacant
places. When this failed, nevertheless, in order to
invalidate the law, it was brought about that Gaius
Lacerius and Marcus Acutius should be chosen
tribunes, without doubt through patrician influence.[1]

XI. It so happened that in that year one of the
tribunes was Gnaeus Trebonius, whose name and
family seemed to make it his duty to defend the
Trebonian law. This man said that what the
Fathers had formerly aimed at (and had been
foiled on their first attempting), the tribunes of
the soldiers had finally extorted; he asseverated
that the Trebonian law had been done away with,
and that the tribunes of the plebs had been appointed not by the votes of the people but at the
dictation of the nobles; that things had come to
such a pass, that they must perforce have either
patricians or the satellites of patricians for tribunes
of the plebs; their sacred laws were being taken

LIVY

A.U.C. 353

patriciorum; eo[1] revolvi rem ut aut patricii aut
patriciorum adseculae habendi tribuni plebis sint;
3 eripi sacratas leges, extorqueri tribuniciam potestatem; id fraude patriciorum, scelere ac proditione
collegarum factum arguere.

4 Cum arderent invidia non patres modo sed etiam
tribuni plebis, cooptati pariter et qui cooptaverant,
tum ex collegio tres, P. Curatius M. Metilius M. Minucius, trepidi rerum suarum, in Sergium Vergini-
umque, prioris anni tribunos militares, incurrunt; in
eos ab se iram plebis invidiamque die dicta avertunt.
5 Quibus dilectus, quibus tributum, quibus diutina
militia longinquitasque belli sit gravis, qui clade
accepta ad Veios doleant, qui amissis liberis fratribus,
propinquis adfinibus, lugubres domos habeant, his
publici privatique doloris exsequendi ius potesta-
temque ex duobus noxiis capitibus datam ab se
6 memorant. Omnium namque malorum in Sergio
Verginioque causas esse; nec id accusatores[2] magis
arguere quam fateri reos, qui noxii ambo alter in
alterum causam conferant, fugam Sergi Verginius,
7 Sergius proditionem increpans Vergini. Quorum
adeo incredibilem amentiam fuisse ut multo veri
similius sit compecto eam rem et communi fraude
8 patriciorum actam. Ab his et prius datum locum
Veientibus ad incendenda opera belli trahendi causa,

---

[1] eo *Weissenborn*: et Ω: et eo *Vorm. ? D*[4].
[2] accusatores *Giers*: accusatorem Ω.

---

[1] Perhaps these three were held accountable for the illegal
step which the college had taken.

38

away, the tribunician power wrested from them. B.C. 401
This was done, he declared, by the knavery of the
patricians, the rascality and the treason of his
colleagues.

Men were burning with resentment, not only
against the patricians, but also against the tribunes
of the plebs, both those who had been co-opted and
those who had co-opted them, when three of the
college, Publius Curatius, Marcus Metilius, and
Marcus Minucius, being alarmed at their own situation,[1] fell violently upon Sergius and Verginius,
the military tribunes of the previous year, and by
appointing them a day for trial turned against them
the anger and displeasure which the plebs had
evinced towards themselves. They reminded their
hearers, that those who were aggrieved by the levy,
or the tax, or the protracted service and the long
duration of the war, those who sorrowed for the
calamity that befell at Veii, those whose houses were
in mourning for the loss of sons, brothers, kinsmen
or connexions,—that all those now had the right and
the power, thanks to the speakers, of avenging the
nation's private wrongs and their own on the two
culprits; for of all their sufferings Sergius and
Verginius were the cause; and this their accusers
were not more forward to maintain than the defendants to confess, who, equally guilty, threw the blame
on one another, Verginius taxing Sergius with his
flight, while Sergius complained of Verginius's
treachery. Their madness had been so incredible,
that it was much more probable that they had done
the thing upon agreement, with the collusion of the
senators; who having before given opportunity to
the Veientes to set fire to their works, in order to

et nunc proditum exercitum, tradita Faliscis Romana
9 castra. Omnia fieri ut consenescat ad Veios iuventus
nec de agris nec de aliis commodis plebis ferre
ad populum tribuni frequentiaque urbana celebrare
actiones et resistere conspirationi patriciorum possint.
10 Praeiudicium iam de reis et ab senatu et ab populo
11 Romano et ab ipsorum collegio [1] factum esse; nam
et senatus consulto eos ab re publica remotos esse,
et recusantes abdicare se magistratu dictatoris metu
ab collegis coercitos esse, et populum Romanum
tribunos creasse qui non idibus Decembribus, die
sollemni, sed extemplo kalendis Octobribus magistratum occiperent, quia stare diutius res publica his
12 manentibus in magistratu non posset; et tamen eos,
tot iudiciis confossos praedamnatosque venire ad
populi iudicium et existimare defunctos se esse
satisque poenarum dedisse quod duobus mensibus
13 citius privati facti sint, neque intellegere nocendi
sibi diutius tum potestatem ereptam esse, non poenam
inrogatam; quippe et collegis abrogatum imperium,
14 qui certe nihil deliquissent. Illos repeterent animos
Quirites quos recenti clade accepta habuissent, cum
fuga trepidum, plenum volnerum ac pavoris [2] inci-
dentem portis exercitum viderint non fortunam aut

---

[1] collegio *Walters*: collegiis (collegis D^2 or D^4a^2) Ω.
[2] pavoris *Gronov.*: pauore Ω.

prolong the war, had now betrayed the army and
delivered up a Roman camp to the Faliscans. They
were doing everything to wear out the young men
before Veii, and prevent the tribunes from bringing
before the people the question of land and other
advantages to the plebs, and from pushing their
measures in well-attended assemblies and thwarting
the conspiracy of the patricians. Judgment was
already given against the accused both by the
senate and by the Roman People, and also by
their own college; for the senate had by its decree
removed them from authority, and when they refused to abdicate their office, their colleagues had
coerced them by threatening to appoint a dictator,
and the Roman People had elected tribunes to
assume their duties, not on the thirteenth of
December, the usual date, but immediately, on
October the first, believing that the state could
endure no longer if the incumbents should remain
in place; yet, in spite of all, these men, stigmatized
and fore-judged by so many adverse verdicts, presented themselves for trial by the people, and
fancied that they were quit and sufficiently mulcted
because they were made private citizens two months
before their time; not perceiving that they had then
merely been deprived of the power to do further
mischief, not punished, since their colleagues, too,
were turned out of office, though they had certainly
done no wrong. Let the Quirites call back the
spirit they had shown when the recent calamity had
occurred, when they had beheld the flight and confusion of their troops, as they stumbled, wounded
and dismayed, through the City gates, accusing
neither fortune nor any of the gods, but these their

A.U.C.
353 15 quemquam deorum, sed hos duces accusantem.   Pro
certo se habere neminem in contione stare qui illo
die non caput domum fortunasque L. Vergini ac
16 M.' Sergi sit exsecratus detestatusque.   Minime
convenire quibus iratos quisque deos precatus sit in
iis sua potestate, cum liceat et oporteat, non uti.
Nunquam deos ipsos admovere nocentibus manus;
satis esse si occasione ulciscendi laesos arment.

A.U.C.
354   XII. His orationibus incitata plebs denis milibus
aeris gravis reos condemnat, nequiquam Sergio
Martem communem belli fortunamque accusante,
Verginio deprecante ne infelicior domi quam militiae
2 esset.   In hos versa ira populi cooptationis tribunorum fraudisque contra legem Treboniam factae
memoriam obscuram fecit.

3   Victores tribuni, ut praesentem mercedem iudicii
plebes haberet, legem agrariam promulgant tribu-
4 tumque conferri prohibent, cum tot exercitibus stipendio opus esset resque militiae[1] ita prospere
gererentur ut nullo bello veniretur ad exitum spei.
Namque Veiis castra quae amissa erant reciperata
castellis praesidiisque firmantur; praeerant tribuni
5 militum M.' Aemilius[2] et K. Fabius.[3]   A M. Furio
in Faliscis, a[4] Cn. Cornelio in Capenate agro hostes
nulli extra moenia inventi; praedae actae incendiis-
que villarum ac frugum vastati fines; oppida nec
6 oppugnata nec obsessa sunt.   At in Volscis depopu-

---

[1] militiae *Gronovius*: miliae *H*: militia Ω.
[2] M.' Aemilius *a*: m. (*or* m̄.) aemilius (aemelius *B*) Ω.
[3] K. Fabius *cf. chap.* x, § 1: q. (*or* quintus) fabius Ω.
[4] a M¹: et Ω.

leaders. They were sure that there was not a man B.C. 401
present in the assembly who had not on that day
cursed and execrated the lives, the houses, and the
fortunes of Lucius Verginius and Manius Sergius.
It was not reasonable that their hearers, having a
legal and moral right in the matter, should not use
their power against those upon whom each one of
them had invoked the wrath of Heaven. The gods
themselves never laid hands upon the guilty; it was
enough if they armed with opportunity those who
had been wronged.

XII. Incited by these speeches, the plebs con- B.C. 400
demned the accused to pay each a fine of 10,000
pounds of bronze. It was in vain that Sergius
blamed Fortune and the common chance of war,
while Verginius begged that he might not be more
unlucky at home than he had been in the campaign.
On them the wrath of the people was poured out,
and the co-optation of the tribunes and the evasion
of the Trebonian law were almost forgotten.

The victorious tribunes, that the plebs might have
an immediate reward for its judgment, proposed a
land-law and forbade the gathering of the war-tax,
notwithstanding that pay was needed for so many
armies, whose campaigning, though successful, yet
failed to realize the desired end in any war. Thus,
at Veii, they recovered the lost camp and strengthened it with fortresses and garrisons, led by the
military tribunes Manius Aemilius and Caeso Fabius;
Marcus Furius in the Faliscan country, and Gnaeus
Cornelius in the territory of Capena, meeting no
enemies afield, drove off booty, and burning farm-
houses and crops, laid waste the land, but the towns
they neither assaulted nor beseiged; in the Volscian

A.U.C.
354 lato agro Anxur nequiquam oppugnatum loco alto
situm et, postquam vis inrita erat, vallo fossaque
obsideri coeptum. Valerio Potito Volsci provincia
evenerat.

7 Hoc statu militarium rerum seditio intestina maiore
mole coorta quam bella tractabantur; et cum tributum conferri per tribunos non posset[1] nec stipendium imperatoribus mitteretur aeraque militaria
flagitaret miles, haud procul erat quin castra quoque
8 urbanae seditionis contagione turbarentur. Inter
has iras plebis in patres cum tribuni plebi nunc illud
tempus esse dicerent stabiliendae libertatis et ab
Sergiis Verginiisque ad plebeios viros fortes ac
9 strenuos transferendi summi honoris, non tamen ultra
processum est quam ut unus ex plebe, usurpandi
iuris causa, P. Licinius Calvus tribunus militum con-
10 sulari potestate crearetur; ceteri patricii creati, P.
Manlius[2] L. Titinius[3] P. Maelius L. Furius Medul-
11 linus L. Publilius[4] Volscus. Ipsa plebes mirabatur
se tantam rem obtinuisse, non is modo qui creatus
erat, vir nullis ante honoribus usus, vetus tantum
12 senator et aetate iam gravis; nec satis constat cur
primus ac potissimus ad novum delibandum honorem
sit habitus. Alii Cn. Corneli fratris, qui tribunus
militum priore anno fuerat triplexque stipendium

---

[1] posset *D?* ϛ: possit Ω.
[2] Manlius *D¹* (*or D²*) ϛ: manilius Ω: mamilius *PFUB*:
mamlius (*or* manilius) *D*.
[3] L. Titinius *Sigon.* (v. xviii. 2, *and Diod.* xiv. xc. 1) p.
titinius Ω: et p. titinius *EDA*.
[4] Publilius *Sigon.* (*C.I.L.* i², *p.* 116): popilius Ω: popu-
lius *U*.

---

[1] Or, perhaps, step-brother.

country, however, after ravaging the fields, they made a futile attack on Anxur, which was seated on an eminence, and finding force to be unavailing, began to invest it with a stockade and trench, under Valerius Potitus, who had got the command against the Volsci.

While military affairs were in this posture, a quarrel that broke out at home aroused more energy than went to their making of wars; and since the tax could not be taken up, on account of the tribunes, and the generals were sent no money, while the soldiers were clamouring for their pay, the camp, too, was like to have been disrupted by the contagion of mutiny in the City. In the midst of this hostility which the plebs felt towards the patricians, though the plebeian tribunes said that the time was now come to establish liberty, and to transfer the highest office from such as Sergius and Verginius to stout and courageous commoners, yet they got no further than the election of one plebeian (by way of asserting their right), namely, Publius Licinius Calvus, to be military tribune with consular powers; the others chosen were patricians: Publius Manlius, Lucius Titinius, Publius Maelius, Lucius Furius Medullinus, Lucius Publilius Volscus. The plebeians themselves were amazed that they had gained so important a point, and not alone the man who had been chosen, one that had held no offices before, but was only a senator of long standing, now well on in years. There is no unanimity of opinion why he was selected as the first and fittest to taste of the new honours. Some think it was the favour of his cousin [1] Gnaeus Cornelius, who as tribune of the soldiers the year before had granted triple pay

45

A.U.C.
355

equitibus dederat, gratia extractum ad tantum honorem credunt, alii orationem ipsum tempestivam de
concordia ordinum patribus plebique gratam habuisse.

13 Hac victoria comitiorum exsultantes tribuni plebis,
quod maxime rem publicam impediebat de tributo
remiserunt. Conlatum oboedienter missumque ad
exercitum est.

XIII. Anxur in Volscis brevi receptum est neglectis
die festo custodiis urbis. Insignis annus hieme
gelida ac nivosa fuit, adeo ut viae clausae, Tiberis
innavigabilis fuerit. Annona ex ante convecta copia

2 nihil mutavit. Et quia P. Licinius, ut ceperat haud
tumultuose magistratum maiore gaudio plebis quam
indignatione patrum, ita etiam gessit, dulcedo invasit proximis comitiis tribunorum militum plebeios

3 creandi. Unus M. Veturius ex patriciis candidatis
locum tenuit: plebeios alios tribunos militum consulari potestate omnes fere centuriae dixere, M. Pomponium Cn. Duillium Voleronem Publilium [1] Cn.
Genucium L. Atilium.

4 Tristem hiemem, sive ex intemperie caeli raptim
mutatione in contrarium facta sive alia qua de causa,
gravis pestilensque omnibus animalibus aestas ex-

5 cepit. Cuius insanabili pernicie quando nec causa
nec finis inveniebatur, libri Sibyllini ex senatus con-

---

[1] Publilium *Sigon.* : publicium (*or* -litium, *or* -licum) Ω.

---

[1] In chap. vii. § 5, there is no mention of pay ; Livy means
that the cavalryman received thrice the pay of the foot-soldier.

to the cavalrymen,[1] that got him his promotion to so great an office; others, that he himself made a timely speech on the harmony of the orders, which pleased both patricians and plebeians. Overjoyed at their victory in this election, the tribunes of the plebs withdrew that opposition to the tax which was the greatest obstacle to the business of the state, and it was obediently paid in and dispatched to the army.

XIII. Anxur of the Volsci was speedily re-captured, a holiday having relaxed the vigilance of their guard. This year was remarkable for so cold and snowy a winter, that the roads were blocked and the Tiber became unnavigable. The price of corn, owing to the supply which they had brought in before, did not go up. Publius Licinius had obtained his magistracy without any disorders, rejoicing the commons more than he offended the patricians, and in the same spirit he conducted it; the people therefore became desirous of returning plebeians at the next election of consular tribunes. Marcus Veturius was the sole patrician candidate to get in; all the other military tribunes with consular authority were commoners, as the result of an all but unanimous vote of the centuries. Their names were Marcus Pomponius, Gnaeus Duillius, Volero Publilius, Gnaeus Genucius, Lucius Atilius.

The severe winter was succeeded, whether in consequence of the sudden change from such inclement weather to the opposite extreme, or for some other reason, by a summer that was noxious and baleful to all living creatures. Unable to discover what caused the incurable ravages of this distemper, or would put an end to them, the senate voted to consult the Sibylline Books. The duumvirs

47

A.U.C.
355

6 sulto aditi sunt. Duumviri sacris faciundis lecti-
sternio tunc primum in urbe Romana facto per dies
octo Apollinem Latonamque et Dianam, Herculem
Mercurium atque Neptunum tribus quam amplissime
7 tum apparari poterat stratis lectis placavere. Privatim quoque id sacrum celebratum est. Tota urbe
patentibus ianuis promiscuoque usu rerum omnium
in propatulo posito, notos ignotosque passim advenas
in hospitium ductos ferunt et cum inimicis quoque
benigne ac comiter sermones habitos, iurgiis ac
8 litibus temperatum; vinctis quoque dempta in eos
dies vincula; religioni deinde fuisse quibus eam
opem di tulissent vinciri.

9　Interim ad Veios terror multiplex fuit tribus in
unum bellis conlatis. Namque eodem quo antea
modo circa munimenta cum repente Capenates
Faliscique subsidio venissent, adversus tres exercitus
10 ancipiti proelio pugnatum est. Ante omnia adiuvit
memoria damnationis Sergi ac Vergini. Itaque e
maioribus [1] castris, unde antea cessatum fuerat, brevi
spatio circumductae copiae Capenates in vallum
Romanum versos ab tergo adgrediuntur; inde pugna
11 coepta et Faliscis intulit terrorem, trepidantesque
eruptio ex castris opportune facta avertit. Repulsos
deinde insecuti victores ingentem ediderunt caedem.
12 Nec ita multo post iam forte [2] oblati populatores
13 Capenatis agri reliquias pugnae absumpsere. Et

---

[1] e maioribus *Perizonius* : maioribus Ω.

[2] iam forte *Conway* : iam palantes (palentes *H*) veluti
forte Ω.

---

[1] From *lectus*, "couch" and *sternere*, "to spread." The
images of the gods were placed on banqueting couches and
served with food.

in charge of the sacred rites then celebrated the B.C. 399
first lectisternium [1] ever held in Rome, and for the
space of eight days sacrificed to Apollo, to Latona
and Diana, to Hercules, to Mercury and to Neptune,
spreading couches for them with all the splendour
then attainable. They also observed the rite in
their homes. All through the City, they say, doors
stood wide open, all kinds of viands were set out for
general consumption, all comers were welcomed,
whether known or not, and men even exchanged
kind and courteous words with personal enemies;
there was a truce to quarrelling and litigation; even
prisoners were loosed from their chains for those
days, and they scrupled thenceforth to imprison men
whom the gods has thus befriended.

Meantime alarms were multiplied at Veii, where
three wars were rolled into one. For, precisely as
before, the Capenates and the Faliscans came
suddenly to raise the siege, and the Romans fought
about their works against three armies, which
attacked them on both sides. What helped them
most, was the recollection how Sergius and Verginius
had been condemned. And so from the principal
camp, where the delay had occurred on the former
occasion, troops were dispatched by a short circuit
and fell upon the Capenates in the rear, as they
faced the rampart of the Romans. Beginning there,
the battle carried terror even among the Faliscans,
who were wavering, when a timely sally from the
camp put them to flight. Then, as they retreated,
the victors pursued them with great slaughter; and
not long after a party that was raiding the territory
of the Capenates happened to fall in with them and
destroyed such as had survived the battle. Of the

49

A.U.C.
355 Veientium refugientes in urbem multi ante portas
caesi, dum prae metu, ne simul Romanus inrumperet,
obiectis foribus extremos suorum exclusere.

A.U.C.
356 XIV. Haec eo anno acta. Et iam comitia tribunorum militum aderant, quorum prope maior patribus
quam belli cura erat, quippe non communicatum
modo cum plebe sed prope amissum cernentibus
2 summum imperium. Itaque clarissimis viris ex com-
posito praeparatis ad petendum quos praetereundi
verecundiam crederent fore, nihilo minus ipsi,
perinde ac si omnes candidati essent, cuncta ex-
perientes non homines modo sed deos etiam exciebant,[1] in religionem vertentes comitia biennio
3 habita: priore anno intolerandam hiemem prodigiis-
que divinis similem coortam, proximo non prodigia,
4 sed iam eventus: pestilentiam agris urbique inlatam
haud dubia ira deum, quos pestis eius arcendae causa
placandos esse in libris fatalibus inventum sit;
comitiis auspicato quae fierent indignum dis visum
honores volgari discriminaque gentium confundi.
5 Praeterquam maiestate petentium, religione etiam
attoniti homines patricios omnes, partem magnam
honoratissimum quemque, tribunos militum consulari
potestate creavere, L. Valerium Potitum quintum
M.[2] Valerium Maximum M. Furium Camillum iterum

---

[1] exciebant *Drakenborch*: excipiebant (-bat *F*) Ω.
[2] quintum M. *D?*: quintum (*or* q̃) Ω: q. (*i. e.* que) *LA?*

Veientes likewise, many, as they fled back to the B.C. 399
town, were slain before the gates, when their friends,
fearing lest the Romans should burst in along with
them, had closed the portals, and barred out the
hindmost of their own people.

XIV. Such were the events of this year. And B.C. 398
now the time drew near for choosing military tribunes
and the Fathers were almost more concerned about
the election than about the war, perceiving that the
highest authority had been not merely shared with
the plebs, but well-nigh lost to themselves. They
therefore arranged that their most distinguished
members should stand,—men whom they believed
the electors would be ashamed to pass over,—and at
the same time they themselves, as if they had all
been candidates, left no stone unturned, and called
to their aid not only men, but the gods as well, by
raising a religious scruple anent the election held
two years before. In the year before the last, they
said, there had been an intolerable winter, like a
warning from Heaven. Last year had come not
prodigies but actual realities: a pestilence had
descended upon the fields and the City, clearly
proceeding from the anger of the gods, whom they
must propitiate in order to avert the plague, as the
fateful Books had indicated; it had seemed to the
gods an affront that an election held under their
auspices should prostitute honours and confound
family distinctions. The people were awed not only
by the dignity of the candidates, but by the fear of
Heaven, and to be military tribunes with consular
powers chose all patricians, and chiefly the most
illustrious among them, as follows: Lucius Valerius
Potitus (for the fifth time), Marcus Valerius Maximus,

51

A.U.C.
356

L. Furium Medullinum tertium Q. Servilium Fide-
6 natem iterum Q. Sulpicium Camerinum iterum. His
tribunis ad Veios nihil admodum memorabile actum
7 est; tota vis in populationibus fuit. Duo summi
imperatores, Potitus a Faleriis, Camillus a Capena
praedas ingentes egere nulla incolumi relicta re cui
ferro aut igni noceri posset.

XV. Prodigia interim multa nuntiari, quorum
pleraque, et quia singuli auctores erant, parum
credita spretaque, et quia hostibus Etruscis, per
2 quos ea procurarent, haruspices non erant : in unum
omnium curae versae sunt, quod lacus in Albano
nemore sine ullis caelestibus aquis causave qua alia
quae rem miraculo eximeret, in altitudinem insolitam
3 crevit. Quidnam eo di portenderent prodigio missi
4 sciscitatum oratores ad Delphicum oraculum. Sed
propior interpres fatis oblatus senior quidam Veiens,
qui inter cavillantes in stationibus ac custodiis milites
Romanos Etruscosque vaticinantis in modum cecinit
priusquam ex lacu Albano aqua emissa foret nun-
5 quam potiturum Veiis Romanum. Quod primo velut
temere iactum sperni, agitari deinde sermonibus
coeptum est, donec unus ex statione Romana percontatus proximum oppidanorum iam per longin-
quitatem belli commercio sermonum facto, quisnam
is esset qui per ambages de lacu Albano iaceret,
6 postquam audivit haruspicem esse, vir haud intacti

Marcus Furius Camillus (for the second time), Lucius B.C. 398 Furius Medullinus (for the third), Quintus Sulpicius Camerinus (for the second). These tribunes achieved absolutely nothing noteworthy at Veii, but employed all their strength in pillaging. The two chief commanders, Potitus and Camillus,—one at Falerii, the other at Capena,—carried off huge spoils and left nothing untouched that iron or fire could destroy.

XV. Meanwhile many portents were reported, most of which, because they had only one witness each to vouch for them, obtained no credence and were slighted; and, besides, when the Etruscans, whose services they employed to avert evil omens, were at war with them, they had no soothsayers. One thing occasioned universal anxiety, namely that the lake in the Alban Wood, without any rains or other cause to make it less than a miracle, rose to an unwonted height. To inquire what the gods could possibly foretell by that prodigy, envoys were sent to the Delphic oracle. But a nearer interpreter of the fates presented himself, an old man of Veii, who, while the Roman and Etruscan soldiers were scoffing at one another as they stood guard at the outposts, declared in a prophetic strain that until the water should be drawn off from the Alban Lake the Romans never could take Veii. At first they made light of this as an idle taunt; then they began to talk it over; presently one of the Roman outpost inquired of the townsman nearest him (for owing to the long continuance of the war they had now got into the way of conversing together) who that man was who threw out mysterious hints regarding the Alban Lake. When he heard that he was a soothsayer, being himself not without a touch of

A U.C.
356 religione animi, causatus de privati portenti pro-
curatione si operae illi esset consulere velle, ad
7 conloquium vatem elicuit. Cumque progressi ambo
a suis longius essent inermes sine ullo metu, prae-
valens iuvenis Romanus senem infirmum in conspectu
omnium raptum nequiquam tumultuantibus Etruscis
8 ad suos transtulit. Qui cum perductus ad imperatorem, inde Romam ad senatum missus esset, scisci-
tantibus quidnam id esset quod de lacu Albano
9 docuisset, respondit profecto iratos deos Veienti
populo illo fuisse die quo sibi eam mentem obiecissent
10 ut excidium patriae fatale proderet. Itaque quae
tum cecinerit divino spiritu instinctus, ea se nec ut
indicta sint revocare posse et tacendo forsitan quae
di immortales volgari velint haud minus quam
11 celanda effando nefas contrahi. Sic [1] igitur libris
fatalibus, sic disciplina Etrusca traditum esse,
quando [2] aqua Albana abundasset, tum si eam
Romanus rite emisisset victoriam de Veientibus dari ;
antequam id fiat deos moenia Veientium desorturos
12 non esse. Exsequebatur inde quae sollemnis deri-
vatio esset. Sed auctorem levem nec satis fidum
super tanta re patres rati decrevere legatos sortesque
oraculi Pythici exspectandas.

A.U.C.
357 XVI. Priusquam a Delphis oratores redirent
Albanive prodigii piacula invenirentur, novi tribuni

---

[1] sic ς: his Ω.
[2] quando *Duker*: ut quando Ω: ut q̄n̄ *A*.

---

[1] A tunnel to drain the flood-waters of the Alban Lake,
1300 yards long and from seven to ten feet high, was actually
cut through the solid rock, not to bring about the capture of
Veii, but to save a few hundred acres of arable land on the
sloping edge within the crater (Tenney Frank, *Economic
History of Rome*, p. 7).

superstition, he alleged a desire to consult him B.C. 398 about the averting of a domestic portent, if he could spare the time, and so enticed the seer to a conference. And when they had walked a little way apart from the friends of both, unarmed and fearing nothing, the stalwart young Roman laid hold of the feeble old man in the sight of them all, and despite an unavailing hubbub raised by the Etruscans, bore him off to his own fellows. There they had him before the general, who sent him on to Rome, to the senate. When the Fathers questioned him what it was he had meant about the Alban Lake, he answered that the gods must surely have been incensed at the people of Veii on the day when they put it into his mind to reveal the destruction destined to befall his native city; and so what he had then uttered under divine inspiration, he could not now unsay and recall; and perhaps in concealing what the immortal gods wished to be published guilt was incurred no less than by disclosing what should be hid. Thus then it was written in the books of fate, thus handed down in the lore of the Etruscans, that when the Alban water should overflow, if then the Romans should duly draw it off, they would be given the victory over the Veientes; until that should come to pass, the gods would not abandon the walls of Veii. He then went on to explain the appointed method of draining it. But the senators, making slight account of his authority, as not sufficiently trustworthy in so grave a matter, determined to wait for their deputies with the response of the Pythian oracle.[1]

XVI. But before these envoys could return from B.C. 397 Delphi or an expiation be devised for the Alban

55

LIVY

militum consulari potestate L. Iulius Iulus[1] L.
Furius[2] Medullinus quartum L. Sergius Fidenas
A. Postumius Regillensis[3] P. Cornelius Maluginensis
2 A Manlius magistratum inierunt. Eo anno Tarquinienses novi hostes exorti. Qui quia[4] multis
simul bellis, Volscorum ad Anxur, ubi praesidium
obsidebatur, Aequorum ad Labicos,[5] qui Romanam
ibi coloniam oppugnabant, ad hoc Veientique et
Falisco et Capenati bello occupatos videbant
Romanos, nec intra muros quietiora negotia esse
3 certaminibus patrum ac plebis, inter haec locum
iniuriae rati esse praedatum in agrum Romanum
cohortes expeditas mittunt: aut enim passuros
inultam eam iniuriam Romanos, ne novo bello se
onerarent, aut exiguo eoque parum valido exercitu
4 persecuturos. Romanis indignitas maior quam cura
populationis Tarquiniensium fuit; eo nec magno
5 conatu suscepta nec in longum dilata res est. A.
Postumius[6] et L. Iulius non iusto dilectu—etenim
ab tribunis plebis impediebantur—sed prope volun-
tariorum quos adhortando incitaverant coacta manu
per agrum Caeretem obliquis tramitibus egressi
redeuntes a populationibus gravesque praeda Tar-
6 quinienses oppressere. Multos mortales obtruncant,
omnes exuunt impedimentis, et receptis agrorum

[1] Iulus *Sigonius*: tullus *HDLA*: utullus *PFBOE*: uitullus
U: silius tullus *MA*[2].

[2] L. Furius ς: p̄ furius Ω : p̄ silius furius *PFUB*: praesilius
(pre- *O*) furius *OE*.

[3] Regillensis *Sigon.*: regiliensis *MOE*: religiensis Ω.

[4] Qui quia *Duker*: quia Ω.

[5] Labicos Ω *at* II. xxxix. 4: lauicos Ω.

[6] A. Postumius ς: aurelius postumius Ω.

[1] For the second time (*cf.* chap. x. § 1).
[2] For the third time (*cf.* chap. viii. § 1).

portent, new military tribunes with consular authority
came in; these were Lucius Julius Iulus,[1] Lucius
Furius Medullinus (for the fourth time), Lucius
Sergius Fidenas, Aulus Postumius Regillensis,
Publius Cornelius Maluginensis, and Aulus Manlius.[2]
In that year a new enemy arose in the Tarquinienses,
who seeing the Romans beset with many wars at
once,—against the Volsci, who were laying siege to
the garrison at Anxur, against the Aequi, who were
attacking the Roman colony at Labici, and also
against the men of Veii, of Falerii, and of Capena,—
and perceiving that affairs within the City were no
less troubled, owing to contentions betwixt the
patricians and the plebs, believed that in these
circumstances they had an opportunity to do the
Romans a hurt, and sent out light-armed detachments to raid their territory; for they thought that
either the Romans would put up with the wrong, to
avoid the burden of another war, or would take the
field with a small and therefore inadequate army.
The indignation of the Romans was greater than
their concern for the damage wrought by the
Tarquinienses; so they neither made strenuous
efforts to prepare, nor deferred taking action to a
distant date. Aulus Postumius and Lucius Iulus,
without holding a regular levy—for this the plebeian
tribunes hindered—but with a company consisting
almost solely of volunteers whom they had induced
to join by their exhortations, marched out by cross-
country ways through the territory of Caere, and
surprised the Tarquinienses as they were returning
from their depradations laden with booty. Many
men they slew, all they stripped of their baggage;
and having recovered the spoils of their own fields,

A.U.C.
357

7 suorum spoliis Romam revertuntur. Biduum ad
recognoscendas res datum dominis; tertio incognita
—erant autem ea pleraque hostium ipsorum—sub
hasta veniere, quodque inde redactum militibus est
divisum.

8   Cetera bella maximeque Veiens incerti exitus
erant. Iamque Romani desperata ope humana fata
et deos spectabant, cum legati ab Delphis venerunt
sortem oraculi adferentes congruentem responso
9 captivi vatis: "Romane, aquam Albanam cave lacu
contineri, cave in mare manare suo flumine sinas;
emissam per agros rigabis dissipatamque rivis exstin-
10 gues; tum tu insiste audax hostium muris, memor
quam per tot annos obsides urbem ex ea tibi his
11 quae nunc panduntur fatis victoriam datam. Bello
perfecto donum amplum victor ad mea templa
portato, sacraque patria, quorum omissa cura est,
instaurata ut adsolet facito."

XVII. Ingens inde haberi captivus vates coeptus,
eumque adhibere tribuni militum Cornelius Postu-
miusque ad prodigii Albani procurationem ac deos
2 rite placandos coepere; inventumque tandem est
ubi neglectas caerimonias intermissumve sollemne
di arguerent: nihil profecto aliud esse quam magistratus vitio creatos Latinas sacrumque in Albano
3 monte non rite concepisse; unam expiationem eorum

---

¹ *i. e.* at public auction, the spear being set up to advertise
such a sale.

returned to Rome. Two days were allowed the owners to identify their property; on the third all that had not been recognized—chiefly things belonging to the enemy themselves—was sold under the spear[1] and the proceeds divided amongst the soldiers.

The other campaigns, especially the one at Veii, were indecisive. And now the Romans, despairing of human aid, were looking to destiny and the gods, when the deputies returned from Delphi, bringing the oracle's response, which corresponded with the utterance of the captive seer: "Roman, see that thou suffer not the Alban water to be confined within the lake, nor to fret its own channel to the sea; thou shalt draw it forth and water the fields withal, and spread it abroad till it be lost in rivulets; after that press boldly on against the walls of the foe, and know that over that city which thou dost beleaguer for so many years, the fates now disclosed have given thee the victory. When thou hast ended the war with conquest, bring to my temple an ample gift, and repeat and accomplish in customary wise the ancestral rites thou hast neglected."

XVII. The captive soothsayer began from that moment to be held in great repute, and the military tribunes, Cornelius and Postumius, set out to employ him about the expiation of the Alban prodigy and the due appeasement of the gods. At length it was discovered wherein the gods taxed them with neglecting ceremonies or omitting a festival: it was assuredly nothing else than that magistrates in whose election there had been a flaw had improperly proclaimed the Latin games and the sacrifice on the

LIVY

esse ut tribuni militum abdicarent se magistratu,
auspicia de integro repeterentur, et interregnum
4 iniretur. Ea ita facta sunt ex senatus consulto.
Interreges tres deinceps fuere, L. Valerius Q.
5 Servilius Fidenas M. Furius Camillus. Nunquam
desitum interim turbari, comitia interpellantibus
tribunis plebis donec convenisset prius ut maior pars
tribunorum militum ex plebe crearetur.
6 Quae dum aguntur, concilia Etruriae ad fanum
Voltumnae habita, postulantibusque Capenatibus ac
7 Faliscis ut Veios communi animo consilioque omnes
Etruriae populi ex obsidione eriperent, responsum
est antea se id Veientibus negasse quia unde consilium non petissent super tanta re auxilium petere
8 non deberent ; nunc iam pro se fortunam suam illis
negare. Maxima iam in parte [1] Etruriae gentem
invisitatam,[2] novos accolas esse,[3] cum quibus nec pax
9 satis fida nec bellum pro certo sit. Sanguini tamen
nominique et praesentibus periculis consanguineorum
id dari ut si qui iuventutis suae voluntate ad id
10 bellum eant non impediant. Eum magnum advenisse
hostium numerum fama Romae erat; eoque mites-
cere discordiae intestinae metu communi, ut fit,
coepere.[4]

[1] maxima iam in parte *Luterbacher*: maxime in ea
parte Ω.
[2] invisitatam *E¹D²*: inuisitatem (*or* inusitatam *or* inuis
sitatam) Ω.
[3] esse *Conway and Walters*: Gallos esse Ω.
[4] coepere *Weissenborn*: coeptae Ω.

---

[1] The Latin Festival (in honour of Jupiter Latiaris, who
presided over the Latin League) was held each year, and was
followed by a sacrifice, on the date proclaimed by the new
consuls, or consular tribunes.

Alban Mount[1]; only one atonement for these errors was open to them, to make the tribunes of the soldiers resign their office, to take the auspices afresh, and to begin an interregnum. By decree of the senate these things were done. There were three successive interreges, Lucius Valerius, Quintus Servilius Fidenas, Marcus Furius Camillus. In the meantime there were continuous disturbances, and the plebeian tribunes blocked the election, until it had first been agreed that the majority of the military tribunes should be chosen out of the commons.

While this was going on, the Etruscans met in council at the Fane of Voltumna; where the Capenates and Faliscans proposed that all the nations of Etruria should unite in a common resolution and design to raise the siege of Veii. The council made answer that they had before refused the Veientes this request, on the ground that they had no right to ask help from those whom they had not cared to look to for advice in so weighty a matter. Just then, however, the plight of their country itself denied the petition. There was now in the greatest part of Etruria a strange race, new settlers, with whom they were neither securely at peace nor yet certain to have war. Nevertheless, out of regard for the blood and the name and the present perils of their kinsmen, they would grant that if any of their young men wished to serve in that war, they might do so without let or hindrance. Of such recruits it was said at Rome that a great number had come in; and so domestic differences began to subside, as generally happens, in the face of a common danger.

XVIII. Haud invitis patribus P. Licinium Calvum praerogativae[1] tribunum militum non petentem creant, moderationis expertae in priore magistratu virum, ceterum iam tum exactae aetatis ; omnesque
2 deinceps ex collegio eiusdem anni refici apparebat, L. Titinium P. Maenium[2] Cn. Genucium L. Atilium. Qui priusquam renuntiarentur iure vocatis tribubus, permissu interregis P. Licinius Calvus ita verba
3 fecit : "Omen concordiae, Quirites, rei maxime in hoc tempus utili, memoria nostri magistratus vos his
4 comitiis petere in insequentem annum video ; sed collegas[3] eosdem reficitis, etiam usu meliores factos, me iam non eundem sed umbram nomenque P. Licini relictum videtis. Vires corporis adfectae, sensus oculorum atque aurium hebetes, memoria
5 labat, vigor animi obtunsus. En vobis" inquit "iuvenem," filium tenens, "effigiem atque imaginem eius quem vos antea tribunum militum ex plebe primum fecistis. Hunc ego institutum disciplina mea vicarium pro me rei publicae do dicoque vosque quaeso, Quirites, delatum mihi ultro honorem huic petenti meisque pro eo adiectis precibus mandetis."
6 Datum id petenti patri, filiusque eius P. Licinius tribunus militum consulari potestate cum iis quos
7 supra scripsimus declaratus. Titinius Genuciusque

[1] praerogativae *Sigonius* : praerogatiua (progatiua *P*) Ω.
[2] P. Maenium Ω : P. Maenium Q. Manlium *Niebuhr* : Q. Manlium P. Maenium *Madvig* (*cf.* v. xii. 10, *and C.I.L.* i,[2] *p.* 118).
[3] sed collegas *Madvig* : sit (*or* et sit *or* et si *or* et ii *or* si et *or* sic) collegas Ω.

[1] The *praerogatives* were the eighteen centuries of knights, which voted first ; if they agreed, the other centuries were not called. See I. xliii. 11.

XVIII. It occasioned the Fathers no displeasure when the prerogative centuries[1] chose Publius Licinius Calvus tribune of the soldiers, without his seeking office; he was a man whose moderation had been proven in his former term, but was now become superannuated. It was clear that all who had been his colleagues in that same year would also be returned, one after the other, to wit: Lucius Titinius, Publius Maenius, Gnaeus Genucius, Lucius Atilius. But before they were declared to the duly assembled tribes, Licinius spoke as follows, having obtained permission of the interrex: "It is an omen of harmony, as I perceive, Quirites, a thing most needful at this juncture, that you seek for the ensuing year, when in your voting you remember our former magistracy; but whereas in my colleagues you are choosing again the same men, and all the better for experience, in me you see no longer the same Publius Licinius, of whom but the shadow and the name are left. My strength of body is decayed, my sight and hearing dulled, memory fails me, and the vigour of my mind is impaired. Here," he cried, laying hold of his son, "here is a young man, the effigy and likeness of him you formerly chose for military tribune first of all plebeians. Him have I bred up in my own principles, and in my stead I give and dedicate him to the state, and I pray you, Quirites, who without my seeking have offered me the office, that you grant it to him, who seeks it, and to the prayers I have added in his behalf." The father was granted his request, and the son, Publius Licinius, was declared military tribune with consular powers, together with those I have named above. Titinius and Genucius, tribunes of the soldiers,

tribuni militum profecti adversus Faliscos Capenates-
que, dum bellum maiore animo gerunt quam consilio,
8 praecipitavere se in insidias. Genucius morte honesta
temeritatem luens ante signa inter primores cecidit;
Titinius in editum tumulum ex multa trepidatione
militibus collectis aciem restituit, nec se tamen aequo
9 loco hosti commisit. Plus ignominiae erat quam
cladis acceptum, quae prope in cladem ingentem
vertit; tantum inde terroris non Romae modo, quo
multiplex fama pervenerat, sed in castris quoque
10 fuit ad Veios. Aegre ibi miles retentus a fuga est
cum pervasisset castra rumor ducibus exercituque
caeso victorem Capenatem ac Faliscum Etruriaeque
11 omnem iuventutem haud procul inde abesse. His
tumultuosiora Romae, iam castra ad Veios oppugnari,
iam partem hostium tendere ad urbem agmine infesto, crediderant; concursumque in muros est et
matronarum, quas ex domo conciverat publicus pavor,
obsecrationes in templis factae, precibusque ab dis
12 petitum, ut exitium ab urbis tectis templisque ac
moenibus Romanis arcerent Veiosque eum averterent
terrorem, si sacra renovata rite, si procurata prodigia
essent.

XIX. Iam ludi Latinaeque instaurata erant, iam
ex lacu Albano aqua emissa in agros, Veiosque fata
2 adpetebant. Igitur fatalis dux ad excidium illius

having marched against the Faliscans and Capenates, B.C. 396 brought more spirit than generalship to their conduct of the war, and plunged into an ambush. Genucius, atoning for his rashness by an honourable death, fell fighting among the foremost, in front of the standards; Titinius rallied his men, who had been thrown into great confusion, on a little eminence, and made a stand, yet he would not risk an engagement on level ground. The disgrace outweighed the defeat, which had almost proved disastrous, so great was the panic which it caused, not only in Rome, where a greatly exaggerated report of the affair had been received, but also in the camp before Veii. There the soldiers could hardly be restrained from flight, for a rumour had run through the camp that the victorious Capenates and Faliscans, having slaughtered the Roman commanders and their army, were close at hand, with all the manhood of Etruria. Accounts even more alarming had been credited at Rome: that the camp at Veii was already under attack; that already a division of the enemy was marching to assail the City. There was a rush to the walls, and the women, drawn from their houses by the general consternation, betook themselves to prayer in the temples, and besought the gods to ward off destruction from the houses and shrines of the City and from the walls of Rome, and to turn that panic against Veii, if the sacred rites had been duly renewed and the portents expiated.

XIX. And now the games and the Latin Festival had been repeated, now the water had been let out from the Alban Lake upon the fields, and the doom of Veii drew on apace. Accordingly the commander destined to destroy that city and to save his country,

65

LIVY

urbis servandaeque patriae, M. Furius Camillus, dictator dictus magistrum equitum P. Cornelium

3 Scipionem dixit. Omnia repente mutaverat imperator mutatus; alia spes, alius animus hominum, fortuna

4 quoque alia urbis videri. Omnium primum in eos qui a Veiis in illo pavore fugerant more militari animadvertit, effecitque ne hostis maxime timendus militi esset. Deinde indicto dilectu in diem certam ipse interim Veios ad confirmandos militum animos

5 intercurrit; inde Romam ad scribendum novum exercitum redit nullo detractante militiam. Peregrina etiam iuventus, Latini Hernicique, operam

6 suam pollicentes ad id bellum venere; quibus cum gratias in senatu egisset dictator, satis iam omnibus ad id bellum paratis ludos magnos ex senatus consulto vovit Veiis captis se facturum aedemque Matutae Matris refectam dedicaturum, iam ante ab rege

7 Ser. Tullio dedicatam. Profectus cum exercitu ab urbe exspectatione hominum maiore quam spe in agro primum Nepesino cum Faliscis et Capenatibus

8 signa confert. Omnia ibi summa ratione consilioque acta fortuna etiam, ut fit, secuta est. Non proelio tantum fudit hostes, sed castris quoque exuit ingentique praeda est potitus; cuius pars maxima ad quaestorem redacta est, haud ita multum militi datum.

9 Inde ad Veios exercitus ductus, densioraque castella

---

[1] Livy's brevity here makes the sentence a little obscure. No doubt the Latins and Hernicans first sent envoys, and these were introduced into the senate and there thanked by the dictator.

[2] *i.e.* votive games in recognition of some special favour of the gods.

Marcus Furius Camillus, was appointed dictator, and
named Publius Cornelius Scipio as his master of the
horse. The change in the command at once made
a change in all things else; there was new hope and
a new spirit, and even the fortune of the City seemed
to be renewed. The dictator's first act was to visit
military punishment upon those who had fled from
Veii in the panic there, and to teach his men that
the enemy was not the worst thing they had to fear.
He then fixed the levy for a certain day, and in the
interval hastened to Veii to encourage his soldiers;
thence he returned to Rome to enroll the new army,
and found no one who refused to serve. Even
foreign troops, Latins and Hernicans, came with
promises to help in this war, and the dictator
thanked them in the senate.[1] All things being now
in readiness for the campaign, Camillus vowed, in pur-
suance of a senatorial decree, to celebrate the Great
Games,[2] if he should capture Veii, and to restore
and dedicate anew the temple of Mater Matuta,
which in time gone by had been consecrated by
King Servius Tullius. Marching out from the City,
where he left a greater feeling of suspense than
of confidence, he first engaged the Faliscans and
Capenates, in the Nepesine country. There all his
measures, being executed with consummate skill and
prudence, were attended, as generally happens, with
good fortune. Not only did he rout the enemy in
battle, but he also deprived them of their camp and
got possession of enormous booty, the chief part of
which was made over to the quaestor, and no great
quantity given to the soldiers. He then led his
army to Veii, where he increased the number of
redoubts, and withdrawing the troops from the

67

facta et a procursationibus, quae multae temere inter
murum ac vallum fiebant, edicto ne quis iniussu
10 pugnaret, ad opus milites traducti. Operum fuit
omnium longe maximum ac laboriosissimum cuniculus
in arcem hostium agi coeptus. Quod ne intermit-
11 teretur opus neu sub terra continuus labor eosdem
conficeret, in partes sex munitorum numerum divisit;
senae horae in orbem operi attributae sunt; nocte
ac die nunquam ante omissum quam in arcem viam
facerent.

XX. Dictator cum iam in manibus videret victoriam
esse, urbem opulentissimam capi, tantumque praedae
fore quantum non omnibus in unum conlatis ante
2 bellis fuisset, ne quam inde aut militum iram ex
malignitate praedae partitae aut invidiam apud patres
ex prodiga largitione caperet, litteras ad senatum
3 misit, deum immortalium benignitate suis consiliis
patientia militum Veios iam fore in potestate populi
4 Romani; quid de praeda faciendum censerent? Duae
senatum distinebant sententiae, senis P. Licini,
quem primum dixisse a filio interrogatum ferunt,
edici palam placere populo ut qui particeps esse
5 praedae vellet in castra Veios iret, altera Ap. Claudi,
qui largitionem novam prodigam inaequalem incon-

---

¹ Livy is perhaps following Licinius Macer (Introd.
p. xxix), in recording the very irregular procedure by which
the tribune passed over the patrician senators to honour his
plebeian father.
² The booty was regularly sold and the proceeds placed in
the treasury.

skirmishes which frequently took place, on the spur
of the moment, in the space between the town wall
and the stockade, by an edict forbidding any man to
fight without orders, he employed them in digging.
Of all the works, much the greatest and most
laborious was a mine they began to drive into the
enemy's citadel. That this work might not be
interrupted nor the same men become exhausted by
perpetually toiling under ground, he divided the
workers into six parties and assigned them six-hour
shifts in rotation; night and day the work went on
unceasingly, till they had made a way into the
citadel.

XX. The dictator saw that victory was at last
within his grasp, and that a city of great wealth was
on the point of being taken, with booty more than
if all previous wars had been put together. Lest,
therefore, he might incur either the resentment of
the soldiers, in consequence of a niggardly division
of the spoils, or the ill-will of the Fathers, if he were
lavish in sharing them out, he wrote to the senate,
that thanks to the favour of the immortal gods, his
own direction, and the patient efforts of his troops,
Veii would presently be in the power of the Roman
People, and asked what disposition they proposed
making of the plunder. The senate was divided
between two opinions; the aged Publius Licinius,
who was the first, they say, that his son called
upon to speak,[1] advised making public proclamation
that the people decreed that whoso desired a share
in the spoils should proceed to the camp at Veii;
the other plan was that of Appius Claudius, who
declared that such largess was without example,[2]
reckless, unfair, and ill-advised; if they were per-

sultam arguens, si semel nefas ducerent captam ex
hostibus in aerario exhausto bellis pecuniam esse,
auctor erat stipendii ex ea pecunia militi numerandi

6 ut eo minus tributi plebes conferret; eius enim doni
societatem sensuras aequaliter omnium domos, non
avidas in direptiones manus otiosorum urbanorum
praerepturas fortium bellatorum praemia esse, cum
ita ferme eveniat ut segnior sit praedator, ut quisque
laboris periculique praecipuam petere partem soleat.

7 Licinius contra suspectam et invisam semper eam
pecuniam fore aiebat causasque criminum ad plebem,
seditionum inde ac legum novarum praebituram;

8 satius igitur esse reconciliari eo dono plebis animos,
exhaustis atque exinanitis tributo tot annorum
succurri, et sentire praedae fructum ex eo bello in
quo prope consenuerint. Gratius id fore laetiusque
quod quisque sua manu ex hoste captum domum
rettulerit quam si multiplex alterius arbitrio accipiat.

9 Ipsum dictatorem fugere invidiam ex eo criminaque;
eo delegasse ad senatum; senatum quoque debere
reiectam rem ad se permittere plebi ac pati habere

10 quod cuique fors belli dederit. Haec tutior visa
sententia est quae popularem senatum faceret.
Edictum itaque est ad praedam Veientem quibus
videretur in castra ad dictatorem proficiscerentur.

---

[1] The patricians also paid the tax; but it bore harder
upon the plebeians, owing to their poverty.

suaded once for all that it was wicked that money B.C. 396
captured from the enemy should lie in the treasury,
which had been exhausted by the wars, he urged
them to pay the soldiers out of it, that the plebs
might have so much the less war-tax to contribute[1];
this was a boon of which all families alike would
feel the benefit, nor would the hands of idle city-
folk, greedy of pillage, pluck away the rewards of
valiant fighting men—since it commonly turned out
that in proportion as a man was prone to seek a
leading share of toil and danger, he was slow in
plundering. Licinius argued, on the other hand,
that this money would breed endless suspicion and
hate, and would furnish grounds for accusations
before the plebs, and so for agitation and revolutionary laws; it was better, therefore, to win over
by this gift the sympathies of the commons, to
succour them, exhausted and impoverished as they
were by so many years' taxation, and to let them
enjoy the spoils and fruits of that war in which they
had well-nigh grown old men; there would in every
instance be more satisfaction and pleasure in what a
man took with his own hand from the enemy and
brought home, than if he received many times its
value at the discretion of another; the dictator
himself would fain avoid the enmity and charges
arising from this business, and therefore had handed
it over to the senate; the senate, likewise, in its
turn, should refer the question to the plebs, and let
every man keep what the fortune of war might give
him. This policy seemed the safer, since it would
make the senate popular. Accordingly, proclamation was made that all who liked might go to the
dictator in camp, to share in the plunder of Veii.

XXI. Ingens profecta multitudo replevit castra.
Tum dictator auspicato egressus cum edixisset ut
2 arma milites caperent, "Tuo ductu" inquit, "Pythice
Apollo, tuoque numine instinctus pergo ad delendam
urbem Veios tibique hinc decimam partem praedae
3 voveo. Te simul, Iuno regina, quae nunc Veios
colis, precor, ut nos victores in nostram tuamque
mox futuram urbem sequare, ubi te dignum amplitu-
4 dine tua templum accipiat." Haec precatus superante
multitudine ab omnibus locis urbem adgreditur, quo
minor ab cuniculo ingruentis periculi sensus esset.
5 Veientes ignari se iam a suis vatibus, iam ab externis
oraculis proditos, iam in partem praedae suae vocatos
deos, alios votis ex urbe sua evocatos hostium templa
novasque sedes spectare, seque ultimum illum diem
6 agere, nihil minus timentes quam subrutis cuniculo
moenibus arcem iam plenam hostium esse, in muros
7 pro se quisque armati discurrunt, mirantes quidnam
id esset quod, cum tot per dies nemo se ab stationibus Romanus movisset, tum velut repentino icti
furore improvidi currerent ad muros.
8   Inseritur huic loco fabula : immolante rege Veientium vocem haruspicis, dicentis qui eius hostiae exta
prosecuisset ei victoriam dari, exauditam in cuniculo

---

¹ The Latin word is a technical term which is used of
carving up, in a specified way, the entrails (*prosiciae*) which
were to be burnt on the altar.

XXI. A vast throng went out, and filled the camp. B.C. 396
Then the dictator, after taking the auspices, came
forth and commanded the troops to arm. " Under
thy leadership," he cried, " Pythian Apollo, and
inspired by thy will, I advance to destroy the city of
Veii, and to thee I promise a tithe of its spoils. At
the same time I beseech thee, Queen Juno, that
dwellest now in Veii, to come with us, when we
have gotten the victory, to our City—soon to be
thine, too—that a temple meet for thy majesty may
there receive thee." These prayers uttered, he set
forward with overwhelming numbers to assault the
town on every side, that the inhabitants might not
perceive the danger pressing upon them from the
mine. The Veientes, unconscious that they were
already given up by their own soothsayers, and by
foreign oracles, that some of the gods had already
been invited to share in their despoiling, while
others having been entreated to quit their city were
beginning to look to new homes in the temples of
their enemies, and that this was the last day they
were themselves to live, feared nothing less than that
their defences were undermined and their citadel
already filled with foemen, and, each for himself,
took up arms and ran out to the ramparts ; marvelling
what it meant that whereas for so many days not a
Roman had stirred from his post, they should now,
as though they had suddenly gone mad, be rushing
blindly against the walls.

At this point men introduce a tale, how, as the
King of the Veientes was sacrificing, the Roman
soldiers in the mine overheard the soothsayer
declare that to him who should cut up [1] the inwards
of that victim would be given the victory, and were

A.U.C.
358

movisse Romanos milites ut adaperto cuniculo exta
9 raperent et ad dictatorem ferrent. Sed in rebus
tam antiquis si quae similia veri sint pro veris accipiantur, satis habeam : haec ad ostentationem scaenae
gaudentis miraculis aptiora quam ad fidem neque
adfirmare neque refellere est operae pretium.

10 Cuniculus delectis militibus eo tempore plenus
in aedem [1] Iunonis, quae in Veientana arce erat,
armatos repente edidit, et pars aversos in muris
invadunt hostes, pars claustra portarum revellunt,
pars cum ex tectis saxa tegulaeque a mulieribus ac
11 servitiis iacerentur, inferunt ignes. Clamor omnia
variis terrentium ac paventium vocibus mixto mulie-
12 rum ac puerorum ploratu complet. Momento temporis deiectis ex muro undique armatis patefactisque
portis cum alii agmine inruerent, alii desertos scan-
derent muros, urbs hostibus impletur ; omnibus locis
13 pugnatur ; deinde multa iam edita caede senescit
pugna, et dictator praecones edicere iubet ut ab
14 inermi abstineatur. Is finis sanguinis fuit. Dedi
inde inermes coepti, et ad praedam miles permissu
dictatoris discurrit. Quae cum ante oculos eius
aliquantum spe atque opinione maior maiorisque
pretii rerum ferretur, dicitur manus ad caelum tollens
15 precatus esse ut si cui deorum hominumque nimia
sua fortuna populique Romani videretur, ut eam

----

[1] in aedem ς: in aede Ω

----

[1] With this sentence compare Livy's Preface, § 6.

moved to open the mine and seize the entrails, B.C. 396
which they bore off to the dictator. But in matters
of so great antiquity I should be content if things
probable were to be received as true : this story,
more fit to be displayed on the stage, that delights
in wonders, than to be believed, it is worth while
neither to affirm nor to refute.[1]

The mine, which was then filled with picked troops,
suddenly discharged its armed men into the temple
of Juno, on the Veientine citadel ; some of them
assailed the backs of their enemies, who were on the
walls ; others wrenched off the bars that made fast
the gates ; others, when the women and slaves cast
down stones and tiles from roofs, fetched fire against
them. The air resounded with shouts ; and fearful
yells and shrieks of despair were blended with the
wailing of women and children. In a moment the
armed soldiers were everywhere hurled from the walls,
and the gates thrown open. A part of the Romans
poured through them in a body, others scaled the
deserted walls ; the city was overrun with enemies ;
the battle raged in every quarter ; then, when there
had already been great carnage, the fighting began
to flag, and the dictator bade the heralds proclaim
that those without arms should be spared. This
ended the slaughter. The unarmed began to give
themselves up, and the Romans scattered, with the
dictator's permission, in quest of booty. When this
was brought before him, and he saw that it was
considerably larger and comprised effects of greater
value than he had hoped or thought, it is said that
he raised his hands to heaven and prayed that if any
god or man deemed his good fortune and that of the
Roman People to be excessive, it might be granted

invidiam lenire quam minimo suo privato incommodo
16 publicoque populi Romani liceret. Convertentem
se inter hanc venerationem traditur memoriae pro-
lapsum cecidisse; idque omen pertinuisse postea
eventu rem coniectantibus visum ad damnationem
ipsius Camilli, captae deinde urbis Romanae, quod
17 post paucos accidit annos, cladem. Atque ille dies
caede hostium ac direptione urbis opulentissimae est
consumptus.

XXII. Postero die libera corpora dictator sub
corona vendidit. Ea sola pecunia in publicum redi-
gitur, haud sine ira plebis; et quod rettulere secum
praedae, nec duci, qui ad senatum, malignitatis auc-
2 tores quaerendo, rem arbitrii sui reiecisset, nec
senatui, sed Liciniae familiae, ex qua filius ad
senatum rettulisset, pater tam popularis sententiae
3 auctor fuisset, acceptum referebant. Cum iam huma-
nae opes egestae a Veiis essent, amoliri tum deum
dona ipsosque deos, sed colentium magis quam
4 rapientium modo, coepere. Namque delecti ex
omni exercitu iuvenes pure lautis corporibus, candida
veste, quibus deportanda Romam regina Iuno adsig-
nata erat, venerabundi templum iniere primo religiose
5 admoventes manus, quod id signum more Etrusco
nisi certae gentis sacerdos attractare non esset

---

[1] Literally, "under the chaplet," alluding to the garlands
worn by captives when they were put up for sale (Aulus
Gellius, VI. iv.).

him to appease that envy with the least harm to his own private interests and to the public welfare of the Roman People. As he turned, while making this prayer, tradition states that he slipped and fell, and that this omen was seen (when men came later to gather its meaning from the event) to point to the condemnation of Camillus himself, and in the second place, to the capture of Rome, a disaster which befell a few years afterwards. So that day was spent in the slaughter of enemies and the sack of a most opulent city.

XXII. On the following day the dictator sold the free-born inhabitants into slavery.[1] This was the only money that went into the state treasury, but the commons were angry about it; as for the booty they brought back themselves, they gave the credit not to their commander, who had referred to the Fathers, that they might support his niggardliness, a matter which had lain within his own discretion, nor yet to the senators, but to the house of the Licinii, whose son had brought to a vote in the senate that popular measure which his father had proposed. When the wealth that belonged to men had now been carried away out of Veii, they began to remove the possessions of the gods and the gods themselves, but more in the manner of worshippers than of pillagers. For out of all the army youths were chosen, and made to cleanse their bodies and to put on white garments, and to them the duty was assigned of conveying Queen Juno to Rome. Reverently entering her temple, they scrupled at first to approach her with their hands, because this image was one that according to Etruscan practice none but a priest of a certain family was wont to

solitus. Dein cum quidam seu spiritu divino tactus
seu iuvenali ioco, "Visne Romam ire, Iuno?" dixis-
6 set, adnuisse ceteri deam conclamaverunt. Inde
fabulae adiectum est vocem quoque dicentis velle
auditam; motam certe sede sua parvi molimenti
adminiculis sequentis modo accepimus levem ac
facilem tralatu fuisse, integramque in Aventinum,
7 aeternam sedem suam quo vota Romani dictatoris
vocaverant, perlatam, ubi templum ei postea idem
qui voverat Camillus dedicavit.

8   Hic Veiorum occasus fuit, urbis opulentissimae
Etrusci nominis, magnitudinem suam vel ultima
clade indicantis, quod decem aestates hiemesque
continuas circumsessa cum plus aliquanto cladium
intulisset quam accepisset, postremo iam fato quoque
urgente, operibus tamen, non vi expugnata est.

  XXIII. Romam ut nuntiatum est Veios captos,
quamquam et prodigia procurata fuerant et vatum
responsa et Pythicae sortes notae, et quantum
humanis adiuvari consiliis potuerat res ducem M.
Furium maximum imperatorum omnium legerant,
2 tamen, quia tot annis varie ibi bellatum erat multae-
que clades acceptae, velut ex insperato immensum
3 gaudium fuit, et priusquam senatus decerneret plena
omnia templa Romanarum matrum grates dis agen-

touch; when one of them, whether divinely inspired B.C. 396 or out of youthful jocularity, asked, " Wilt thou go, Juno, to Rome?"—whereat the others all cried out that the goddess had nodded assent. It was afterwards added to the story that she had also been heard to say that she was willing. At all events we are told that she was moved from her place with contrivances of little power, as though she accompanied them voluntarily, and was lightly and easily transferred and carried safe and sound to the Aventine, the eternal home to which the prayers of the Roman dictator had called her; and there Camillus afterwards dedicated to her the temple which he himself had vowed.

Such was the fall of Veii, the wealthiest city of the Etruscan race, which gave evidence of its greatness even in its final overthrow; since after a blockade of ten continuous summers and winters, during which time it had inflicted considerably heavier losses than it had sustained, it yet was ultimately taken, when at last even destiny fought against it, by siege-works and not by force.

XXIII. When word came to Rome that Veii was taken, although the portents had been averted and the answers of the soothsayers and the Pythian oracle were known; and though they had done all that human wisdom could do to help, in choosing Marcus Furius Camillus, greatest of all generals, to lead them; nevertheless, because they had warred there so many years with varying fortune and had suffered many a reverse, their joy, as though unexpected, knew no bounds; and ere the senate could act, the temples were all thronged with Roman matrons giving thanks to the gods. The

tium erant. Senatus in quadriduum, quot dierum
4 nullo ante bello, supplicationes decernit. Adventus
quoque dictatoris omnibus ordinibus obviam effusis
celebratior quam ullius unquam antea fuit, triumphusque omnem consuetum honorandi diei illius [1]
5 modum aliquantum excessit. Maxime conspectus
ipse est curru equis albis iuncto urbem invectus ;
parumque id non civile modo sed humanum etiam
6 visum. Iovis Solisque equis aequiperatum dictatorem
in religionem etiam trahebant, triumphusque ob
eam unam maxime rem clarior quam gratior fuit.
7 Tum Iunoni reginae templum in Aventino locavit
dedicavitque Matutae Matris ; atque his divinis
humanisque rebus gestis dictatura se abdicavit.
8   Agi deinde de Apollinis dono coeptum. Cui
se decimam vovisse praedae partem cum diceret
Camillus, pontifices solvendum religione populum
9 censerent, haud facile inibatur ratio iubendi referre
praedam populum, ut ex ea pars debita in sacrum
10 secerneretur. Tandem eo quod lenissimum videbatur decursum est, ut qui se domumque religione
exsolvere vellet, cum sibimet ipse praedam aesti-
masset suam, decimae pretium partis in publicum
11 deferret, ut ex eo donum aureum, dignum amplitudine templi ac numine dei, ex dignitate populi

---

[1] diei illius F^3_5 : diem illius (illus H) Ω.

---

[1] Livy is probably mistaken in ascribing the unpopularity
of the triumph to the supposed presumption of Camillus,
since it was traditional for the triumphator to suggest a
likeness to Jupiter, both in his chariot and in his costume.
Resentment over the disposal of the booty is more likely to
have been the reason.

[2] This temple was in the cattle-market, the Forum
Boarium.

senate decreed supplications for four days, a longer
period than in any former war. Moreover, as the
dictator drew near, all sorts and conditions of men
ran forth to meet him in such numbers as had never
welcomed a general before, and the triumph far
exceeded the measure of honour usual on that day.
He was himself the most conspicuous object in it, as
he rode into the City on a chariot drawn by white
horses; an act which struck men as being not only
undemocratic, but irreverent, for they were troubled
at the thought that in respect to his steeds the
dictator was made equal to Jupiter and the sun-god;
and the triumph, chiefly for this one reason, was more
brilliant than popular.[1] He then let the contract
for the temple of Queen Juno on the Aventine, and
dedicated one to Mater Matuta;[2] and having fulfilled these obligations to gods and men, laid down
the dictatorship.

The next thing to be discussed was the gift to
Apollo, to whom Camillus said that he had solemnly
promised a tenth part of the spoils. The pontiffs
ruled that the people must discharge this obligation,
but it was not easy to devise a method for compelling
them to return the booty, that out of it the due
proportion might be set apart for the sacred object.
They finally resorted to what seemed the least
oppressive plan, namely, that whosoever wished to
acquit himself and his household of obligation on
the score of the vow, should appraise his own share
of the spoils, and pay in a tenth part of its value to
the public treasury, to the end that it might be
converted into an offering of gold befitting the
grandeur of the temple and the power of the god
and corresponding to the majesty of the Roman

81

A.U.C.
358 Romani fieret. Ea quoque conlatio plebis animos
12 a Camillo alienavit. Inter haec pacificatum legati a
Volscis et Aequis venerunt, impetrataque pax, magis
ut fessa tam diutino bello adquiesceret civitas quam
quod digni peterent.

A.U.C.
359 XXIV. Veiis captis sex tribunos militum consulari
potestate insequens annus habuit, duos P. Cornelios,
Cossum et Scipionem, M. Valerium Maximum iterum
K. Fabium Ambustum tertium [1] L. Furium Medul-
2 linum quintum Q. Servilium tertium. Corneliis
Faliscum bellum, Valerio ac Servilio Capenas sorte
evenit. Ab iis non urbes vi aut operibus temptatae,
sed ager est depopulatus praedaeque rerum agrestium
actae; nulla felix arbor, nihil frugiferum in agro
3 relictum. Ea clades Capenatem populum subegit;
pax petentibus data; in Faliscis bellum restabat.
4 Romae interim multiplex seditio erat, cuius leniendae causa coloniam in Volscos, quo tria milia civium
Romanorum scriberentur, deducendam censuerant,
triumvirique ad id creati terna iugera et septunces
5 viritim diviserant. Ea largitio sperni coepta, quia
spei maioris avertendae solacium obiectum censebant: cur enim relegari plebem in Volscos, cum
pulcherrima urbs Veii agerque Veientanus in con-
6 spectu sit, uberior ampliorque Romano agro? Urbem

---

[1] tertium *Sigon.* (*C.I.L.* i², *p.* 118): iterum (*wanting in
V*) Ω.

---

[1] See chap. xxii. § 1 and chap. xxiii. § 5.
[2] The *iugerum* contained 28,800 square feet, while the
English acre contains 43,560.

People. This contribution still further alienated B.C. 396
the affections of the commons from Camillus.[1] In
the midst of these affairs came envoys from the
Volsci and the Aequi seeking peace, and their suit
was granted, more that the state, worn out with
so long a war, might be at rest, than because the
petitioners deserved it.

XXIV. The year which followed the capture of B.C. 395
Veii had six consular tribunes, to wit, the two
Publii Cornelii, Cossus and Scipio, Marcus Valerius
Maximus (for the second time), Caeso Fabius
Ambustus (for the third), Lucius Furius Medullinus
(for the fifth), Quintus Servilius (for the third). To
the Cornelii was allotted the Faliscan war, to
Valerius and Servilius the war with Capena. They
attempted no cities, either by assault or by siege,
but wasted the countryside and despoiled the
farmers of their possessions, leaving not one fruit-
tree in the land nor any productive plant. This
devastation overcame the resistance of the Capenates ;
they begged for peace and it was granted. In the
Faliscan country the war went on.

At Rome, meanwhile, there were disturbances of
many sorts, to quiet which the senate had voted to
plant a colony on the Volscian frontier, and to enroll
for that destination three thousand Roman citizens,
to each of whom a board of three, appointed for the
purpose, had proposed to assign three iugera [2] and
seven-twelfths. This donation men were disposed
to spurn, regarding it as a sop intended to divert
their hopes from greater things : for why should the
plebs be banished to the Volscian country, when the
fair city of Veii and the Veientine lands (more
fertile and extensive than those of Rome) were there

83

LIVY

quoque urbi Romae vel situ vel magnificentia publi-
corum privatorumque tectorum ac locorum praepone-
7 bant. Quin illa quoque actio movebatur, quae post
captam utique Romam a Gallis celebratior fuit,
8 transmigrandi Veios. Ceterum partem plebis, partem
senatus destinabant ad habitandos [1] Veios, duasque
urbes communi re publica [2] incoli a populo Romano
posse.
9 Adversus quae cum optimates ita tenderent ut
morituros se citius dicerent in conspectu populi
Romani quam quicquam earum rerum rogaretur;
10 quippe nunc in una urbe tantum dissensionum esse:
quid in duabus [3] fore? victamne ut quisquam vic-
trici patriae praeferret sineretque maiorem fortunam
captis esse Veiis, quam incolumibus fuerit? Postremo
11 se relinqui a civibus in patria posse: ut relinquant
patriam atque cives nullam vim unquam subacturam,
et T. Sicinium—is enim ex tribunis plebis rogationis
eius lator erat—conditorem Veios sequantur relicto
deo Romulo, dei filio, parente et auctore urbis Romae.

XXV. Haec cum foedis certaminibus agerentur—
nam partem tribunorum plebi patres in suam senten-
2 tiam traxerant,—nulla res alia manibus temperare
plebem cogebat quam quod, ubi rixae committendae
causa clamor ortus esset, principes senatus primi tur-

---

[1] ad habitandos *Heerwagen*: a habitandos *P*: habitandos
Ω: habitando *V*.
[2] communi re publica (republica) *Weissenborn*: communi
re *V*: communes reipublicae Ω.
[3] duabus *DLA*: duabus urbibus Ω.

---

[1] See chap. xlix.
[2] Only two, in fact, according to chap. xxix. § 6, but one
was enough to veto the motion.

in plain sight? The city, too, they preferred to
the City of Rome, whether for situation, or for the
splendour of its public and private buildings and its
places. Nay, they even mooted the plan which
certainly had a great following later, when the
Gauls had captured Rome, of migrating to Veii.[1]
For the rest, they intended that half of the plebs
and half of the senate should dwell in Veii, regarding
it as possible for the Roman people to inhabit two
cities with a common polity.

This proposal the patricians opposed with such
vehemence as to declare that they would sooner die
in the sight of the Roman People than suffer anything of the sort to come to a vote; for when there
was already so much dissension in a single city,
what would it be in two? Was it possible that any
man should prefer a vanquished to a victorious city,
and suffer Veii captured to enjoy a greater fortune
than Veii free? In fine, it was conceivable that
they should be left behind in their native city by
their fellow Romans; but to forsake their country
and their fellow-citizens no violence should ever
force them; they had no mind to follow Titus
Sicinius—the tribune of the plebs who had proposed
the bill—to Veii, as their founder, abandoning the
god and god's son Romulus, the Father and Author
of the Roman City.

XXV. These differences gave rise to disgraceful
contentions—for the Fathers had won over some of
the tribunes[2] to their opinion—and the only thing
that compelled the plebs to stay their hands was
this, that as often as they raised a shout, in order
to begin a riot, the leaders of the senate were the
first to confront the mob, bidding them visit blows,

A.U.C.
359

bae offerentes se peti feririque atque occidi iubebant.

3 Ab horum aetatibus dignitatibusque et honoribus violandis dum abstinebatur, et ad reliquos similes conatus verecundia irae obstabat.

4 Camillus identidem omnibus locis contionabatur: haud mirum id quidem esse, furere civitatem, quae damnata voti omnium rerum potiorem curam quam 5 religione se exsolvendi habeat. Nihil de conlatione dicere, stipis verius quam decumae, quando ea se quisque privatim obligaverit, liberatus sit populus.

6 Enimvero illud se tacere suam conscientiam non pati quod ex ea tantum praeda quae rerum moventium sit decuma designetur: urbis atque agri capti, quae et ipsa voto contineatur, mentionem nullam fieri.

7 Cum ea disceptatio, anceps senatui visa, delegata ad pontifices esset, adhibito Camillo visum collegio, quod eius ante conceptum votum Veientium fuisset et post votum in potestatem populi Romani venisset, eius partem decimam Apollini sacram esse. Ita in 8 aestimationem urbs agerque venit. Pecunia ex aerario prompta, et tribunis militum consularibus ut aurum ex ea coemerent negotium datum. Cuius cum copia non esset, matronae coetibus ad eam rem consultandam habitis communi decreto pollicitae tribunis militum aurum, et omnia ornamenta sua in 9 aerarium detulerunt. Grata ea res ut quae maxime

wounds, and death on them. The grey hairs of B.C. 395 these men, their distinctions, and their honours, they shrank from outraging, and shame thwarted their rage in all similar attempts.

Camillus harangued the people constantly, and in all places. It was no wonder, he said, that the citizens had gone mad, since, bound though they were to carry out their vow, they were more concerned about everything else than about the discharge of their obligation. He would say nothing of their penny contribution—a truer name for it than tithe—since in this regard each man had bound himself as an individual, and the state was freed; but there was one thing his conscience would not suffer him to pass over in silence; to wit, that the tithe should be defined as consisting of that part only of the booty which was movable; and that nothing should be said of the captured city and its territory, which were likewise included in the vow.

Unable to agree on this point, the senate referred it to the pontiffs, who decided, after consulting with Camillus, that so far as these things had belonged to the Veientes before the vow was made, and had subsequently come into the possession of the Roman People, a tithe thereof was sacred to Apollo. Thus the city and the land came into the estimate. Money was drawn from the treasury, and the tribunes of the soldiers with consular rank were directed to purchase gold with it; and there being not enough of this metal, the matrons held meetings to consider the need, and binding themselves by a common resolution to supply the tribunes with gold, brought in all their ornaments to the treasury. No act was ever more acceptable to the senate, and to

senatui unquam fuit; honoremque ob eam munificentiam ferunt matronis habitum ut pilento ad sacra
ludosque, carpentis festo profestoque uterentur.
10 Pondere ab singulis auri accepto aestimatoque ut
pecuniae solverentur, crateram auream fieri placuit
quae donum Apollini Delphos portaretur.

11   Simul ab religione animos remiserunt, integrant
seditionem tribuni plebis; incitatur multitudo in
12 omnes principes, ante alios in Camillum; eum praedam Veientanam publicando sacrandoque ad nihilum
redegisse. Absentes ferociter increpant; praesen-
tium, cum se ultro iratis offerrent, verecundiam
13 habent. Simul extrahi rem ex eo anno viderunt,
tribunos plebis latores legis in annum eosdem
reficiunt; et patres hoc idem de intercessoribus legis
adnisi. Ita tribuni plebis magna ex parte iidem
refecti.

XXVI. Comitiis tribunorum militum patres summa
ope evicerunt ut M. Furius Camillus crearetur.
Propter bella simulabant parari ducem; sed largitioni
2 tribuniciae adversarius quaerebatur. Cum Camillo
creati tribuni militum consulari potestate L. Furius
Medullinus sextum C. Aemilius L. Valerius Publicola
3 Sp. Postumius P. Cornelius iterum. Principio anni
tribuni plebis nihil moverunt, donec M. Furius

---

[1] The proposed law mentioned in chap. xxiv. § 7.
[2] For the third time. See chap. xiv. § 5.
[3] i. e., their proposal to divide up the lands of Veii.
[4] Either Scipio or Cossus (chap. xxiv. § 1), or possibly
Maluginensis (chap. xiv. § 1).

honour the matrons for their generosity, it is said to B.C. 395
have voted that they might drive in four-wheeled
carriages to festivals and games, and in two-wheeled
cars on holy and working days. When the gold
received from each had been appraised, in order
that the moneys might be repaid, it was determined
to make a golden bowl and carry it to Delphi as an
offering to Apollo.

No sooner had they eased their minds of the vow,
than the tribunes of the commons began again their
agitation, inflaming the populace against all the
nobles, but especially against Camillus, whom they
charged with having reduced to naught the spoils of
Veii, by devoting them to the state and to religion.
If any of the leaders were absent, they were fiercely
denounced; being present they outfaced their angry
critics and shamed them into silence. As soon as
the people saw that the question would be carried
over from that year, they worked for the re-election
of the tribunes of the plebs who were backing the
measure; [1] and the patricians exerted themselves to
do the same for its opponents. So, for the most
part, the same tribunes were returned to office.

XXVI. At the voting for military tribunes, the B.C. 394
senators with much ado obtained the election of
Marcus Furius Camillus. [2] The need of a commander
for the wars was their pretext, but what they really
wanted was a man who would combat the lavishness
of the tribunes. [3] With Camillus were elected to that
office, Lucius Furius Medullinus (for the sixth time),
Gaius Aemilius, Lucius Valerius Publicola, Spurius
Postumius, and (for the second time) Publius Cornelius. [4] At the outset of the year the tribunes of
the commons made no move, until Marcus Furius

A.U.C.
360
Camillus in Faliscos, cui id bellum mandatum erat
proficisceretur.   Differendo deinde elanguit res, et
Camillo, quem adversarium maxime metuebant,
4 gloria in Faliscis crevit.   Nam cum primo moenibus
se hostes tenerent tutissimum id rati, populatione
agrorum atque incendiis villarum coegit eos egredi
5 urbe.   Sed timor longius progredi prohibuit ; mille
fere passuum ab oppido castra locant nulla re alia
fidentes ea satis tuta esse quam difficultate aditus,
asperis confragosisque circa et partim artis partim
6 arduis viis.   Ceterum Camillus captivum indidem [1]
ex agris secutus ducem castris multa nocte motis
prima luce aliquanto superioribus locis se ostendit.
7 Trifariam Romani muniebant, alius exercitus proelio
intentus stabat.   Ibi impedire opus conatos hostes
fundit fugatque ; tantumque inde pavoris Faliscis
iniectum est ut effusa fuga castra sua quae propiora
8 erant praelati urbem peterent.   Multi caesi volnera-
tique priusquam paventes portis inciderent.   Castra
capta ; praeda ad quaestores redacta cum magna
militum ira ; sed severitate imperii victi eandem
9 virtutem et oderant et mirabantur.   Obsidio inde
urbis et munitiones, et interdum per occasionem
impetus oppidanorum in Romanas stationes proelia-

----

[1] indidem *Kern* : indecem *M* : indicem Ω.

Camillus should march against the Faliscans, for to B.C. 394
him this war had been committed. Then came
delays, and men's enthusiasm waned, while Camillus,
the opponent whom they chiefly feared, won fresh
renown in the Faliscan country. For though at first
the enemy kept within their walls, deeming this
their safest course, he compelled them, by ravaging
their fields and burning their farm-houses, to come
out of their city. Still, they were afraid to advance
very far, and pitched their camp about a mile from
the town, trusting that it was quite safe, without
other reason than the difficulty of approaching it;
for the ground about it was rough and broken, and
the roads were either narrow or steep. But Camillus,
employing a prisoner taken in that very region for
his guide, broke camp in the dead of night, and
showed himself at earliest dawn in a considerably
superior position. The Romans, divided into three
shifts, began to build a rampart, the soldiers who
were not working standing by in readiness to fight.
There, when the enemy sought to hinder the work,
he defeated and routed them; and so great was the
panic that came over the Faliscans, that they fled
in disorder past their camp, which was the nearer
refuge, and made for the town; and many were
slain or wounded, before, in their terror, they could
rush in through the gates. The camp was taken,
and the booty was paid over to the quaestors. This
incensed the troops, but they were overborne by the
strictness of the discipline, and admired, while they
detested, their general's probity. Then came a
blockade of the town, and the construction of siege-
works; and sometimes, when opportunity offered,
the townsfolk would raid the Roman outposts and

A.U.C.
360

que parva fieri, et teri tempus neutro inclinata spe,
cum frumentum copiaeque aliae ex ante convecto
largius obsessis quam obsidentibus suppeterent.
10 Videbaturque aeque diuturnus futurus labor ac Veiis
fuisset, ni fortuna imperatori Romano simul et
cognitae rebus bellicis virtutis specimen et maturam
victoriam dedisset.

XXVII. Mos erat Faliscis eodem magistro liberorum et comite uti, simulque plures pueri, quod hodie
quoque in Graecia manet, unius curae demandaban-
tur. Principum liberos, sicut fere fit, qui scientia
2 videbatur praecellere erudiebat. Is cum in pace
instituisset pueros ante urbem lusus exercendique
causa producere, nihil eo more per belli tempus
intermisso, modo[1] brevioribus modo longioribus
spatiis trahendo eos a porta lusu sermonibusque
variatis, longius solito ubi res dedit progressus inter
stationes eos hostium castraque inde Romana in
3 praetorium ad Camillum perduxit. Ibi scelesto
4 facinori scelestiorem sermonem addit, Falerios se in
manus Romanis tradidisse, quando eos pueros quorum
parentes capita ibi rerum sint in potestatem[2] dedi-
5 derit. Quae ubi Camillus audivit, "Non ad similem"
inquit "tui nec populum nec imperatorem scelestus
6 ipse cum scelesto munere venisti. Nobis cum Faliscis

---

[1] modo *Hertz* : dum modo Ω.
[2] in potestatem *Ald.* : in potestate Ω.

skirmishes would ensue. Time wore on, without b.c. 394
bringing hope to either side; the besieged had corn
and other supplies, which they had laid up before-
hand in greater abundance than the besiegers; and
it began to seem as though the struggle would be
as long drawn out as at Veii, had not Fortune, at
one stroke, given the Roman general an opportunity
to display the magnanimity already familiar from
his exploits in war, and an early victory.

XXVII. It was customary amongst the Faliscans
to employ the same person as teacher and attendant
of their children, and they used to intrust a number
of lads at the same time to the care of one man, a
practice which still obtains in Greece. The children
of the chief men, as is commonly the case, were
under the tuition of one who was regarded as their
foremost scholar. This man had in time of peace
got into the way of leading the boys out in front of
the city for play and exercise, and during the war
made no change in his routine, but would draw
them sometimes a shorter, sometimes a longer distance from the gate, with this and that game and
story, until being farther away one day than usual,
he seized the opportunity to bring them amongst the
enemy's outposts, and then into the Roman camp,
to the headquarters of Camillus. He then followed up
his villainous act with an even more villainous speech,
saying that he had given Falerii into the hands of
the Romans, having delivered up to them the
children of those whose fathers were in power there.
On hearing this Camillus answered : "Neither the
people nor the captain to whom you are come, you
scoundrel, with your scoundrel's gift, is like yourself. Between us and the Faliscans is no fellow-

93

A.U.C.
360
quae pacto fit humano societas non est : quam in-
generavit natura utrisque est eritque.   Sunt et belli
sicut pacis iura, iusteque ea non minus quam fortiter
7 didicimus gerere.   Arma habemus non adversus eam
aetatem cui etiam captis urbibus parcitur, sed adversus
armatos et ipsos, qui nec laesi nec lacessiti a nobis
8 castra Romana ad Veios oppugnarunt.   Eos tu
quantum in te fuit novo scelere vicisti : ego Romanis
artibus, virtute opere armis, sicut Veios vincam.''
9 Denudatum deinde eum manibus post tergum in-
ligatis reducendum Falerios pueris tradidit, virgasque
eis quibus proditorem agerent in urbem verberantes
10 dedit. Ad quod spectaculum concursu populi primum
facto, deinde a magistratibus de re nova vocato
senatu tanta mutatio animis est iniecta ut qui modo
efferati odio iraque Veientium exitum paene quam
Capenatium pacem mallent, apud eos pacem universa
11 posceret civitas.   Fides Romana, iustitia imperatoris
in foro et curia celebrantur ; consensuque omnium
legati ad Camillum in castra, atque inde permissu
Camilli Romam ad senatum, qui dederent Falerios
12 proficiscuntur.   Introducti ad senatum ita locuti
traduntur : " Patres conscripti, victoria cui nec deus
nec homo quisquam invideat victi a vobis et impera-

94

ship founded on men's covenants; but the fellowship
which nature has implanted in both sides is there
and will abide. There are rights of war as well as of
peace, and we have learnt to use them justly no less
than bravely. We bear no weapons against those
tender years which find mercy even in the storming
of a city, but against those who are armed themselves, who, without wrong or provocation at our
hands, attacked the Roman camp at Veii. Those
people you have done your best to conquer by an
unheard-of crime. I shall conquer them, as I conquered Veii, in the Roman way, by dint of courage,
toil, and arms." He then had the fellow stripped,
his hands bound behind his back, and gave him up
to the boys to lead back to Falerii, providing them
with rods to scourge the traitor as they drove him
into town. To behold this spectacle, there was at
first a great gathering together of the people, and presently the magistrates called a meeting of the senate
about the strange affair, and men underwent such a
revulsion of feeling, that those who a short time
before, in the fury of their hate and resentment
would almost have preferred the doom of Veii to the
peace of Capena, were now calling for peace, with
the voice of an entire city. The honesty of the
Romans, and the justice of their general, were
praised in market-place and senate-house, and, with
the consent of all, envoys proceeded to Camillus in
his camp, and thence, by his permission, to the
Roman senate, to surrender Falerii. Being introduced into the Curia they are said to have spoken
as follows: " Conscript Fathers, you and your
general have won a victory over us which no one,
whether God or man, could begrudge you, and we

tore vestro dedimus nos vobis, rati, quo nihil victori
pulchrius est, melius nos sub imperio vestro quam
13 legibus nostris victuros. Eventu huius belli duo
salutaria exempla prodita humano generi sunt : vos
fidem in bello quam praesentem victoriam maluistis ;
14 nos fide provocati victoriam ultro detulimus. Sub
dicione vestra sumus ; mittite qui arma, qui obsides,
15 qui urbem patentibus portis accipiant. Nec vos fidei
nostrae nec nos imperii vestri paenitebit." Camillo
et ab hostibus et a civibus gratiae actae. Faliscis in
stipendium militum eius anni, ut populus Romanus
tributo vacaret, pecunia imperata. Pace data exercitus Romam reductus.

XXVIII. Camillus, meliore multo laude quam cum
triumphantem albi per urbem vexerant equi insignis,
iustitia fideque hostibus victis cum in urbem redisset,
taciti[1] eius verecundiam non tulit senatus quin sine
2 mora voti liberaretur ; crateramque auream donum
Apollini Delphos legati qui ferrent, L. Valerius L.
Sergius A. Manlius, missi longa una nave haud procul freto Siculo a piratis Liparensium excepti deve-
3 huntur Liparas. Mos erat civitatis velut publico
latrocinio partam praedam dividere. Forte eo anno
in summo magistratu erat Timasitheus quidam,
4 Romanis vir similior quam suis ; qui legatorum nomen

---

[1] taciti *Gronovius V* : tacite Ω.

give ourselves into your hands, believing (than which B.C. 394
nothing can be more honourable to a victor) that
we shall be better off under your government than
under our own laws. The outcome of this war has
afforded the human race two wholesome precedents :
you have set fair-dealing in war above immediate
victory ; and we, challenged by your fair-dealing,
have freely granted you that victory. We are under
your sway ; send men to receive our arms and
hostages, and our city, the gates of which stand
open. Neither shall you be disappointed in our
fidelity nor we in your rule." Camillus was thanked
both by his enemies and by his fellow citizens. The
Faliscans were commanded to pay the soldiers for
that year, that the Roman People might be exempted
from the war tax. Peace being granted, the Roman
army was led home.

XXVIII. Camillus, having returned to the City
distinguished by a far better kind of glory than
when he had entered it in triumph drawn by white
horses—for he had conquered his enemies by justice
and fair-dealing—uttered no reproaches, but the
senators were ill-at-ease till they should free him,
without delay, from the obligation of his vow. And
so, to carry the golden bowl as a gift to Apollo at
Delphi, they appointed Lucius Valerius, Lucius
Sergius, and Aulus Manlius, who, being dispatched
in a single warship, were captured by Liparaean
pirates not far from the Sicilian Straits and carried to
Liparae. It was the manner of that people to divide
up the booty which they had obtained by a kind of
public piracy, but it chanced that year that one
Timasitheus was chief magistrate, a man more re-
sembling the Romans than his own countrymen ;

97

donumque et deum cui mitteretur et doni causam
veritus ipse multitudinem quoque, quae semper ferme
regenti est similis, religionis iustae implevit adduc-
tosque in publicum hospitium legatos cum praesidio
etiam navium Delphos prosecutus, Romam inde
5 sospites restituit. Hospitium cum eo senatus consulto est factum donaque publice data.

Eodem anno in Aequis varie bellatum, adeo ut in
incerto fuerit et apud ipsos exercitus et Romae vicis-
6 sent victine essent. Imperatores Romani fuere ex tribunis militum C. Aemilius Sp. Postumius. Primo
rem communiter gesserunt ; fusis inde acie hostibus
Aemilium praesidio Verruginem obtinere placuit,
7 Postumium fines vastare. Ibi eum incomposito
agmine neglegentius ab re bene gesta euntem adorti
Aequi terrore iniecto in proximos compulere tumulos ; pavorque inde Verruginem etiam ad praesidium
8 alterum est perlatus. Postumius suis in tutum receptis cum contione advocata terrorem increparet
ac fugam, fusos esse ab ignavissimo ac fugacissimo
hoste, conclamat universus exercitus merito se ea
audire et fateri admissum flagitium, sed eosdem cor-
recturos esse neque diuturnum id gaudium hostibus

who, himself revering the title of the envoys and
their gift, as well as the god to whom it was being
sent and the cause of the oblation, imbued also the
people, who are almost always like their ruler, with
a due sense of religious awe; and after entertaining the ambassadors in the guest-house of the
state, even sent ships to convoy them to Delphi,
and thence brought them safely back to Rome. A
covenant of hospitality was made with him by decree
of the senate, and gifts were presented him in the
name of the state.

The same year there was a war with the Aequi,
of so varied fortune that it was not clear, either at
the front itself or in Rome, whether the upshot had
been victory or defeat. The Roman generals were
two of the military tribunes, Gaius Aemilius and
Spurius Postumius. At first they exercised the
command conjointly; afterwards, when they had
routed the enemy in battle, they arranged that
Aemilius should hold Verrugo with a garrison, while
Postumius should lay waste the country. As he was
leading his troops in irregular formation, somewhat
carelessly in consequence of his success, the Aequi
fell upon them and throwing them into confusion
drove them to the nearest hills, whence the panic
spread even to Verrugo, to the other army.
Postumius having rallied his men in a position of
safety, called them together and chid them for
their alarm and flight, telling them they had been
discomfited by the most craven and fugitive of
foes. Whereat the army cried out as one man, that
they deserved his reproaches, and confessed the
enormity of their misconduct, but promised that
they would themselves mend it, and that their

99

9 fore. Poscentes ut confestim inde ad castra hostium
duceret—et in conspectu erant posita in plano—
nihil poenae recusabant ni ea ante noctem expug-
10 nassent. Conlaudatos corpora curare paratosque esse
quarta vigilia iubet. Et hostes nocturnam fugam
ex tumulo Romanorum ut ab ea via quae ferebat
Verruginem excluderent, fuere obvii, proeliumque
ante lucem—sed luna pernox erat—commissum est.
11 Haud[1] incertius diurno proelium fuit ; sed clamor
Verruginem perlatus, cum castra Romana crederent
oppugnari, tantum iniecit pavoris ut nequiquam re-
tinente atque obsecrante Aemilio Tusculum palati
12 fugerent. Inde fama Romam perlata est Postumium
exercitumque occisum. Qui, ubi prima lux metum
insidiarum effuse sequentibus sustulit, cum perequi-
tasset aciem promissa repetens, tantum iniecit ardoris
13 ut non ultra sustinuerint impetum Aequi. Caedes
inde fugientium, qualis ubi ira magis quam virtute
res geritur, ad perniciem hostium facta est ; tris-
temque ab Tusculo nuntium nequiquam exterrita
civitate litterae a Postumio laureatae sequuntur,
victoriam populi Romani esse, Aequorum exercitum
deletum.

XXIX. Tribunorum plebis actiones quia nondum

---

[1] Haud *Madvig* : et haud (aut *FB*) Ω.

enemies' joy should be short-lived. Demanding to be led forthwith against the camp of the Aequi— which was in full sight in the plain where they had pitched it—they professed themselves willing to undergo any punishment if they should not have stormed it before nightfall. Postumius commended them and bade them sup and be ready at the fourth watch. The enemy, too, that they might cut off any retreat by night along the road to Verrugo, from the hill where the Romans lay, were afield and met them, and the battle began before daylight, but there was a moon all night. They could see to fight as well as in the daytime; but the shouts were heard in Verrugo, the soldiers believed the Roman camp was being attacked, and so great was their consternation that, despite the efforts of Aemilius to check them and despite his appeals, they fled in a scattered rout to Tusculum. From thence a rumour was carried to Rome that Postumius and the army were destroyed. But Postumius, as soon as the first rays of light had removed all fear of ambuscades in case of a wide-spread pursuit, rode down the line, reminding his men of the promises they had given him, and inspired such ardour that the Aequi could no longer withstand their charge, and were slaughtered while they fled (as happens when rage is more concerned than valour), till their army was clean destroyed; and the gloomy tidings from Tusculum which had thrown the City into a needless fright, were succeeded by a laurel-wreathed letter from Postumius, announcing the victory of the Roman People and the annihilation of the Aequian army.

XXIX. The measures introduced by the tribunes

LIVY

invenerant finem, et plebs continuare latoribus legis
tribunatum et patres reficere intercessores legis ad-
2 nisi sunt; sed plus suis comitiis plebs valuit. Quem
dolorem ulti patres sunt senatus consulto facto ut
consules, invisus plebi magistratus, crearentur. Annum post quintum· decimum creati consules L.
3 Lucretius Flavus Ser.[1] Sulpicius Camerinus. Principio huius anni ferociter, quia nemo ex collegio inter-
cessurus erat, coortis ad perferendam legem tribunis
plebis nec segnius ob id ipsum consulibus resistenti-
bus omnique civitate in unam eam curam conversa
Vitelliam coloniam Romanam in suo agro Aequi
4 expugnant. Colonorum pars maxima incolumis, quia
nocte proditione oppidum captum liberam per aversa
5 urbis fugam dederat, Romam perfugere. L. Lucretio
consuli ea provincia evenit. Is cum exercitu profectus acie hostes vicit, victorque Romam ad maius
6 aliquanto certamen redit. Dies dicta erat tribunis
plebis biennii superioris A. Verginio et Q. Pomponio,
quos defendi patrum consensu ad fidem senatus
pertinebat; neque enim eos aut vitae ullo crimine
alio aut gesti magistratus quisquam arguebat praeterquam quod gratificantes patribus rogationi tri-
7 buniciae intercessissent. Vicit tamen gratiam senatus

---

[1] Ser. ς (*C.I.L.* i², *p.* 119 *and Diod.* xv. viii. 1):
Sergius Ω.

---

[1] Providing for the division of the Roman People between
Rome and Veii. See chap. xxiv. § 7.

of the plebs being still undecided, the commons strove to prolong the tenure of the supporters of the bill,[1] and the patricians to re-elect the tribunes who had vetoed it; but in the election of their own magistrates the plebeians proved the stronger, a disappointment which the Fathers avenged by passing a resolution in the senate providing for the election of consuls—a magistracy odious to the plebs. There had been no consuls for fifteen years, when they elected Lucius Lucretius Flavus, and Servius Sulpicius Camerinus. In the beginning of this year, the tribunes united in a spirited attempt— for none of the college was disposed to object—to carry the bill; and the consuls, for that very reason, were quite as active in opposing them. While the whole body politic was absorbed in this one concern, Vitellia, a Roman colony, was captured by the Aequi, in whose territory it was situated. The greatest part of the settlers escaped, for the place was taken by treachery at night and their flight through the opposite quarter of the town was unopposed, and made their way to Rome in safety. To Lucius Lucretius the consul fell the command in this affair. Marching out with his army, he defeated the enemy in a battle and returned victorious to the City, where he found a far more serious struggle impending. A day of trial had been appointed for the plebeian tribunes of two years before, namely Aulus Verginius and Quintus Pomponius, to defend whom the senate, as the patricians all agreed, was in honour bound; for no man brought any charge against their lives or the conduct of their office, except their having, out of complaisance to the Fathers, opposed the tribunician law. But the in-

plebis ira, et pessimo exemplo innoxii denis milibus

8 gravis aeris condemnati sunt. Id aegre passi patres.
Camillus palam sceleris plebem arguere, quae iam in
suos versa non intellegeret se pravo iudicio de tribunis intercessionem sustulisse, intercessione sublata

9 tribuniciam potestatem evertisse [1]; nam quod illi
sperarent effrenatam licentiam eius magistratus
patres laturos, falli eos. Si tribunicia vis tribunicio
auxilio repelli nequeat, aliud telum patres inventu-

10 ros esse. Consulesque increpabat quod fide publica
decipi tribunos eos taciti tulissent qui senatus auctoritatem secuti essent. Haec propalam contionabun-
dus in dies magis augebat iras hominum.

XXX. Senatum vero incitare adversus legem haud
desistebat: ne aliter descenderent in forum, cum
dies ferendae legis venisset, quam ut qui meminissent
sibi pro aris focisque et deum templis ac solo in quo

2 nati essent dimicandum fore. Nam quod ad se privatim attineat, si suae gloriae sibi inter dimicationem
patriae meminisse sit fas, sibi amplum quoque esse
urbem ab se captam frequentari, cottidie se frui

---

[1] evertisse *Rhenanus* : euertissent Ω.

fluence of the senators was out-weighed by the B.C. 393
resentment of the plebs, and a shameful precedent
was set, when the innocent men were condemned
each to pay a fine of 10,000 asses. This roused
the indignation of the senate. Camillus frankly
denounced the depravity of the commons, who
having turned against their own representatives,
failed to perceive that they had by their wicked
judgment of the tribunes done away with the veto,
and that in doing away with the veto they had overthrown the tribunician power. For if they supposed
that the unbridled licence of that office would be
tolerated by the Fathers, they were mistaken; if
tribunician violence could not be resisted by the
help of tribunes, the senators must find some other
weapon. He rebuked the consuls also, because they
had, without protesting, allowed those tribunes who
had followed the guidance of the senate to suffer for
their reliance on the guarantee of state protection.
By such sentiments, publicly expressed in speeches,
he angered the people more and more from day to
day.

XXX. As to the senate, he ceased not to encourage it in opposing the law: they must go down
into the Forum, when the day should arrive for
voting on it, in no other spirit than that of men
who realized that they had to fight for hearth
and home, for the temples of their gods, and for
the soil of their birth. So far, indeed, as the
question touched his private interest, it would
actually be an honour to him, if it were not sinful
to be thinking of his own renown while his country
was struggling for life, that the city he had won
should be thronged with people; that he should

A.U.C.
361

monumento gloriae suae et ante oculos habere urbem latam in triumpho suo, insistere omnes vestigiis
3 laudum suarum; sed nefas ducere desertam ac relictam ab dis immortalibus incoli urbem, et in captivo solo habitare populum Romanum et victrice patria victam mutari.

4 His adhortationibus principis[1] concitati patres, senes iuvenesque, cum ferretur lex agmine facto in forum venerunt, dissipatique per tribus suos quisque
5 tribules prensantes orare cum lacrimis coepere ne eam patriam pro qua fortissime felicissimeque ipsi ac patres eorum dimicassent desererent, Capitolium, aedem Vestae, cetera circa templa deorum osten-
6 tantes; ne exsulem, extorrem populum Romanum ab solo patrio ac dis penatibus in hostium urbem agerent, eoque rem adducerent ut melius fuerit non capi
7 Veios, ne Roma desereretur. Quia non vi agebant sed precibus et inter preces multa deorum mentio erat, religiosum parti maximae fuit, et legem una[2]
8 plures tribus antiquarunt quam iusserunt. Adeoque ea victoria laeta patribus fuit ut postero die referentibus consulibus senatus consultum fieret ut agri Veientani septena iugera plebi dividerentur, nec patribus familiae tantum, sed ut omnium in domo

---

[1] principis ς: principes Ω.
[2] una A²ς: unam Ω.

---

[1] Livy is thinking of the custom which grew up later of exhibiting in the triumphal procession models or pictures of towns, rivers, and mountains, belonging to the conquered nation.

[2] There were at this time twenty-one tribes.

daily be reminded of his glory, and have before his B.C. 393
eyes the town which had figured in his triumph;[1]
that all men should tread in the footsteps of his
fame. But he thought it an offence against Heaven
that a city deserted and forsaken by the immortal
gods should be inhabited, and that the Roman
People should dwell on conquered soil, exchanging
their victorious City for a vanquished one.

These earnest words of their leading member so
stirred the senators, old men as well as young, that
on the day the law was proposed they formed in
a body and came into the Forum, where they dispersed among the tribes, and canvassing every man
his own tribesmen, began with tears to beseech them,
that they would not forsake that City for which both
they and their fathers had fought with the greatest
courage and good fortune. They pointed to the
Capitol, to the shrine of Vesta, and to the other
temples standing all about them; they begged them
not to drive the Roman People, an exile, and a
wanderer from its native land and its household
gods, to the city of its enemies, nor to carry things
so far that it would be better that Veii had not been
taken, so that Rome might not be deserted. Since
the patricians used not force but entreaties, and in
their entreaties made many a reference to the gods,
the greater part felt the prick of conscience, and the
law was rejected by one more tribe than voted in its
favour.[2] And so greatly did this victory rejoice the
Fathers, that next day, at the instance of the consuls,
a decree was passed by the senate, that seven *iugera*
of the Veientine land should be apportioned to every
plebeian, and not alone to the heads of families, but
so as to reckon in all the free-born members of the

A.U.C.
361 liberorum capitum ratio haberetur, vellentque in eam
spem liberos tollere.

A.U.C.
362 XXXI. Eo munere delenita plebe nihil certatum
2 est quo minus consularia comitia haberentur. Creati
consules L. Valerius Potitus M. Manlius, cui Capitolino postea fuit cognomen. Hi consules magnos
ludos fecere, quos M. Furius dictator voverat Veienti
3 bello. Eodem anno aedes Iunonis reginae ab eodem
dictatore eodemque bello vota dedicatur, celebra-
tamque dedicationem ingenti matronarum studio
tradunt.

4 Bellum haud memorabile in Algido cum Aequis
gestum est, fusis hostibus prius paene quam manus
consererent. Valerio, quod perseverantior iis caedendis [1] in fuga fuit, triumphus, Manlio ut ovans ingrede-
5 retur urbem, decretum est. Eodem anno novum
bellum cum Volsiniensibus exortum ; quo propter
famem pestilentiamque in agro Romano ex siccitate
caloribusque nimiis ortam exercitus duci nequivit.
Ob quae Volsinienses Sappinatibus [2] adiunctis super-
6 bia inflati ultro agros Romanos incursavere ; bellum
inde duobus populis indictum.

C. Iulius censor decessit ; in eius locum M. Cornelius suffectus, quae res postea religioni fuit quia eo

---

[1] iis caedendis *Weissenborn* : caedendis (*or* ce-) Ω : cae-
d..dis *V* : gaedendis *M* : gerendis *BP²FU* (*omitted by* P) :
gerendis (*with* c *above*) E.
[2] Sappinatibus *Mommsen* (*cf. chap.* xxxii. § 2) : salpinati-
bus Ω : sapienatibus *V* : scalpinatibus *M*.

---

[1] At VI. xvii. 5 Livy implies that Manlius was given the
cognomen because of his defence of the Capitol (chap. xlvii.),
but at IV. xlii. 2 a L. Manlius Capitolinus had been mentioned,
and the surname was probably due to the family's residing on
the Capitoline.

household, that with such a prospect before them B.C. 393
men might be willing to rear children.

XXXI. Appeased by this largess, the plebs made B.C. 392
no objection to an assembly for the election of consuls, and the choice fell on Lucius Valerius Potitus
and Marcus Manlius, afterwards surnamed Capitolinus.[1] These consuls celebrated the Great Games,
which Marcus Furius the dictator had vowed in the
war with Veii. This year saw also the dedication of
a temple to Queen Juno, vowed by the same dictator
in the same war; and tradition relates that the
ceremony was attended by throngs of enthusiastic
matrons.

A campaign in no way memorable was fought with
the Aequi on Mount Algidus, the enemy being
routed before they had well begun to fight. Valerius
was the more persistent in cutting them down as
they fled, and to him was decreed a triumph ; Manlius was allowed to enter the City in an ovation.[2]
In this year also a new war broke out, namely with
the people of Volsinii. Owing to a famine and
pestilence which arose in the Roman territories on
account of drought and excessive heat, it was impossible to send an army against them ; and in consequence of this the Volsinienses, having added the
Sappinates[3] to their forces, were puffed up with
pride and made an incursion themselves into the
fields of the Romans. War was then declared
against both nations.

Gaius Julius, the censor, died, and Marcus Cornelius was substituted in his place, a circumstance

---

[2] A lesser triumph, in which the victorious general entered
the City on foot.

[3] Sappinum, a town otherwise unknown, is presumed to
have been situated near Volsinii.

A.U.C.
362
lustro Roma est capta; nec deinde unquam in de-
7 mortui locum censor sufficitur. Consulibusque morbo
implicitis placuit per interregnum renovari auspicia.
8 Itaque cum ex senatus consulto consules magistratu
se abdicassent, interrex creatur M. Furius Camillus,
qui P. Cornelium Scipionem, is deinde L. Valerium
9 Potitum interregem prodidit. Ab eo creati sex tribuni militum consulari potestate ut, etiam si cui
eorum incommoda valetudo fuisset, copia magistratuum rei publicae esset.

A.U.C.
363
XXXII. Kalendis Quinctilibus magistratum occepere L. Lucretius Ser. Sulpicius M. Aemilius L.
Furius Medullinus septimum Agrippa Furius C.
2 Aemilius iterum. Ex his L. Lucretio et C. Aemilio
Volsinienses[1] provincia evenit, Sappinates[2] Agrippae
Furio et Ser. Sulpicio. Prius cum Volsiniensibus
3 pugnatum est. Bellum numero hostium ingens,
certamine haud sane asperum fuit. Fusa primo
concursu acies; in fugam versa milia octo armatorum
ab equitibus interclusa positis armis in deditionem
4 venerunt. Eius belli fama effecit, ne se pugnae
committerent Sappinates; moenibus armati se tuta-
bantur. Romani praedas passim et ex Sappinati[3]
agro et ex Volsiniensi nullo eam vim arcente egerunt;

---

[1] Volsinienses *Madvig*: Vols. . . . ses *V*: uolsiniensis
(*or* uuls-) Ω.
[2] Sappinates *HDL* (*here and in* § 4): salpinates (salpp-
P) Ω: sal sappinates *M*: *wanting in V.*
[3] Sappinati *Mommsen*: salpinati Ω: sa . pinati *V*.

---

[1] Thereafter the survivor resigned and two new censors
were appointed (IX. xxxiv. 21).

which was afterwards thought to have offended the B.C. 392
gods, because in this lustrum Rome was captured;
nor from that day has a censor ever been appointed
in the room of one who has died.[1] The consuls, too,
caught the plague, and it was voted that fresh
auspices should be obtained by means of an interregnum. Accordingly, when the consuls, in obedience
to the senate's decree, had abdicated, Marcus Furius
Camillus was appointed interrex, and named as his
successor Publius Cornelius Scipio, who, in turn,
named Lucius Valerius Potitus interrex; under whom
they elected six military tribunes of consular rank,
so that even if any of them should fall ill the state
might still have magistrates.

XXXII. On the first day of July they entered B.C. 391
office, to wit, Lucius Lucretius, Servius Sulpicius,
Marcus Aemilius, Lucius Furius Medullinus (for the
seventh time), Furius Agrippa, and (for the second
time) Gaius Aemilius. Of these, Lucius Lucretius
and Gaius Aemilius were assigned the war with
Volsinii as their province, while the Sappinates fell to
Furius Agrippa and Servius Sulpicius. The Volsinienses were encountered first, in a campaign of
great magnitude in respect to the enemy's numbers,
though the engagement with them was no very
sharp affair. Their line broke at the first assault,
and in the rout eight thousand soldiers were cut off
by the cavalry, and laying down their arms, surrendered. When the Sappinates heard of this
campaign, they refused to risk a battle, but retired
within their walls and prepared to defend themselves. The Romans plundered right and left, both
the lands of Sappinum and those of Volsinii, without
finding any to resist their force, until the Volsini-

A.U.C. 363

5 donec Volsiniensibus fessis bello ea condicione ut res
populo Romano redderent stipendiumque eius anni
exercitui praestarent, in viginti annos indutiae datae.
6 Eodem anno M. Caedicius de plebe nuntiavit
tribunis se in Nova via, ubi nunc sacellum est supra
aedem Vestae, vocem noctis silentio audisse clariorem
humana, quae magistratibus dici iuberet Gallos ad-
7 ventare. Id, ut fit, propter auctoris humilitatem
spretum et quod longinqua eoque ignotior gens erat.
Neque deorum modo monita ingruente fato spreta,
sed humanam quoque opem, quae una erat, M.
8 Furium ab urbe amovere. Qui die dicta ab L. Apuleio
tribuno plebis propter praedam Veientanam, filio
quoque adulescente per idem tempus orbatus cum
accitis domum tribulibus clientibusque, quae [1] magna
pars plebis erat, percontatus animos eorum responsum tulisset se conlaturos quanti damnatus esset,
9 absolvere eum non posse, in exsilium abiit, precatus
ab dis immortalibus si innoxio sibi ea iniuria fieret,
primo quoque tempore desiderium sui civitati in-
gratae facerent. Absens quindecim milibus gravis
aeris damnatur.

XXXIII. Expulso cive quo manente, si quicquam humanorum certi est, capi Roma non potuerat, adventante fatali urbi clade legati ab Clusinis veniunt

[1] clientibusque, quae ς: clientibus quae (que *E*: quae E^2 *or* E^3: q *BD*: q que D^4) Ω: eo clientibus quae *M*: et clientilus quae A^1: *wanting in V*.

enses wearied of the war ; and upon their agreeing B.C. 391
to restore the goods of the Roman People and
furnish pay for the army for that campaign, they
were granted a truce of twenty years.

The same year Marcus Caedicius, a plebeian,
reported to the tribunes, that in the Nova Via,
where the chapel now stands above the temple of
Vesta, he had heard in the silence of the night a
voice more distinct than a man's, which bade him
tell the magistrates that the Gauls were approaching.
This portent was neglected, as often happens, because of the informant's humble station, and because
that race was remote and therefore not well known.
And not only did they reject the warnings of
Heaven, as their doom drew nearer, but they even
sent away from the City the only human assistance
present with them, in the person of Marcus Furius.
He had been indicted by Lucius Apuleius, tribune of
the plebs, on account of the spoils of Veii, just at
the time of losing his youthful son. Summoning to
his house his fellow tribesmen and his clients (who
formed a good part of the plebs), he sounded their
feelings, and having been answered that they would
make up such an amount as he might be fined, but
that they could not acquit him, he departed into
exile, beseeching the immortal gods that if he were
an innocent man to whom that wrong was done they
would speedily make his thankless fellow citizens
wish to have him back. He was fined in his absence
in the sum of 15,000 asses.

XXXIII. After the expulsion of that citizen whose
presence, if anything in this life is certain, would
have made the capture of Rome impossible, disaster
approached the ill-fated City with the arrival of

113

A.U.C.
363

2 auxilium adversus Gallos petentes. Eam gentem
traditur fama dulcedine frugum maximeque vini,
nova tum voluptate, captam Alpes transisse agrosque
3 ab Etruscis ante cultos possedisse; et invexisse in
Galliam vinum inliciendae gentis causa Arruntem
Clusinum ira corruptae uxoris ab Lucumone, cui
tutor is fuerat,[1] praepotente iuvene et a quo expeti
poenae, nisi externa vis quaesita esset, nequirent;
4 hunc transeuntibus Alpes ducem auctoremque Clusium oppugnandi fuisse. Equidem haud abnuerim
Clusium Gallos ab Arrunte seu quo alio Clusino
5 adductos; sed eos qui oppugnaverint Clusium non
fuisse qui primi Alpes transierint satis constat.
Ducentis quippe annis ante quam Clusium oppugnarent urbemque Romam caperent, in Italiam Galli
6 transcenderunt; nec cum his primum Etruscorum
sed multo ante cum iis qui inter Appenninum Alpes-
que incolebant saepe exercitus Gallici pugnavere.
7   Tuscorum ante Romanum imperium late terra
marique opes patuere. Mari supero inferoque, quibus Italia insulae modo cingitur, quantum potuerint
nomina sunt argumento, quod alterum Tuscum com-
8 muni vocabulo gentis, alterum Hadriaticum[2] ab
Hatria,[3] Tuscorum colonia, vocavere Italicae gentes;
Graeci eadem Tyrrhenum atque Adriaticum vocant.
9 Ei[4] in utrumque mare vergentes incoluere urbibus

---

[1] is fuerat *Conway*: ipse fuerat V: is (es M) fuerat ipse
Ω: fuerat ipse A^2.

[2] Hadriaticum ς: hadriatium V: atriaticum $MPFUB$:
adriaticum $M^2OEHDLA$.

[3] ab Hatria *Conway* (*The Italic Dialects, p.* 450): mare ab
atria (*or* adria) Ω.

[4] vocant. Ei ς: uocant et Ω: uocante. $PFBE$? : nocantes
U: uocat. Et M^2: uocant. Et M^3: uocant OE^3.

envoys from the men of Clusium seeking help
against the Gauls. The story runs that this race,
allured by the delicious fruits and especially the
wine—then a novel luxury—had crossed the Alps
and possessed themselves of lands that had before
been tilled by the Etruscans; and that wine had
been imported into Gaul expressly to entice them,
by Arruns of Clusium, in his anger at the seduction
of his wife by Lucumo. This youth, whose guardian
he had been, was so powerful that he could not have
chastised him without calling in a foreign force.
He it was who is said to have guided the Gauls
across the Alps, and to have suggested the attack on
Clusium. Now I would not deny that Arruns or
some other citizen brought the Gauls to Clusium,
but that those who besieged Clusium were not the
first who had passed the Alps is generally agreed.
Indeed it was two hundred years before the attack
on Clusium and the capture of Rome, that the Gauls
first crossed over into Italy; neither were the
Clusini the first of the Etruscans with whom they
fought; but long before that the Gallic armies had
often given battle to those who dwelt between the
Apennines and the Alps.

The Tuscan sway, down to the rise of the Roman
domination, stretched over a wide expanse of land
and sea. How great their power was on the upper
and the lower seas, by which Italy is surrounded
like an island, is apparent from the names, since the
Italian races have called one of them Tuscan, the
general designation of the race, and the other
Hadriatic, from Hatria, an Etruscan colony; and
the Greeks know the same seas as Tyrrhenian and
Adriatic. In the lands which slope on either side

A.U.C.
363

duodenis terras, prius cis Appenninum ad inferum
mare, postea trans Appenninum totidem, quot capita
10 originis erant, coloniis missis, quae trans Padum
omnia loca, excepto Venetorum angulo qui sinum
11 circumcolunt maris, usque ad Alpes tenuere. Alpinis
quoque ea gentibus haud dubie origo est, maxime
Raetis,[1] quos loca ipsa efferarunt ne quid ex antiquo
praeter sonum linguae, nec eum incorruptum,
retinerent.

XXXIV. De transitu in Italiam Gallorum haec
accepimus : Prisco Tarquinio Romae regnante Cel-
tarum, quae pars Galliae tertia est, penes Bituriges summa imperii fuit ; ii regem Celtico dabant.
2 Ambigatus is fuit, virtute fortunaque cum sua tum
publica praepollens, quod in imperio eius Gallia adeo
frugum hominumque fertilis fuit ut abundans multi-
3 tudo vix regi videretur posse. Hic magno natu ipse
iam exonerare praegravante turba regnum cupiens,
Bellovesum ac Segovesum, sororis filios, impigros
iuvenes, missurum se esse in quas di dedissent augu-
riis sedes ostendit : quantum ipsi vellent numerum
4 hominum excirent, ne qua gens arcere advenientes
posset. Tum Segoveso sortibus dati Hercynei saltus ;

---

[1] Raetis *Madvig* : raetiis(*or* retiis *or* reciis) Ω : ratiis *D*?:
ratus *A*.

---

[1] The *Hyrcinei saltus* were the upland districts of South
Germany (including the Black Forest, Bohemia, and the
Hartz) where both Caesar and Tacitus intimate that Celts
had formerly established settlements (*B.G.* VI. xxiv. ;
Germ. xxviii.).

B.C. 391

towards one of these seas, they had twice twelve
cities; first the twelve on this side the Apennines,
towards the lower sea; to which afterwards they
added the same number beyond the Apennines,
sending over as many colonies as there were original
cities, and taking possession of all the transpadane
region (except the angle belonging to the Veneti
who dwell about the gulf) as far as the Alps. The
Alpine tribes have also, no doubt, the same origin,
especially the Raetians; who have been rendered so
savage by the very nature of the country as to
retain nothing of their ancient character save the
sound of their speech, and even that is corrupted.

XXXIV. Concerning the migration of the Gauls
into Italy we are told as follows: While Tarquinius
Priscus reigned at Rome, the Celts, who make up
one of the three divisions of Gaul, were under the
domination of the Bituriges, and this tribe supplied
the Celtic nation with a king. Ambigatus was then
the man, and his talents, together with his own and
the general good fortune, had brought him great
distinction; for Gaul under his sway grew so rich
in corn and so populous, that it seemed hardly
possible to govern so great a multitude. The king,
who was now an old man and wished to relieve his
kingdom of a burdensome throng, announced that
he meant to send Bellovesus and Segovesus, his
sister's sons, two enterprising young men, to find
such homes as the gods might assign to them by
augury; and promised them that they should head
as large a number of emigrants as they themselves
desired, so that no tribe might be able to prevent
their settlement. Whereupon to Segovesus were by
lot assigned the Hercynian highlands [1]; but to Bello-

LIVY

Belloveso haud paulo laetiorem in Italiam viam di
5 dabant. Is quod eius ex populis abundabat, Bituriges
Arvernos Senones Haeduos [1] Ambarros Carnutes Au-
lercos excivit. Profectus ingentibus peditum equitumque copiis in Tricastinos [2] venit.

6   Alpes inde oppositae erant; quas inexsuperabiles
visas haud equidem miror nulladum via, quod quidem
continens memoria sit, nisi de Hercule fabulis credere
7 libet, superatas. Ibi cum velut saeptos montium alti-
tudo teneret Gallos circumspectarentque quanam per
iuncta caelo iuga in alium orbem terrarum transirent,
religio etiam tenuit quod allatum est advenas quae-
8 rentes agrum ab Saluum gente oppugnari. Massi-
lienses erant ii, navibus a Phocaea profecti. Id Galli
fortunae suae omen rati adiuvere ut quem primum in
terram egressi occupaverant locum patientibus Saluis [3]
communirent. Ipsi per Taurinos saltus saltumque
9 Duriae Alpes [4] transcenderunt; fusisque acie Tuscis
haud procul Ticino flumine, cum in quo consederant
agrum Insubrium appellari audissent, cognominem
Insubribus, pago Haeduorum, ibi omen sequentes
loci condidere urbem; Mediolanium appellarunt.

   XXXV. Alia subinde manus Cenomanorum [5] Eti-

---

[1] Haeduos *H. J. Mueller* : aeduos Ω.

[2] Tricastinos ς (*cf.* XXI. xxxi. 9): tricaspinos Ω : tris
caspinos *D*.

[3] patientibus Saluis *Valesius* : patientibus (petentibus *B*)
siluis Ω.

[4] saltumque Duriae Alpes *Conway* : saltusque iuriae alpes
H : saltusque iuliae alpis (alpes M^1 *or* $M^2 A^2$) Ω : saltusque (*or*
quae) iuliae alte (alta *U*) alpis (alpes F^2) *PE?FBU*.

[5] Cenomanorum *Glareanus* : germanorum Ω.

---

[1] Tribes in central Gaul some of whose names survive in
the modern Bourges, Auvergne, Sens, and Chartres. The
Tricastini were in the Roman province (Provence).

vesus the gods proposed a far pleasanter road, into B.C. 391
Italy. Taking out with him the surplus population
of his tribes, the Bituriges, Arverni, Senones,
Haedui, Ambarri, Carnutes, and Aulerci, he marched
with vast numbers of infantry and cavalry into the
country of the Tricastini.[1]

There the Alps stood over against them ; and I
for one do not wonder that they seemed insuperable,
for as yet no road had led across them—as far back
at all events as tradition reaches—unless one
chooses to believe the stories about Hercules.
While they were there fenced in as it were by the
lofty mountains, and were looking about to discover
where they might cross, over heights that reached
the sky, into another world, superstition also held
them back, because it had been reported to them
that some strangers seeking lands were beset by the
Salui. These were the Massilians, who had come in
ships from Phocaea. The Gauls, regarding this as
a good omen of their own success, lent them assistance, so that they fortified, without opposition
from the Salui, the spot which they had first seized
after landing. They themselves crossed the Alps
through the Taurine passes and the pass of the
Duria ; routed the Etruscans in battle not far from the
river Ticinus, and learning that they were encamped
in what was called the country of the Insubres, who
bore the same name as an Haeduan canton, they
regarded it as a place of good omen, and founded a
city there which they called Mediolanium.[2]

XXXV. Presently another band, consisting of
Cenomani led by Etitovius, followed in the tracks

[2] Now Milan.

A.U.C
363

tovio duce vestigia priorum secuta eodem saltu
favente Belloveso cum transcendisset Alpes, ubi nunc
2 Brixia ac Verona urbes sunt locos tenuere. Libui
considunt post hos Salluviique[1] prope antiquam
gentem Laevos Ligures incolentes circa Ticinum
amnem. Poenino deinde[2] Boii Lingonesque trans-
gressi cum iam inter Padum atque Alpes omnia
tenerentur, Pado ratibus traiecto non Etruscos modo
sed etiam Umbros agro pellunt; intra Appenninum
3 tamen sese tenuere. Tum Senones, recentissimi
advenarum, ab Utente flumine usque ad Aesim fines
habuere. Hanc gentem Clusium Romamque inde
venisse comperio : id parum certum est, solamne an
ab omnibus Cisalpinorum Gallorum populis adiutam.
4 Clusini novo bello exterriti cum multitudinem,
cum formas hominum invisitatas cernerent et genus
armorum, audirentque saepe ab iis cis Padum
ultraque legiones Etruscorum fusas, quamquam adversus Romanos nullum eis ius societatis amicitiaeve
erat, nisi quod Veientes consanguineos adversus
populum Romanum non defendissent, legatos Ro-
5 mam qui auxilium ab senatu peterent, misere. De
auxilio nihil impetratum; legati tres M. Fabi Ambusti filii missi, qui senatus populique[3] Romani
nomine agerent cum Gallis ne a quibus nullam
iniuriam accepissent socios populi Romani atque
6 amicos oppugnarent. Romanis eos bello quoque, si

---

[1] Salluviique *Madvig*: salluui (*or* salluii *or* saluuii) qui Ω.
[2] poenino deinde $E^3\varsigma$: poeni nonne inde M: poeninon
deinde *Vorm.* M^2 (*or* M^1) UO^1E^1H: paeni non deinde PL:
peninon deinde FBA: poeninen deinde O: poenis non deinde
E: pene noti D^3 (*over erasure*).
[3] populique A^1 (*or* A^2) ς *Ald.*: populi Ω.

of the earlier emigrants; and having, with the B.C. 391 approval of Bellovesus, crossed the Alps by the same pass, established themselves where the cities of Brixia and Verona are now. After these the Libui came and settled, and the Salluvii—taking up their abode hard by the ancient tribe of the Laevi Ligures, about the river Ticinus. Then, over the Poenine Pass, came the Boii and Lingones, who finding everything taken up between the Po and the Alps, crossed the Po on rafts, and drove out not only the Etruscans, but also the Umbrians from their lands; nevertheless, they kept on the further side of the Apennines. Then the Senones, the latest to come, had their holdings from the river Utens all the way to the Aesis. This was the tribe, I find, which came to Clusium and from thence to Rome, but whether alone or assisted by all the peoples of Cisalpine Gaul, is uncertain.

The men of Clusium, alarmed by this strange invasion, when they beheld the numbers and the unfamiliar figures of the men and their novel weapons, and heard that on many a field, this side the Po and beyond it, they had put to flight the levies of Etruria; though they had no rights of alliance or of friendship with the Romans, except that they had refused to defend their kinsmen the Veientes against the Roman People; did yet dispatch envoys to Rome to ask help of the senate. As for the help, they were unsuccessful; but the three sons of Marcus Fabius Ambustus were sent as ambassadors to remonstrate with the Gauls, in the name of the senate and the Roman People, against their attack on those who had done them no wrong, and were the Roman People's allies and friends. The Romans,

A.U.C.
363

res cogat, tuendos esse ; sed melius visum bellum
ipsum amoveri, si posset, et Gallos, novam gentem,
pace potius cognosci quam armis.

A.U.C.
364

XXXVI. Mitis legatio, ni praeferoces legatos
Gallisque magis quam Romanis similes habuisset.
Quibus postquam mandata ediderunt in concilio
2 Gallorum datur responsum : etsi novum nomen
audiant Romanorum, tamen credere viros fortes esse,
quorum auxilium a Clusinis in re trepida sit implora-
3 tum ; et quoniam legatione adversus se maluerint
quam armis tueri socios, ne se quidem pacem quam
illi adferant aspernari, si Gallis egentibus agro, quem
latius possideant quam colant Clusini, partem finium
4 concedant ; aliter pacem impetrari non posse. Et
responsum coram Romanis accipere velle, et si nege-
tur ager coram iisdem Romanis dimicaturos, ut
nuntiare domum possent quantum Galli virtute cete-
5 ros mortales praestarent. Quodnam id ius esset
agrum a possessoribus petere aut minari arma Romanis quaerentibus et quid in Etruria rei Gallis
esset, cum illi se in armis ius ferre et omnia fortium
virorum esse ferociter dicerent, accensis utrimque

they said, would be obliged to defend them, even
going to war, if circumstances should make it
necessary; but it had seemed preferable that the
war itself should, if possible, be accommodated,
and that they should make the acquaintance of
the Gauls—a new race to them—in a friendly rather
than in a hostile manner.

XXXVI. It was a peaceful embassy, had it not
been for the violence of the ambassadors, who were
more like Gauls than Romans. To them, when they
had made known their mission in the council, the
Gauls replied, that although they then heard for the
first time the name of Roman, they could yet believe
them to be stout-hearted men, since the Clusini had
sought their aid in time of danger; and inasmuch
as they had chosen to defend their allies by negotia-
tion rather than by the sword, they would not, for
their own part, spurn the peace which the Romans
proposed, if the men of Clusium, who possessed more
land than they could till, would surrender to the
Gauls, who needed land, a portion of their territory;
on no other terms could they consider granting peace.
They added that they desired to be answered in the
presence of the Romans, and that if land were
refused them, it was under the eyes of these same
Romans that they meant to fight, that they might
be able to tell their friends how greatly the Gauls
excelled all other men in prowess. When the
Romans asked what conceivable right they had to
demand land of its occupants under threat of war,
and what business Gauls had in Etruria, they were
truculently informed, that the new-comers carried
their right at the point of the sword and that all
things belonged to the brave. So, angry passions

animis ad arma discurritur et proelium conseritur.
6 Ibi iam urgentibus Romanam urbem fatis legati
contra ius gentium arma capiunt. Nec id clam esse
potuit cum ante signa Etruscorum tres nobilissimi
fortissimique Romanae iuventutis pugnarent ; tantum
7 eminebat peregrina virtus. Quin etiam Q. Fabius
evectus extra aciem equo ducem Gallorum ferociter
in ipsa signa Etruscorum incursantem per latus
transfixum hasta occidit ; spoliaque eius legentem
Galli agnovere, perque totam aciem Romanum lega-
8 tum esse signum datum est. Omissa inde in Clusinos
ira receptui canunt minantes Romanis. Erant qui
extemplo Romam eundum censerent; vicere seniores
ut legati prius mitterentur questum iniurias postu-
latumque ut pro iure gentium violato Fabii dede-
9 rentur. Legati Gallorum cum ea, sicut erant
mandata, exposuissent, senatui nec factum placebat
Fabiorum et ius postulare barbari videbantur ; sed
ne id quod placebat decerneretur in tantae nobilita-
10 tis viris ambitio obstabat. Itaque ne penes ipsos culpa
esset cladis forte Gallico bello acceptae, cognitionem
de postulatis Gallorum ad populum reiciunt; ubi
tanto plus gratia atque opes valuere ut quorum de
poena agebatur tribuni militum consulari potestate

being kindled on both sides, they ran to their B.C. 390
weapons and joined battle; and the envoys, impelled
by the fate which was even then urging Rome to its
doom, took up arms, in defiance of the law of
nations. Nor could it pass unnoticed, when in the
very fore-front of the Tuscan line there were fighting
three of the noblest and most valiant of the Roman
youth, so conspicuous was the strangers' bravery.
Nay, Quintus Fabius even rode out in front of the
line, and meeting the Gallic leader as he charged
boldly at the very standards of the Etruscans, ran
his spear through his side and killed him. As he
was engaged in despoiling his man, the Gauls
recognized him, and the word passed through all the
army that it was the Roman envoy. Thereupon,
they gave over their anger at the Clusini and sounded
the retreat, uttering threats against the Romans.
Some were for marching at once on Rome; but the
older men brought them over to send envoys first
to complain of their wrongs, and to demand the
surrender of the Fabii, in satisfaction for their
violation of the law of nations. When the Gallic
emissaries had stated their mission according to
instructions, the senate disapproved of the conduct
of the Fabii and felt the demands of the barbarians
to be just; but private interest could not suffer
them, in the case of men of such exalted station, to
decree what they approved. And so, that the blame
might not rest with the senate, if a Gallic war should
chance to bring disaster, they referred the demands
of the Gauls to the people for consideration; and
with them wealth and influence carried so much
more weight, that the men whose punishment was
under discussion were elected consular tribunes for

A.U.C.
364
11 in insequentem annum crearentur.   Quo facto haud
secus quam dignum erat infensi Galli bellum propalam minantes ad suos redeunt.   Tribuni militum
cum tribus Fabiis creati Q. Sulpicius Longus Q.
Servilius quartum P. Cornelius [1] Maluginensis.

XXXVII. Cum tanta moles mali instaret—adeo
obcaecat animos fortuna ubi vim suam ingruentem
refringi non volt—civitas quae adversus Fidenatem
ac Veientem hostem aliosque finitimos populos ultima experiens auxilia dictatorem multis tempestati-
2 bus dixisset, ea tunc invisitato atque inaudito hoste
ab Oceano terrarumque ultimis oris bellum ciente,
nihil extraordinarii imperii aut auxilii quaesivit.
3 Tribuni quorum temeritate bellum contractum erat
summae rerum praeerant, dilectumque nihilo accura-
tiorem quam ad media bella haberi solitus erat,
4 extenuantes etiam famam belli, habebant.   Interim
Galli postquam accepere ultro honorem habitum
violatoribus iuris humani elusamque legationem suam
esse, flagrantes ira, cuius impotens est gens, confestim signis convolsis citato agmine iter ingredi-
5 untur.   Ad quorum praetereuntium raptim tumultum
cum exterritae urbes ad arma concurrerent fugaque
agrestium fieret, Romam se ire magno clamore signi-
ficabant quacumque ibant, equis virisque longe ac
6 late fuso agmine immensum obtinentes loci.   Sed
antecedente fama nuntiisque Clusinorum, deinceps

---

[1] P. Cornelius *H. J. Mueller* (*cf. Diod.* xv. xx. 1): p.
seruilius (*omitted by H*) Ω.

---

[1] According to Dionysius of Halicarnassus (XII. xix) four
legions were embodied, and so many allies and auxiliary
troops that at the Allia the Roman army numbered 40,000
(*cf.* Plut. Cam. XVIII).

the ensuing year. At this the Gauls were enraged, B.C. 390 as they had every right to be, and returned to their people with open threats of war. The tribunes of the soldiers chosen with the three Fabii were Quintus Sulpicius Longus, Quintus Servilius (for his fourth term), and Publius Cornelius Maluginensis.

XXXVII. Now that so heavy a calamity drew towards,—such is the blindness Fortune visits on men's minds when she would have her gathering might meet with no check,—that state which against the Fidenates and Veientes and other neighbouring tribes had on many occasions resorted to the last expedient and named a dictator—that state, I say, though now an enemy never yet seen or heard of was rousing up war from the ocean and the remotest corners of the world, had recourse to no unusual authority or help. The tribunes whose rashness had brought on the war were in supreme command; they conducted the levy with no greater care than had usually been employed in preparing for ordinary campaigns,[1] and even disparaged the rumoured seriousness of the danger. The Gauls, meanwhile, on learning that honours had actually been conferred on men who had violated the rights of mankind and insulted their embassy, were consumed with wrath (a passion which their race is powerless to control), and straightway catching up their standards, set their column in rapid motion. As they marched swiftly and noisily on, the terrified cities armed in haste, and the peasants fled; but they signified with loud cries, wherever they came, that Rome was their goal, and their horse and foot in an extended line covered a vast tract of ground. Yet, though rumour and the report of the Clusini preceded them, and

127

inde aliorum populorum, plurimum terroris Romam
7 celeritas hostium tulit, quippe quibus velut tumultuario exercitu raptim ducto aegre ad undecimum
lapidem occursum est, qua flumen Allia Crustuminis
montibus praealto defluens alveo haud multum infra
8 viam Tiberino amni miscetur. Iam omnia contra
circaque hostium plena erant, et nata in vanos
tumultus gens truci cantu clamoribusque variis
horrendo cuncta compleverant sono.

XXXVIII. Ibi tribuni militum non loco castris
ante capto, non praemunito vallo quo receptus esset,
non deorum saltem, si non hominum memores, nec
auspicato nec litato, instruunt aciem diductam in
cornua, ne circumveniri multitudine hostium pos-
2 sent; nec tamen aequari frontes poterant cum ex-
tenuando infirmam et vix cohaerentem mediam aciem
haberent. Paulum erat ab dextera editi loci, quem
subsidiariis repleri placuit; eaque res ut initium
3 pavoris ac fugae, sic una salus fugientibus fuit. Nam
Brennus regulus Gallorum in paucitate hostium
artem maxime timens, ratus ad id captum superiorem
locum ut ubi Galli cum acie legionum recta fronte
concucurrissent subsidia in aversos transversosque
4 impetum darent, ad subsidiarios signa convertit, si eos

---

¹ The exact position of the battlefield is uncertain, as the
town Crustumerium has disappeared and left no trace. A
brook called *Fosso Maestro*, which empties into the Tiber
about eleven miles from Rome, has been thought to be the
ancient Allia.

after that successive messages from other peoples, B.C. 390 the utmost consternation was wrought in Rome by the enemy's swiftness, which was such that the army, albeit levied as it were *en masse* and hurriedly led out, barely covered eleven miles before confronting him, at the point where the river Allia descends in a very deep channel from the Crustuminian mountains, and mingles, not far south of the highway, with the waters of the Tiber.[1] The Gauls had already overrun all the ground in front and on both sides, and—the race being naturally given to vainglorious outbursts—their wild songs and discordant shouts filled all the air with a hideous noise.

XXXVIII. There the tribunes of the soldiers, without having selected a place for a camp or fortified a position to which they might retreat, and, forgetting even the gods, to say nothing of men, without auspices or sacrificial omens, drew up their line with the wings extended to prevent being outflanked by the numbers of the enemy; yet could not stretch their front as wide as his, though they thinned it till the centre was weak and scarce held together. There was a little eminence on the right which they decided to occupy with their reserves, a measure which, though it was the beginning of their panic and flight, was also the sole salvation of the fugitives. For Brennus, the Gallic chieftain, seeing the Romans to be so few, was especially apprehensive of a stratagem. He supposed that they had seized the higher ground for this purpose, that when the Gauls had made a frontal attack on the battle-line of the legions, the reserves might assail them in the flank and rear. He therefore directed his assault against the reserves, not doubting that, if he could

129

A.U.C.
364
loco depulisset haud dubius facilem in aequo campi
tantum superanti multitudini victoriam fore ; adeo
non fortuna modo sed ratio etiam cum barbaris
5 stabat.   In altera acie nihil simile Romanis, non
apud duces, non apud milites erat.   Pavor fugaque
occupaverat animos et tanta omnium[1] oblivio ut
multo maior pars Veios in hostium urbem, cum
Tiberis arceret, quam recto itinere Romam ad
6 coniuges ac liberos fugerent.   Parumper subsidiarios
tutatus est locus ; in reliqua acie simul est clamor
proximis ab latere, ultimis ab tergo auditus, ignotum
hostem prius paene quam viderent, non modo non
temptato certamine sed ne clamore quidem reddito,
7 integri intactique fugerunt ; nec ulla caedes pugnantium fuit ; terga caesa suomet ipsorum certamine
8 in turba impedientium fugam.   Circa ripam Tiberis,
quo armis abiectis totum sinistrum cornu defugit,
magna strages facta est, multosque imperitos nandi
aut invalidos, graves loricis aliisque tegminibus, hau-
9 sere gurgites ; maxima tamen pars incolumis Veios
perfugit, unde non modo praesidii quicquam sed ne
10 nuntius quidem cladis Romam est missus.   Ab dextro cornu, quod procul a flumine et magis sub monte
steterat, Romam omnes petiere et ne clausis quidem
portis urbis in arcem confugerunt.

[1] omnium *Gronovius D?* : hominum Ω

130

dislodge them, it would be easy for his greatly B C. 390 superior numbers to obtain a victory in the plain. Thus not only luck but generalship as well were on the side of the barbarians. In the other army there was no resemblance to Romans, either amongst officers or private soldiers. Terror and dismay had got hold of their spirits, and such complete forgetfulness of everything that a much greater number fled to Veii, a hostile city, though the Tiber was across their way, than by the straight road to Rome, to their wives and children. For a little while the reserves were protected by their position. In the rest of the field, no sooner had those who were nearest heard the shouting on their flank, and those who were farthest the outcry in their rear, than— fresh and unhurt—they ran away from their strange enemies, almost before they had caught sight of them; and so far were they from risking a combat, that they did not even return their battle-cry. None were slain in fight; but they were cut down from behind as they blocked their escape by their own struggles in the disordered rout. On the bank of the Tiber, whither the whole left wing had fled, after throwing away their arms, there was great slaughter, and many who could not swim, or lacked the strength, weighed down by their corslets and other armour, sank beneath the flood. Nevertheless, the chief part got safely to Veii, whence they not only sent no succours to Rome, but dispatched not even a messenger to tell of the defeat. From the right wing, which had stood at a distance from the river and closer to the foot of the mountain, the fugitives all made for Rome, and without stopping even to shut the city gates, sought refuge in the Citadel.

XXXIX. Gallos quoque velut obstupefactos miraculum victoriae tam repentinae tenuit, et ipsi pavore defixi primum steterunt, velut ignari quid accidisset; deinde insidias vereri; postremo caesorum spolia legere armorumque cumulos, ut mos eis est, coacer- 2 vare; tum demum postquam nihil usquam hostile cernebatur viam ingressi, haud multo ante solis occasum ad urbem Romam perveniunt. Ubi cum praegressi equites non portas clausas, non stationem pro portis excubare, non armatos esse in muris rettulissent, aliud priori simile miraculum eos sustinuit; 3 noctemque veriti et ignotae situm urbis inter Romam atque Anienem consedere exploratoribus missis circa moenia aliasque portas quaenam hostibus in perdita 4 re consilia essent. Romani cum pars maior ex acie Veios petisset quam Romam, nemo superesse quemquam praeter eos qui Romam refugerant crederet,[1] complorati omnes pariter vivi mortuique totam prope 5 urbem lamentis impleverunt. Privatos deinde luctus stupefecit publicus pavor, postquam hostes adesse nuntiatum est; mox ululatus cantusque dissonos vagantibus circa moenia turmatim barbaris audiebant. 6 Omne inde tempus suspensos ita tenuit animos usque ad lucem alteram ut identidem iam in urbem futurus videretur impetus: primo adventu, quia

---

[1] crederet $F^3A^1_5$: crederent Ω.

XXXIX. The very Gauls themselves, stunned by B.C. 390 the marvellous victory they had so suddenly gained, at first stood rooted to the spot with amazement, like men that knew not what had happened; then they feared an ambush; after that they fell to collecting the spoils of the slain and erecting piles of arms, as their custom is; then at last having discovered no hostile movement anywhere, they began their march, and a little before sunset reached the environs of Rome. There, when the cavalry had reconnoitred and had reported that the gates were not closed, that no out-guards were watching before the gates, that no armed men were on the walls, astonishment held them spell-bound as before; and fearful of the night and the lie of the unknown City, they went into camp between Rome and the Anio, after sending off patrols about the walls and the rest of the gates, to find out what the enemy in their desperate case could possibly be at. As for the Romans, inasmuch as more, on escaping from the battle, had fled to Veii than to Rome, and no one supposed that any were left alive except those who had found refuge in the City, they mourned for all alike, both the living and the dead, and well nigh filled the City with lamentation. But presently their personal griefs were overwhelmed in a general panic, with the announcement that the enemy was at hand; and soon they could hear the dissonant howls and songs of the barbarians, as their squadrons roamed about the walls. During all the time that intervened before the following morning their hearts were in such suspense, that each moment they anticipated an immediate attack: on the first arrival of the enemy, because they had come close to the

LIVY

accesserant ad urbem—mansuros enim ad Alliam
7 fuisse nisi hoc consilii foret ;—deinde sub occasum
solis, quia haud multum diei supererat, ante noctem
rati sunt [1] invasuros ; tum in noctem dilatum con-
8 silium esse, quo plus pavoris inferrent. Postremo
lux appropinquans exanimare, timorique perpetuo
ipsum malum continens fuit cum signa infesta portis
sunt inlata. Nequaquam tamen ea nocte neque insequenti die similis illi quae ad Alliam tam pavide
9 fugerat civitas fuit. Nam cum defendi urbem
posse tam parva relicta manu spes nulla esset, placuit
cum coniugibus ac liberis iuventutem militarem
senatusque robur in arcem Capitoliumque concedere,
10 armisque et frumento conlato inde ex loco munito [2]
deos hominesque et Romanum nomen defendere ;
11 flaminem sacerdotesque Vestales sacra publica a
caede, ab incendiis procul auferre, nec ante deseri
cultum eorum quam non superessent qui colerent.
12 Si arx Capitoliumque, sedes deorum, si senatus, caput
publici consilii, si militaris iuventus superfuerit imminenti ruinae urbis, facilem iacturam esse seniorum
13 relictae in urbe utique periturae turbae. Et quo id
aequiore animo de plebe multitudo ferret, senes
triumphales consularesque simul se cum illis palam
dicere obituros nec his corporibus quibus non arma

---

[1] rati sunt *Walters* (*Class. Quart.* V (1911) *p.* 14): rati
(ratu *B*) se Ω: rati *V*: enim *Walters* (*Oxford Text*).
[2] inde ex loco munito *Reid*: ex loco inde munito Ω.

City—for they would have stopped at the Allia, had
this not been their design ;—again, towards sundown,
because there was little daylight left, they thought
that they would enter the City before nightfall ;
then they concluded that they had put it off till
night, to strike more fear into them. Finally the
approach of dawn put them beside themselves, and
close upon these restless apprehensions came the
evil they were dreading, when the hostile forces
entered the city gates. Yet neither that night nor
the following day did the citizens at all resemble
those who had fled in such consternation at the
Allia. For having no hopes that they could protect
the City with so small a force as remained to them,
they resolved that the men of military age and the
able-bodied senators should retire into the Citadel
and the Capitol, with their wives and children ; and,
having laid in arms and provisions, should from that
stronghold defend the gods, the men, and the name
of Rome ; that the flamen and the priestesses of
Vesta should remove the sacred objects pertaining
to the State far from the bloodshed and the flames,
nor should their cult be abandoned till none should
be left to cherish it. If the Citadel and the Capitol,
where dwelt the gods; if the senate, the source of
public wisdom ; if the young men capable of bearing
arms survived the impending destruction of the City,
they could easily bear to lose the crowd of old men
left behind them, who were bound to die in any
case. And in order that the multitude of commoners might endure it with the more composure,
the old men who had triumphed and those who had
been consuls declared publicly that they would
perish with those others, nor burden with bodies

ferre, non tueri patriam possent, oneraturos inopiam
armatorum.

XL. Haec inter seniores morti destinatos iactata
solacia. Versae inde adhortationes ad agmen iuvenum quos in Capitolium atque in arcem proseque-
bantur, commendantes virtuti eorum iuventaeque
urbis per trecentos sexaginta annos omnibus bellis
2 victricis quaecumque reliqua esset fortuna. Digre-
dientibus qui spem omnem atque opem secum ferebant ab iis qui captae urbis non superesse statuerant
3 exitio cum ipsa res speciesque miserabilis erat, tum
muliebris fletus et concursatio incerta nunc hos nunc
illos sequentium rogitantiumque viros natosque cui
se fato darent, nihil quod humani superesset mali [1]
4 relinquebant. Magna pars tamen earum in arcem
suos persecutae sunt nec prohibente ullo nec vocante,
quia quod utile obsessis ad minuendam imbellem
5 multitudinem id parum humanum erat. Alia maxime
plebis turba, quam nec capere tam exiguus collis nec
alere in tanta inopia frumenti poterat, ex urbe effusa
6 velut agmine iam uno petiit Ianiculum. Inde pars
per agros dilapsi, pars urbes petunt finitimas, sine
ullo duce aut consensu suam quisque spem, sua
consilia communibus deploratis sequentes.[2]
7 Flamen interim Quirinalis virginesque Vestales

[1] humani superesset mali *Finckh*: humanis superesset
malis Ω.
[2] sequentes *Madvig*: exsequentes (exe- *B*) Ω.

incapable of bearing arms in defence of the country B.C. 390 the scanty stores of the fighting men.

XL. Such were the consolations which the old men appointed to die exchanged among themselves; then, directing their encouragement to the band of youths whom they were escorting to the Capitol and the Citadel, they committed to their valour and their young strength whatever fortune might yet be in store for a City that for three hundred and sixty years had been victorious in every war. On the departure of those who carried with them all hope and help, from those who had resolved not to survive the capture and destruction of their City, though the separation was a pitiful thing to see, yet the tears of the women, as they ran distractedly up and down, and following now these, now those, demanded of husbands and sons to what fate they were consigning them, supplied the final touch of human wretchedness. Still, the greater part of them followed their sons into the Citadel, though none either forbade or encouraged it, since what would have helped the besieged to lessen the number of non-combatants would have been inhuman. Another host—consisting chiefly of plebeians—too large for so small a hill to receive, or to support with so meagre a supply of corn, streamed out of the City as though forming at last one continuous line, and took their way towards Janiculum. Thence some of them scattered through the country-side, and others made for the towns near by. They had neither leader nor concerted plan; each followed the promptings of his own hopes and his own counsels, in despair of the commonwealth.

Meanwhile the flamen of Quirinus and the Vestal

A.U.C.
394

omissa rerum suarum cura, quae sacrorum secum ferenda, quae quia vires ad omnia ferenda deerant
relinquenda essent consultantes, quisve ea locus fideli
8 adservaturus custodia esset, optimum ducunt condita
in doliolis sacello proximo aedibus flaminis Quirinalis,
ubi nunc despui religio est, defodere ; cetera inter
se onere partito ferunt [1] via quae sublicio ponte ducit
9 ad Ianiculum. In eo clivo eas cum L. Albinius de
plebe homo conspexisset plaustro coniugem ac liberos
avehens [2] inter ceteram turbam quae inutilis bello
10 urbe excedebat salvo etiam tum discrimine divi-
narum humanarumque rerum religiosum ratus sacerdotes publicas sacraque populi Romani pedibus ire
ferrique ac suos in vehiculo conspici, descendere
uxorem ac pueros iussit, virgines sacraque in plaus-
trum imposuit et Caere, quo iter sacerdotibus erat,
pervexit.

XLI. Romae interim satis iam omnibus, ut in tali
re, ad tuendam arcem compositis turba seniorum
domos regressi adventum hostium obstinato ad
2 mortem animo exspectabant. Qui eorum curules
gesserant magistratus, ut in fortunae pristinae honorumque ac virtutis insignibus morerentur, quae
augustissima vestis est tensas ducentibus triumph-
antibusve, ea vestiti medio aedium eburneis sellis

---

[1] ferunt ⌐: feruntur Ω.
[2] avehens *Madvig*: uehens ⌐: habens Ω.

---

[1] Cars used in the games of the Circus to carry the images
of the Gods.
[2] The curule chair was inlaid with ivory. At this period
the only curule magistrates were dictators, masters of the
horse, consuls, and censors.

virgins, with no thought for their own belongings, B.C. 390 were consulting which of the sacred things they should carry with them, and which, because they were not strong enough to carry them all, they must leave behind, and, finally, where these objects would be safe. They judged it best to place them in jars and bury them in the shrine adjoining the flamen's house, where it is now forbidden to spit; the rest of the things they carried, sharing the burden amongst them, along the road which leads by the Sublician Bridge to Janiculum. As they mounted the hill they were perceived by a plebeian named Lucius Albinius, who had a waggon in which he was conveying his wife and children, amidst the throng of those who, unfit for war, were leaving the City. Preserving even then the distinction between divine and human, and holding it sacrilege that the priestesses of his country should go afoot, bearing the sacred objects of the Roman People, while his family were seen in a vehicle, he commanded his wife and children to get down, placed the virgins and their relics in the waggon, and brought them to Caere, whither the priestesses were bound.

XLI. At Rome meantime such arrangements for defending the Citadel as the case admitted of were now fairly complete, and the old men returned to their homes to await the coming of their enemies with hearts that were steeled to die. Such of them as had held curule magistracies, that they might face death in the trappings of their ancient rank and office, as beseemed their worth, put on the stately robes which are worn by those who conduct the *tensae* [1] or celebrate a triumph, and, thus habited, seated themselves on ivory chairs [2] in the middle of

3 sedere. Sunt qui M. Folio pontifice maximo prae-
fante carmen devovisse eos se pro patria Quiriti-
busque Romanis tradant.

4 Galli et quia interposita nocte a contentione pugnae remiserant animos et quod nec in acie ancipiti
usquam certaverant proelio nec tum impetu aut vi
capiebant urbem, sine ira, sine ardore animorum
ingressi postero die urbem patente Collina porta in
forum perveniunt, circumferentes oculos ad templa
5 deum arcemque solam belli speciem tenentem. Inde
modico relicto praesidio ne quis in dissipatos ex
arce aut Capitolio impetus fieret, dilapsi ad praedam
vacuis occursu hominum viis pars in proxima quaeque tectorum agmine ruunt, pars ultima, velut ea
6 demum intacta et referta praeda, petunt. Inde
rursus ipsa solitudine absterriti, ne qua fraus hostilis
vagos exciperet, in forum ac propinqua foro loca
7 conglobati redibant [1]; ubi eos, plebis aedificiis ob-
seratis, patentibus atriis principum, maior prope
cunctatio tenebat aperta quam clausa invadendi;
8 adeo haud secus quam venerabundi intuebantur in
aedium vestibulis sedentes viros praeter ornatum
habitumque humano augustiorem maiestate etiam
quam voltus gravitasque oris prae se ferebat simil-
limos dis.

[1] redibant F^3 (or F^2)D^3A^2: rediebant Ω.

their houses. Some historians record that Marcus B.C. 390
Folius, the pontifex maximus, led in the recitation
of a solemn vow, by which they devoted themselves
to death, in behalf of their country and the Roman
Quirites.

The Gauls found their lust for combat cooled by
the night which had intervened. At no point in the
battle had they been pushed to desperate exertions,
nor had they now to carry the City by assault. It
was therefore without rancour or excitement that
they entered Rome, on the following day, by the
Colline Gate (which lay wide open), and made their
way to the Forum, gazing about them at the temples
of the gods and at the Citadel, which alone presented
some show of war. Thence, after leaving a moderate
guard to prevent any attack upon their scattered
forces from Citadel or Capitol, they dispersed in
quest of booty through streets where there was none
to meet them, some rushing in a body into whatever
houses were nearest, while others sought out the
most remote, as though supposing that only such
would be intact and full of plunder. But being
frightened out of these by their very solitude, lest
the enemy should by some ruse entrap them as they
wandered apart, they came trooping back to the
Forum and the places near it. There they found the
dwellings of the plebeians fastened up, but the halls
of the nobles open ; and they hesitated almost more
to enter the open houses than the shut,—so nearly
akin to religious awe was their feeling as they beheld
seated in the vestibules, beings who, besides that
their ornaments and apparel were more splendid
than belonged to man, seemed also, in their majesty
of countenance and in the gravity of their expression,
most like to gods.

9   Ad eos velut simulacra versi cum starent, M.
Papirius, unus ex iis, dicitur Gallo barbam suam,
ut tum omnibus promissa erat, permulcenti scipione
eburneo in caput incusso iram movisse atque ab eo
initium caedis ortum, ceteros in sedibus suis truci-
10 datos ; post principum caedem nulli deinde mortalium
parci, diripi tecta, exhaustis inici ignes.

XLII. Ceterum, seu non omnibus delendi urbem
libido erat, seu ita placuerat principibus Gallorum
et ostentari quaedam incendia terroris causa, si
compelli ad deditionem caritate sedum suarum
2 obsessi possent, et non omnia concremari tecta ut
quodcumque superesset urbis, id pignus ad flectendos
hostium animos haberent, nequaquam perinde atque
in capta urbe primo[1] die aut passim aut late vagatus
3 est ignis.   Romani ex arce plenam hostium urbem
cernentes vagosque per vias omnes cursus, cum alia
atque alia parte nova aliqua clades oreretur, non
mentibus solum consipere,[2] sed ne auribus quidem
4 atque oculis satis constare poterant.   Quocumque
clamor hostium,[3] mulierum puerorumque ploratus,
sonitus flammae et fragor ruentium tectorum avertisset, paventes ad omnia animos oraque et oculos
flectebant velut ad spectaculum a fortuna positi

---

[1] primo *H. J. Mueller* : prima Ω.
[2] consipere *Lipsius* : concipere Ω : incipere *E.*
[3] clamor hostium *A*[2] (*or A*[3]) ς : clamor sonitus hostium Ω.

While they stood reverentially before them, as
if they had been images, it is related that a Gaul
stroked the beard of one of them, Marcus Papirius,—
which he wore long, as they all did then,—whereat
the Roman struck him over the head with his ivory
mace, and, provoking his anger, was the first to be
slain; after that the rest were massacred where
they sat; and when the nobles had been murdered,
there was no mercy then shown to anyone; the
houses were ransacked, and after being emptied
were given to the flames.

XLII. But whether it was that not all the Gauls
desired to destroy the City, or that their leaders had
resolved to make a certain show of burning, to
inspire alarm, in hopes that the besieged might be
driven to capitulate by affection for their homes, but
not to burn up all the houses, in order that they
might hold whatever remained of the City as a
pledge to work on the feelings of their enemies—
however this may have been, the fire spread by no
means so freely or extensively on the first day as
is commonly the case in a captured town. As the
Romans looked down from their fastness and saw
the City full of enemies running up and down in all
the streets, while first in one quarter and then in
another some new calamity would be occurring, they
were unable, I do not say to keep their heads, but
even to be sure of their ears and eyes. Wherever
the shouting of the invaders, the lamentations of
the women and children, the crackling of the flames,
and the crash of falling buildings drew their
attention, trembling at each sound, they turned
their thoughts and their gaze that way, as though
Fortune had placed them there to witness the

occidentis patriae nec ullius rerum suarum relicti
5 praeterquam corporum vindices, tanto ante alios
miserandi magis qui unquam obsessi sunt quod
interclusi a patria obsidebantur, omnia sua cernentes
6 in hostium potestate. Nec tranquillior nox diem tam
foede actum excepit; lux deinde noctem inquieta[1]
insecuta est, nec ullum erat tempus quod a novae
7 semper cladis alicuius spectaculo cessaret. Nihil
tamen tot onerati atque obruti malis flexerunt
animos quin, etsi omnia flammis ac ruinis aequata
vidissent, quamvis inopem parvumque quem tenebant collem libertati relictum virtute defenderent;
8 et iam cum eadem cottidie acciderent, velut adsueti
malis abalienaverant ab sensu rerum suarum animos,
arma tantum ferrumque in dextris velut solas reliquias
spei suae intuentes.

XLIII. Galli quoque per aliquot dies in tecta
modo urbis nequiquam bello gesto cum inter incendia ac ruinas captae urbis nihil superesse praeter
armatos hostes viderent nec quicquam tot cladibus
territos nec flexuros ad deditionem animos ni vis
adhiberetur, experiri ultima et impetum facere in
2 arcem statuunt. Prima luce signo dato multitudo
omnis in foro instruitur; inde clamore sublato ac
testudine facta subeunt. Adversus quos Romani

---

[1] inquieta *Gronovius*: inquietam Ω.

pageant of their dying country. Of all their B.C. 390
possessions nothing was left them to defend save
their persons alone; and so much more wretched
was their plight than that of all others who have
ever been beleaguered, that they were cut off from
their native City and confined where they could see
all that belonged to them in the power of their
enemies. Nor was the night more tranquil, after a
day of such distress; and the night was followed by
a restless day, with never a moment that had not
still some fresh calamity to unfold. Yet, oppressed
as they were, or rather overwhelmed, by so many
misfortunes, nothing could alter their resolve;
though they should see everything laid low in
flames and ruins, they would stoutly defend the
hill they held, however small and naked, which
was all that Liberty had left. And now that the
same events were occurring every day, like men
grown used to grief, they had ceased to feel their
own misfortunes, looking solely to their shields and
the swords in their right hands as their only
remaining hope.

XLIII. The Gauls likewise, having vainly for
some days waged war against only the buildings of
Rome, when they saw that there was nothing left
amidst the smouldering ruins of the captured City
but armed enemies, who for all their disasters were
not a jot appalled nor likely to yield to anything
but force, took a desperate resolution to attack the
Citadel. At daybreak the signal was made; and
the entire host, having formed up in the Forum,
gave a cheer, and raising their shields above their
heads and locking them, began the ascent. The
defenders on the other hand did nothing rashly

145

nihil temere nec trepide; ad omnis aditus stationibus
firmatis, qua signa ferri videbant ea robore virorum
opposito scandere hostem sinunt, quo successerit
magis in arduum eo pelli posse per proclive facilius
3 rati. Medio fere clivo restitere, atque inde ex loco
superiore, qui prope sua sponte in hostem inferebat
impetu facto, strage ea ac[1] ruina fudere Gallos ut
nunquam postea nec pars nec universi temptaverint
4 tale pugnae genus. Omissa itaque spe per vim
atque arma subeundi obsidionem parant, cuius ad
id tempus immemores et quod in urbe fuerat frumentum incendiis urbis absumpserant, et ex agris
5 per eos ipsos dies raptum omne Veios erat. Igitur
exercitu diviso partim per finitimos populos praedari
placuit, partim obsideri arcem, ut obsidentibus
frumentum populatores agrorum praeberent.

6 Proficiscentis Gallos ab urbe ad Romanam experi-
endam virtutem fortuna ipsa Ardeam, ubi Camillus
7 exsulabat, duxit; qui maestior ibi fortuna publica
quam sua cum dis hominibusque accusandis senes-
ceret, indignando mirandoque ubi illi viri essent qui
secum Veios Faleriosque cepissent, qui alia bella
8 fortius semper quam felicius gessissent, repente audit
Gallorum exercitum adventare atque de eo pavidos

---

[1] strage ea ac *Madvig*: strage ac Ω.

or in confusion. At all the approaches they had
strengthened the guard-posts, and where they saw
the enemy advancing they stationed their best
soldiers, and suffered them to come up, persuaded
that the higher they mounted up the steep the
easier it would be to drive them down.   They made
their stand about the middle of the declivity, and
there, launching their attack from the higher ground,
which seemed of itself to hurl them against the foe,
dislodged the Gauls, with such havoc and destruction
that they never attempted to attack in that manner
again, with either a part or the whole of their
strength. So, relinquishing all hope of getting up
by force of arms, they prepared for a blockade.
Having never till that moment considered such a
thing, they had destroyed all the corn in the City
with their conflagrations, and what was in the fields
had all been hurriedly carried off, within the last
few days, to Veii.   They therefore arranged to
divide their army, and employ part of it to pillage
the neighbouring nations and part to invest the
Citadel, in order that those who held the lines might
be provisioned by the foragers.

  When the Gauls departed from the City, Fortune's
own hand guided them to Ardea, that they might
make trial of Roman manhood. Camillus was languishing there in exile, more grieved by the nation's
calamity than by his own ; and as he sorrowfully
inveighed against gods and men, and asked, with
wonder and humiliation, where those heroes were
who had shared with him in the capture of Veii and
Falerii, and whose gallantry in other wars had ever
outrun their success, of a sudden he heard that the
army of the Gauls was coming, and that the Ardeates

147

Ardeates consultare. Nec secus quam divino spiritu
tactus cum se in mediam contionem intulisset absti-
nere suetus ante talibus conciliis, (XLIV.) "Ardeates"
inquit, "veteres amici, novi etiam cives mei, quando
et vestrum beneficium ita tulit et fortuna hoc eguit
mea, nemo vestrum condicionis meae oblitum me
huc processisse putet; sed res ac periculum commune cogit quod quisque possit in re trepida prae-
2 sidii in medium conferre. Et quando ego vobis pro
tantis vestris in me meritis gratiam referam, si nunc
cessavero? Aut ubi usus erit mei vobis, si in bello
non fuerit? Hac arte in patria steti et invictus
3 bello, in pace ab ingratis civibus pulsus sum. Vobis
autem, Ardeates, fortuna oblata est et pro tantis
populi Romani beneficiis, quanta ipsi meministis—
nec enim exprobranda ea¹ apud memores sunt—
gratiae referendae et huic urbi decus ingens belli
4 ex hoste communi pariendi. Quae effuso agmine
adventat gens est cui natura corpora animosque
magna magis quam firma dederit; eo in certamen
5 omne plus terroris quam virium ferunt. Argumento
sit clades Romana. Patentem cepere urbem: ex
arce Capitolioque iis exigua resistitur manu: iam
obsidionis taedio victi abscedunt vagique per agros
6 palantur. Cibo vinoque raptim hausto repleti, ubi

¹ exprobranda ea *Alschefski U*: exprobrandae *P*: exprobranda *VOEHA*: exprobrande *MD?FB*: exprobandae *E²*:
exprobanda *L*: exprobrando *D²* or *D⁴A²*.

in alarm were deliberating what to do about it. With B.C. 390 an inspiration nothing less than divine, he pushed into the midst of their conference,—though before accustomed to avoid these councils—and there, (XLIV.) "Men of Ardea," he said, "my ancient friends, and of late my fellow citizens,—since your goodness would have it so and my own fortune has made it necessary,—let none of you suppose me to have come forward in forgetfulness of my condition; but circumstances and our common peril oblige every man at this crisis to contribute what he can to the general defence. And when shall I show gratitude for your great kindnesses to me, if I am backward now? Or when shall you have need of me, if not in war? 'Twas by this art that I stood secure in my native City: unbeaten in war, I was driven out in time of peace by the thankless citizens. But you, men of Ardea, have now an opportunity of requiting the Roman People for such great benefits as you yourselves are mindful of,—nor need I cast up to you things which you remember;—and your city has an opportunity to win from our common enemy great renown in war. That people now drawing near in loose array has been endowed by nature with bodily size and courage, great indeed but vacillating; which is the reason that to every conflict they bring more terror than strength. This may be seen in their defeat of the Romans. They captured the City, which lay wide open; but a handful of men in the Citadel and the Capitol are holding them at bay; already, oppressed by the tedium of the siege, they are departing and roaming aimlessly through the country-side. They greedily gorge themselves with food and wine, and when

A.U.C.
364 nox adpetit prope rivos aquarum sine munimento,
sine stationibus ac custodiis passim ferarum ritu
sternuntur, nunc ab secundis rebus magis etiam
7 solito incauti. Si vobis in animo est tueri moenia
vestra nec pati haec omnia Galliam fieri, prima
vigilia capite arma frequentesque[1] me sequimini ad
caedem, non ad pugnam. Nisi vinctos somno velut
pecudes trucidandos tradidero, non recuso eundem
Ardeae rerum mearum exitum, quem Romae habui."

XLV. Aequis iniquisque persuasum erat tantum
bello virum neminem usquam ea tempestate esse.
Contione dimissa corpora curant intenti quam mox
signum daretur. Quo dato primae silentio noctis ad
2 portas Camillo praesto fuere. Egressi haud procul
urbe, sicut praedictum erat, castra Gallorum intuta
neglectaque ab omni parte nacti cum ingenti clamore
3 invadunt. Nusquam proelium, omnibus locis caedes
est; nuda corpora et soluta somno trucidantur. Extremos tamen pavor cubilibus suis excitos, quae aut
unde vis esset ignaros, in fugam et quosdam in
hostem ipsum improvidos tulit. Magna pars in
agrum Antiatem delati incursione ab oppidanis in
palatos facta circumveniuntur.

4 Similis in agro Veienti Tuscorum facta strages

---

[1] frequentesque V: frequentes Ω.

night approaches they erect no rampart, and without B.C. 390
pickets or sentries, throw themselves down anywhere
beside a stream, in the manner of wild beasts. Just
now success has rendered them even more careless
than they are wont to be. If you have a mind to
protect your city and not to suffer all this country
to become Gaul, arm yourselves in the first watch,
and follow me in force, not to a battle but a
massacre. If I do not deliver them up to you fast
asleep, to be butchered like cattle, I am ready to
submit at Ardea to the same fate that I endured at
Rome."

XLV. Well-wishers and opponents were alike
persuaded that there was no such warrior in those
days anywhere. Breaking up the council, they
supped, and waited intently for the signal. On its
being given, in the silence of the early night, they
presented themselves before Camillus at the gates.
They had not left the city very far behind them,
when they came to the camp of the Gauls, unguarded, just as he had prophesied, and open on
every side, and, giving a loud cheer, rushed upon it.
There was no resistance anywhere: the whole place
was a shambles, where unarmed men, relaxed in
sleep, were slaughtered. Those, however, who were
farthest off were frightened from the places where
they lay, and ignorant of the nature of the attack
or its source, fled panic-stricken, and some ran un-
awares straight into the enemy. The most of them
were carried into the territory of Antium, where
they wandered about until the townspeople sallied
out and cut them off.

A similar overthrow was experienced, in the region
of Veii, by the Etruscans. So far were they from

est, qui urbis iam prope quadringentesimum annum
vicinae, oppressae ab hoste invisitato, inaudito, adeo
nihil miseriti sunt ut in agrum Romanum eo tempore
incursiones facerent plenique praedae Veios etiam
praesidiumque, spem ultimam Romani nominis, in
5 animo habuerint oppugnare. Viderant eos milites
Romani vagantes per agros et congregato agmine
praedam prae se agentis, et castra cernebant haud
6 procul Veiis posita. Inde primum miseratio sui,
deinde indignitas atque ex ea ira animos cepit:
Etruscisne [1] etiam, a quibus bellum Gallicum in se
7 avertissent, ludibrio esse clades suas? Vix tempe-
ravere animis quin extemplo impetum facerent;
compressi a Q. Caedicio centurione, quem sibimet
8 ipsi praefecerant, rem in noctem sustinuere. Tantum par Camillo defuit auctor: cetera eodem ordine
eodemque fortunae eventu gesta. Quin etiam ducibus captivis, qui caedi nocturnae superfuerant, ad
aliam manum Tuscorum ad salinas profecti nocte
insequenti ex improviso maiorem caedem edidere,
duplicique victoria ovantes Veios redeunt.

XLVI. Romae interim plerumque obsidio segnis
et utrimque silentium esse ad id tantum intentis
Gallis ne quis hostium evadere inter stationes posset,
cum repente iuvenis Romanus admiratione in se

---

[1] Etruscisne *Vorm.?* ς: etruscin *MPHDLA*: etruscis
P²FUBOED³A³.

---

[1] Established according to tradition, by King Ancus (I.
xxxiii. 9), on the right bank of the Tiber, not far from Ostia.

pitying a City that had been their neighbour for B.C. 390
close upon four hundred years, and was now overwhelmed by an enemy never seen or heard of before,
that they chose that time to make incursions into
the lands of the Romans; and laden with spoils,
even meditated an attack on Veii and its garrison,
the last hope of the Roman name. The Roman
soldiers had seen them, as they ranged through the
fields and afterwards, gathering in a body, drove
the booty off before them, and could descry their
camp, which was pitched not far from Veii. This
made them at first to compassionate themselves;
then they were seized with resentment, which soon
gave way to rage: were even the Etruscans, whom
they had saved from the Gauls by incurring war
themselves, to make sport of their calamities? They
could hardly curb an impulse to assail them on the
instant; but being restrained by the centurion
Quintus Caedicius, whom they had chosen to be
their commander, postponed the affair till dark.
The only thing wanting was a leader like Camillus;
in all else the order followed was the same, and the
same success was achieved. Indeed, under the
guidance of captives who had survived the nocturnal
massacre, they set out on the following night and
came to another band of Etruscans, at the salt-
works,[1] whom they surprised and defeated with
even greater carnage; and so, rejoicing in their
double victory, returned to Veii.

XLVI. At Rome meanwhile the siege was for the
most part languishing and all was quiet on both
sides, the Gauls being solely concerned with preventing the escape of any enemy through their
lines, when suddenly a young Roman attracted the

A.U.C.
364

2 cives hostesque convertit. Sacrificium erat statum
in Quirinali colle genti Fabiae. Ad id faciendum
C. Fabius Dorsuo Gabino cinctu incinctus[1] sacra
manibus gerens cum de Capitolio descendisset, per
medias hostium stationes egressus nihil ad vocem
cuiusquam terroremve motus in Quirinalem collem
3 pervenit; ibique omnibus sollenniter peractis eadem
revertens similiter constanti vultu graduque, satis
sperans propitios esse deos quorum cultum ne mortis
quidem metu prohibitus deseruisset, in Capitolium
ad suos rediit seu attonitis Gallis miraculo audaciae
seu religione etiam motis, cuius haudquaquam
neglegens gens est.
4   Veiis interim non animi tantum in dies sed etiam
vires crescebant. Nec Romanis solum eo conveni-
entibus ex agris qui aut proelio adverso aut clade
captae urbis palati fuerant, sed etiam ex Latio
voluntariis confluentibus ut in parte praedae essent,
5 maturum iam videbatur repeti patriam eripique ex
hostium manibus; sed corpori valido caput deerat.
6 Locus ipse admonebat Camilli, et magna pars militum erat qui ductu auspicioque eius res prospere
gesserant; et Caedicius negare se commissurum cur
sibi aut deorum aut hominum quisquam imperium
finiret potius quam ipse memor ordinis sui posceret
7 imperatorem. Consensu omnium placuit ab Ardea

---

[1] cinctu incinctus *Walters*: cinctus (cintus *B*: cunctus
F) Ω : cinctu *V Rhenanus*.

---

[1] This was a mode of girding up the toga traditional in
religious ceremonies.

wondering admiration of fellow citizens and foes.
There was an annual sacrifice to be made on the
Quirinal Hill by the family of the Fabii. To celebrate it Gaius Fabius Dorsuo, in the Gabinian
cincture,[1] with the sacred vessels in his hands,
descended from the Capitol, passed out through the
midst of the enemy's pickets, and regardless of any
words or threats, proceeded to the Quirinal, where
he duly accomplished all the rites. He then
returned by the same way, with the like resolute
countenance and gait, in the full assurance of the
favour of the gods whose service not even the fear
of death could cause him to neglect, and rejoined
his friends on the Capitol, leaving the Gauls dumbfounded by his astonishing audacity, or perhaps even
moved by religious awe, a sentiment to which that
race is far from indifferent.

At Veii, all this while, they were gathering from
day to day, not courage merely, but strength as
well. Not only were Romans coming in from the
country-side,—men who had been wanderers since
the defeat, or the capture of the City,—but
volunteers were also pouring in from Latium, that
they might share in the spoils. It seemed therefore
that the time was now ripe to return to their native
City and wrest it from the hands of the enemy ; but
their strong body lacked a head. The place itself
reminded men of Camillus, and there were many
of the soldiers who had fought successfully under
his leadership and auspices. Moreover, Caedicius
declared that he would suffer neither god nor man
to put an end to his authority, but, remembering
his station, would himself demand the appointment
of a general. With the consent of all they resolved

A.U.C.
364

Camillum acciri, sed antea consulto senatu, qui
Romae esset: adeo regebat omnia pudor, discrimina-
8 que rerum prope perditis rebus servabant. Ingenti
periculo transeundum per hostium custodias erat.
Ad eam rem Pontius Cominus,[1] impiger iuvenis,
operam pollicitus incubans cortici secundo Tiberi ad
9 urbem defertur. Inde qua proximum fuit a ripa,
per praeruptum eoque neglectum hostium custodiae
saxum in Capitolium evadit, et ad magistratus ductus
10 mandata exercitus edit. Accepto inde senatus consulto uti comitiis curiatis revocatus de exsilio iussu
populi Camillus dictator extemplo diceretur milites-
que haberent imperatorem quem vellent, eadem de-
11 gressus [2] nuntius Veios contendit; missique Ardeam
legati ad Camillum Veios eum perduxere, seu—
quod magis credere libet non prius profectum ab
Ardea quam compererit [3] legem latam, quod nec
iniussu populi mutari finibus posset nec nisi dictator
dictus auspicia in exercitu habere—lex curiata lata
est dictatorque absens dictus.

XLVII. Dum haec Veiis agebantur, interim arx
Romae Capitoliumque in ingenti periculo fuit.
2 Namque Galli seu vestigio notato humano, qua
nuntius a Veiis pervenerat, seu sua sponte animad-
verso ad Carmentis[1] saxo ascensu aequo, nocte

---

[1] Cominus *E Sigonius* (*Conway, Italic Dialects, p.* 15):
quominus Ω: comminus *MO?*: cominius *E²* (or *E³*) ς.
[2] degressus *Sigonius*: digressus (digresū *B*: digressu
B¹) Ω.
[3] compererit ς: comperit Ω: comperet *M*.

---

[1] The mother of Evander, whose name appears in I. vii. 8
in the form Carmenta.

to send for Camillus from Ardea, but not till the B.C. 390 senate at Rome had been consulted; so modest were they in their conduct of everything, preserving the proper distinctions even in their well-nigh desperate case. It was necessary at enormous risk to pass the enemy's outposts. This an active youth named Pontius Cominus undertook to do, and supporting himself on a strip of cork, floated down the Tiber to the City. Once there, he passed by the shortest way from the bank up a cliff so steep that the enemy had neglected to guard it, to the Capitol, and being brought before the magistrates delivered to them the message from the army. Then, on the senate's resolving that the *curiate comitia* should recall Camillus from exile, and that, even as the people commanded he should straightway be appointed dictator, and the soldiers have the general they desired, the messenger returned by the same route and came in haste to Veii; whence envoys were despatched to Ardea for Camillus, and fetched him to Veii; or rather—as I prefer to believe that he did not quit Ardea until he had learnt that the law was passed, since he could not change his residence without the People's command, nor take the auspices in the army till he had been appointed dictator—the curiate law was passed and Camillus declared dictator, in his absence.

XLVII. While this was going on at Veii, the Citadel of Rome and the Capitol were in very great danger. For the Gauls had noticed the tracks of a man, where the messenger from Veii had got through, or perhaps had observed for themselves that the cliff near the shrine of Carmentis [1] afforded an easy ascent. So on a starlit night they first sent

sublustri cum primo inermem qui temptaret viam
praemisissent, tradentes inde arma ubi quid iniqui
esset, alterni innixi sublevantesque in vicem et
3 trahentes alii alios, prout postularet locus, tanto
silentio in summum evasere ut non custodes solum
fallerent, sed ne canes quidem, sollicitum animal ad
4 nocturnos strepitus, excitarent.   Anseres non fe-
fellere quibus sacris Iunonis in summa inopia cibi
tamen abstinebatur.   Quae res saluti fuit; namque
clangore eorum alarumque crepitu excitus M. Manlius
qui triennio ante consul fuerat, vir bello egregius,
armis arreptis simul ad arma ceteros ciens vadit, et
dum ceteri trepidant, Gallum qui iam in summo
5 constiterat umbone ictum deturbat.   Cuius casus
prolapsi cum proximos sterneret, trepidantes alios
armisque omissis ˈsaxa quibus adhaerebant manibus
amplexos trucidat.[1]   Iamque et alii congregati telis
missilibusque saxis proturbare hostes, ruinaque tota
6 prolapsa acies in praeceps deferri.   Sedato deinde
tumultu reliquum noctis, quantum in turbatis mentibus poterat, cum praeteritum quoque periculum
7 sollicitaret, quieti datum est.   Luce orta vocatis
classico ad concilium militibus ad tribunos, cum et
recte et perperam facto pretium deberetur, Manlius
primum ob virtutem laudatus donatusque non ab

---

[1] trucidat ς: trucidant Ω.

forward an unarmed man to try the way; then B.C. 390 handing up their weapons when there was a steep place, and supporting themselves by their fellows or affording support in their turn; they pulled one another up, as the ground required, and reached the summit, in such silence that not only the sentries but even the dogs—creatures easily troubled by noises in the night—were not aroused. But they could not elude the vigilance of the geese, which, being sacred to Juno, had, notwithstanding the dearth of provisions, not been killed. This was the salvation of them all; for the geese with their gabbling and clapping of their wings woke Marcus Manlius,—consul of three years before and a distinguished soldier,—who, catching up his weapons and at the same time calling the rest to arms, strode past his bewildered comrades to a Gaul who had already got a foothold on the crest and dislodged him with a blow from the boss of his shield. As he slipped and fell, he overturned those who were next to him, and the others in alarm let go their weapons and grasping the rocks to which they had been clinging, were slain by Manlius. And by now the rest had come together and were assailing the invaders with javelins and stones, and presently the whole company lost their footing and were flung down headlong to destruction. Then after the din was hushed, the rest of the night—so far as their excitement would permit, when even a past peril made them nervous—was given up to sleep. At dawn the trumpet summoned the soldiers to assemble before the tribunes. Good conduct and bad had both to be requited. First Manlius was praised for his courage and presented with gifts, not only by

tribunis solum militum sed consensu etiam militari;
8 cui universi selibras farris et quartarios vini ad
aedes eius, quae in arce erant, contulerunt,—rem
dictu parvam, ceterum inopia fecerat eam argu-
mentum ingens caritatis, cum se quisque victu suo
fraudans detractum corpori atque usibus necessariis
9 ad honorem unius viri conferret. Tum vigiles eius
loci qua fefellerat adscendens hostis citati; et cum
in omnes more militari se animadversurum Q.
10 Sulpicius[1] tribunus militum pronuntiasset, consen-
tiente clamore militum in unum vigilem conici-
entium culpam deterritus, a ceteris abstinuit, reum
haud dubium eius noxae adprobantibus cunctis de
11 saxo deiecit. Inde intentiores utrimque custodiae
esse, et apud Gallos, quia volgatum erat inter Veios
Romamque nuntios commeare, et apud Romanos ab
nocturni periculi memoria.

XLVIII. Sed ante omnia obsidionis bellique mala
2 fames utrumque exercitum urgebat, Gallos pestilentia
etiam, cum loco iacente inter tumulos castra habentes, tum ab incendiis torrido et vaporis pleno
cineremque non pulverem modo ferente cum quid
3 venti motum esset. Quorum intolerantissima gens
umorique ac frigori adsueta cum aestu et anguore
vexata volgatis velut in pecua morbis morerentur,
iam pigritia singulos sepeliendi promisce acervatos

---

[1] Q. Sulpicius *Sigonius* (*cf. chap.* xxxvi. § 11): p. (*or*
publius *or* pubblius) sulpicius (*or* sulpitius) Ω.

the tribunes of the soldiers, but by agreement B.C. 390
amongst the troops, who brought each half a pound
of spelt and a gill of wine to his house, which stood
in the Citadel. It is a little thing to tell, but the
scarcity made it a great token of affection, since
everyone robbed himself of his own sustenance and
bestowed what he had subtracted from his physical
necessities to do honour to one man. Then the
watchmen of the cliff which the enemy had scaled
without being discovered were called up. Quintus
Sulpicius, the tribune, announced his intention to
punish them all in the military fashion ; but deterred
by the cries of the soldiers, who united in throwing
the blame upon a single sentinel, he spared the
others. This man was guilty beyond a doubt, and
was flung from the rock with the approval of all.
From that time the guards on both sides were more
alert : the Gauls, because it had been put about that
messengers were passing between Veii and Rome,
the Romans, from their recollection of the peril of
the night.

XLVIII. But worse than all the evils of the
blockade and the war was the famine with which
both armies were afflicted. The Gauls suffered also
from a pestilence, being encamped between hills on
low ground, parched and heated by the conflagration,
where the air was filled with ashes, as well as dust,
whenever a breeze sprang up. These annoyances
were intolerable to a race accustomed to damp and
cold, and when, distressed by the suffocating heat,
they began to sicken of diseases that spread as
though the victims had been cattle, they were soon
too slothful to bury their dead singly, and piling the
bodies up in promiscuous heaps, they burned them,

161

LIVY

cumulos hominum urebant; bustorumque inde Gal-
4 licorum nomine insignem locum fecere. Induciae
deinde cum Romanis factae et conloquia permissu
imperatorum habita; in quibus cum identidem Galli
famem obicerent eaque necessitate ad deditionem
vocarent, dicitur avertendae eius opinionis causa
multis locis panis de Capitolio iactatus esse in
5 hostium stationes. Sed iam neque dissimulari neque
ferri ultra fames poterat. Itaque dum dictator dilectum per se Ardeae habet, magistrum equitum
L. Valerium a Veiis adducere exercitum iubet, parat
instruitque quibus haud impar adoriatur hostes
6 interim Capitolinus exercitus stationibus vigiliisque
fessus superatis tamen humanis omnibus malis cum
famem unam natura vinci non sineret, diem de die
prospectans ecquod auxilium ab dictatore appareret
7 postremo spe quoque iam non solum cibo deficiente
et cum stationes procederent prope obruentibus
infirmum corpus armis, vel dedi vel redimi se quacumque pactione possent iussit, iactantibus non
obscure Gallis haud magna mercede se adduci
8 posse ut obsidionem relinquant. Tum senatus
habitus tribunisque militum negotium datum ut
paciscerentur. Inde inter Q. Sulpicium[2] tribunum militum et Brennum regulum Gallorum

---

[1] vigiliisque D^4: et uigiliis O: uigiliis Ω.

[2] Q. Sulpicium *Sigonius* (*cf. chap.* xlvii. § 9): p. sulpiciu.
(-tum L) Ω.

---

[1] Livy tells us in XXII. xiv. 11, that the *Busta Gallica*
were in the middle of the City, but the exact site cannot be
determined.

causing the place to be known from that circum- B.C. 390
stance as the Gallic Pyres.[1] A truce was afterwards
made with the Romans, and the commanders allowed
their soldiers to talk together.   Since in these
conversations the Gauls used frequently to taunt
their enemies with their famished state, and call on
them to yield to that necessity and surrender, the
Romans are said, in order to do away with this
opinion, to have cast bread down from the Capitol
in many places, into the outposts of the enemy.
Yet at last they could neither dissemble their hunger
nor endure it any longer. The dictator was now
holding a levy of his own at Ardea, and having
ordered the master of the horse, Lucius Valerius, to
bring up his army from Veii, was mustering and
drilling a force with which he might cope with the
Gauls on equal terms. But the army on the Capitol
was worn out with picket duty and mounting guard;
and though they had got the better of all human
ills, yet was there one, and that was famine, which
nature would not suffer to be overcome. Day after
day they looked out to see if any relief from the
dictator was at hand; but at last even hope, as well
as food, beginning to fail them, and their bodies
growing almost too weak to sustain their armour
when they went out on picket duty, they declared
that they must either surrender or ransom themselves, on whatever conditions they could make; for
the Gauls were hinting very plainly that no great
price would be required to induce them to raise the
siege. Thereupon the senate met, and instructed the
tribunes of the soldiers to arrange the terms. Then,
at a conference between Lucius Sulpicius the
tribune and the Gallic chieftain Brennus, the affair

conloquio transacta res est, et mille pondo auri
pretium populi gentibus mox imperaturi factum.
9 Rei foedissimae per se adiecta indignitas est:
pondera ab Gallis allata iniqua, et tribuno recu-
sante additus ab insolente Gallo ponderi gladius,
auditaque intoleranda Romanis vox, Vae victis.[1]

XLIX. Sed diique et homines prohibuere re-
demptos vivere Romanos. Nam forte quadam, priusquam infanda merces perficeretur, per altercationem
nondum omni auro adpenso, dictator intervenit au-
ferrique aurum de medio et Gallos summoveri iubet.
2 Cum illi renitentes pactos dicerent sese, negat eam
pactionem ratam esse quae, postquam ipse dictator
creatus esset, iniussu suo ab inferioris iuris magistratu facta esset, denuntiatque Gallis ut se ad
3 proelium expediant. Suos in acervum conicere
sarcinas et arma aptare ferroque non auro reciperare[2] patriam iubet, in conspectu habentes fana
deum et coniuges et liberos et solum patriae deforme
belli malis et omnia quae defendi repetique et ulcisci
4 fas sit. Instruit deinde aciem, ut loci natura patiebatur, in semirutae solo urbis et natura inaequali, et
omnia quae arte belli secunda suis eligi praepararive
5 poterant providit. Galli nova re trepidi arma capi-

---

[1] Vae victis *Duker*: uae (ue *PF?UOA*: ut *F*[3]) uictis esse
Ω: . . . . ictis esse *V*.
[2] reciperare *Conway and Walters (cf. their note on* I. xii. 1):
recuperare (*and in* § 7) Ω.

was settled, and a thousand pounds of gold was B.C. 390
agreed on as the price of a people that was destined
presently to rule the nations. The transaction was
a foul disgrace in itself, but an insult was added
thereto: the weights brought by the Gauls were dis-
honest, and on the tribune's objecting, the insolent
Gaul added his sword to the weight, and a saying
intolerable to Roman ears was heard,—Woe to the
conquered!

XLIX. But neither gods nor men would suffer
the Romans to live ransomed. For, by some chance,
before the infamous payment had been consum-
mated, and when the gold had not yet, owing to the
dispute, been all weighed out, the dictator appeared
and commanded the gold to be cleared away and
the Gauls to leave. They objected vehemently, and
insisted on the compact; but Camillus denied the
validity of that compact which, subsequently to his
own appointment as dictator, an inferior magistrate
had made without his authorization, and warned
them to prepare for battle. His own men he
ordered to throw their packs in a heap, make ready
their weapons, and win their country back with iron
instead of gold; having before their eyes the temples
of the gods, their wives and their children, the soil
of their native land, with the hideous marks of war
upon it, and all that religion called upon them to
defend, recover, or avenge. He then drew up his
line, as well as the ground permitted, on the
naturally uneven surface of the half-ruined City,
and saw to it that his soldiers had every advantage
in choice of position and in preparation which the
art of war suggested. The Gauls were taken aback;
they armed, and, with more rage than judgment,

LIVY

A.U.C.
364

unt iraque magis quam consilio in Romanos incurrunt. Iam verterat fortuna, iam deorum opes
humanaque consilia rem Romanam adiuvabant.
Igitur primo concursu haud maiore momento fusi
6 Galli sunt quam ad Alliam vicerant. Iustiore altero
deinde proelio ad octavum lapidem Gabina via, quo
se ex fuga contulerant, eiusdem ductu auspicioque
Camilli vincuntur. Ibi caedes omnia obtinuit ; castra
7 capiuntur et ne nuntius quidem cladis relictus. Dictator reciperata ex hostibus patria triumphans in
urbem redit, interque iocos militares, quos incon-
ditos iaciunt, Romulus ac parens patriae conditorque
alter urbis haud vanis laudibus appellabatur.

8 Servatam deinde bello patriam iterum in pace
haud dubie servavit cum prohibuit migrari Veios, et
tribunis rem intentius agentibus post incensam urbem
et per se inclinata magis plebe ad id consilium ; eaque
causa fuit non abdicandae post triumphum dictaturae
senatu obsecrante ne rem publicam in incerto relinqueret statu. L. Omnium primum, ut erat diligen-
tissimus religionum cultor, quae ad deos immortales
2 pertinebant rettulit et senatus consultum facit : fana
omnia, quoad [1] ea hostis possedisset, restituerentur
terminarentur expiarenturque, expiatioque eorum in

---

[1] quoad *Mommsen :* quod Ω.

charged the Romans. But now fortune had turned; B.C. 390 now the might of Heaven and human wisdom were engaged in the cause of Rome. Accordingly, at the first shock the Gauls were routed with as little effort as they had themselves put forth to conquer on the Allia. They afterwards fought a second, more regular engagement, eight miles out on the Gabinian Way, where they had rallied from their flight, and again the generalship and auspices of Camillus overcame them. Here the carnage was universal; their camp was taken; and not a man survived to tell of the disaster. The dictator, having recovered his country from her enemies, returned in triumph to the city; and between the rough jests uttered by the soldiers, was hailed in no unmeaning terms of praise as a Romulus and Father of his Country and a second Founder of the City.

His native City, which he had saved in war, he then indubitably saved a second time, now that peace was won, by preventing the migration to Veii: though the tribunes were more zealous for the plan than ever, now that the City lay in ashes, and the plebs were of themselves more inclined to favour it. This was the reason of his not resigning the dictatorship after his triumph, for the senate besought him not to desert the state in its hour of uncertainty. L. His first act, in conformity with his scrupulous attention to religion, was to lay before the senate such matters as pertained to the immortal gods, and to obtain the passage of a decree that all shrines, in so far as they had been in the enemy's possession, should be restored, their boundaries established, and rites of purification celebrated, and that the duumvirs should

A.U.C.
364

3 libris per duumviros quaereretur; cum Caeritibus
hospitium publice fieret quod sacra populi Romani
ac sacerdotes recepissent, beneficioque eius populi
4 non intermissus honos deorum immortalium esset;
ludi Capitolini fierent, quod Iuppiter optimus maximus suam sedem atque arcem populi Romani in re
trepida tutatus esset; collegiumque ad eam rem M.
Furius dictator constitueret ex iis [1] qui in Capitolio
5 atque arce habitarent. Expiandae etiam vocis nocturnae quae nuntia cladis ante bellum Gallicum
audita neglectaque esset mentio inlata, iussumque
6 templum in Nova via Aio Locutio [2] fieri. Aurum
quod Gallis ereptum erat quodque ex aliis templis
inter trepidationem in Iovis cellam conlatum, cum
quo [3] referri oporteret confusa memoria esset, sacrum
7 omne iudicatum et sub Iovis sella poni iussum. Iam
ante in eo religio civitatis apparuerat quod cum in
publico deesset aurum, ex quo summa pactae mer-
cedis Gallis confieret, a matronis conlatum accepe-
rant ut sacro auro abstineretur. Matronis gratiae
actae honosque additus ut earum sicut virorum post
8 mortem sollemnis laudatio esset. His peractis, quae
ad deos pertinebant quaeque per senatum agi po-

---

[1] iis ⌠ : hiis *A* : eis *VU* : his Ω.
[2] in Nova via Aio Locutio *Sigonius* (*cf. Gellius* XVI. xvii.
2, *Cic. Div.* I. 101, II. 69) : in noua ia locutio *M* : in noua iam
locutio (*or similar corruptions*) Ω.
[3] quo *Mommsen* : quo re *V* : in quae (inique *H*) Ω.

---

[1] The Sybilline Books.
[2] The god of Utterance. This " temple " is evidently the
"chapel" spoken of at chap. xxxii. § 2.

search the Books[1] for the proper rites; that a covenant B.C. 390
of hospitality should be entered into by the state
with the people of Caere, because they had received
the holy things of the Roman People and its priests,
and thanks to their good offices worship of the immortal gods had not been interrupted; that Capitoline
Games should be held, because Jupiter Optimus
Maximus had protected his own abode and the Citadel
of the Roman People in its time of danger; and that
Marcus Furius the dictator should to that end con-
stitute a board consisting of men who lived on the
Capitol and the Citadel. A proposal was made, too,
for propitiating the voice which was heard in the
night to foretell disaster before the Gallic War, and
was disregarded, and a temple was ordered to be built
in the Nova Via to Aius Locutius.[2] The gold which
had been carried away from the Gauls and that
which had been collected from other temples during
the alarm and carried into the shrine of Jupiter,
since there was no clear recollection where it ought
to be returned, was all adjudged to be sacred and
ordered to be deposited under the throne of Jupiter.
Even before this the scrupulousness of the citizens
had been apparent in this connexion, for when the
gold in the public coffers was insufficient to make up
to the Gauls the stipulated sum, they had accepted
what the matrons got together, that they might not
touch the sacred gold. For this a vote of thanks
was given to the matrons, and they were granted
the honour of having eulogies pronounced at their
funerals, as in the case of the men. After these
measures, which related to the gods and lay within
the competence of the senate, had been enacted,
then, and only then, heeding the importunity of the

A.U.C.
364

terant, tum demum agitantibus tribunis plebem
adsiduis contionibus, ut relictis ruinis in urbem
paratam Veios transmigrarent, in contionem uni-
verso senatu prosequente escendit atque ita verba
fecit :

LI. " Adeo mihi acerbae sunt, Quirites, conten-
tiones cum tribunis plebis, ut nec tristissimi exsilii
solacium aliud habuerim, quoad Ardeae vixi, quam
quod procul ab his certaminibus eram, et ob eadem
haec non si miliens senatus consulto [1] populique
2 iussu revocaretis, rediturus unquam fuerim. Nec
nunc me ut redirem mea voluntas mutata sed vestra
fortuna perpulit ; quippe ut in sua sede maneret
patria, id agebatur, non ut ego utique in patria
essem. Et nunc quiescerem ac tacerem libenter,
nisi haec quoque pro patria dimicatio esset ; cui
deesse, quoad vita suppetat, aliis turpe, Camillo
3 etiam nefas est. Quid enim repetiimus,[2] quid ob-
sessam ex hostium manibus eripuimus, si reciperatam
ipsi deserimus ? Et cum victoribus Gallis capta tota
urbe Capitolium tamen atque arcem dique et homines Romani tenuerint,[3] victoribus Romanis reciperata urbe arx quoque et Capitolium deseretur, et
plus vastitatis huic urbi secunda nostra fortuna
4 faciet quam adversa fecit ? Equidem si nobis cum
urbe simul positae traditaeque per manus religiones

---

[1] si miliens senatus consulto *Weissenborn* : si mille Sīē S *M* :
simile senatus consulti *V* : simillae sic (*or other corruptions*) Ω.
[2] repetiimus ϛ : repetimus Ω.
[3] tenuerint *Conway* : tenuerint habitauerint Ω (*but there is
a punct. in a space before and in one after* habitauerint *in
PFO, and after it in E, and D⁴ marks it as interpolated, while
F writes it with a capital* H) : tenuerint et habitauerint *V*.

B.C. 390

tribunes, who were urging the plebs unceasingly to quit their ruins and emigrate to a city ready to their hand at Veii, Camillus went up into the assembly, attended by the entire senate, and discoursed as follows :

LI. "So painful to me, Quirites, are these controversies with the tribunes of the plebs, that my most bitter exile knew no other solace but this, all the time that I lived at Ardea, that I was far away from these contentions. And they are likewise the cause that though you had a thousand times recalled me by resolution of the senate and the people's vote, I intended never to return. Nor have I now been induced to do so by any change in my desires, but by the alteration in your fortunes. For the issue was this, that my countrymen should abide in their own home, not that I, at any or all costs, should be with my countrymen. Even now I would gladly stop and hold my peace, were not this too the quarrel of my country ; whom to fail while life endures is in other men disgraceful, but in Camillus impious. For why did we seek to win her back, why rescue her, when besieged, from the hands of the enemy, if, now that she is recovered, we voluntarily abandon her ? And although, while the Gauls were victorious and in possession of the entire City, the Capitol nevertheless and the Citadel were held by the gods and men of Rome, shall we now, when the Romans are victorious and the City is regained, desert even Citadel and Capitol ? Shall our prosperity make Rome more desolate than our adversity has done ? Indeed, if we had no religious rites established with the founding of the City and by tradition handed down,

171

nullae essent, tamen tam evidens numen hac tempestate rebus adfuit Romanis ut omnem neglegentiam
5 divini cultus exemptam hominibus putem. Intue-
mini enim horum deinceps annorum vel secundas
res vel adversas; invenietis omnia prospera evenisse
6 sequentibus deos, adversa spernentibus. Iam omnium
primum Veiens bellum—per quot annos quanto labore gestum!—non ante cepit finem quam monitu
7 deorum aqua ex lacu Albano emissa est. Quid haec
tandem urbis nostrae clades nova? Num ante exorta
est quam spreta vox caelo emissa de adventu Gallorum, quam gentium ius ab legatis nostris violatum,
quam a nobis, cum vindicari deberet, eadem negle-
8 gentia deorum praetermissum? Igitur victi captique
ac redempti tantum poenarum dis hominibusque de-
9 dimus ut terrarum orbi documento essemus. Adversae
deinde res admonuerunt religionum. Confugimus in
Capitolium ad deos, ad sedem Iovis optimi maximi;
sacra in ruina rerum nostrarum alia terra[1] celavimus,
alia avecta in finitimas urbes amovimus ab hostium
oculis; deorum cultum deserti ab dis hominibusque
10 tamen non intermisimus. Reddidere igitur patriam
et victoriam et antiquum belli decus amissum; et
in hostes qui caeci avaritia in pondere auri foedus ac
fidem fefellerunt verterunt terrorem fugamque et
caedem.

[1] terra ς *Gronovius* : terrae Ω.

yet so manifest has at this time the divine purpose B.C. 390 been in the affairs of Rome, that I for one should suppose it no longer possible for men to neglect the worship of the gods. For consider these past few years in order, with their successes and reverses; you will find that all things turned out well when we obeyed the gods, and ill when we spurned them. First of all, the war with Veii. How many years we fought, and with what painful exertion! And the end came not, until, admonished by Heaven, we drew the water off from the Alban Lake. What, I beseech you, of this strange disaster that lately overwhelmed our City? Did it come before we disregarded the voice from Heaven that announced the approach of the Gauls? before the law of nations was violated by our envoys? before we, that ought to have punished their fault, had passed it by, with the same indifference towards the gods? Therefore were we conquered, led captive, and put to ransom; and suffered such punishments at the hands of gods and men as to be a warning to all the world. Adversity then turned our thoughts upon religion. We fled for refuge to the Capitol and its gods, to the seat of Jupiter Optimus Maximus; of our holy things, some, in the ruin of our fortunes, we concealed in the earth, others we removed to neighbouring cities out of sight of our enemies; in the worship of the gods, albeit forsaken of gods and men, yet were we unceasing. Therefore have they given us our native land again, and victory, and our ancient renown in war that we had forfeited; and against our enemies, who, blinded with greed, broke treaty and troth in the weighing of the gold, have they turned dismay and rout and slaughter.

A.U.C.
364

LII. " Haec culti neglectique numinis tanta momenta [1] in rebus humanis cernentes ecquid sentitis, Quirites, quantum vixdum e naufragiis prioris culpae cladisque emergentes paremus nefas? Urbem auspicato inauguratoque conditam habemus; nullus locus in ea non religionum deorumque est plenus; sacrificiis sollemnibus non dies magis stati quam loca sunt, in quibus fiant. Hos omnes deos publicos privatosque, Quirites, deserturi estis? Quam par vestrum factum ei est,[2] quod in obsidione nuper in egregio adulescente C. Fabio non minore hostium admiratione quam vestra conspectum est, cum inter Gallica tela degressus [3] ex arce sollemne Fabiae gentis in colle Quirinali obiit? An gentilicia sacra ne in bello quidem intermitti, publica sacra et Romanos deos etiam in pace deseri placet, et pontifices flaminesque neglegentiores publicarum religionum esse quam privatus in sollemni gentis fuerit? Forsitan aliquis dicat aut Veiis ea nos facturos aut huc inde missuros sacerdotes nostros qui faciant; quorum neutrum fieri salvis caerimoniis potest. Et ne omnia generatim sacra omnesque percenseam deos, in Iovis epulo num alibi quam in Capitolio pulvinar suscipi potest? Quid de aeternis Vestae ignibus signoque quod imperii pignus custodia eius templi tenetur loquar? Quid de ancilibus vestris, Mars Gradive

---

[1] momenta ç : monumenta (or -nim-) Ω : munimenta *MBO*.
[2] factum ei est *Drakenborch* : factum est Ω.
[3] degressus *Sigonius* (*cf. chap.* xlvi § 10) : digressus Ω.

---

[1] On the 15th of November the senate held a stately banquet at which a couch was placed for Jupiter, and Juno and Minerva occupied stools on either side of the god.
[2] The image of Pallas (Palladium), fabled to have been brought to Italy by Aeneas.

LII. "As you consider these momentous effects B.C. 390
upon the affairs of men, of serving the deity and of
neglecting him, do you begin, Quirites, to perceive
how, though yet scarce clear of the wreckage of our
former guilt and calamity, we are headed towards
a grievous sin? We have a City founded with due
observance of auspice and augury; no corner of it
is not permeated by ideas of religion and the gods;
for our annual sacrifices, the days are no more fixed
than are the places where they may be performed.
Do you intend, Quirites, to abandon all these gods,
both of state and of family? How squares your
conduct with that of the noble young man Gaius
Fabius in the recent siege, which the enemy beheld
with no less astonishment and admiration than yourselves, when he descended from the Citadel through
the missiles of the Gauls and offered the annual
sacrifice of the Fabian clan on the Quirinal Hill?
What? Would you suffer no interruption, even in
war, of family rites, but desert the national worship
and the gods of Rome in time of peace? Would
you have the pontiffs and the flamens less careful
of the ceremonies of the state religion than a private
citizen has been of the anniversary of his clan?
Perhaps someone may say that we shall either do
these things at Veii, or thence dispatch our priests
to Rome to do them; but of these courses neither
can be followed without violation of the sacred
usages. For, not to enumerate all the kinds of
rites and all the gods, is it possible at the feast of
Jupiter [1] that the couch should be spread elsewhere
than in the Capitol? Why need I speak of Vesta's
eternal fires, and the image [2] which is preserved as a
pledge of empire in her temple? or of your sacred

tuque, Quirine pater? Haec omnia in profano deseri
placet sacra aequalia urbi, quaedam vetustiora origine urbis?

8 "Et videte quid inter nos ac maiores intersit. Illi
sacra quaedam in monte Albano Laviniique [1] nobis
facienda tradiderunt. An ex hostium urbibus Romam ad nos transferri sacra religiosum fuit, hinc
sine piaculo in hostium urbem Veios transferemus?

9 Recordamini, agite dum, quotiens sacra instaurentur,
quia aliquid ex patrio ritu neglegentia casuve praetermissum est. Modo quae res post prodigium
Albani lacus nisi instauratio sacrorum auspiciorum-
que renovatio adfectae Veienti bello rei publicae

10 remedio fuit? At etiam, tamquam veterum religionum memores, et peregrinos deos transtulimus Romam et instituimus novos. Iuno regina transvecta
a Veiis nuper in Aventino quam insigni ob excellens
matronarum studium celebrique dedicata est die!

11 Aio Locutio [2] templum propter caelestem vocem
exauditam in Nova via iussimus fieri; Capitolinos
ludos sollemnibus aliis addidimus collegiumque ad

12 id novum auctore senatu condidimus; quid horum
opus fuit suscipi, si una cum Gallis urbem Romanam
relicturi fuimus, si non voluntate mansimus in Capitolio per tot menses obsidionis, sed ab hostibus metu

13 retenti sumus? De sacris loquimur et de templis;

---

[1] Laviniique *Gronovius*: lauinioque *MHDL* '*antiqua lectio*'
Rhenanus; lauinoque Ω.
[2] Aio Locutio *Gebhard*: aputu locutio *V*: ad locutio *D*:
ad locucio *A*: allocutio (*and similar corruptions*) Ω.

---

[1] See I. xx. 4, and note.

shields,[1] O Mars Gradivus and Quirinus our Father? B.C. 390
All these would you leave behind on unconsecrated
ground—things coeval with the City, and some more
ancient than its origin?

"And mark what a difference between us and our
forefathers! They handed down to us certain rites
to be solemnized on the Alban Mount and in
Lavinium. But if we scrupled to transfer sacred
rites from hostile cities to ourselves in Rome, can
we shift them without sin from Rome to Veii, city
of our enemies? Recollect, I beg you, how often
sacrifices are renewed because some point of antique
ritual has been, through carelessness or accident,
omitted. What was it, a while ago, after the portent
of the Alban Lake, that brought relief to the
commonwealth—then in the throes of war with
Veii—if not a renewal of the sacred rites and
auspices? But, more than that, like men mindful
of their old religious fervour, we have both brought
in foreign deities to Rome and established new
ones. Queen Juno was lately conveyed from Veii
and enshrined on the Aventine, and how notable
was that day, for the zeal of the matrons and the
throng! We have ordered a temple to be built for
Aius Locutius because of the voice from heaven,
clearly heard in the Nova Via. We have added
Capitoline Games to the other annual festivals, and
by authority of the senate have established a new
college for this purpose. Was there any of these
things we needed to have undertaken, if we meant
to retire from Rome along with the Gauls; if we
remained not voluntarily in the Capitol, through so
many months of siege, but constrained by fear of
the enemy? We talk of sacred rites and temples;

177

quid tandem de sacerdotibus? Nonne in mentem
venit quantum piaculi committatur? Vestalibus
nempe una illa sedes est, ex qua eas nihil unquam
praeterquam urbs capta movit; flamini Diali noctem
unam manere extra urbem nefas est; hos Veientis
14 pro Romanis facturi estis sacerdotes, et Vestales tuae
te deserent, Vesta, et flamen peregre habitando in
singulas noctes tantum sibi reique publicae piaculi
15 contrahet? Quid alia quae auspicato agimus omnia
fere intra pomerium, cui oblivioni aut cui negle-
16 gentiae damus? Comitia curiata, quae rem militarem
continent, comitia centuriata, quibus consules tribu-
nosque militaris creatis, ubi auspicato, nisi ubi ad-
17 solent, fieri possunt? Veiosne haec transferemus?
An comitiorum causa populus tanto incommodo
in desertam hanc ab dis hominibusque urbem
conveniet?

LIII. "At enim apparet quidem pollui omnia [1] nec
ullis piaculis expiari posse, sed res ipsa cogit vastam
incendiis ruinisque relinquere urbem et ad integra
omnia Veios migrare nec hic aedificando inopem
2 plebem vexare. Hanc autem iactari magis causam
quam veram esse, ut ego non dicam, apparere vobis,
Quirites, puto, qui meministis ante Gallorum adventum salvis tectis publicis privatisque, stante incolumi

---

[1] quidem pollui omnia *Madvig*: quidem P (*or* I) . . . . .
nia *V*: *the other MSS. omit* at enim—expiari posse.

---

[1] Livy has in mind one important exception: the centuriate
comitia met outside the pomerium, usually in the Campus
Martius.

pray, what about the priests? Do you never think B.C. 390
what a sacrilege you are about? The Vestals surely
have but that one dwelling-place, from which nothing ever caused them to remove but the capture
of the City; the Flamen Dialis may not lie for a
single night outside the City, without sin. Will you
make these priests Veientine instead of Roman?
Shall thy Virgins forsake thee, Vesta, and the
Flamen, as he dwells abroad, bring, night after
night, such guilt upon himself and the republic?
What about the other matters nearly all of which [1]
we transact, after taking auspices, within the
pomerium? To what oblivion and neglect do we
consign them? The curiate comitia which deals
with the business of war, the centuriate comitia,
where you elect the consuls and military tribunes—
where can these be held, with due observance of
the auspices, save in the customary places? Shall
we transfer them to Veii? Or shall the people, for
the sake of the comitia assemble with enormous
inconvenience in this City, forsaken of god and
man?

LIII. "'But,' you will say, 'while it is obvious
that everything will be polluted beyond all possi-
bility of purification, yet the situation itself compels
us to leave a City which fires and falling buildings
have made a wilderness, and emigrate to Veii, where
everything is untouched, nor vex the helpless commons with building here.' But that this is rather a
pretext than a true reason is, I think, apparent to you,
Quirites, without my saying so; for you remember
how, before the coming of the Gauls, when our
roof-trees, public and private, were unharmed and
our City stood uninjured, that this same proposal was

179

urbe, hanc eandem rem actam esse ut Veios trans-
3 migraremus. Et videte quantum inter meam sententiam vestramque intersit, tribuni. Vos, etiamsi
tunc faciendum non fuerit, nunc utique faciendum
putatis : ego contra—nec id mirati sitis priusquam
quale sit audieritis—etiamsi tum migrandum fuisset
incolumi tota urbe, nunc has ruinas relinquendas
4 non censerem. Quippe tum causa nobis in urbem
captam migrandi victoria esset, gloriosa nobis ac
posteris nostris ; nunc haec migratio nobis misera
5 ac turpis, Gallis gloriosa est. Non enim reliquisse
victores sed amisisse victi patriam videbimur : hoc
ad Alliam fuga, hoc capta urbs, hoc circumsessum
Capitolium necessitatis imposuisse, ut desereremus
penates nostros exsiliumque ac fugam nobis ex eo
loco conscisceremus quem tueri non possemus. Et
Galli evertere potuerunt Romam, Romani [1] restituere
6 non videbuntur potuisse ? Quid restat nisi ut, si iam
novis copiis veniant—constat enim vix credibilem
multitudinem esse—et habitare in capta ab se,
7 deserta a vobis hac urbe velint, sinatis ? Quid ? si
non Galli hoc sed veteres hostes vestri, Aequi
Volscive, faciant ut commigrent Romam, velitisne
illos Romanos, vos Veientes esse ? An non [2] malitis
hanc solitudinem vestram quam urbem hostium
esse ? Non equidem video quid magis nefas sit.
Haec scelera, quia piget aedificare, haec dedecora

---

[1] Romani *Madvig* : quam Romani Ω.
[2] An non *Conway and Walters (note)* : an Ω : Non L^2 : non
D? : ñ *HLA*.

---

[1] Chap. xxiv. § 7.

urged, of migrating to Veii.[1] And consider, tribunes, B.C. 390 how wide is the difference between my view and yours. You think that even if then it ought not to have been done, yet now at any rate it ought; I on the contrary—and be not astonished at this, till you have heard what my meaning is,—even if it had been right to migrate then, with the City all intact, should not think it right to abandon these ruins now. For then our victory would have been a reason for migrating to a captured city—a reason glorious to ourselves and our posterity; but now such a removal is for us a wretched and humiliating course, and a glory to the Gauls. For we shall not seem to have left our country as victors, but to have lost it as men vanquished. It will be thought that the rout on the Allia, the capture of the City, the blockade of the Capitol, have compelled us to forsake our family gods, and sentence ourselves to banishment and exile from that place which we were powerless to defend. Have Gauls then been able to cast Rome down; and must Romans appear unable to have raised her up? What remains, if they should presently come with fresh forces—for all agree that their numbers are scarce to be believed,—and should wish to dwell in this City which they have captured and you have abandoned, but that you should suffer them? What if not the Gauls but your ancient foes the Volsci and Aequi should migrate to Rome? Should you like them to be Romans, and yourselves Veientes? Or should you not prefer this to be your wilderness, rather than the city of your enemies? For my part I do not see what could be more abominable. Are you ready to stomach these outrages, these infamies, because it

A.U.C.
364

8 pati parati estis? Si tota urbe nullum melius ampli-
usve tectum fieri possit quam casa illa conditoris est
nostri, non in casis ritu pastorum agrestiumque
habitare est satius inter sacra penatesque nostros
9 quam exsulatum publice ire? Maiores nostri, con-
venae pastoresque, cum in his locis nihil praeter
silvas paludesque esset, novam urbem tam brevi
aedificarunt: nos Capitolio atque arce[1] incolumi,
stantibus templis deorum aedificare incensa piget?
Et quod singuli facturi fuimus, si aedes nostrae de-
flagrassent, hoc in publico incendio universi recusa-
mus facere?

LIV. "Quid tandem? Si fraude, si casu Veiis incendium ortum sit, ventoque, ut fieri potest, diffusa
flamma magnam partem urbis absumat, Fidenas inde
aut Gabios aliamve quam urbem quaesituri sumus
2 quo transmigremus? Adeo nihil tenet solum patriae
nec haec terra quam matrem appellamus, sed in
superficie tignisque caritas nobis patriae pendet? Et
3 quidem—fatebor vobis, etsi minus iniuriae vestrae[2]
meminisse iuvat—cum abessem, quotienscumque
patria in mentem veniret, haec omnia occurrebant,
colles campique et Tiberis et adsueta oculis regio et
hoc caelum sub quo natus educatusque essem; quae
vos, Quirites, nunc moveant potius caritate sua ut
maneatis in sede vestra, quam postea, cum relique-
4 ritis eam, macerent desiderio. Non sine causa di

---

[1] atque arce *Wesenberg*: arce Ω.
[2] iniuriae vestrae *Conway and Walters*: iniuriae vestrae
quam meae calamitatis (quam calamitatis meae *HDLA*) Ω.

---

[1] The *casa Romuli* stood on the Palatine, on the side next
the Circus Maximus, and a hut which went by this name
was preserved and venerated as late as Livy's own time.

irks you to build? If in all the City no house could B.C. 390
be put up better or bigger than is the famous Hut
of our Founder,[1] would it not be better to live in
huts, as shepherds and rustics do, amongst our
sacred monuments and our household gods, than
to go forth as a nation into exile? Our ancestors,
refugees and herdsmen, at a time when there was
nothing in this region but forests and marshes, built
quickly a new City; and are we loath, though Capitol
and Citadel are untouched and the temples of the
gods are standing, to rebuild what has been destroyed
by fire? And what each would have done for himself, if his house had been burned, shall we refuse
to do together after this common conflagration?

LIV. "Or suppose that by crime or chance a fire
should break out at Veii, and that the wind should
spread the flames, as may easily happen, until they
consume a great part of the city; are we to quit
it, and seek out Fidenae, or Gabii, or any other town
you like, and migrate thither? Have the soil of
our native City and this land which we call our
mother so slight a hold on us? Is our love of
country confined to buildings and rafters? And in
truth I will confess to you—though I like not to
recall the wrong you did me—that as often, during
my absence, as I thought of my native place, all
these objects came into my mind: the hills and the
fields and the Tiber and the region familiar to my
eyes, and this sky beneath which I had been born
and reared. And I wish these things may rather
move you now with love, Quirites, to make you
abide in your own home, than afterwards, when
you have left it, torment you with vain regrets.
Not without cause did gods and men select this

hominesque hunc urbi condendae locum elegerunt,
saluberrimos colles, flumen opportunum, quo ex
mediterraneis locis fruges devehantur, quo maritimi commeatus accipiantur, mare vicinum ad com-
moditates nec expositum nimia propinquitate ad peri-
cula classium externarum, regionem Italiae mediam,[1]
5 ad incrementum urbis natum unice locum.   Argumento est ipsa magnitudo tam novae urbis.   Trecen-
tensimus sexagensimus quintus annus urbis, Quirites,
agitur; inter tot veterrimos populos tam diu bella
geritis, cum interea, ne singulas loquar urbes, non
coniuncti cum Aequis Volsci, tot tam valida oppida,
non universa Etruria tantum terra marique pollens
atque inter duo maria latitudinem obtinens Italiae
6 bello vobis par est.   Quod cum ita sit, quae, malum,
ratio est haec expertis alia[2] experiri, cum, iam ut
virtus vestra transire alio possit, fortuna certe loci
7 huius transferri non possit?   Hic Capitolium est, ubi
quondam capite humano invento responsum est eo
loco caput rerum summamque imperii fore; hic cum
augurato liberaretur Capitolium, Iuventas Terminus-
que maximo gaudio patrum vestrorum moveri se non
passi; hic Vestae ignes, hic ancilia caelo demissa,
hic omnes propitii manentibus vobis di."

LV. Movisse eos Camillus cum alia oratione tum
ea quae ad religiones pertinebat maxime dicitur; sed

---

[1] regionem Italiae mediam *Madvig*: regionum (geonum *E*
regionum *E¹ or E²*) Italiae medium Ω.
[2] haec expertis alia *Walters*: expertis alia *MOHDLA*:
expertis latos alia *PFUE*: expertis latos aia *B*.

place for establishing our City—with its healthful B.C. 390
hills; its convenient river, by which crops may be
floated down from the midland regions and foreign
commodities brought up; its sea, near enough for
use, yet not exposing us, by too great propinquity,
to peril from foreign fleets; a situation in the heart
of Italy—a spot, in short, of a nature uniquely
adapted for the expansion of a city. This is proved
by the very greatness of so new a place. It is now,
Quirites, in its three hundred and sixty-fifth year.
Amongst all these ancient nations you have for so
long a time been waging wars; and all this while—
to say nothing of single cities—neither the Volsci
joined with the Aequi, and all their powerful towns,
nor all Etruria, with its enormous strength on land
and water, and its occupancy of the entire breadth
of Italy from sea to sea, has been a match for you
in war. Since this is so, what a plague is the reason
why you that have experienced these things should
experiment with others? Granting that your valour
may go elsewhere, yet surely the fortune of this
place could not be taken along! Here is the Capitol,
where men were told, when of old they discovered
there a human head, that in that place should be
the head of the world and the seat of empire;
here, when the Capitol was being cleared with
augural rites, Juventas and Terminus, to the vast
joy of your fathers, refused to be removed; here
are Vesta's fires, here the shields that were sent
down from heaven, here are all the gods propitious,
if you remain."

LV. The speech of Camillus is said to have moved
them, particularly where he touched upon religion;
but the doubtful issue was resolved by a word

rem dubiam decrevit vox opportune emissa, quod
cum senatus post paulo de his rebus in curia Hostilia
haberetur cohortesque ex praesidiis revertentes forte
agmine forum transirent, centurio in comitio excla-
mavit: "Signifer, statue signum; hic manebimus
2 optime." Qua voce audita et senatus accipere se
omen ex curia egressus conclamavit et plebs circumfusa adprobavit. Antiquata deinde lege promisce
3 urbs aedificari coepta. Tegula publice praebita est;
saxi materiaeque caedendae, unde quisque vellet ius
factum praedibus acceptis eo anno aedificia perfectu-
4 ros. Festinatio curam exemit vicos dirigendi, dum
omisso sui alienique discrimine in vacuo aedificant.
5 Ea est causa ut veteres cloacae, primo per publicum
ductae, nunc privata passim subeant tecta, formaque
urbis sit occupatae magis quam divisae similis.

that was let fall in the nick of time.   It was B.C. 390 while the senate, a little later, was deliberating about these matters in the Curia Hostilia; some cohorts returning from guard-duty were marching through the Forum, and as they came to the Comitium a centurion cried out, "Standard-bearers, fix your ensign; here will be our best place to remain." Hearing this sentence the senators came out from the Curia and shouted their acceptance of the omen, and the commons gathering round them signified approval. The bill was then rejected, and people began in a random fashion to rebuild the City. The state supplied tiles, and granted everybody the right to quarry stone and to hew timber where he liked, after giving security for the completion of the structures within that year. In their haste men were careless about making straight the streets, and paying no attention to their own and others' rights, built on the vacant spaces. This is the reason that the ancient sewers, which were at first conducted through the public ways, at present frequently run under private dwellings, and the appearance of the City is like one where the ground has been appropriated rather than divided.

LIBRI V PERIOCHA

In obsidione Veiorum tabernacula[1] militibus facta sunt.
Ea res cum esset nova, indignationem tribunorum plebis
movit querentium non dari plebi nec per hiemem militiae
requiem. Equites tum primum equis suis mereri coeperunt. Cum inundatio ex lacu Albano facta esset, vates
qui eam rem interpretaretur ex hostibus captus est.
Furius Camillus dictator X annis obsessos Veios cepit,
simulacrum Iunonis[2] Romam transtulit, decimam praedae
Delphos Apollini misit. Idem[3] tribunus militum cum
Faliscos obsideret, proditos hostium filios parentibus remi-
sit statimque deditione facta Faliscorum victoriam iustitia
consecutus est. Cum alter ex censoribus C. Iulius deces-
sisset, in locum eius M. Cornelius suffectus est. Nec id
postea factum est, quoniam eo lustro a Gallis Roma capta
est. Furius Camillus, cum dies ei a L. Apuleio tribuno
pl. dicta esset, in exilium abit. Cum Galli Senones Clusium
obsiderent et legati a senatu missi ad conponendam inter
eos et Clusinos pacem pugnantes contra Gallos starent in
acie Clusinorum, hoc facto eorum concitati Senones urbem
infesto exercitu petierunt, fusisque ad Aliam Romanis
cepere urbem praeter Capitolium, quo se iuventus contu-
lerat ; maiores natu cum insignibus honorum quos quisque
gesserat in vestibulis aedium sedentes occiderunt Et cum
per aversam partem Capitoli iam in summum evasissent,
proditi clangore anserum M. Manli praecipue opera

---

[1] tabernacula *MSS* : hibernacula *Vascosanus* (*cf.* V. xi.).
[2] Iunonis *om. MSS*.
[3] Idem *edito princeps* : item *MSS*.

188

SUMMARY OF BOOK V

At the siege of Veii winter quarters were constructed
for the soldiers. This, being a new departure, stirred the
ire of the tribunes of the plebs, who complained that the
plebs were given no rest from warfare even in winter.
The cavalry began then for the first time to serve on their
own mounts. An inundation from the Alban Lake having
occurred, a soothsayer was captured from the enemy that
he might explain it. Furius Camillus the dictator captured Veii in a ten years' siege, transferred to Rome the
image of Juno, and sent a tithe of the spoils to Apollo at
Delphi. When the same man was besieging the Falisci
as military tribune, he restored to their parents the sons
of the enemy who had been betrayed, whereupon the
Falisci surrendered and he obtained the victory by his
justice. On the death of one of the censors, Gaius Julius,
Marcus Cornelius was chosen to fill out his term, but this
was never afterwards done because in that five-year period
Rome was taken. Furius Camillus, having been cited for
trial by the tribune Lucius Apuleius, a tribune of the
plebs, went into exile. When the Gallic Senones were
besieging Clusium and the envoys sent by the senate to
arrange a peace between them and the Clusini fought in
the army of the Clusini, the Senones were angered and
marched to the attack of Rome. Defeating the Romans on
the Allia they captured the City, all but the Capitol, in
which the Romans of fighting age had taken refuge, and
slew the elders, who, dressed in the insignia of the offices
which they had held, were sitting in the vestibules of their
houses. And when, climbing up on the other side of the
Capitol, they had already come out on the top of it, they
were betrayed by the gabbling of geese and—chiefly by the
efforts of Marcus Manlius—were flung down. Later the

LIBRI V PERIOCHA

deiecti [1] sunt. Coactis deinde propter famem Romanis eo [2]
descendere ut M. pondo auri darent et hoc [3] pretio finem
obsidionis emerent, Furius Camillus dictator absens creatus
inter ipsum conloquium quo de pacis condicionibus agebatur cum exercitu venit et Gallos post sextum mensem urbe
expulit ceciditque. Dictum est ad Veios migrandum esse
propter incensam et dirutam urbem, quod consilium
Camillo auctore discussum est. Movit populum vocis
quoque omen ex centurione auditae qui, cum in forum
venisset, manipularibus suis dixerat: "Sta miles, hic
optime manebimus." Aedis Iovi Capitolino facta est,
quod ante urbem captam vox audita erat adventare Gallos.

[1] deiecti *editio princeps*: detecti *MSS.*
[2] eo *inserted by Gronovius.*
[3] et hoc *editio princeps*: ut hoc *MSS.*

Romans were reduced so low by hunger as to offer a thousand pounds of gold and with this price to purchase an end of the siege. Furius Camillus, having been appointed dictator in his absence, came up with his army in the midst of this very conference about the terms of peace, and six months after their coming drove out the Gauls from Rome and cut them to pieces. Men said that they ought to remove to Veii because the City had been burned and overthrown, but this counsel was rejected, at the instance of Camillus. The people were moved also by the omen of certain words that a centurion was heard to utter, when having come into the Forum he said to his company : "Halt, soldiers, we shall do well to stop here." A temple was erected to Jupiter Capitolinus, because a voice had been heard before the capture of the City, which declared that the Gauls were coming.

BOOK VI

LIBER VI

I. Quae ab condita urbe Roma ad captam
eandem [1] Romani sub regibus primum, consulibus
deinde ac dictatoribus decemvirisque ac tribunis
consularibus gessere, foris bella, domi seditiones,
2 quinque libris exposui, res cum vetustate nimia
obscuras, velut quae magno ex intervallo loci vix
cernuntur, tum quod parvae et rarae per eadem
tempora litterae fuere, una custodia fidelis memoriae
rerum gestarum, et quod, etiam si quae in com-
mentariis pontificum aliisque publicis privatisque
erant monumentis, incensa urbe pleraeque interiere.
3 Clariora deinceps certioraque ab secunda origine
velut ab stirpibus laetius feraciusque renatae urbis
gesta domi militiaeque exponentur.
4   Ceterum primo quo adminiculo erecta erat eodem
innixa M. Furio principe stetit, neque eum abdicare
5 se dictatura nisi anno circumacto passi sunt. Comitia
in insequentem annum tribunos habere, quorum in
magistratu capta urbs esset, non placuit; res ad

---

[1] eandem ⟨ *Muretus*: urbem eandem (*or* eandem urbem) Ω.

---

[1] Livy means the year (ending June 30th) for which the
consular tribunes were elected whom Camillus, as dictator,
superseded.

BOOK VI

I. The history of the Romans from the founding B.C. 389
of the City of Rome to the capture of the same—
at first under kings and afterwards under consuls
and dictators, decemvirs and consular tribunes—their
foreign wars and their domestic dissensions, I have
set forth in five books, dealing with matters which
are obscure not only by reason of their great antiquity—like far-off objects which can hardly be
descried—but also because in those days there
was but slight and scanty use of writing, the sole
trustworthy guardian of the memory of past events,
and because even such records as existed in the
commentaries of the pontiffs and in other public
and private documents, nearly all perished in the
conflagration of the City. From this point onwards
a clearer and more definite account shall be given
of the City's civil and military history, when, beginning for a second time, it sprang up, as it were
from the old roots, with a more luxuriant and fruitful
growth.

Now it stood at first by leaning on the same support by which it had raised itself up, that is on
Marcus Furius, its foremost citizen; neither would
men suffer him to resign the dictatorship till the
completion of the year.[1] That elections for the
ensuing year should be held by the tribunes, in
whose magistracy the City had been captured, was
considered inadvisable, and the state reverted to an

195

6 interregnum rediit. Cum civitas in opere ac labore
assiduo reficiendae urbis teneretur, interim Q. Fabio,
simul primum magistratu abiit, ab Cn. Marcio tribuno
plebis dicta dies est, quod in Gallos,[1] ad quos missus

7 erat orator, contra ius gentium pugnasset ; cui
iudicio eum mors, adeo opportuna ut voluntariam

8 magna pars crederet, subtraxit. Interregnum in-
itum : P. Cornelius Scipio interrex et post eum
M. Furius Camillus.[2] Is tribunos militum consulari
potestate creat L. Valerium[3] Publicolam iterum L.
Verginium P. Cornelium A. Manlium L. Aemilium
L. Postumium.

9 Hi ex interregno cum extemplo magistratum
inissent, nulla de re prius quam de religionibus

10 senatum consuluere. In primis foedera ac leges—
erant autem eae duodecim tabulae et quaedam
regiae leges — conquiri, quae comparerent,[4] iusserunt. Alia ex eis edita etiam in volgus : quae
autem ad sacra pertinebant, a pontificibus maxime
ut religione obstrictos haberent multitudinis animos

11 suppressa. Tum de diebus religiosis agitari coeptum,
diemque a. d. XV Kal. Sextiles, duplici clade insignem, quo die ad Cremeram Fabii caesi, quo
deinde ad Alliam cum exitio urbis foede pugnatum, a
posteriore clade Alliensem appellarunt reique[5] nullius

---

[1] in Gallos *Cobet* : legatus (-tos *Ot* : -tis *E*) Ω.
[2] Camillus *Duker* : camillus iterum Ω.
[3] L. Valerium *Glareanus, Sigonius* (v. xxvi. 2, vi. v. 7):
a ualerium *P²FUBt* : ā ualerium *VOEHL* : am ualerium *M* :
ualerium *DA* : m. ualerium *A¹* (αὖλον *Diod.* xv. xxii).
[4] comparerent *A³ʒ* : non comparerent *V* : comparerent
(comparare *B*) Ω.
[5] reique *Karsten* : insignemque rei (*A adds* publice) Ω.

---

[1] On July 6th at the earliest.

interregnum. While the citizens were engrossed in unremitting toil and labour to restore the City, Quintus Fabius had no sooner quitted his magistracy than he was indicted by Gnaeus Marcius, a tribune of the plebs, on the ground of his having fought in violation of the law of nations against the Gauls, to whom he had been sent as an envoy—a trial which he escaped by a death so opportune that the majority believed it voluntary. The interregnum began: Publius Cornelius Scipio was interrex; and after him Marcus Furius Camillus, who effected the election, as tribunes of the soldiers with consular authority, of Lucius Valerius Publicola (for the second time) Lucius Verginius, Publius Cornelius, Aulus Manlius, Lucius Aemilius, and Lucius Postumius.

Having, immediately [1] after the interregnum, entered upon their term, they consulted the senate before everything else on questions of religious observance. Among the first decrees they passed was one for searching out the treaties and laws— to wit, the twelve tables and certain laws of the kings,—so far as they could be discovered. Some of these were made accessible even to the common people, but such as dealt with sacred rites were kept private by the pontiffs, chiefly that they might hold the minds of the populace in subjection through religious fear. Then they proceeded to deliberate about days of evil omen. The 18th of July was notorious for a double misfortune, since it was on that day that the Fabii were massacred at the Cremera and that subsequently the rout at the Allia occurred, which resulted in the destruction of the City. From the latter disaster they named it the Day of the Allia, and forbade any public or

A.U.C.
365 12 publice privatimque agendae fecerunt. Quidam,
quod postridie Idus Quintiles non litasset Sulpicius
tribunus militum neque inventa pace deum post
diem tertium obiectus hosti exercitus Romanus
esset, etiam postridie Idus rebus divinis supersederi
iussum; inde, ut postridie Kalendas quoque ac
Nonas eadem religio esset, traditum putant.

II. Nec diu licuit quietis consilia erigendae ex
2 tam gravi casu rei publicae secum agitare. Hinc
Volsci, veteres hostes, ad exstinguendum nomen
Romanum arma ceperant: hinc Etruriae principum
ex omnibus populis coniurationem de bello ad fanum
3 Voltumnae factam mercatores adferebant. Novus
quoque terror accesserat defectione Latinorum
Hernicorumque, qui post pugnam ad lacum Regillum factum per annos prope centum nunquam
ambigua fide in amicitia populi Romani fuerant.
4 Itaque cum tanti undique terrores circumstarent
appareretque omnibus non odio solum apud hostes
sed contemptu etiam inter socios nomen Romanum
5 laborare, placuit eiusdem auspiciis defendi rem
publicam cuius reciperata[1] esset, dictatoremque
6 dici M. Furium Camillum. Is dictator C. Servilium
Ahalam magistrum equitum dixit, iustitioque indicto
dilectum iuniorum habuit ita ut seniores quoque,

---

[1] reciperata, *Walters and Conway* (*cf. their note on* I. xii.
1): recuperata Ω.

B.C. 389

private business to be done that day. Some think, because Sulpicius had, on the day after the Ides of July, made an unacceptable sacrifice, and, without having gained the divine approval, had two days later exposed the Roman army to the enemy, that therefore religious rites were omitted also on the days after the several Ides; and that afterwards it became traditional that the morrow after Kalends and Nones should likewise be avoided, from the same scruple.

II. But the Romans were not left long to the peaceful consideration of plans for raising their state after its grievous fall. On the one hand the Volsci, their ancient foes, had armed for the purpose of extinguishing the Roman name: on the other, merchants brought word from Etruria that the leading men of all her nations had met at the shrine of Voltumna and conspired to make war. A fresh alarm, too, was occasioned by the revolt of the Latins and the Hernici, who since the battle fought at Lake Regillus had continued for close upon a hundred years, with unquestioned loyalty, in the friendship of the Roman People. And so, when such dangers threatened them on every side, and it was clear to all that the name of Rome was not only held in hatred by her enemies, but even in contempt by her allies, it was resolved that the republic should be defended under the same auspices under which it had been redeemed and that Marcus Furius Camillus should be named dictator. Being appointed dictator he designated Gaius Servilius Ahala master of the horse, and after proclaiming a cessation of legal business, held a levy of the juniors, yet without excluding such of the older men as still

quibus aliquid roboris superesset, in verba sua
iuratos centuriaret.

7   Exercitum conscriptum armatumque trifariam
divisit.   Partem unam in agro Veiente Etruriae
opposuit, alteram ante urbem castra locare iussit;
8 tribuni militum his A. Manlius, illis, qui adversus
Etruscos mittebantur, L. Aemilius praepositus;
tertiam partem ipse ad Volscos duxit nec procul
a Lanuvio — ad Mecium is locus dicitur — castra
9 oppugnare est adortus.   Quibus ab contemptu, quod
prope omnem deletam a Gallis Romanam iuventutem
crederent, ad bellum profectis tantum Camillus
auditus imperator terroris intulerat ut vallo se ipsi,
vallum congestis arboribus saepirent, ne qua intrare
10 ad munimenta hostis posset.   Quod ubi animadvertit Camillus, ignem in obiectam saepem coici
iussit; et forte erat vis magna venti versa in hostem;
11 itaque non aperuit solum incendio viam, sed flammis
in castra tendentibus vapore etiam ac fumo crepitu-
que viridis materiae flagrantis ita consternavit
hostes ut minor moles superantibus vallum militibus
munitum [1] in castra Volscorum Romanis fuerit quam
transcendentibus saepem incendio absumptam fuerat.
12 Fusis hostibus caesisque cum castra impetu cepisset
dictator, praedam militi dedit, quo minus speratam

---

[1] vallum militibus munitum V; uallum Ω.

possessed any vigour, to whom also he administered B.C. 389
the oath and mustered them into centuries.

Having enrolled the army and equipped it, he
divided it into three parts. One division he stationed
in the Veientine district to confront Etruria; a
second he ordered to encamp before the City.
These divisions were put under the command of
military tribunes, Aulus Manlius for the home troops,
Lucius Aemilius for those which were being dispatched against the Etruscans. The third division
he led himself against the Volsci, and not far from
Lanuvium—*ad Mecium* the place is called—advanced
to attack their camp. The enemy had gone to
war from a feeling of contempt for the Romans,
believing that their fighting strength had been
nearly wiped out by the Gauls, but merely on hearing that Camillus was their general, they were so
terrified that they protected themselves with a
rampart and the rampart with a barricade of logs,
that the Romans might nowhere be able to pene-
trate to their defences. On perceiving this, Camillus
ordered his men to throw fire on the barrier. It
so happened that there was a high wind blowing
towards the enemy, which not only caused the
blaze to open a path, but what with the flames
making towards the camp, and the heat and smoke
and the crackling of the green wood, so alarmed
the enemy, that the Roman soldiers experienced
less difficulty in scaling the fortifications of the
Volscian camp than they had met with in crossing
the burnt barricade. Having routed and slain his
enemies and taken their camp by assault, the
dictator gave the booty to his soldiers, an act
which, coming unexpectedly from a commander who

LIVY

13 minime largitore duce, eo militi gratiorem. Per-
secutus deinde fugientes cum omnem Volscum
agrum depopulatus esset, ad deditionem Volscos
14 septuagesimo demum anno subegit. Victor ex Volscis in Aequos transiit et ipsos bellum molientes;
exercitum eorum ad Bolas oppressit, nec castra
modo sed urbem etiam adgressus impetu primo
cepit.

III. Cum in ea parte in qua caput rei Romanae
Camillus erat ea fortuna esset, aliam in partem terror
2 ingens ingruerat. Etruria prope omnis armata Sutrium, socios populi Romani, obsidebat; quorum
legati opem rebus adfectis orantes cum senatum
adissent, decretum tulere ut dictator primo quoque
3 tempore auxilium Sutrinis ferret. Cuius spei moram
cum pati fortuna obsessorum non potuisset con-
fectaque paucitas oppidanorum opere, vigiliis, volneribus, quae semper eosdem urgebant, per pactionem
urbe hostibus tradita inermis cum singulis emissa
vestimentis miserabili agmine penates relinqueret,
4 eo forte tempore Camillus cum exercitu Romano
intervenit. Cui cum se maesta turba ad pedes pro-
volvisset principumque orationem necessitate ultima
expressam fletus mulierum ac puerorum, qui exsilii
comites trahebantur, excepisset, parcere lamentis

---

[1] Writing of Tarquinius Superbus, Livy says (I. liii. 2)
that he began a war with the Volsci which was to last more
than two hundred years after his time. It is not known
where he could have found the seventy years tradition.

was by no means open-handed, was all the more
acceptable to the men. Then after pursuing the
fugitives and laying waste all the Volscian country-
side, he forced the Volsci to surrender at last, after
seventy years of war.[1] The victor, leaving the
Volsci, crossed over to the Aequi, who were themselves making preparations for war; their army he
surprised at Bolae, and carried not only their camp
but their city, too, at the first assault.

III. While affairs were thus prosperous in that
region where Camillus commanded for Rome, in
another direction a great danger threatened. Well-
nigh the whole of Etruria was in arms and was
laying siege to Sutrium, an ally of the Roman
People. Envoys of the Sutrines had appeared before the senate to beg for assistance in their distress,
and had obtained a decree that the dictator should
march to the aid of their people at the earliest
opportunity. But the plight of the besieged would
not admit of their waiting till this hope was realized;
and the population of the little town, exhausted
with the labour, guard-mounting, and wounds, which
fell always to the lot of the same men, had come
to terms, and having surrendered their city to the
enemy, were leaving their homes in a sad procession,
unarmed and with but a single garment each, when,
as it chanced, Camillus appeared on the scene with
a Roman army. The disconsolate rabble cast themselves at his feet, while their leading men addressed
him with words drawn from them by the direst
necessity and accompanied by the wailing of the
women and children, who were being dragged along
as the companions of their exile. He bade the
Sutrines spare their lamentations; the Etruscans

A.U.C.
365

Sutrinos iussit: Etruscis se luctum lacrimasque
5 ferre. Sarcinas inde deponi Sutrinosque ibi con-
sidere modico praesidio relicto, arma secum militem
ferre iubet. Ita expedito exercitu profectus ad
Sutrium, id quod rebatur, soluta omnia rebus, ut fit,
secundis invenit, nullam stationem ante moenia,
patentes portas, victorem vagum praedam ex ho-
6 stium tectis egerentem. Iterum igitur eodem die
Sutrium capitur; victores Etrusci passim trucidantur
ab novo hoste, nec se conglobandi coeundique in
7 unum aut arma capiundi datur spatium. Cum pro
se quisque tenderent ad portas, si qua forte se in
agros eicere possent, clausas — id enim primum
8 dictator imperaverat — portas inveniunt. Inde alii
arma capere, alii, quos forte armatos tumultus occupaverat, convocare suos ut proelium inirent; quod
accensum ab desperatione hostium fuisset, ni praecones per urbem dimissi poni arma et parci inermi
iussissent nec praeter armatos quemquam violari.
9 Tum etiam quibus animi in spe ultima obstinati ad
decertandum fuerant, postquam data spes vitae est,
iactare passim arma inermesque, quod tutius fortuna
10 fecerat, se hosti offerre. Magna multitudo in custo-

were those to whom he was bringing grief and tears. B.C. 389 He then gave orders that the packs should be set down; that the Sutrines should stop there, with a small guard which he left them; and that his soldiers should take their weapons and follow him. So, with his army in light marching order, he set out for Sutrium, where he was not surprised to find everything at loose ends, as a consequence—common enough—of their success; there was no outpost before the walls; the gates were open; and the victors had dispersed and were fetching the booty out of the houses of their enemies. For the second time, therefore, on the same day, Sutrium was captured. The victorious Etruscans were everywhere slaughtered by the new enemy, and had no time given them to assemble and unite their forces or to arm. As they tried, every man for himself, to reach the gates, if by chance they might somehow escape out into the fields, they found them shut, for so the general had ordered in the beginning. After that some caught up their swords; others, whom the sudden attack had found already armed, tried to call their fellows together for a battle, and this would have been hotly fought, because of the enemy's despair, had not heralds been dispatched through the town who made proclamation that arms should be laid down and the unarmed receive quarter, and that none should suffer any violence except those that carried weapons. Then even such as had in their extremity resolved to fight to the death, now that hope of life was held out to them, began everywhere to throw down their swords, and to go unarmed—for fortune had made this the safer way—to meet their enemies. The

dias divisa ; oppidum ante noctem redditum Sutrinis inviolatum integrumque ab omni clade belli, quia non vi captum sed traditum per condiciones fuerat.

IV. Camillus in urbem triumphans rediit trium simul 2 bellorum victor. Longe plurimos captivos ex Etruscis ante currum duxit, quibus sub hasta venumdatis tantum aeris redactum est ut, pretio pro auro matronis persoluto, ex eo quod supererat tres paterae 3 aureae factae sint, quas cum titulo nominis Camilli ante Capitolium incensum in Iovis cella constat ante pedes Iunonis positas fuisse.

4 Eo anno in civitatem accepti qui Veientium Capenatiumque ac Faliscorum per ea bella transfugerant ad Romanos, agerque his novis civibus 5 adsignatus. Revocati quoque in urbem senatus consulto a Veiis, qui aedificandi Romae pigritia occupatis ibi vacuis tectis Veios se contulerant. Et primo fremitus fuit aspernantium imperium ; dies deinde praestituta capitalisque poena, qui non remigrasset Romam, ex ferocibus universis singulos, metu 6 suo quemque, oboedientes fecit. Et Roma cum frequentia crescere, tum tota simul exsurgere aedificiis et re publica impensas adiuvante et aedilibus velut publicum exigentibus opus et ipsis privatis—

---

[1] A sign that booty was to be sold at auction.
[2] See v. i. 6-7.
[3] July 6th, 83 B.C. The restoration of the temple was completed 69 B.C.

great throng was divided among companies of B.C. 389
guards; and before night the town was restored
to the Sutrines, unharmed and without scathe of
war, because it had not been carried by assault, but
had been surrendered upon terms.

IV. Camillus returned to the City and triumphed B.C. 388
for his victories in three simultaneous wars. By far
the greatest number of the captives led before his
chariot were Etruscans; they were sold under the
spear,[1] and fetched so large a sum that after the
matrons had been repaid for their gold,[2] the surplus
sufficed to make three golden bowls, which were
inscribed, as is well known, with the name of
Camillus, and kept, until the burning of the
Capitol,[3] in the chapel of Jupiter, at Juno's
feet.

This year were received into the state such of
the Veientes, Capenates, and Faliscans as had come
over to the Romans in the course of these wars, and
lands were allotted to these new citizens. There
were also recalled from Veii to the City, by senatorial
decree, those who being too indolent to build in
Rome had taken possession of empty houses in Veii
and had gone there to live. They had indeed murmured at first, and had flouted the order; but the
designation of a day and the threat of a capital
penalty for failure to return to Rome reduced them
from a defiant group to obedient individuals, as each
became alarmed for himself. Rome was now growing
in numbers, and in every part at once new buildings
were springing up; the state contributed towards
the costs, and the aediles forwarded the work as
though it had been public business, while the
citizens themselves, incited by their desire to be

admonebat enim desiderium usus — festinantibus ad effectum operis; intraque annum nova urbs stetit.

7 Exitu anni comitia tribunorum militum consulari potestate habita. Creati T. Quinctius Cincinnatus Q. Servilius Fidenas quintum L. Iulius Iulus[1] L. Aquilius Corvus L. Lucretius Tricipitinus Ser.[2] Sul-
8 picius Rufus. Exercitum alterum in Aequos, non ad bellum — victos namque se fatebantur — sed ab odio ad pervastandos fines, ne quid ad nova consilia relinqueretur virium, duxere, alterum in agrum Tar-
9 quiniensem; ibi oppida Etruscorum Cortuosa et Contenebra vi capta. Ad Cortuosam nihil certaminis fuit: improviso adorti primo clamore atque impetu cepere; direptum oppidum atque incensum est.
10 Contenebra paucos dies oppugnationem sustinuit, laborque continuus, non die non nocte remissus, subegit eos. Cum in sex partes divisus exercitus Romanus senis horis in orbem succederet proelio, oppidanos eosdem integro semper certamini paucitas fessos obiceret, cessere tandem, locusque invadendi
11 urbem Romanis datus est. Publicari praedam tribunis placebat; sed imperium quam consilium segnius fuit; dum cunctantur, iam militum praeda erat nec nisi per invidiam adimi poterat.
12 Eodem anno, ne privatis tantum operibus cresceret urbs, Capitolium quoque saxo quadrato substructum

---

[1] L. Iulius Iulus *Sigon.* (*C.I.L.* i², *p.* 116): l. iulius VM : iulius. l. *PFB* : iulius *U* : iulius tullius *OE¹L³A* : iulius tullius l *E* : iullus tullius *HTD* : iullus tullus L : lucius iulius *A²*.

[2] Servius *A²₅* : seruilius (*cf. Diod.* xv. xxiii. 1) Ω.

using it, hurried their building to a conclusion; B.C. 388 and within the year there was a new City standing.

At the close of the year an election of military tribunes with consular powers was held. Those chosen were Titus Quinctius Cincinnatus, Quintus Servilius Fidenas (for the fifth time), Lucius Julius Iulus, Lucius Aquilius Corvus, Lucius Lucretius Tricipitinus, and Servius Sulpicius Rufus. These men led one army against the Aequi, not to war— for they confessed themselves vanquished—but from hatred, in order to waste their territories and leave them with no strength to make new trouble; with another they invaded the district of Tarquinii, where they captured by assault the Etruscan towns Cortuosa and Contenebra. At Cortuosa there was no struggle: in a surprise attack they carried the place at the first shout and onset, and then sacked and burned it. Contenebra held out for a few days, but the continuous fighting, without respite either day or night, overcame them. The Roman army had been divided into six corps, of which each in its turn went into battle for six hours; while the townsmen were so few that the same men were exposed to an attack that was constantly renewed, until at last they gave way and afforded the Romans an opening to enter the City. The tribunes decided that the booty should go to the state, but were less prompt in issuing orders than in planning; and, while they procrastinated, it was already in the hands of the soldiers and could not be taken away without offending them.

That same year, that the City might not grow in private buildings only, the Capitol was provided with a substructure of hewn stone, a work which even

209

LIVY

est, opus vel in hac magnificentia urbis conspicien
dum.

V. Iam et tribuni plebis civitate aedificando
occupata contiones suas frequentare legibus agrariis
2 conabantur. Ostentabatur in spem Pomptinus ager,
tum primum post accisas a Camillo Volscorum res
3 possessionis haud ambiguae. Criminabantur multo
eum infestiorem agrum ab nobilitate esse, quam a
Volscis fuerit ; ab illis enim tantum, quoad vires et
4 arma habuerint,[1] incursiones eo factas ; nobiles
homines in possessionem agri publici grassari, nec,
nisi antequam omnia praecipiant divisus sit, locum
5 ibi plebi fore. Haud magno opere plebem moverunt[2]
et infrequentem in foro propter aedificandi curam
et eodem exhaustam impensis eoque agri immemorem,
ad quem instruendum vires non essent.

6 In civitate plena religionum, tunc etiam ab recenti clade superstitiosis principibus, ut renovarentur
auspicia res ad interregnum rediit. Interreges deinceps M. Manlius Capitolinus, Ser. Sulpicius Camerinus,
7 L. Valerius Potitus. Hic demum tribunorum militum consulari potestate comitia habuit ; L. Papirium
C. Cornelium C. Sergium L. Aemilium iterum L.

---

[1] habuerint *Madvig*: habuerunt Ω.
[2] moverunt *Madvig*: mouerant (*or* -rat) Ω: moueunt *M*:
mouent *M*² (*or M*¹).

210

amidst the present splendours of the City is deserving B.C. 388
of remark.

V. And now, while the citizens were taken up B.C. 387
with building, the tribunes of the plebs were trying
to attract crowds to their meetings by proposals for
agrarian laws. They held out hopes of the Pomptine
district, of which the Romans had then for the
first time—since the defeat inflicted on the Volsci
by Camillus—acquired undisputed control. The
tribunes brought the charge that this district was
worse plagued by the nobility than it had been by
the Volsci; for the latter, as long as they were
strong enough and had arms, had done no more
than make incursions into it; but the nobles
were taking violent possession of the public domain,
and unless it should be parcelled out before they
seized it all, there would be no room there for
the commons. They made no great impression
on the plebs, who were seldom in the Forum,
because they were so intent on building, and,
exhausted with the expense thereby incurred, had
no thought of land, which they lacked the means
of stocking.

The citizens were much given to religious fears,
and at that time, owing to the recent calamity, even
the leaders were a prey to superstition; so, in order
that new auspices might be had, the state went into
an interregnum. The office of interrex was successively held by Marcus Manlius Capitolinus, Servius
Sulpicius Camerinus, and Lucius Valerius Potitus.
Finally, the last-named held an election of military
tribunes and announced that the choice had fallen
on Lucius Papirius, Gaius Cornelius, Gaius Sergius,
Lucius Aemilius (for the second time), Lucius

211

A.U.C.
367

Menenium[1] L. Valerium Publicolam tertium creat; ii[2] ex interregno magistratum occepere.

Eo anno aedis Martis Gallico bello vota dedicata
8 est a T. Quinctio duumviro sacris faciendis. Tribus quattuor ex novis civibus additae, Stellatina Tromentina Sabatina Arniensis; eaeque viginti quinque tribuum numerum explevere.

A.U.C.
368

VI. De agro Pomptino ab L. Sicinio tribuno plebis actum ad frequentiorem iam populum mobilioremque
2 ad cupiditatem agri quam fuerat. Et de Latino Hernicoque bello mentio facta in senatu maioris belli cura, quod Etruria in armis erat, dilata est.

3 Res ad Camillum tribunum militum consulari potestate rediit; collegae additi quinque: Ser. Cornelius Maluginensis Q. Servilius Fidenas sextum L. Quinctius Cincinnatus L. Horatius Pulvillus P.
4 Valerius. Principio anni aversae curae hominum sunt a bello Etrusco, quod fugientium ex agro Pomptino agmen repente inlatum in urbem attulit Antiates in armis esse Latinorumque populos iuven-
5 tutem suam summisisse[3] ad id bellum, eo abnuentes publicum fuisse consilium quod non prohibitos tantummodo voluntarios dicerent militare ubi vellent.

---

[1] C. Cornelium C. Sergium L. Aemilium iterum L. Menenium *Sigonius*: Cn. Sergium L. Aemilium iterum Licinium Menenium (*H. omits* L. Aemilium Menenium) Ω.

[2] creat ; ii *Alschefski*: creat (*or* creati) hii (*or* hi) Ω.

[3] suam summisisse ς: summisisse (*but F. has* sub- *and various MSS. misspell* -misisse) Ω: suam misisse *VMA²* "*antiqua lectio*" *Rhenanus.*

---

[1] The *duumviri* had charge of the Sibylline Books, which they were directed to consult in times of stress to ascertain what expiation Heaven demanded for the sins of the people.

Menenius and Lucius Valerius Publicola (for the B.C. 387
third time). These men took office at the conclusion
of the interregnum.

In that year the temple of Mars vowed in the
Gallic war was dedicated by Titus Quinctius, duumvir
for sacrifices.[1] Four additional tribes were formed
out of the new citizens, the Stellatina, Tromentina,
Sabatina, and Arniensis; these filled up the number
of tribes to twenty-five.

VI. The question of the Pomptine territory was B.C. 386
brought up by Lucius Sicinius, a tribune of the
plebs, in popular meetings which were now more
numerously attended, and by men more easily induced to covet land, than had been the case before.
The senate talked also of war with the Latins and
the Hernici, but dread of a greater war—Etruria
being up in arms—caused them to defer it.

The government passed to Camillus, as tribune of
the soldiers with consular authority. He was given
five colleagues: Servius Cornelius Maluginensis,
Quintus Servilius Fidenas (for a sixth term), Lucius
Quinctius Cincinnatus, Lucius Horatius Pulvillus,
and Publius Valerius. Early in the year the general
concern was diverted from the Etruscan war, when
a band of fugitives from the Pomptine district
suddenly appeared in Rome with tidings that the
Antiates were in arms. The Latin communities, so
they reported, had sent their soldiers to help in the
war, but asserted that their government was not
involved, since they had merely, as they said, not
forbidden their young men to serve, as volunteers,
where they liked.

Their number was raised to ten in 367 B.C. and later (in
51 B.C.) to fifteen.

213

6 Desierant iam ulla contemni bella. Itaque senatus dis agere gratias quod Camillus in magistratu
esset: dictatorem quippe dicendum eum fuisse si
privatus esset; et collegae fateri regimen omnium

7 rerum, ubi quid bellici terroris ingruat, in viro uno
esse, sibique destinatum id animo [1] esse Camillo sum-
mittere imperium, nec quicquam de maiestate sua
detractum credere quod maiestati eius viri conces-
sissent. Conlaudatis ab senatu tribunis et ipse

8 Camillus confusus animo gratias egit. Ingens inde
ait onus a populo Romano sibi, qui se [2] iam quartum
creasset, magnum a senatu talibus de se iudiciis [3]
maximum tam honoratorum [4] collegarum obsequio

9 iniungi. Itaque si quid laboris vigiliarumque adici
possit, certantem secum ipsum adnisurum ut tanto
de se consensu civitatis opinionem, quae maxima sit,

10 etiam constantem efficiat. Quod ad bellum atque
Antiates attineat, plus ibi minarum quam periculi
esse; se tamen, ut nihil timendi, sic nihil contem-

11 nendi auctorem esse. Circumsederi urbem Romanam
ab invidia et odio finitimorum; itaque et ducibus
pluribus et exercitibus administrandam rem publicam

12 esse. "Te" inquit, "P. Valeri,[5] socium imperii
consiliique legiones mecum adversus Antiatem ho-

13 stem ducere placet; te, Q. Servili, altero exercitu

[1] id animo *V*: in animo Ω: animo *L*.
[2] se *Madvig*: se dictatorem Ω.
[3] iudiciis *Karsten*: iudiciis eius ordinis Ω: iudiciis con-
cordiis *U*.
[4] honoratorum *Ald.*: honorato *V*ς: honoratum (honer-
BHT) Ω.
[5] P. Valeri ς (*cf.* § 3): L. Valeri Ω.

The Romans had ceased by this time to make light B.C. 386
of any wars. And so the senate gave thanks to the
gods that Camillus was in office, for in sooth they
would have been obliged to make him dictator, if he
had been a private citizen; and his colleagues
declared that the general control, when any warlike
danger threatened, belonged to one man alone, and
that they were resolved to subordinate their own
authority to Camillus; nor did they believe that
there was any derogation of their own dignity in
such concessions as they might make to his. The
senate commended the tribunes, and Camillus himself, deeply moved, expressed his thanks. A heavy
responsibility he said, was placed upon him by the
Roman People, who had now elected him for the
fourth time; no small one by the senate, in so judging
of him; but the greatest of all proceeded from
the deference accorded him by such distinguished
colleagues. Accordingly, if it were possible to add
to his exertions and his vigilance, he should vie with
himself in an effort to make the very high opinion
which his fellow citizens so unanimously entertained
of him an abiding one. As for the war with the
men of Antium, there was more bluster in that
quarter than real danger; nevertheless, as he would
have them fear nothing, so he would counsel them
to despise nothing. The City of Rome was ringed
about by the envy and ill-will of her neighbours;
consequently there needed several generals and
armies to administer the interests of the state. "It
is my wish," said he, "that you, Publius Valerius,
should share my authority and deliberations, and
join me in leading the legions against the enemy at
Antium; that you, Quintus Servilius, should organize

instructo paratoque ad urbem[1] castra habere, in-
tentum, sive Etruria se interim, ut nuper, sive nova
haec cura, Latini atque Hernici moverint; pro
certo habeo ita rem gesturum, ut patre avo teque
14 ipso ac sex tribunatibus dignum est. Tertius exercitus ex causariis senioribusque a L. Quinctio[2]
scribatur, qui urbi moenibusque praesidio sit. L.
Horatius arma, tela, frumentum quaeque alia belli
15 tempora poscent provideat. Te, Ser. Corneli, praesidem huius publici consilii, custodem religionum,
comitiorum, legum, rerum omnium urbanarum collegae facimus."

16   Cunctis in partes muneris sui benigne pollicentibus
operam, Valerius, socius imperii lectus, adiecit M.
Furium sibi pro dictatore seque ei pro magistro
17 equitum futurum; proinde, quam opinionem de
unico imperatore, eam spem de bello haberent. Se
vero bene sperare patres et de bello et de pace
18 universaque re publica erecti gaudio fremunt, nec
dictatore unquam opus fore rei publicae, si tales
viros in magistratu habeat, tam concordibus iunctos
animis, parere atque imperare iuxta paratos lau-
demque conferentes potius in medium quam ex
communi ad se trahentes.

   VII. Iustitio indicto dilectuque habito Furius ac

---

[1] ad urbem *V*: in urbem *A*: in urbe Ω.
[2] a L. Quinctio ⊊ (*cf* § 3); ab quinctio *V*; a tito quinctio
Ω: attito quinctio *L*.

and equip a second army, and maintain your camp
near Rome, on the alert, in case any move should be
made in the meantime from Etruria, as happened
recently, or from this new source of anxiety, the
Latins and Hernici; certain I am that you will
discharge the commission in a manner worthy of
your father, your grandfather, and yourself, and of
your six tribuneships. Let a third army be enrolled
by Lucius Quinctius, out of those who are invalided
or over age, to defend the City and the walls. Let
Lucius Horatius provide arms, missiles, corn, and
what else the exigencies of the war demand. You,
Servius Cornelius, we, your colleagues, appoint to be
president of this state council, guardian of religious
rites, of the elections, the laws, and all the affairs of
the City."

All promised loyally to do their best in their
respective departments of their office; and Valerius,
who had been selected to share in the command,
added that he should regard Marcus Furius as a
dictator and himself as his master of the horse; in
proportion therefore to men's confidence in their
unique commander should be their hopes of the
outcome of the war. Whereat the senators in their
enthusiasm shouted that they hoped right well of
the war, and of the peace, and of the common weal
in general; adding that the state would never need
a dictator if it might have such men in office, united
in such loving concord, equally ready to command
and obey, and rather contributing to the common
stock of glory than drawing upon it for their own
behoof.

VII. After proclaiming a suspension of legal
business and holding a levy, Furius and Valerius set

LIVY

Valerius ad Satricum profecti, quo non Volscorum
modo iuventutem Antiates ex nova subole lectam
sed ingentem Latinorum Hernicorumque vim [1] con-
civerant ex integerrimis diutina pace populis. Itaque
novus hostis veteri adiunctus commovit animos mi-
2 litis Romani. Quod ubi aciem iam instruenti Camillo
centuriones renuntiaverunt, turbatas militum mentes
esse, segniter arma capta, cunctabundosque et re-
sistentes egressos castris esse, quin voces quoque
auditas cum centenis hostibus singulos pugnaturos
et aegre inermem tantam multitudinem, nedum
3 armatam, sustineri posse, in equum insilit et ante
signa obversus in aciem ordines interequitans :

"Quae tristitia, milites, haec, quae insolita cunctatio est ? Hostem an me an vos ignoratis ? Hostis
est quid aliud quam perpetua materia virtutis glori-
4 aeque vestrae ? Vos contra me duce, ut Falerios
Veiosque captos et in capta patria Gallorum legiones
caesas taceam, modo trigeminae victoriae triplicem
triumphum ex his ipsis Volscis et Aequis [2] et ex
5 Etruria egistis. An me, quod non dictator vobis
sed tribunus signum dedi, non agnoscitis ducem ?
Neque ego maxima imperia in vos desidero, et vos
in me nihil praeter me ipsum intueri decet ; neque

---

[1] Hernicorumque vim *Madvig* : hernicorumque Ω.
[2] et Aequis Ω : ex Aequis *Heusinger* : et ex Aequis, *H. J.
Mueller.*

---

[1] *i.e.*, since the disastrous defeat they had suffered in 389
(chap. ii. § 12).

out for Satricum, where the Antiates had collected ^{B.C. 386} not only the fighting men of the Volsci, recruited from a new generation,[1] but also a large force of Latins and Hernici, nations which, having been long at peace, were extremely strong. The consequence of this addition of new enemies to their old ones was to trouble the spirit of the Roman soldiers. But when the centurions reported to Camillus, as he was already drawing up his line, that the men were demoralized; that they had been loath to arm and had hesitated and delayed in leaving the camp, nay, that some had even been heard to say that they would be one against a hundred in the battle, and that so great a host could hardly be withstood even though unarmed, much less when provided with weapons—being told of this, I say, Camillus vaulted upon his horse, and riding along the ranks in front of the standards, faced his troops and thus addressed them:

"Soldiers, what means this gloom and this unwonted reluctance? Are you strangers to the enemy, or to me, or to yourselves? The enemy—what else are they but inexhaustible material for you to fashion into glorious deeds of valour? As for yourselves, when acting as my soldiers, though I say nothing of your capturing Falerii and Veii and routing the Gallic legions in your captured City, you celebrated, only the other day, a three-fold triumph for a triple victory over these very Volsci and Aequi and over Etruria. Or is it that I, having given you the signal not as dictator but as tribune of the soldiers, am not recognized as your commander? And yet neither do I desire supreme authority over you, nor ought you to regard in me anything but myself; for

A.U.C.
368

enim dictatura mihi unquam animos fecit, ut ne
6 exsilium quidem ademit. Iidem igitur omnes sumus,
et cum eadem omnia in hoc bellum adferamus, quae
in priora attulimus, eundem eventum belli exspec-
temus. Simul concurreritis, quod quisque didicit
ac consuevit faciet: vos vincetis, illi fugient."

VIII. Dato deinde signo ex equo desilit et proximum signiferum manu arreptum secum in hostem
2 rapit "Infer, miles," clamitans "signum." Quod
ubi videre, ipsum Camillum, iam ad munera corporis
senecta invalidum, vadentem in hostes, procurrunt
pariter omnes clamore sublato "Sequere impera-
3 torem" pro se quisque clamantes. Emissum etiam
signum Camilli iussu in hostium aciem ferunt, idque
4 ut repeteretur concitatos antesignanos; ibi primum
pulsum Antiatem, terroremque non in primam tan-
5 tum aciem sed etiam ad subsidiarios perlatum. Nec
vis tantum militum movebat excitata praesentia
ducis, sed quod Volscorum animis nihil terribilius
6 erat quam ipsius Camilli forte oblata species; ita
quocumque se intulisset victoriam secum haud
dubiam trahebat. Maxime id evidens fuit, cum in
laevum cornu prope iam pulsum arrepto repente
equo cum scuto pedestri advectus conspectu suo
proelium restituit ostentans vincentem ceteram
7 aciem. Iam inclinata res erat, sed turba hostium

the dictatorship could never give me resolution, nor B.C. 386 could even exile deprive me of it. We are all, therefore, exactly as we were, and since we bring the same qualities in all respects to this campaign that we brought to earlier ones, let us look forward to the same result. As soon as you have joined battle, every man will do what he has learned and has become accustomed to: you will conquer, they will run away."

VIII. He then sounded the charge, and leaping from his horse, caught hold of the nearest standard-bearer and hurried him towards the enemy, calling out: "Forward soldiers!" But when they saw Camillus, who for bodily feats was now grown old and infirm, advancing in person against the foe, they all gave a cheer and rushed forward together, and every man took up the cry of "Follow the General!" It is even said that Camillus bade the standard-bearer hurl his ensign into the press of enemies, and urging the front ranks to recover it, then for the first time discomfited the Antiates. The panic did not stop with the first line, but spread even to the troops in support. It was not only the dash of the Roman soldiers, inspired by their leader's presence, which overcame them; for nothing so daunted the spirits of the Volsci as the sight of Camillus himself, when they happened to encounter him—so surely, wherever he went, did he carry victory with him. This was especially apparent on the left. That wing had already nearly given way, when Camillus suddenly threw himself upon a horse, and, armed with an infantry-shield, rode up and by his presence retrieved the battle, calling out that the rest of the army was conquering. The fortune of the day had now turned,

et fuga impediebatur [1] et longa caede conficienda
multitudo tanta fesso militi erat, cum repente ingentibus procellis fusus imber certam magis victoriam
8 quam proelium diremit. Signo deinde receptui dato
nox insecuta quietis Romanis perfecit bellum. Latini namque et Hernici relictis Volscis domos profecti sunt, malis consiliis pares adepti eventus;
9 Volsci, ubi se desertos ab eis videre, quorum fiducia
rebellaverant, relictis castris moenibus Satrici se
includunt. Quos primo Camillus vallo circumdare
et aggere atque operibus oppugnare est adortus.
10 Quae postquam nulla eruptione impediri videt,
minus esse animi ratus in hoste quam ut in eo
tam lentae spei victoriam exspectaret, cohortatus
milites, ne tamquam Veios oppugnantes in opere
longinquo sese tererent, victoriam in manibus esse,
ingenti militum alacritate moenia undique adgressus
scalis oppidum cepit. Volsci abiectis armis sese
dediderunt.

IX. Ceterum animus ducis rei maiori, Antio,
imminebat : id caput Volscorum, eam fuisse ori-
2 ginem proximi belli. Sed quia nisi magno apparatu,
tormentis machinisque, tam valida urbs capi non poterat, relicto ad exercitum collega Romam est profectus,

---

[1] fuga impediebatur *HTLR* : fuga im(*or* in-)pediebat Ω :
fugam impediebat ς.

222

but the enemy's numbers were an obstacle even to their flight, and a great multitude remained for the weary soldiers to dispatch with long-drawn massacre, when suddenly great gusts of wind brought on a downpour of rain, which broke off what was rather a certain victory than a battle. Thereupon the recall was sounded, and the night that followed finished the campaign for the Romans, while they slept. For the Latins and Hernici abandoned the Volsci and marched off to their homes, their evil counsels rewarded with as evil an outcome; and the Volsci, perceiving themselves to be deserted by those on whom they had relied in their rebellion, forsook their camp and shut themselves up within the walls of Satricum. Camillus at first set about confining them with a palisade and mound, intending to lay siege to them; but finding the enemy made no sorties to interrupt the work, he concluded they had not sufficient resolution to make him wait so long for victory. He therefore encouraged his troops not to wear themselves out with protracted toil, as though they were besieging Veii, when victory was within their grasp; and with great alacrity on the part of the soldiers, he approached the walls from every side and captured the town with scaling-ladders. The Volsci threw away their weapons and surrendered.

IX. But the general's thoughts were turning to a matter of greater moment, namely Antium, which, as being the Volscian capital, he held responsible for the last war. But because, without extensive equipment of artillery and engines, it was impossible to take so strong a town, he left his colleague in command of the army and proceeded to Rome, that he might

3 ut senatum ad excidendum Antium hortaretur. Inter
sermonem eius — credo rem Antiatem diuturniorem
manere dis cordi fuisse — legati ab Nepete ac Sutrio
auxilium adversus Etruscos petentes veniunt, brevem
occasionem esse ferendi auxilii memorantes. Eo
4 vim Camilli ab Antio fortuna avertit. Namque cum
ea loca opposita Etruriae et velut claustra inde
portaeque essent, et illis occupandi ea cum quid
novi molirentur, et Romanis reciperandi tuendique
5 cura erat. Igitur senatui cum Camillo agi placuit
ut omisso Antio bellum Etruscum susciperet;
legiones urbanae quibus Quinctius praefuerat ei
6 decernuntur. Quamquam expertum exercitum ad-
suetumque imperio qui in Volscis erat mallet, nihil
recusavit; Valerium tantummodo imperii socium de-
poposcit. Quinctius Horatiusque successores Valerio
in Volscos missi.

7 Profecti ab urbe Sutrium Furius et Valerius
partem oppidi iam captam ab Etruscis invenere,
ex parte altera intersaeptis itineribus aegre oppida-
8 nos vim hostium ab se arcentes. Cum Romani
auxilii adventus tum Camilli nomen celeberrimum
apud hostes sociosque et in praesentia rem incli-
natam sustinuit et spatium ad opem ferendam dedit.
9 Itaque diviso exercitu Camillus collegam in eam

---

[1] With this remark compare I. iv. 1.

urge the senate to undertake the destruction of B.C. 386
Antium. While he was speaking—I suppose it was
Heaven's will that the Antian state should continue
somewhat longer [1]—envoys from Nepete and Sutrium
appeared, who asked for help against the Etruscans,
saying that the opportunity of lending aid would
soon be past. To this quarter Fortune diverted the
energies of Camillus, away from Antium. For since
these places were on the frontier of Etruria, and
were the barriers, so to speak, and gateways of that
region, the Etruscans were concerned to seize them,
as often as they had any new design in hand, and
the Romans to recover or defend them. The senate
therefore resolved to request of Camillus that he
should relinquish Antium and undertake the Etruscan war, and voted him the city levies which had been
under the command of Quinctius. Although Camillus
would have preferred the army, disciplined and used
to his authority, which lay in the Volscian country,
he made no objection, only stipulating that Valerius
should be associated with him in the command.
Quinctius and Horatius were dispatched to succeed
Valerius against the Volsci.

Leaving the City and marching to Sutrium, Furius
and Valerius found that a part of the town was
already captured by the Etruscans, and that in
the other part the townspeople had barricaded the
streets and were defending themselves with great
difficulty from the onslaughts of their enemies. The
arrival of succour from Rome, and particularly the
great reputation which Camillus enjoyed with both
friends and foes, checked for the moment the disastrous course of events and afforded time to render
assistance. Accordingly, Camillus divided the army,

225

partem circumductis copiis quam hostes tenebant
moenia adgredi iubet, non tam a spe [1] scalis capi
urbem posse quam ut aversis eo hostibus et oppidanis
iam pugnando fessis laxaretur labor et ipse spatium
10 intrandi sine certamine moenia haberet. Quod
cum simul utrimque factum esset ancepsque terror
Etruscos circumstaret, et moenia summa vi oppugnari et intra moenia esse hostem viderent, porta
11 se quae una forte non obsidebatur trepidi uno
agmine eiecere. Magna caedes fugientium et in
urbe et per agros est facta. Plures a Furianis intra
moenia caesi; Valeriani expeditiores ad persequendum [2] fuere, nec ante noctem, quae conspectum
ademit, finem caedendi fecere.

12 Sutrio recepto restitutoque sociis Nepete exercitus
ductus, quod per deditionem acceptum iam totum
Etrusci habebant.

X. Videbatur plus in ea urbe recipienda laboris
fore, non eo solum quod tota hostium erat, sed
etiam quod parte Nepesinorum prodente civitatem
2 facta erat deditio; mitti tamen ad principes eorum
placuit ut secernerent se ab Etruscis fidemque quam
3 implorassent ab Romanis, ipsi praestarent. Unde

---

[1] tam a spe *A²* *Heerwagen*: tanta spe Ω.
[2] persequendum *M. Mueller*: persequendos Ω.

and directed his colleague to make a circuit with his B.C. 386
forces and to attack the walls on the side which
was held by the enemy. His hope was not so
much that the city would be taken by escalade, as
that the enemy might be diverted to that quarter
—easing thereby the strain upon the townsmen,
who were already worn out with fighting—and that
he might himself have an opportunity of entering
the place without encountering resistance. But
on this plan being put into effect simultaneously at
both points, the Etruscans, finding themselves threatened on either side and seeing that the walls were
being violently assailed and that the enemy was
inside the city, threw themselves out by the only
gate which chanced to be unguarded, in one panic-
stricken throng. Great was the carnage they suffered
as they fled, both in the city and in the fields.
Furius's men slew more within the walls; the
soldiers of Valerius were more lightly equipped for
pursuit, and kept up the massacre until night made
it impossible to see.

Having retaken Sutrium and restored it to our
allies, the army marched to Nepete, which had surrendered to the Etruscans, who were now in complete
possession.

X. It appeared likely that this town would be
more troublesome to recover, not only because it
was wholly in the hands of the enemy, but also because
a faction of the Nepesini had betrayed their state
and arranged the capitulation. It was nevertheless
decided to send word to their leaders, that they should
sever themselves from the Etruscans and extend to
the Romans the same trusty aid which they had
requested at their hands. When the reply came

A.U.C.
368

cum responsum allatum esset nihil suae potestatis
esse, Etruscos moenia custodiasque portarum tenere,
primo populationibus agri terror est oppidanis ad-
4 motus; deinde, postquam deditionis quam societatis
fides sanctior erat, fascibus sarmentorum ex agro
conlatis ductus ad moenia exercitus completisque
fossis scalae admotae, et clamore primo impetuque
5 oppidum capitur. Nepesinis inde edictum ut arma
ponant, parcique iussum inermi : Etrusci pariter
armati atque inermes caesi. Nepesinorum quoque
auctores deditionis securi percussi : innoxiae multitudini redditae res, oppidumque cum praesidio
6 relictum. Ita duabus sociis urbibus ex hoste receptis victorem exercitum tribuni cum magna gloria
Romam reduxerunt.

Eodem anno ab Latinis Hernicisque res repetitae
quaesitumque cur per eos annos militem ex instituto
7 non dedissent. Responsum frequenti utriusque gentis concilio est nec culpam in eo publicam nec
consilium fuisse quod suae iuventutis aliqui apud
8 Volscos militaverint ; eos tamen ipsos pravi consilii
poenam habere, nec quemquam ex his reducem esse :
militis autem non dati causam terrorem adsiduum
a Volscis fuisse, quam pestem adhaerentem lateri
suo tot super alia aliis bellis exhauriri nequisse.

228

back that they were powerless, that the Etruscans B.C. 386
held the walls and guarded the gates, the Romans
first laid waste their fields, in an effort to frighten
the townsfolk; then, when the sanctity of their
surrender proved to be more binding on them than
that of their alliance, they gathered osiers from the
fields and made fascines, and the army being led
against the walls filled up the moat, erected scaling-
ladders, and carried the town at the first shout and
charge. The Nepesini were then commanded to lay
down their weapons and the order was given to spare
such as were unarmed. The Etruscans were put to
death, whether armed or not. Of the Nepesini,
too, those who were responsible for the surrender
were executed; the innocent populace were given
back their possessions, and the town was left
with a garrison. After thus regaining from the
enemy two cities of the allies, the victorious
army under its tribunes marched gloriously back
to Rome.

The same year demands for reparation were made
upon the Latins and the Hernici, and they were
asked why, during recent years, they had furnished
no soldiers, as they had agreed to do. Both nations
replied in plenary assemblies that no blame or evil
purpose attached to the state because a few of their
young men had served with the Volsci. These men
had, for that matter, paid the penalty for their dis-
torted judgment, and not one of them had come
back; as to their having furnished no soldiers, this
had been due to their constant fear of the Volsci
—a pest that clung so fast to them that with all
that long succession of wars they had been unable
to shake it off. On learning of this answer, the

9 Quae relata patribus magis tempus quam causam
non visa belli habere.

XI. Insequenti anno A. Manlio P. Cornelio T. et
L. Quinctiis Capitolinis L. Papirio Cursore iterum
C. Sergio[1] iterum[2] tribunis consulari potestate
2 grave bellum foris, gravior domi seditio exorta,
bellum ab Volscis adiuncta Latinorum atque Hernicorum defectione, seditio, unde minime timeri
potuit, a patriciae gentis viro et inclitae famae,
3 M. Manlio Capitolino. Qui nimius animi cum alios
principes sperneret, uni invideret, eximio simul
honoribus atque virtutibus, M. Furio, aegre ferebat
4 solum eum in magistratibus, solum apud exercitus[3]
tantum iam eminere ut iisdem auspiciis creatos non
pro collegis sed pro ministris habeat, cum interim,
si quis vere aestimare velit, a M. Furio recuperari
patria ex obsidione hostium non potuerit, nisi a se
5 prius Capitolium atque arx servata esset; et ille
inter aurum accipiendum et in spem pacis solutis
animis Gallos adgressus sit, ipse armatos capien-
tesque arcem depulerit; illius gloriae pars virilis
apud omnes milites sit qui simul vicerint, suae
victoriae neminem omnium mortalium socium esse
6 constet.[4] His opinionibus inflato animo, ad hoc

---

[1] iterum C. Sergio *added by Glareanus and Sigonius from
chap.* v. § 7 *and chap.* xxvii. § 2.

[2] iterum A^2 *or* A^4: ii Ω: duobus M^3OE: u L: iii H:
iis U.

[3] solum apud exercitus *Madvig*: solum apud exercitus
esse Ω.

[4] esse constet *Harant*: esse Ω.

senators were of opinion that they lacked not so
much the ground for war as a favourable opportunity.

XI. In the following year, when the consular
tribunes were Aulus Manlius, Publius Cornelius,
Titus and Lucius Quinctius Capitolinus, Lucius
Papirius Cursor (for the second time) and Gaius
Sergius (for the second time), a serious foreign war
broke out, and an even more serious domestic
schism. The war was set on foot by the Volsci, in
conjunction with a revolt on the part of the Latins
and Hernici ; the schism originated where such a
thing was least to be apprehended, with a man of
patrician family and high renown, Marcus Manlius
Capitolinus. This man, scorning, in his overweening
pride, the other nobles, but envying the one who
excelled them all in honours and good qualities,
namely Marcus Furius, could ill endure that Camillus
should at last have attained to such solitary eminence,
both amongst the magistrates and in the armies, as
to have those who had been chosen under the same
auspices not for colleagues but for servants ; whereas—if one considered the situation fairly—it would
have been impossible for Marcus Furius to redeem
his native City from the leaguer of her enemies,
unless Manlius himself had before that saved the
Capitol and Citadel. Camillus had assailed the
Gauls while they were receiving the gold and while
their resolution was relaxed by thoughts of peace ;
but he himself had driven them back, as they
came on, sword in hand, in the act of taking the
Citadel. Of the glory of Camillus a goodly portion
belonged to all the soldiers who had conquered with
him : in his own victory it was acknowledged that
no mortal soever had a share. Puffed up with these

231

A.U.C.
369

vitio quoque ingenii vehemens et impotens, postquam inter patres non quantum aequum censebat

7 excellere suas opes animadvertit, primus [1] omnium
ex patribus popularis factus cum plebeiis magistratibus consilia communicare ; criminando patres,
alliciendo ad se plebem iam aura,[2] non consilio ferri

8 famaeque magnae malle quam bonae esse. Et non
contentus agrariis legibus, quae materia semper
tribunis plebi seditionum fuisset, fidem [3] moliri
coepit : acriores quippe aeris alieni stimulos esse, qui
non egestatem modo atque ignominiam minentur
sed nervo ac vinculis corpus liberum territent.

9 Et erat aeris alieni magna vis re [4] damnossima etiam
divitibus, aedificando, contracta. Bellum itaque
Volscum, grave per se, oneratum Latinorum atque
Hernicorum defectione, in speciem causae iactatum

10 ut maior potestas quaereretur ; sed nova consilia
Manli magis compulere senatum ad dictatorem
creandum. Creatus A. Cornelius Cossus magistrum
equitum dixit T. Quinctium Capitolinum.

XII. Dictator etsi maiorem dimicationem pro-
positam domi quam foris cernebat, tamen, seu quia
celeritate ad bellum opus erat, seu victoria trium-
phoque dictaturae ipsi vires se additurum ratus,
dilectu habito in agrum Pomptinum, quo a Volscis
exercitum inductum [5] audierat, pergit.

2   Non dubito, praeter satietatem tot iam libris

---

[1] primus U'_{ς} *Tan. Faber* : primu' U : primo O : primum Ω.
[2] plebem iam auram *Vorm. ? MHTD* : plebem iam auriam
$L.$: plebeiā auria A : plebeiam auram F^2 (plebeiam P)
$FUBOET^2D^3A^2$.
[3] fidem *Sigonius* (*after Faernus*) : idem (*or* Idem) Ω :
omitted by A.   [4] re $_{\varsigma}$ Freinsheim : res Ω.
[5] inductum F^2U : indictum (inditum A) Ω : induci indictum MA^2 : indictum induci OE : induci F^3 (*margin*).

opinions, and being besides, through a defect of _{B.C. 385} nature, impetuous and passionate, when he perceived that his abilities did not bring him that leadership amongst the nobles which he thought they merited, he was the first of all the patricians to turn demagogue and to cast in his lot with the plebeian magistrates. He abused the nobles, he courted the favour of the plebs; and swept along by the breath of popularity and not by good counsel chose rather to be reputed great than virtuous. Moreover, not content with agrarian proposals, which had ever served the tribunes to stir up sedition, he began an attack on credit; for he held that debt was a sharper goad, since it not only threatened poverty and shame, but terrified the freeman with the thought of shackles and imprisonment. And in fact there had been a vast piling up of debts, by reason of a thing that is ruinous even to the rich, to wit, building. And so the Volscian war, grave in itself and made still graver by the defection of the Latins and Hernici, was alleged as a reason for seeking a greater authority; but the revolutionary schemes of Manlius were the more compelling cause of the senate's naming a dictator. They appointed Aulus Cornelius Cossus, who appointed as his master of the horse Titus Quinctius Capitolinus.

XII. The dictator perceived that a greater struggle was impending at home than abroad. But either the war demanded haste, or he believed that by a victory and triumph he could add power to the dictatorship itself. So he mustered his forces and proceeded to the Pomptine territory, which he had heard was invaded by a Volscian army.

I doubt not that those who are surfeited with

A.U.C.
369
adsidua bella cum Volscis gesta legentibus illud
quoque succursurum, quod mihi percensenti pro-
piores temporibus harum rerum auctores miraculo
fuit, unde totiens victis Volscis et Aequis suffecerint

3 milites. Quod cum ab antiquis tacitum praetermissum sit, cuius tandem ego rei praeter opinionem,
quae sua cuique coniectanti esse potest, auctor sim ?

4 Simile veri est aut intervallis bellorum, sicut nunc
in dilectibus fit Romanis, alia atque alia subole
iuniorum ad bella instauranda totiens usos esse,
aut non ex iisdem semper populis exercitus scriptos,

5 quamquam eadem semper gens bellum intulerit, aut
innumerabilem multitudinem liberorum capitum in
eis fuisse locis quae nunc vix seminario exiguo
militum relicto servitia Romana ab solitudine vin-

6 dicant. Ingens certe, quod inter omnes auctores
conveniat, quamquam nuper Camilli ductu atque
auspicio accisae res erant, Volscorum exercitus fuit;
ad hoc Latini Hernicique accesserant et Circeiensium quidam et coloni etiam a Velitris Romani.

7   Dictator castris eo die positis, postero cum auspicato prodisset hostiaque caesa pacem deum adorasset,
laetus ad milites iam arma ad propositum pugnae
signum, sicut edictum erat, luce prima capientes

8 processit. "Nostra victoria est, milites," inquit,

---

[1] A red flag flown from the general's tent.

reading in all these books about endless wars waged B.C. 385
with the Volsci will ask, as with great astonishment
I did myself, on examining the historians who were
nearer in point of time to those events, where the
so oft defeated Volsci and Aequi got their supply of
soldiers. But since the ancients have passed over
this question in silence, what can I adduce other
than an opinion such as everyone can by conjecture
arrive at for himself? It is probable either that in
the intervals between wars successive generations
sprang up—as happens nowadays in the levies of
the Romans—which they used for their frequent
renewals of war; or that it was not always the same
tribes from which they enrolled their armies—though
it was always the same nation which made war; or
else that there was an innumerable multitude of
freemen in those regions which in our day scarce
afford a scanty seed-plot for soldiers, and are only
saved from becoming a waste desert by gangs of
Roman slaves. In any case, all the authorities would
agree that the army of the Volsci was an enormous
one, although their state had recently suffered a
heavy blow from the generalship and auspices of
Camillus. There were, besides, additional forces of
Latins and Hernici, as well as a certain number
from Circei, and even Roman colonists from Velitrae.

On the morning after he had made his camp, the
dictator took the auspices, and coming forth from
his tent offered up a victim and besought the favour
of Heaven. He then with great cheerfulness presented himself before the soldiers, who were already
arming by the first rays of light, as they had been
warned to do when the signal for battle[1] should be
displayed. "Ours is the victory, soldiers," he ex-

" si quid di vatesque eorum in futurum vident.
Itaque, ut decet certae spei plenos et cum imparibus
manus conserturos, pilis ante pedes positis gladiis
tantum dextras armemus. Ne procurri quidem ab
acie velim, sed obnixos vos stabili gradu impetum
9 hostium excipere. Ubi illi vana iniecerint missilia
et effusi stantibus vobis se intulerint, tum micent
gladii et veniat in mentem unicuique deos esse qui
Romanum adiuvent, deos qui secundis avibus in
10 proelium miserint. Tu T. Quincti, equitem intentus
ad primum initium moti certaminis teneas ; ubi
haerere iam aciem conlato pede videris, tum terrorem equestrem occupatis alio pavore infer invec-
11 tusque ordines pugnantium dissipa." Sic eques, sic
pedes, ut praeceperat, pugnant ; nec dux legiones
nec fortuna fefellit ducem.

XIII. Multitudo hostium, nulli rei praeterquam
numero freta et oculis utramque metiens aciem,
2 temere proelium iniit, temere omisit ; clamore
tantum missilibusque telis et primo pugnae impetu
ferox gladios et conlatum pedem et voltum hostis
3 ardore animi micantem ferre non potuit. Impulsa
frons prima et trepidatio subsidiis inlata ; et suum
terrorem intulit eques ; rupti inde multis locis
ordines motaque omnia et fluctuanti similis acies

claimed, "if the gods and the soothsayers who B.C. 385
interpret them can at all see what is coming. And
so, as befits men who with sure confidence are about
to fight with those who are no match for them, let
us lay our javelins at our feet and arm our right
hands with swords only. I would have none run out
from the line, but all stand firmly planted and receive the onset of our enemies. When they have
discharged their missiles without effect, and come
thronging upon you where you stand, then let your
blades flash out, and let every man of you bethink
him that the gods are the Roman's helpers, that the
gods have with fair omens sent him into battle.
Do you, Titus Quinctius, hold back your cavalry and
watch for the first beginning of the mellay ; when
you see that the lines are already close-locked, foot
to foot, then loose the terrors of your horse against
them, while they are taken up with another fear ;
charge them as they fight, and break their ranks."
Like horse, like foot, as they were bidden, so they
fought ; the general failed not his legions, nor
fortune the general.

XIII. The hostile multitude, relying on numbers
only and measuring both armies with their eyes
recklessly began the fight and as recklessly gave it
up ; their boldness went no further than the battle-
cry, the discharge of missiles, and the first fury of
the onset ; the play of swords, when foot met foot,
and the glance of the foeman that darted out the
fire of his spirit, they could not abide. Their front
was first driven in and communicated its disorder
to the supports ; the horsemen, too, inspired a terror
of their own ; next the ranks were broken at many
points, and all was in commotion, and the line re-

A.U.C.
369

erat. Dein postquam cadentibus primis iam ad se quisque perventuram caedem cernebat, terga vertunt. 4 Instare[1] Romanus; et donec armati confertique abibant, peditum labor in persequendo fuit; postquam iactari arma passim fugaque per agros spargi aciem hostium animadversum est, tum equitum turmae emissae dato signo ne in singulorum morando caede spatium ad evadendum interim multitudini 5 darent: satis esse missilibus ac terrore impediri cursum obequitandoque agmen teneri dum adsequi 6 pedes et iusta caede conficere hostem posset. Fugae sequendique non ante noctem finis fuit. Capta quoque ac direpta eodem die castra Volscorum, praedaque omnis praeter libera corpora militi con- 7 cessa est. Pars maxima captivorum ex Latinis atque Hernicis fuit, nec omnium[2] de plebe, ut credi posset mercede militasse, sed principes quidam iuventutis inventi, manifesta fides publica ope Volscos 8 hostes adiutos. Circeiensium quoque quidam cogniti et coloni a Velitris; Romamque omnes missi percontantibus primoribus patrum eadem quae dictatori defectionem sui quisque populi haud perplexe indicavere.

XIV. Dictator exercitum in stativis tenebat minime dubius bellum cum iis populis patres

[1] instare $A^2\varsigma$: stare Ω.
[2] omnium F^3B : hominum Ω.

sembled a surging wave. Then, as soon as each B.C. 385 began to see that with the fall of those in front his own turn to be killed would soon be coming, they turned and fled. The Romans pressed on after them, and as long as they retained their arms and withdrew in masses, it was the infantry's task to pursue them; but when the enemy were seen to be throwing away their weapons on every hand and their army to be dispersed in flight over the fields; then the cavalry squadrons were let loose, with orders not to stop to kill single fugitives and afford meanwhile an opportunity to the main body of escaping; it was sufficient if by darting missiles at them to alarm them, and by riding across their path, they should hold the column in check, till the infantry could overtake the enemy and utterly destroy them. Flight and pursuit continued until nightfall. The Volscian camp was also captured the same day and sacked, and all the booty except the persons of freemen was turned over to the soldiers. The chief part of the prisoners consisted of Latins and Hernici, not all of whom were plebeians, such as might be supposed to have served as mercenaries, but certain youths of high rank were discovered, a clear proof that their states had publicly countenanced the Volscian enemy. Some, again, were recognized as being from Circei and from the colony at Velitrae. They were all sent to Rome, and being questioned by the chief senators, gave the same answers they had given the dictator, and in no uncertain terms laid bare the defection of their respective peoples.

XIV. The dictator maintained his army in camp, not doubting in the least that the senate would

A.U.C.
369

iussuros, cum maior domi exorta moles coegit acciri
Romam eum gliscente in dies seditione, quam solito

2 magis metuendam auctor faciebat. Non enim iam
orationes modo M. Manli sed facta, popularia in
speciem, tumultuosa eadem qua mente fierent

3 intuenti[1] erant. Centurionem, nobilem militaribus
factis, iudicatum pecuniae cum duci vidisset, medio
foro cum caterva sua accurrit et manum iniecit;
vociferatusque de superbia patrum ac crudelitate
feneratorum et miseriis plebis, virtutibus eius viri

4 fortunaque, "tum vero ego" inquit "nequiquam
hac dextra Capitolium arcemque servaverim, si civem
commilitonemque meum tamquam Gallis victoribus
captum in servitutem ac vincula duci videam."

5 Inde rem creditori palam populo solvit libraque et
aere liberatum emittit, deos atque homines obtes-
tantem ut M. Manlio, liberatori suo, parenti plebis

6 Romanae, gratiam referant. Acceptus extemplo in
tumultuosam turbam et ipse tumultum augebat,
cicatrices acceptas Veienti Gallico aliisque deinceps

7 bellis ostentans: se militantem, se restituentem
eversos penates, multiplici iam sorte exsoluta,

---

[1] intuenti *Gronovius*: intuenda Ω.

---

[1] Actually the senate could only recommend a declaration
of war, the ultimate decision resting with the *comitia
centuriata*.

[2] Symbolical of the *sale* by which the debtor was conceived
to be transferred from the ownership of his creditor to that
of Liberty.

declare war on those nations;[1] when a greater disturbance broke out at home and obliged them to summon him to the City, where the sedition was increasing from day to day, and occasioned more than the usual alarm by reason of the man who was behind it. For now not only the speeches of Manlius, but his actions as well, while ostensibly democratic, were really revolutionary, considering the purpose which inspired them. A centurion renowned for military prowess had been condemned for debt. As he was being led away, Manlius caught sight of him, and hastening to his side through the midst of the Forum with his band of retainers, he laid hold of him, and exclaiming at the arrogance of the patricians, the heartlessness of the money-lenders, the sufferings of the plebs, and the merits and misfortunes of this man, "Then in very truth," he cried, "was it all in vain that with this right hand I saved the Capitol and the Citadel, if I am to see my fellow citizen and fellow soldier carried off a captive—as though the Gauls had conquered us—to servitude and chains!" He then paid the money to the creditor in full sight of the people, and with the ceremony of the scales and bronze[2] redeemed the debtor and set him free, invoking the blessing of gods and men on Marcus Manlius, his liberator, the father of the Roman plebs. Being at once received into the midst of a tumultuous throng, he added to the tumult by displaying the scars he had received in the Veientine, the Gallic, and other successive wars. While he had himself been fighting, he said, and rebuilding his ruined home, he had been overwhelmed with usury, though he had paid already many times the amount of the capital

241

mergentibus semper sortem usuris, obrutum fenore

8 esse; videre lucem, forum, civium ora M. Manli
opera; omnia parentum beneficia ab illo se habere;
illi devovere corporis vitaeque ac sanguinis quod
supersit; quodcumque sibi cum patria penatibus
publicis ac privatis iuris fuerit, id cum uno homine

9 esse. His vocibus instincta plebes cum iam unius
hominis esset, addita alia commodioris [1] ad omnia

10 turbanda consilii res. Fundum in Veienti, caput
patrimonii, subiecit praeconi, "ne quem vestrum"
inquit, "Quirites, donec quicquam in re mea supere-
rit, iudicatum addictumve duci patiar." Id vero ita
accendit animos ut per omne fas ac nefas secuturi
vindicem libertatis viderentur.

11 Ad hoc domi contionantis in modum sermones
pleni criminum in patres; inter quos, omisso [2] discrimine vera an vana iaceret, thesauros Gallici auri
occultari a patribus [3] nec iam possidendis publicis
agris contentos esse nisi pecuniam quoque publicam
avertant; ea res si palam fiat, exsolvi plebem aere

12 alieno posse. Quae ubi obiecta spes est, enimvero
indignum facinus videri: cum conferendum ad redi-

---

[1] commodioris A_5 : commotioris Ω : accommodatioris *Wesenberg*.

[2] omisso $_5$ *Drakenborch* : cum omisso Ω.

[3] occultari a patribus *Gronovius* : occultari a patribus iecit (iniecit *U*) Ω.

debt, for the interest always swallowed up the B.C. 385
principal ; that he beheld the light of day, the Forum,
the faces of his fellow citizens, he owed to the
generosity of Marcus Manlius, at whose hands he
had experienced all the loving-kindness of parents ;
to him he solemnly devoted his remaining strength
and life and blood ; what ties soever bound him to
native land and the gods of his state and family,
bound him to one man alone. Excited by these
words, the commons were already at the beck of a
single man, when Manlius did another thing even
better calculated to promote a general embroilment.
For he gave a farm in the Veientine district, which
formed the main part of his fortune, to an auctioneer
to sell,—"that I may not suffer one of your number,
Quirites," said he, "to be condemned, made over,
and carried off to slavery, so long as anything of my
estate remains." At this their ardour was so kindled
that it was clear that in every measure, right or
wrong, they would follow the champion of their
liberty.

Besides this he delivered in his house harangues
that were full of accusation against the patricians ;
amongst other things, he declared, with reckless indifference to truth or falsehood, that the patricians
were concealing treasures of Gallic gold, and were
no longer content with possessing the state lands,
unless they could also divert to their own use the
money of the state—money which, if it were employed for the common weal, would suffice to clear
the plebs of debt. On this hope being held out
to them, the commons felt that they were indeed
ill-used. When, they said, it had been necessary to
raise gold for the redemption of their City from the

243

mendam civitatem a Gallis aurum fuerit, tributo
conlationem factam, idem aurum ex hostibus captum
13 in paucorum praedam cessisse. Itaque exseque-
bantur quaerendo ubi tantae rei furtum occultare-
tur; differentique et tempore suo se indicaturum
dicenti ceteris omissis eo versae erant omnium curae,
apparebatque nec veri indicii gratiam mediam nec
falsi offensionem fore.

XV. Ita suspensis rebus dictator accitus ab
exercitu in urbem venit. Postero die senatu habito
cum satis periclitatus voluntates hominum discedere
senatum ab se vetuisset, stipatus ea multitudine,
sella in comitio posita, viatorem ad M. Manlium
2 misit; qui dictatoris iussu vocatus, cum signum
suis dedisset adesse certamen, agmine ingenti ad
3 tribunal venit. Hinc senatus, hinc plebs, suum
quisque intuentes ducem, velut in acie constiterant.
4 Tum dictator silentio facto : "utinam" inquit "mihi
patribusque Romanis ita de ceteris rebus cum
plebe conveniat, quemadmodum quod ad te attinet
eamque rem quam de te sum quaesiturus conven-
5 turum satis confido. Spem factam a te civitati video
fide incolumi ex thesauris Gallicis, quos primores

Gauls, it had been collected by taxation; but this b.c. 385
same gold, after being captured from the enemy,
had become the spoil of a few. They therefore
persistently demanded to be told where all that
stolen money was hid; and when he put them off
with the promise that he would tell them at the
proper time, they dropped their other concerns and
became one and all so absorbed in this, that it was
evident he would reap no little gratitude if his
report proved true, and no small offence if it turned
out to be false.

XV. Such was the critical state of affairs when
the dictator was sent for from the army and came to
Rome. Next day he held a meeting of the senate,
and having satisfied himself of the people's support,
he commanded the senators not to leave him, and
coming forth with a great company of them into the
Comitium, he there set up his curule chair and
dispatched an officer for Marcus Manlius. Being
thus summoned by order of the dictator, Manlius
signalled to his friends that the struggle was at
hand, and advanced with a great train of followers
to the tribunal. On this side were ranged the
senators, on that the plebs, looking, every man
of them, to his respective leader, as though they
had formed up for battle. Then, having obtained
silence, the dictator began: "I would," said he,
"that I and the senators of Rome might agree with
the plebs in all things else as readily as I am con-
fident we shall do regarding you and the demand
I am about to make of you. I perceive that you
have caused the citizens to hope that the money
which has been lent may be repaid, without injury
to credit, out of Gallic treasure which prominent

patrum occultent, creditum solvi posse. Cui ego
rei tantum abest ut impedimento sim ut contra te,
M. Manli, adhorter, liberes fenore plebem Romanam
et istos incubantes publicis thesauris ex praeda
6 clandestina evolvas. Quod nisi facis, sive ut et ipse
in parte praedae sis sive quia vanum indicium est,
in vincla te duci iubebo nec diutius patiar a te
multitudinem fallaci spe concitari."

7 Ad ea Manlius nec se fefellisse ait, non adversus
Volscos, totiens hostes quotiens patribus expediat,
nec adversus Latinos Hernicosque, quos falsis criminibus in arma agant, sed adversus se ac plebem Roma-
8 nam dictatorem creatum esse ; iam omisso bello quod
simulatum sit, in se impetum fieri ; iam dictatorem
profiteri patrocinium feneratorum adversus plebem ;
iam sibi ex favore multitudinis crimen et perniciem
9 quaeri. "Offendit" inquit "te, A. Corneli, vosque,
patres conscripti, circumfusa turba lateri meo?
Quin eam diducitis[1] a me singuli vestris beneficiis,
intercedendo, eximendo de nervo cives vestros, pro-
hibendo iudicatos addictosque duci, ex eo, quod
afluit opibus vestris sustinendo necessitates aliorum?
10 Sed quid ego vos de vestro impendatis, hortor?
Sortem reliquam[2] ferte : de capite deducite quod
usuris pernumeratum est ; iam nihilo mea turba

---

[1] diducitis *Vorm?* *MPFBOET*[2] (*but* *M* *has* quine audi
ducitis) : deducitis *UHTDLA*.
[2] reliquam *Madvig* : aliquam Ω : aliquando *E.S. Thompson*.

patricians are concealing. This proposal I am so B.C. 385 far from hindering, that on the contrary I exhort you, Marcus Manlius, to free the Roman plebs from usury, and dislodge from their secret hoards those men who are brooding jealously over the public treasure; which if you do not, whether that you may share the spoil yourself, or because your story is a lie, I shall order you into custody, nor suffer you any longer to excite the multitude with delusive hopes."

To this Manlius replied that he had not failed to perceive that the appointment of a dictator was aimed, not at the Volsci, who were enemies whenever it suited the convenience of the patricians, nor at the Latins and Hernici, whom they were driving by false accusations to take up arms, but at himself and the Roman plebs. And now they had dropped their pretended war and were attacking him; now the dictator was coming out as the champion of the money-lenders against the plebs; and they were seeking now to derive from the people's friendliness to him some charge that might lead to his destruction. "Does it offend you," he asked, "Aulus Cornelius, and you, Conscript Fathers, that a crowd attends me? Why do you not take it from me by doing, each of you, acts of kindness, by saving debtors, by rescuing your fellow citizens from prison, by preventing the enslavement of those who have been condemned and assigned, by employing your superfluity of wealth to sustain the necessities of others? But why should I ask of you that you spend of your own money? Receive what is outstanding of the original debts, after deducting from the principal what has been paid in interest, and

247

11 quam ullius conspectior erit. At enim quid ita
solus ego civium curam ago? Nihilo magis quod
respondeam habeo quam si quaeras quid ita solus
Capitolium arcemque servaverim. Et tum universis
12 quam potui opem tuli et nunc singulis feram. Nam
quod ad thesauros Gallicos attinet, rem suapte
natura facilem difficilem interrogatio facit. Cur
enim quaeritis quod scitis? cur quod in sinu vestro
est excuti iubetis potius quam ponatis, nisi aliqua
13 fraus subest? Quo magis argui praestigias iubetis
vestras, eo plus vereor ne abstuleritis observantibus
etiam oculos. Itaque non ego vobis ut indicem
praedas vestras, sed vos id cogendi estis ut in
medium proferatis."

XVI. Cum mittere ambages dictator iuberet et
aut peragere verum indicium cogeret aut fateri
facinus insimulati falso crimine senatus oblataeque
vani furti invidiae, negantem arbitrio inimicorum
2 se locuturum in vincla duci iussit. Arreptus a
viatore "Iuppiter" inquit "optime maxime Iunoque
regina ac Minerva ceterique di deaeque, qui Capitolium arcemque incolitis, sicine vestrum militem ac
praesidem sinitis vexari ab inimicis? Haec dextra,
qua Gallos fudi a delubris vestris, iam in vinclis et
3 catenis erit? Nullius nec oculi nec aures indigni-
tatem ferebant; sed invicta sibi quaedam patientis-

my retinue will soon attract no more notice than any man's. But why, you will ask, am I the only man to be concerned for my fellow citizens? I can no more answer you than if you were to ask why I was the only man to save the Capitol and Citadel. As then—to the best of my ability—I helped the people at large, so now will I help single persons. And touching the Gallic treasure—the thing itself is simple, but your questioning makes it difficult. For why do you ask about a thing you know? Why do you bid us shake out what is in your purses, and not rather lay it down yourselves—unless there is some cheat involved? The more you bid us expose your sleight-of-hand, the more I fear you may have robbed us even of our eyes, while we were watching you. And so it is not I that must be forced to tell of your plunder, but you that must be compelled to give it up."

XVI. But the dictator bade him cease to quibble, and insisted that he should either make his indictment good or confess to the crime of having accused the senate falsely and exposed it to the unmerited odium of a charge of theft; and when Manlius refused to speak at the pleasure of his enemies, he commanded him to be imprisoned. On being arrested by the attendant, Manlius cried out, "Jupiter Optimus Maximus, and Queen Juno and Minerva, and all ye other gods and goddesses that dwell in the Capitol and in the Citadel, is it thus ye suffer your soldier and protector to be tormented by his adversaries? Shall this right arm wherewith I routed the Gauls from your shrines be now chained and fettered?" There was none that could endure to behold or hear this shame; but there were

A.U.C.
369

sima iusti imperii civitas fecerat, nec adversus dictatoriam vim aut tribuni plebis aut ipsa plebs 4 attollere oculos aut hiscere audebant. Coniecto in carcerem Manlio satis constat magnam partem plebis vestem mutasse, multos mortales capillum ac barbam promisisse obversatamque vestibulo carceris maestam turbam.

5 Dictator de Volscis triumphavit, invidiaeque magis triumphus quam gloriae fuit; quippe domi non militiae partum eum actumque de cive non de hoste fremebant: unum defuisse tantum superbiae, quod 6 non M. Manlius ante currum sit ductus. Iamque haud procul seditione res erat; cuius leniendae causa postulante nullo largitor voluntarius repente senatus factus Satricum coloniam duo milia civium Romanorum deduci iussit. Bina iugera et semisses 7 agri adsignati; quod cum et parvum et paucis datum et mercedem esse prodendi M. Manli interpretaren-8 tur, remedio inritatur seditio. Et iam magis insignis et sordibus et facie reorum turba Manliana erat, amotusque post triumphum abdicatione dictaturae terror et linguam et animos liberaverat hominum.

XVII. Audiebantur itaque propalam voces expro-brantium multitudini, quod defensores suos semper

---

1 About one and two-thirds acres. The allotment of Veientine land had been seven *iugera*.

certain rules of conduct which the citizens, deeply B.C. 385
submissive to regular authority, had made inviolable;
nor did either the tribunes of the plebs or the plebs
themselves dare to lift their eyes or open their mouths
against the power of the dictator. But after Manlius
was cast into gaol, it is certain that a great part
of the people put on mourning, and that many men
permitted their hair and beards to grow, and that
a mournful throng hung about the entrance to the
prison.

The dictator triumphed over the Volsci, but
gained more ill-will thereby than glory; for men
murmured that he had earned it, not in the field, but
at home, not over an enemy, but over a citizen; one
thing only had been lacking to his arrogance, in that
Marcus Manlius had not been led before his car. By
this time the feeling was grown well-nigh seditious;
and to appease it the senate—though none demanded
it—became all at once a voluntary giver, and commanded two thousand Roman citizens to be led out
to plant a colony at Satricum. Two *iugera* and a
half [1] of land were allotted them; but since they
chose to regard it as too little, and only given to a
few, and as being the price of Manlius's condemnation, the remedy but aggravated the sedition.
And now the Manlian party were more conspicuous
than before, both for their sordid dress and for the
sorrowful countenances of defendants; men's fears
had been removed by the abdication of the dictator,
following his triumph, and their tongues and spirits
had been set free.

XVII. Accordingly one began to hear the opinion
openly expressed that the people were to blame,
because they always by their favours raised their

in praecipitem locum favore tollat, deinde in ipso
2 discrimine periculi destituat : sic Sp. Cassium in
agros plebem vocantem, sic Sp. Maelium ab ore
civium famem suis impensis propulsantem oppressos,
sic M. Manlium mersam et obrutam fenore partem
civitatis in libertatem ac lucem extrahentem prodi-
3 tum inimicis ; saginare plebem populares suos [1] ut
iugulentur. Hocine patiendum fuisse, si ad nutum
dictatoris non responderit vir consularis ? Fingerent
mentitum ante atque ideo non habuisse quod tum
responderet ; cui servo unquam mendacii poenam
4 vincula fuisse ? Non obversatam esse memoriam
noctis illius quae paene ultima atque aeterna nomini
Romano fuerit ? Non speciem agminis Gallorum per
Tarpeiam rupem scandentis ? Non ipsius M. Manli,
qualem eum armatum, plenum sudoris ac sanguinis,
ipso paene Iove erepto ex hostium manibus vidissent ?
5 Selibrisne farris gratiam servatori patriae relatam ?
Et quem prope caelestem, cognomine certe Capitolino
Iovi parem fecerint eum pati vinctum in carcere, in
tenebris obnoxiam carnificis arbitrio ducere animam ?
Adeo in uno omnibus satis auxilii fuisse, nullam opem
6 in tam multis uni esse ? Iam ne nocte quidem turba
ex eo loco dilabebatur refracturosque carcerem mina-
bantur, cum repente id [2] quod erepturi erant, ex

---

[1] populares suos Ω (*cf. Walters and Conway ad loc.*) :
populares *Duker* : suos *Madvig* : populares viros *Kraffert*.
[2] repente id *Luterbacher* : remisso id Ω : remisso F³ *Douia-
tius Crévier* : remisso eo ς.

---

champions to a dizzy eminence, and then at the B.C. 385
critical juncture left them in the lurch : it had
been so with Spurius Cassius and with Spurius
Maelius, of whom the former was destroyed while
summoning the people to the land, and the latter
while endeavouring at his own expense to stave off
starvation from his fellow citizens; it was so with
Marcus Manlius, who, finding a part of the citizens
overwhelmed and sunk in debt, was dragging them
out into light and liberty, when they betrayed him
to his adversaries; the plebs fattened their own
defenders for the shambles. Was this the penalty
a consular must undergo, if he answered not when
the dictator nodded to him? Let them assume
that he had lied before, and for that reason was
then unable to reply: what slave had ever been
cast into prison for a lie? Did they not recall that
night which had almost been the last eternal night
of the Roman name? Could they not see the line
of Gauls scaling the Tarpeian Rock? Could they
not see Marcus Manlius himself, as they had seen
him, covered with sweat and blood, when he had
rescued as it were Jupiter himself from the hands
of our enemies? Had their half-pound measures
of meal requited the saviour of their country? [1]
Would they suffer one whom they had well-nigh
made a god, and in surname, at any rate, the equal
of Jupiter Capitolinus, to be confined in prison, and
to draw his breath in darkness, at the mercy of the
executioner? When one man had been quite able
to help them all, was there no help in so many men
for one? By this time the crowd would not even
leave the place at night and were threatening that
they would force the gaol, when suddenly, just as

senatus consulto Manlius vinclis liberatur. Quo facto non seditio finita, sed dux seditioni datus est.

7 Per eosdem dies Latinis et Hernicis, simul colonis Circeiensibus et a Velitris, purgantibus se Volsci crimine belli captivosque repetentibus ut suis legibus in eos animadverterent, tristia responsa reddita, tristiora colonis, quod cives Romani patriae oppu- 8 gnandae nefanda consilia inissent. Non negatum itaque tantum de captivis, sed, in quo ab sociis tamen temperaverant, denuntiatum senatus verbis facesserent propere ex urbe ab ore atque oculis populi Romani, ne nihil eos legationis ius, externo non civi comparatum, tegeret.

XVIII. Recrudescente Manliana seditione sub exitum[1] anni comitia habita, creatique tribuni militum consulari potestate Ser.[2] Cornelius Malugi- nensis iterum P. Valerius Potitus iterum M. Furius Camillus quintum Ser. Sulpicius Rufus iterum C. Papirius Crassus T. Quinctius Cincinnatus iterum. 2 Cuius principio anni et patribus et plebi peroppor- tune externa pax data: plebi, quod non avocata dilectu spem cepit, dum tam potentem haberet ducem, fenoris expugnandi: patribus, ne quo externo terrore avocarentur animi ab sanandis domesticis

---

[1] exitum *Madvig*: exitu (*or* excitu) Ω.
[2] Ser. *Sigonius*: sergius Ω.

they were about to rescue Manlius, the senate voted to release him—an act which, instead of ending the sedition, supplied it with a leader.

At about this time came Latins and Hernici, with colonists from Circeii and from Velitrae, to clear themselves of the charge of joining in the Volscian war and to ask for the release of the captives, that they might punish them in accordance with their own laws. They were harshly answered—especially the colonists, because, though Roman citizens, they had formed the impious design of attacking their native country. And so they were not only denied the captives, but received a rebuke which the allies were spared; being commanded in the name of the senate to make haste and depart the City, out of the presence and sight of the Roman People, lest they should find no protection in the rights of envoys, which were meant for foreigners, not for citizens.

XVIII. The sedition of Manlius was breaking out afresh, towards the end of the year, when an election was held which resulted in the choice of the following consular tribunes: Servius Cornelius Maluginensis (for the second time), Publius Valerius Potitus (for the second), Marcus Furius Camillus (for the fifth), Servius Sulpicius Rufus (for the second), Gaius Papirius Crassus, and (for the second time) Titus Quinctius Cincinnatus. The peace which was enjoyed in the early part of this year was equally advantageous to the patricians and to the plebs; to the plebs because, not being called to service by the levy, they had hopes that they might be able under their powerful leader to storm the stronghold of usury; to the patricians, because they desired not to be diverted by any foreign peril from healing the

255

LIVY

3 malis. Igitur cum pars utraque acrior aliquanto
coorta esset, iam [1] propinquum certamen aderat.
Et Manlius advocata domum plebe cum principibus
novandarum rerum interdiu noctuque consilia agitat,
plenior aliquanto animorum irarumque quam antea
4 fuerat. Iram accenderat ignominia recens in animo
ad contumeliam inexperto : spiritus dabat, quod nec
ausus esset idem in se dictator quod in Sp. Maelio
Cincinnatus Quinctius fecisset, et vinculorum suorum
invidiam non dictator modo abdicando dictaturam
fugisset, sed ne senatus quidem sustinere potuisset.
5 His simul inflatus exacerbatusque iam per se accensos
incitabat plebis animos.

"Quousque tandem ignorabitis vires vestras, quas
natura ne beluas quidem ignorare voluit ? Numerate
saltem quot ipsi sitis, quot adversarios habeatis.
6 Quot enim clientes circa singulos fuistis patronos, tot
nunc adversus unum hostem eritis.[2] Si singuli singulos adgressuri essetis, tamen acrius crederem vos pro
libertate quam illos pro dominatione certaturos.
7 Ostendite modo bellum ; pacem habebitis. Videant
vos paratos ad vim ; ius ipsi remittent. Audendum
est aliquid universis, aut omnia singulis patienda.
8 Quousque me circumspectabitis ? Ego quidem nulli
vestrum deero ; ne fortuna mea desit videte. Ipse

---

[1] iam *Gronovius* : iam in *MA*[2] : in Ω.

[2] *The words* Quot enim—eritis *are given their position in
the context by Walters and Conway* : *the MSS. have them after*
certaturos. *The correction was suggested by the omission in*
HTDLA of si singuli singulos adgressuri essetis, *for which*
DL give his (*corruption of* h.s. = hic supple), *while the missing*
words are restored by the correctors of TDA. See Walters and
Conway, ad loc.

sores of the state. Accordingly both sides had taken the field with much more spirit, and the hour of conflict was now at hand. Manlius indeed was inviting the plebeians to his house, and night and day discussing with their leaders plans for accomplishing the revolution, for he was much bolder and more resentful than before. His wrath had been kindled by his recent humiliations, for his pride was a stranger to insult; and his courage had waxed, as he considered that the dictator had not dared to serve him as Quinctius Cincinnatus had served Spurius Maelius, and that his imprisonment had aroused such hatred as not only the dictator had resigned his office to escape, but even the senate had been unable to endure. At once elated and exasperated by these thoughts, he began to work upon the already excited emotions of the plebs.

"How long, pray," he asked them, "will you remain ignorant of your own strength, which nature has willed that even brutes shall know? At least count up your numbers and the number of your adversaries. For as many as you were that gathered as clients about a single patron, so many shall you now be against a single enemy. If you were going to meet them man for man, I should still believe that you would fight more fiercely for your liberty than they for domination. Make but a show of war, and you shall have peace. Let them see you ready to resist, and they will give you your rights of their own accord. We must all unite in some bold stroke, or else, divided, submit to every evil. How long will you keep looking round for me? It is true I shall not fail a single one of you; but you must see to it that fortune fail not me. I myself, your champion,

vindex vester, ubi visum inimicis est, nullus repente fui ; et vidistis in vincula duci universi eum qui a 9 singulis vobis vincula depuleram. Quid sperem, si plus in me audeant inimici ? An exitum Cassi Maelique exspectem ? Bene facitis, quod abominamini. Di prohibebunt haec ; sed nunquam propter me de caelo descendent ; vobis dent mentem oportet ut prohibeatis, sicut mihi dederunt armato togatoque ut vos a barbaris hostibus, a superbis defenderem 10 civibus. Tam parvus animus tanti populi est ut semper vobis auxilium adversus inimicos satis sit, nec ullum, nisi quatenus imperari vobis sinatis, certamen adversus patres noritis ? Nec hoc natura 11 insitum vobis est, sed usu possidemini. Cur enim adversus externos tantum animorum geritis ut imperare illis aequum censeatis ? Quia consuestis cum eis pro imperio certare, adversus hos temptare magis 12 quam tueri libertatem. Tamen, qualescumque duces habuistis, qualescumque ipsi fuistis, omnia adhuc quantacumque petistis, obtinuistis, seu vi seu fortuna 13 vestra. Tempus est etiam [1] maiora conari. Experimini modo et vestram felicitatem et me, ut spero, feliciter expertum ; minore negotio qui imperet patribus imponetis quam qui resisterent imperanti- 14 bus imposuistis. Solo aequandae sunt dictaturae

---

[1] etiam Ω : omitted by *O* : iam *Gronovius.*

was suddenly brought to naught, when it pleased B.C. 384 your enemies; and you all beheld that man dragged off to prison who had protected each of yourselves from imprisonment. What can I expect, if my enemies grow bolder? Must I look forward to dying like Cassius and Maelius? You do well to express abhorrence. The gods *will* forbid such a thing; but they will never come down from heaven on my account; they must give you the inspiration to forbid it, as they gave me, in war and in peace, the inspiration to defend you from the barbarity of your foes and the arrogance of your fellow citizens. Is there so little spirit in this great people that you are always satisfied with the help your tribunes lend you against your adversaries, and never quarrel with the senators, save as to the length you will suffer them to go in ruling you? And this is no native trait in you, but you are slaves by use. Why, pray, are you so high and mighty with foreigners as to deem your-selves meet to be their lords? It is because you have been used to vie with them for sovereignty; but against these men, though you make attempts at gaining your liberty, you are not used to defend it. Nevertheless, with such leaders as you have had, and such courage as you yourselves could muster, you have thus far obtained, by violence or good fortune, whatever you have sought. The time has come to attempt even greater things. Do but make trial of your own good fortune and of me, whom, as I think, you have already happily proved; you will find it less trouble to impose a ruler on the patricians, than you encountered in imposing tribunes on them to resist their rule. Dictatorships and consulships must be levelled with

259

consulatusque, ut caput attollere Romana plebes
possit. Proinde adeste; prohibete ius de pecuniis
dici; ego me patronum profiteor plebis, quod mihi
15 cura mea et fides nomen induit: vos si quo insigni
magis imperii honorisve nomine vestrum appellabitis
ducem, eo utemini potentiore ad obtinenda ea quae
16 voltis." Inde de regno agendi ortum initium dicitur;
sed nec cum quibus nec quem ad finem consilia
pervenerint satis planum traditur.

XIX. At in parte altera senatus de secessione in
domum privatam plebis, forte etiam in arce positam,
2 et imminenti mole libertati[1] agitat. Magna pars
vociferantur Servilio Ahala opus esse, qui non in
vincla duci iubendo inritet publicum hostem sed
3 unius iactura civis finiat intestinum bellum. De-
curritur ad leniorem verbis sententiam, vim tamen
eandem habentem, ut videant magistratus ne quid
ex perniciosis consiliis M. Manli res publica detri-
4 menti capiat. Tum tribuni consulari potestate
tribunique plebi—nam et ei,[2] quia eundem suae[3]
potestatis, quem libertatis omnium, finem cernebant,
patrum auctoritati se dediderant—hi tum[4] omnes
5 quid opus facto sit consultant. Cum praeter vim et
caedem nihil cuiquam occurreret, eam autem ingentis
dimicationis fore appareret, tum M. Menenius et Q.
6 Publilius[5] tribuni plebis: "Quid patrum et plebis

---

[1] libertati ς: libertatis Ω.
[2] et ei *Crévier and Stroth*: et Ω: ei *U*: ex *B*: *erased in F.*
[3] suae *Walters and Conway*: et suae Ω.
[4] hi tum *E*ς: hii tum Ω: ii tum *P²U*: ii tantum *F?B*:
hi tantum *F³*.   [5] Publilius *Glareanus*: publius Ω.

the ground, that the Roman plebs may be enabled B.C. 384
to lift its head. Stand by me, then; prevent all
court-proceedings regarding moneys; I avow myself
the patron of the commons—a title with which my
zeal and loyalty have invested me: if you choose to
give your leader a more striking title of authority
or honour, you will find him the more able to make
good your wishes." It was thus, they say, that the
agitation for kingly power was begun; but there
is no very clear tradition with whom or to what
length his plans were matured.

XIX. On the other side the senate were discussing
the secret gathering of the plebs in a private house
—a house, too, that, as it happened, was situated in
the Citadel—and the grave danger that threatened
liberty. The majority exclaimed that a Servilius
Ahala was needed, one who would not exasperate
a public enemy by ordering his imprisonment, but
would sacrifice a single citizen to end a domestic war.
However, they had recourse to a proposal which
sounded milder, though its force was identical,
namely, that the magistrates should see to it that the
republic took no harm by the ruinous devices of
Marcus Manlius. Thereupon the consular tribunes
and the tribunes of the plebs—for they too, perceiving
that their own authority would come to an end with
the general liberty, had made their submission to
the Fathers—all these men, I say, thereupon took
counsel together, what was needful to be done.
They could none of them see any way but violence
and bloodshed, which would clearly involve a mighty
struggle, when Marcus Menenius and Quintus Publilius, tribunes of the plebs, addressed them as follows:
" Why do we make a conflict between patricians and

certamen facimus, quod civitatis esse adversus unum
pestiferum civem debet? Quid cum plebe adgredimur,
eum quem per ipsam plebem tutius adgredi est ut
7 suis ipse oneratus viribus ruat? Diem dicere ei nobis
in animo est. Nihil minus populare quam regnum
est. Simul multitudo illa non secum certari viderint
et ex advocatis iudices facti erunt et accusatores de
plebe patricium reum intuebuntur et regni crimen
in medio, nulli magis quam libertati favebunt suae."

XX. Adprobantibus cunctis diem Manlio dicunt.
Quod ubi est factum, primo commota plebs est,
2 utique postquam sordidatum reum viderunt nec cum
eo non modo patrum quemquam sed ne cognatos
quidem aut adfines, postremo ne fratres quidem A.
et T. Manlios, quod ad eum diem nunquam usu
venisset, ut in tanto discrimine non et proximi
3 vestem mutarent: Ap. Claudio in vincula ducto C.
Claudium inimicum Claudiamque omnem gentem
sordidatam fuisse; consensu opprimi popularem
virum, quod primus a patribus ad plebem defecisset.
4   Cum dies venit, quae praeter coetus multitudinis
seditiosasque voces et largitionem et fallax indicium
pertinentia proprie ad regni crimen ab accusatoribus
obiecta sint reo, apud neminem auctorem invenio;

plebeians out of what ought to be the quarrel of the B.C. 384
state with a single pestilent citizen? Why in attacking
him do we attack the plebs as well, when it is safer to
attack him by the help of this same plebs, that his
very strength may bring about his ruin? We propose
to summon him to trial. Nothing is less popular than
kingly power. As soon as the populace, perceiving
that our quarrel is not with them, are changed
from supporters into judges, and see that the prosecu-
tors are plebeians, the defendant a patrician, and the
accusation that of seeking to set up a kingdom, they
will not favour any man at the expense of their own
liberty."

XX. This argument won universal approbation,
and Manlius was indicted. The first effect of this was
to rouse great feeling in the commons, especially
when they saw the defendant meanly clad and not
attended by a single senator, or even by his kinsmen
or connexions, or indeed by his own brothers, Aulus
and Titus Manlius. That a man's nearest friends
should not join him in assuming mourning in an hour
so fraught with danger to him, was something that
had never until that day occurred. They remembered
that on the imprisonment of Appius Claudius, his
enemy Gaius Claudius and all the Claudian family had
gone into mourning; and they concluded that there
must be a general conspiracy to put down the people's
friend because he had been the first to forsake the
patricians for the plebs.

The day of the trial came, but I do not find it
stated in any authority what facts were alleged by
his accusers that bore directly on the charge of
plotting to establish a kingdom, except gatherings
of the populace and seditious expressions and his

263

LIVY

5 nec dubito haud parva fuisse, cum damnandi mora
plebi non in causa sed in loco fuerit. Illud no-
tandum videtur, ut sciant homines quae et quanta
decora foeda cupiditas regni non ingrata solum sed
6 invisa etiam reddiderit: homines prope quadrin-
gentos produxisse dicitur, quibus sine fenore ex-
pensas pecunias tulisset, quorum bona venire, quos
7 duci addictos prohibuisset; ad haec decora quoque
belli non commemorasse tantum sed protulissse etiam
conspicienda, spolia hostium caesorum ad triginta,
dona imperatorum ad quadraginta, in quibus insignes
8 duas murales coronas, civicas octo; ad hoc servatos
ex hostibus cives [1] inter quos C. Servilium magistrum
equitum absentem nominatum; et cum ea quoque quae
bello gesta essent pro fastigio rerum oratione etiam
magnifica, facta dictis aequando, memorasset, nudasse
9 pectus insigne cicatricibus bello acceptis et identidem
Capitolium spectans Iovem deosque alios devocasse
ad auxilium fortunarum suarum precatusque [2] esse
ut, quam mentem sibi Capitolinam arcem protegenti
ad salutem populi Romani dedissent, eam populo
Romano in suo discrimine darent, et orasse singulos
universosque ut Capitolium atque arcem intuentes,
ut ad deos immortales versi, de se iudicarent.
10   In campo Martio cum centuriatim populus cita-

---

[1] cives *Rhenanus*: ciues produxit (*or* produx̄) Ω.
[2] precatusque *Rhenanus*: precatumque Ω : peccatumque
E.

---

[1] The Campus Martius, from which they could see the
Capitol (*cf.* § 10).
[2] A mural crown was conferred on the soldier who was the
first to scale the enemy's wall, a civic crown on one who had
saved a fellow citizen (Aulus Gellius v. vi. 11).
[3] The *comitia centuriata* being a military organisation might

largesses and false witness ; and yet I doubt not they B.C. 381
were of moment, since the reluctance of the plebs to
condemn him was not owing to his cause but to the
place.[1] One thing appears worthy of remark, that
men may know what great and glorious achievements
a vile lust for regal power rendered not merely thankless but actually hateful. It is said that he brought
forward nearly four hundred men to whom he had
lent money without interest, thus saving their goods
from being sold and their persons from enslavement ;
that besides this the military distinctions which he not
only enumerated but produced for all to see, comprised the spoils of thirty enemies whom he had slain,
and some forty decorations from his generals, amongst
which were conspicuous two mural and eight civic
crowns ;[2] that he told, besides, of citizens saved from
the enemy, and among these named Gaius Servilius,
the master of the horse, who was not present. And
after rehearsing his services in war, in a speech as
magnificent as the height of his achievements and
equalling his deeds with its words, he is said to have
bared his breast, marked with the scars of battle, and
gazing at the Capitol to have called on Jupiter and
the other gods to help him, that they might inspire
the Roman People in his hour of danger with the
same spirit they had given him when he defended
the Capitoline Hill ; and to have implored the Romans
one and all to fix their eyes on the Capitol and
Citadel, and turn to the immortal gods while they
judged him.

In the Campus Martius, when the people were
being called by centuries,[3] and the defendant,

not assemble within the pomerium. The meeting referred to
in the preceding paragraph was a *contio.*

retur et reus ad Capitolium manus tendens ab
hominibus ad deos preces avertisset, apparuit tribunis, nisi oculos quoque hominum liberasset tanti
memoria decoris, nunquam fore in praeoccupatis
11 beneficio animis vero crimini locum. Ita prodicta
die in Petelinum lucum extra portam Flumentanam,
unde conspectus in Capitolium non esset, concilium
populi indictum est. Ibi crimen valuit et obstinatis
animis triste iudicium invisumque etiam iudicibus
12 factum. Sunt qui per duumviros, qui de perduel-
lione anquirerent creatos, auctores sint damnatum.
Tribuni de saxo Tarpeio deiecerunt; locusque idem
in uno homine et eximiae gloriae monumentum et
poenae ultimae fuit.

13   Adiectae mortuo notae sunt: publica una, quod,
cum domus eius fuisset ubi nunc aedes atque
officina Monetae est, latum ad populum est ne quis
14 patricius in arce aut Capitolio habitaret; gentilicia
altera, quod gentis Manliae decreto cautum est ne
quis deinde M. Manlius vocaretur. Hunc exitum
habuit vir, nisi in libera civitate natus esset, me-
15 morabilis. Populum brevi, postquam periculum ab
eo nullum erat, per se ipsas recordantem virtutes
desiderium eius tenuit. Pestilentia etiam brevi con-
secuta nullis occurrentibus tantae cladis causis ex
16 Manliano supplicio magnae parti videri orta: vio-

---

¹ The *Porta Flumentana* was at a point in the wall between
the Aventine and the Capitoline.

² For another instance of this procedure, see I. xxvi. 5.

³ The temple of Juno Moneta, vowed by Lucius Furius
Camillus (345 B.C.) was dedicated June 1st, 344. Money
was coined in this temple.

⁴ As a matter of fact, no patrician Marcus Manlius of a
later date is known to us.

stretching forth his hands to the Capitol, had turned B.C. 384
from men to make his prayers to the gods, the tribunes clearly saw that unless they could also eman-
cipate men's eyes from the associations of so glorious
a deed, no accusation, however true, could ever find
lodgment in their grateful hearts.   And so they adjourned the day of trial and appointed a council of
the people to meet in the Peteline Wood outside the
Flumentane Gate,[1] whence no prospect of the Capitol
was afforded.   There they made good their charge ;
men steeled their hearts and pronounced a dolorous
judgment, abhorrent to the very ones who rendered
it.   Some authorities assert that he was condemned
by duumvirs appointed to deal with a charge of
treason.[2] The tribunes flung him from the Tarpeian
Rock, and the same spot served to commemorate
extraordinary fame and the extremity of punishment,
as experienced by the self-same man.

   To his death were added marks of ignominy : one
of a public nature, because the people were asked to
vote that, since his house had stood where the temple
and mint of Moneta now are,[3] no patrician might
dwell in the Citadel or the Capitol ; the other
proceeding from his family, in that the Manlian clan
made a decree forbidding anyone thenceforth to
bear the name of Marcus Manlius.[4] Such was the
end of a man who, had he not been born in a free
state, would have left a memorable name.   In a short
time the people, remembering—now that he was no
longer a source of danger—only his good qualities,
regretted him.   Moreover a pestilence soon ensued,
and occasioned a mortality out of all proportion to
any visible causes, and this many people ascribed to
the execution of Manlius : the Capitol, they said, had

latum Capitolium esse sanguine servatoris nec dis
cordi fuisse poenam eius oblatam prope oculis suis,
a quo sua templa erepta e manibus hostium essent.

XXI. Pestilentiam inopia frugum et volgatam
utriusque mali famam anno insequente multiplex
bellum excepit L. Valerio quartum A. Manlio
tertium Ser. Sulpicio tertium L. Lucretio,[1] L.
Aemilio tertium M. Trebonio tribunis militum con-
2 sulari potestate. Hostes novi praeter Volscos, velut
sorte quadam prope in aeternum exercendo Romano
militi datos, Circeiosque et Velitras colonias iam diu
molientes defectionem et suspectum Latium Lanu-
vini etiam, quae fidelissima urbs fuerat, subito
3 exorti. Id patres rati contemptu accidere, quod
Veliternis civibus suis tam diu impunita defectio
esset, decreverunt ut primo quoque tempore ad
4 populum ferretur de bello eis indicendo. Ad quam
militiam quo paratior plebes esset, quinqueviros
Pomptino agro dividendo et triumviros Nepete
5 coloniae deducendae creaverunt. Tum, ut bellum
iuberent, latum ad populum est et nequiquam dis-
suadentibus tribunis plebis omnes tribus bellum
6 iusserunt. Apparatum eo anno bellum est, exercitus
propter pestilentiam non eductus, eaque cunctatio
colonis spatium dederat deprecandi senatum; et
magna hominum pars eo ut legatio supplex Romam

---

[1] Lucretio (*or* -cio) Ω : Lucretio tertium *Glareanus.*

---

[1] Livy has perhaps made a slip in ascribing this action to
the *tribes*, as it was regularly the assembly of *centuries* which
declared war.

been polluted by the blood of its saviour, and the B.C. 384
gods had not been pleased that the man who had
rescued their temples from the hands of the enemy,
should be punished almost under their very eyes.

XXI. The pestilence was succeeded by a scarcity B.C. 383
of corn, and in the following year, when the rumour
of these two misfortunes had got abroad, by various
wars. The consular tribunes were Lucius Valerius
(for the fourth time), Aulus Manlius (for the third),
Servius Sulpicius (for the third), Lucius Lucretius,
Lucius Aemilius (for the third time) and Marcus Trebonius. Besides the Volsci, who had been provided,
as it were by a kind of fatality, to furnish perpetual
occupation for the Roman arms, and the colonies of
Circei and Velitrae, which had long been scheming
a rebellion, and the Latins, whose loyalty was suspected, a new enemy suddenly rose up at Lanuvium,
a city which until then had been very faithful.
Believing that they were now actuated by contempt,
on finding the revolt of the Veliterni, who were
Roman citizens, to go so long unpunished, the senate
decreed that a proposal should be laid before the
people, at the earliest possible moment, for declaring
war on them; and, to make the plebs readier for
this campaign, they appointed five commissioners to
divide up the Pomptine land, and three to conduct
a colony to Nepete. They then asked the people
for a declaration of war, and notwithstanding the
opposition of the plebeian tribunes, all the tribes
voted for war.[1] Preparations for the campaign were
made that year, but owing to the pestilence the
army did not take the field. This delay would have
given the colonists time to sue the senate for pardon—
and in fact a majority of them were in favour of

7 mitteretur inclinabat, ni privato, ut fit, periculo
publicum implicitum esset auctoresque defectionis
ab Romanis metu, ne soli crimini subiecti piacula
irae Romanorum dederentur, avertissent colonias a
8 consiliis pacis. Neque in senatu[1] solum per eos
legatio impedita est sed magna pars plebis incitata
ut praedatum in agrum Romanum exirent. Haec
9 nova iniuria exturbavit omnem spem pacis. De
Praenestinorum quoque defectione eo anno primum
fama exorta; arguentibusque eos Tusculanis et
Gabinis et Labicanis, quorum in fines incursatum
erat, ita placide ab senatu responsum est ut minus
credi de criminibus, quia nollent ea vera esse,
appareret.

XXII. Insequenti anno Sp. et L. Papirii[2] novi
tribuni militum consulari potestate Velitras legiones
duxere, quattuor collegis Ser. Cornelio Maluginensi
tertium Q. Servilio C. Sulpicio L. Aemilio quartum,[3]
ad praesidium urbis et si qui ex Etruria novi motus
nuntiarentur—omnia enim inde suspecta erant—
2 relictis. Ad Velitras adversus maiora paene auxilia
Praenestinorum quam ipsam colonorum multitudinem
secundo proelio pugnatum est ita ut propinquitas
urbis hosti et causa maturioris fugae et unum ex
3 fuga receptaculum esset. Oppidi oppugnatione
tribuni abstinuere, quia et anceps erat nec in perniciem coloniae pugnandum censebant. Litterae

---

[1] in senatu ς : in senatum Ω.
[2] Papirii ς : papirius (or -pyr-) Ω : papilius T.
[3] quartum ς : quartum tribunis Ω.

sending an embassy to Rome to make submission— B.C. 383
but danger to the commonwealth was bound up, as
often happens, with that of individuals, and the ring-
leaders of the revolt were so afraid of the Romans—
lest they alone might be charged with the crime and
offered up as a sacrifice to Roman indignation—that
they turned the colonies away from peaceful counsels.
Moreover, not content with merely opposing the
embassy in their senate, they egged on a great part
of the commons to go out and pillage the Roman
lands; and this new outrage destroyed all hope of
peace. The Praenestines, too, were that year, for
the first time, reported as disloyal; evidence against
them was given by the Tusculans, the Gabini, and
the Labicani, whose borders they had invaded; but
the senate returned so mild an answer that it was
evident that they refused to believe in the charges
because they wished them not to be true.

XXII. The next year Spurius and Lucius Papirius, B.C.
the new consular tribunes, led the levies to Velitrae, 382–381
while their four colleagues, Servius Cornelius Maluginensis (in his third term), Quintus Servilius, Gaius
Sulpicius, and Lucius Aemilius (in his fourth term),
remained behind to protect the City and to guard
against any fresh commotion which might be reported
from Etruria—a quarter from which everything was
suspected. Near Velitrae the Romans defeated an
army in which auxiliaries from Praeneste almost out-
numbered the colonists themselves; but the city was
so close at hand that, as it occasioned their early
retreat, so it afforded them their only refuge. The
tribunes abstained from attacking the place; they
were not certain of succeeding, nor did they think it
right to aim at the extermination of the colony. In

Romam ad senatum cum victoriae nuntiis acriores
in Praenestinum quam in Veliternum hostem missae.

4   Itaque ex senatus consulto populique iussu bellum
Praenestinis indictum; qui coniuncti Volscis anno
insequente Satricum, coloniam populi Romani, per-
tinaciter a colonis defensam, vi expugnarunt foede-
5 que in captis exercuere victoriam. Eam rem aegre
passi Romani M. Furium Camillum sextum[1] tribunum militum creavere. Additi collegae A. et L.
Postumii Regillenses[2] ac L. Furius cum L. Lucretio
et M. Fabio Ambusto.

6   Volscum bellum M. Furio extra ordinem decretum; adiutor ex tribunis sorte L. Furius datur,
non tam e re publica quam ut collegae materia ad
omnem laudem esset et publice, quod rem temeritate
eius prolapsam restituit et privatim, quod ex errore
gratiam potius eius sibi quam suam gloriam petiit.[3]

7 Exactae iam aetatis Camillus erat, comitiisque iurare
parato in verba excusandae valetudini solita[4] consensus populi restiterat; sed vegetum ingenium in
vivido pectore vigebat virebatque integris sensibus,
et civiles iam res haud magnopere obeuntem bella
8 excitabant. Quattuor legionibus quaternum milium

---

[1] sextum (vi) Ω: vi (*or* iii)*P*: iii *O?E*: septimum (vii) ς
Drakenborch.

[2] Regillenses *Mommsen C.I.L.* 1¹ *p.* 444 *marg.*: regilienses
Ω: religienses *UHDLA.*

[3] petiit ς; petit Ω.

[4] solita *Rhenanus*: solitae (*or* -te) Ω: litae (*or* -te)
HDTLA.

the letter which they sent to the senate in Rome, announcing the victory, they were more severe upon the enemies from Praeneste than upon those of Velitrae.

And so, by resolution of the senate and popular enactment, war was proclaimed against the people of Praeneste; who, uniting in the following year with the Volsci, attacked the Roman colony of Satricum, and having carried it, despite the obstinate resistance of the colonists, abused their victory by cruel treatment of the captives. This incensed the Romans, and they elected Marcus Furius Camillus tribune of the soldiers, for the sixth time. To be his colleagues they gave him Aulus and Lucius Postumius Regillensis and Lucius Furius, together with Lucius Lucretius and Marcus Fabius Ambustus.

The Volscian war was entrusted, out of the regular course, to Marcus Furius. Of the other tribunes, Lucius Furius was assigned him by lot for his assistant, not so much (it should seem) for the good of the commonwealth, as that he might be the source of all honour to his colleague; who gained it in his public capacity because he made good what the other's rashness had lost, and as a man because he used the error of Lucius to earn his gratitude rather than glory for himself. Camillus was now extremely old. At the election he was prepared to excuse himself by taking the customary oath on the score of health, had not the unanimous wishes of the people prevented him. But a lusty spirit flourished in his sturdy breast, and his senses were as keen as ever; and though he no longer much concerned himself with politics, wars excited him. He enrolled four legions, each of four thousand men, appointed

273

scriptis, exercitu indicto ad portam Esquilinam in
posteram diem, ad Satricum profectus. Ibi eum ex-
pugnatores coloniae haudquaquam perculsi, fidentes
militum numero, quo aliquantum praestabant opperie-
9 bantur. Postquam appropinquare Romanos senserunt,
extemplo in aciem procedunt, nihil dilaturi quin
periculum summae rerum facerent: ita paucitati
hostium nihil artes imperatoris unici, quibus solis
confiderent, profuturas esse.

XXIII. Idem ardor et in Romano exercitu erat
et in altero duce, nec praesentis dimicationis fortunam ulla res praeterquam unius viri consilium
atque imperium morabatur, qui occasionem iuvan-
darum ratione virium trahendo bello quaerebat.
2 Eo magis hostis instare nec iam pro castris tantum
suis explicare aciem sed procedere in medium campi
et vallo prope hostium signa inferendo superbam
3 fiduciam virium ostentare. Id aegre patiebatur
Romanus miles, multo aegrius alter ex tribunis
militum, L. Furius, ferox cum aetate et ingenio
tum multitudinis ex incertissimo sumentis animos
4 spe inflatus. Hic per se iam milites incitatos insuper instigabat elevando, qua una poterat, aetate
auctoritatem collegae, iuvenibus bella data dictitans
et cum corporibus vigere et deflorescere animos;
5 cunctatorem ex acerrimo bellatore factum et, qui
adveniens castra urbesque primo impetu rapere sit

the army to assemble on the following day B.C. 382–381
at the Esquiline Gate, and marched on Satricum.
There the conquerors of the colony were waiting for
him, undismayed, for they confided in their numbers,
in which they possessed a considerable superiority.
On perceiving the approach of the Romans they
formed up at once. It was their purpose to engage
immediately in a decisive battle; for so the numer-
ical weakness of their enemies would derive no help
from the skill of their unique commander, which
constituted—so they assumed—their sole reliance.

XXIII. There was the same ardour in the Roman
army, and in one of its generals. The hazard of an
immediate battle was only postponed by the wisdom
and the authority of one man, who sought an opportunity to supplement his resources with strategy, by
prolonging the campaign. This made the enemy the
more urgent, and, no longer content with deploying
their line before the camp, they advanced into
the middle of the field, and, marching up almost to
the rampart of the Romans, displayed the proud confidence which their strength gave them. The Roman
soldiers were mortified at this, and even more mortified was one of their two tribunes, Lucius Furius.
His youth and native disposition made him head
strong, and the utterly baseless enthusiasm of the
rank and file filled him with assurance. The soldiers
were already in a state of excitement, but he further
instigated them by disparaging his colleague in the
only possible way, on the score of age. Wars, he
insisted, were the province of youth; the growth and
decay of the spirit kept pace with those of the body;
the most energetic of soldiers was become a procras-
tinator, and he who had been wont to storm a camp

275

solitus, eum residem intra vallum tempus terere,
quid accessurum suis decessurumve hostium viribus
6 sperantem? Quam occasionem, quod tempus, quem
insidiis instruentem[1] locum? Frigere ac torpere
7 senis consilia. Sed Camillo cum vitae satis tum
gloriae esse; quid attinere cum mortali corpore
uno civitatis, quam immortalem esse deceat, pati
consenescere vires?

8 His sermonibus tota in se averterat castra, et
cum omnibus locis posceretur pugna, "Sustinere"
inquit, "M. Furi, non possumus impetum militum,
et hostis, cuius animos cunctando auximus, iam
minime toleranda superbia insultat; cede unus
omnibus et patere te vinci consilio ut maturius bello
9 vincas." Ad ea Camillus, quae bella suo unius
auspicio gesta ad eam diem essent, negare in eis
neque se neque populum Romanum aut consilii sui
aut fortunae paenituisse; nunc scire se collegam
habere iure imperioque parem, vigore aetatis prae-
10 stantem; itaque se quod ad exercitum attineat,
regere consuesse, non regi: collegae imperium se
non posse impedire. Dis bene iuvantibus ageret
11 quod e re publica duceret: aetati suae se veniam
eam[2] petere, ne in prima acie esset; quae senis
munia in bello sint, iis se non defuturum. Id a

---

[1] instruentem Ω: instruendis *Gron.* : instruendis quaer-
entem *Alschefski.*

[2] eam *Tanaquil Faber* : etiam Ω.

or a city on the first approach, was sitting still and
wasting time behind intrenchments. What accession
to his own strength did he look for, or what diminu-
tion of the enemy's? What opportunity, what
favourable moment, what ground for an ambush was
he making ready? The old man's strategy was cold
and torpid. But why, though Camillus had had
enough both of life and of glory, should they permit
the state, which ought to be immortal, to sink into
decrepitude in company with the mortal body of
one man?

When he had won over the entire army by these
speeches, and the men were everywhere demanding
battle, he said to his colleague: "Marcus Furius,
we can no longer resist the enthusiasm of the
soldiers; and the enemy, whose courage we have
augmented by our delay, is insulting us with an
arrogance no longer to be endured. Give way, for
you are alone against us all, and suffer yourself to
be overcome in counsel, that you may overcome the
sooner in war." To this Camillus replied that in
the wars which up to that day had been conducted
under his sole auspices neither the Roman People
nor himself had repented of his strategy or fortune;
he was aware that he had now a colleague of equal
commission and authority, and of more vigorous
years; and so, although—as regarded the army—he
was accustomed not to be governed but to govern,
yet he had no power to thwart the commands of his
associate. Let him proceed, with Heaven's blessing,
to do what he thought best for the commonwealth:
for his own grey hairs he begged this favour, that
he might not be assigned to the front; of such
duties as belonged to an old man he would not be

dis immortalibus precari ne qui casus suum consilium
laudabile efficiat.

12   Nec ab hominibus salutaris sententia nec a dis
tam piae preces auditae sunt.   Primam aciem auctor
pugnae instruit, subsidia Camillus firmat validamque
stationem pro castris opponit ; ipse edito loco spec-
tator intentus in eventum alieni consilii constitit.
XXIV. Simul primo concursu concrepuere arma,
2 hostis dolo non metu pedem rettulit.   Lenis ab
tergo clivus erat inter aciem et castra ; et, quod
multitudo suppeditabat, aliquot validas cohortes in
castris armatas instructasque reliquerant, quae inter
commissum iam certamen, ubi vallo appropinquasset
3 hostis, erumperent.   Romanus cedentem hostem effuse
sequendo in locum iniquum pertractus opportunus
huic eruptioni fuit ; versus itaque in victorem terror
et novo hoste et supina valle Romanam inclinavit
4 aciem.   Instant Volsci recentes qui e castris impetum
fecerant ; integrant et illi pugnam qui simulata
cesserant fuga.   Iam non recipiebat se Romanus miles
sed immemor recentis ferociae veterisque decoris
terga passim dabat atque effuso cursu castra re-
5 petebat, cum Camillus subiectus ab circumstantibus
in equum et raptim subsidiis oppositis " Haec est "
inquit, " milites, pugna, quam poposcistis ?   Quis
6 homo, quis deus est quem accusare possitis ?   Vestra
278

B.C.
382-381

negligent. One thing he entreated of the immortal
gods : that no mischance might occur, to make his
own appear to have been the wiser plan. But
neither did men heed these salutary words, nor the
immortal gods his loyal prayers. The man responsible for the engagement marshalled the battle-line.
Camillus provided adequate supports, and stationed
a strong out-guard before the camp; he then took
up his post on an eminence, and watched intently
for the issue of another's strategy. XXIV. At the
very instant of the first clash of arms the enemy
gave ground, not out of fear, but guile. Behind
them the ground sloped gently up from the battle-
line to their camp ; and having plenty of men they
had left a few strong cohorts armed and drawn up
within the camp, which were to sally forth when
the fighting had got under way, and the Romans
had approached the rampart. The Romans pursued
the retreating enemy without order, and were drawn
into an unfavourable position, where this attack
could be made upon them with advantage. Thus
the victors were threatened in their turn, and, what
with the new foe and the declivity, the Roman line
gave way. They were closely pressed by the fresh
Volsci who had made the sortie, and those, too, who
had pretended flight renewed the battle. And now
the Roman soldiers were no longer retiring in order,
but regardless of their late impetuosity and their
ancient fame, had turned their backs and were
everywhere in full flight towards the camp; when
Camillus was lifted into the saddle by his attendants,
and rapidly throwing his reserves into the fight,
"Soldiers," he cried, "is this the battle you
demanded? What man, what god is there, whom

illa temeritas, vestra ignavia haec est.   Secuti alium
ducem sequimini nunc Camillum et quod ductu meo
soletis vincite.   Quid vallum et castra spectatis?
Neminem vestrum illa nisi victorem receptura sunt."

7   Pudor primo tenuit effusos; inde, ut circumagi
signa obvertique aciem viderunt in hostem, et dux,
praeterquam quod tot insignis triumphis, etiam aetate
venerabilis inter prima signa ubi pluribus labor
periculumque erat se offerebat, increpare singuli se
quisque et alios, et adhortatio in vicem totam alacri

8 clamore pervasit aciem.   Neque alter tribunus rei
defuit sed missus a collega restituente peditum
aciem ad equites, non castigando—ad quam rem
leviorem auctorem eum culpae societas fecerat—
sed ab imperio totus ad preces versus orare singulos
universosque ut se reum fortunae eius diei crimine

9 eximerent: "Abnuente ac prohibente collega temeritati[1] me omnium potius socium quam unius
prudentiae dedi.   Camillus in utraque vestra fortuna
suam gloriam videt; ego, ni restituitur pugna, quod
miserrimum est, fortunam cum omnibus infamiam

10 solus sentiam."   Optimum visum est in fluctuante
acie[2] tradi equos et pedestri pugna invadere hostem.
Eunt insignes armis animisque qua premi parte

---

[1] temeritati T^2_5: temeritatis Ω: temeritatos H.
[2] in fluctuante acie *Heerwagen*: in fluctuantem aciem
(aciem *omitted by* H) Ω: inter fluctuantem aciem *Gronovius*.

B.C.
382–381

you could accuse? Yours was the rashness then, now the infamy is yours. You have followed another leader: follow now Camillus, and, as your habit is when I am leading, conquer. Why do you look on the rampart and the camp? Not one of you shall find entrance there, save as a victor."

A sense of shame at first checked their headlong flight; then, as they saw the standards face about and the line form up against the enemy, while their general, distinguished for his many triumphs and rendered venerable by his age, exposed himself at the front amidst the ensigns, where the fighting and the danger were the greatest, they began each and every one to cry out against themselves and their fellows, and their mutual encouragements ran through the entire army in a ringing cheer. Nor was the other tribune behindhand, but being sent by his colleague—who was re-forming the line of foot—to rally the horse, he did not chide them—for his share in their fault would have made this of little use—but turning wholly from commands to entreaties, he besought them one and all to save him from the guilt of that day's mishap, for which he was responsible. "Notwithstanding," he said, "the refusal and the opposition of my colleague, I gave my adhesion to the general recklessness in preference to the prudence of one man. Camillus sees glory for himself, whichever way your fortune turns; but I, if the battle is not restored, shall experience the utter misery of sharing with everybody the disaster, while enduring the infamy alone." It seemed best, as the battle-line was wavering, to dismiss the horses and attack the enemy on foot. Conspicuous for their arms and their courage, they advanced where

A.U.C.
372-373

maxime peditum copias vident. Nihil neque apud
duces neque apud milites remittitur a summo cer-
11 tamine animi. Sensit ergo eventus virtutis enixae
opem, et Volsci, qua modo simulato metu cesserant,
ea in veram fugam effusi, magna pars et in ipso
certamine et post in fuga caesi, ceteri in castris,
quae capta eodem impetu sunt; plures tamen capti
quam occisi.

XXV. Ubi in recensendis captivis cum Tusculani
aliquot noscitarentur, secreti ab aliis ad tribunos
adducuntur percontantibusque fassi publico consilio
2 se militasse. Cuius tam vicini belli metu Camillus
motus extemplo se Romam captivos ducturum ait,
ne patres ignari sint Tusculanos ab societate descisse :
castris exercituique interim, si videatur, praesit col-
3 lega. Documento unus dies fuerat, ne sua consilia
melioribus praeferret ; nec tamen aut ipsi aut in
exercitu cuiquam satis placato animo Camillus laturus
culpam eius videbatur, qua data in tam praecipitem
4 casum res publica esset ; et cum in exercitu tum
Romae constans omnium fama erat, cum varia fortuna in Volscis gesta res esset, adversae pugnae
fugaeque in L. Furio culpam, secundae decus omne
5 penes M. Furium esse. Introductis in senatum
captivis cum bello persequendos Tusculanos patres

---

¹ Niebuhr thinks that this battle was a pure invention, for
there is no indication that it had any effect : Satricum was
not taken, nor was a triumph decreed.

B.C.
382–381

they saw the foot-soldiers hardest pressed. Neither generals nor soldiers relaxed their utmost efforts, and the help afforded by their brave exertions was felt in the result. The Volsci fled in a genuine panic over the ground where they had lately pretended fear. Great numbers of them were slain both in the battle itself and in the flight which followed ; the others were cut down in the camp, which was captured in the same charge ; but more were made prisoners than were slain.[1]

XXV. In taking account of the prisoners, they recognized some as being Tusculans. These were separated from the rest and brought before the tribunes, to whom they confessed, on being questioned, that they had served at the bidding of the state. The danger of so near a war disturbed Camillus, who declared that he would straightway carry the prisoners to Rome, that the Fathers might not be kept in ignorance how the Tusculans had broken the alliance. In the meantime he proposed that his colleague should, if agreeable, take charge of the camp and the army. A single day had taught Lucius Furius not to prefer his own to wiser counsels, yet neither he nor anyone in the army supposed that Camillus would condone his fault, which had plunged the commonwealth into such desperate peril ; and everybody, not in the army only, but also in Rome, agreed in saying, that in the ups and downs of the Volscian war, the responsibility for the defeat and flight lay with Lucius Furius, and all the credit for the victory with Camillus. But when the prisoners had been introduced into the senate, and the Fathers, having decided that they must make war on Tusculum, had

LIVY

censuissent Camilloque id bellum mandassent, adiu-
torem sibi ad eam rem unum petit permissoque
ut ex collegis optaret quem vellet, contra spem
6 omnium L. Furium optavit; qua moderatione animi
cum collegae levavit infamiam, tum sibi gloriam
ingentem peperit.

Nec fuit cum Tusculanis bellum : pace constanti
vim Romanam arcuerunt[1] quam armis non poterant.
7 Intrantibus fines Romanis non demigratum ex
propinquis itineri[2] locis, non cultus agrorum intermissus, patentibus portis urbis togati obviam
frequentes imperatoribus processere ; commeatus
exercitui comiter in castra ex urbe et ex agris de-
8 vehitur. Camillus castris ante portas positis, eademne
forma pacis quae in agris ostentaretur etiam intra
9 moenia esset scire cupiens, ingressus urbem ubi
patentes ianuas et tabernis apertis proposita omnia
in medio vidit intentosque opifices suo quemque
operi et ludos litterarum strepere discentium vocibus ac repletas semitas inter volgus aliud puerorum
et mulierum huc atque illuc euntium, qua quemque
10 suorum usuum causae ferrent, nihil usquam non
pavidis modo sed ne mirantibus quidem simile,
circumspiciebat omnia, anquirens[3] oculis ubinam
11 bellum fuisset ; adeo nec amotae rei usquam nec
oblatae ad tempus vestigium ullum erat, sed ita

---

[1] arcuerunt E^3T^1 (or T^2)D^x : arcuerant *PFUB* : arguerunt
MEHTDLA.
[2] itineri ς: itineris Ω : itineribus ς.
[3] anquirens *Gebhard* : inquirens Ω.

9

designated Camillus to conduct it, he requested that B.C. 382–381
he might have a single lieutenant to assist him, and
being permitted to select any one of his colleagues
whom he might desire, contrary to everybody's
expectation he selected Lucius Furius—an instance
of magnanimity which, while it lightened the disgrace of his colleague, also brought great honour
to himself.

But no war was, in fact, waged with the Tusculans :
by their steadfast adherence to peace they saved
themselves from violation by the Romans, as they
could not have done by resorting to arms. When the
Romans entered their territory, they did not withdraw
from the places near the line of march, nor break off
their labour in the fields ; the gates of their city stood
wide open ; the citizens, wearing the toga, came out
in great numbers to meet the generals ; and provisions
for the army were obligingly brought into the camp
from the city and the farms. Camillus set up his
camp before the gates, and desirous of knowing
whether the same aspect of peace prevailed within
the walls that was displayed in the country, entered
the city and beheld the house-doors open, the shops
with their shutters off and all their wares exposed,
the craftsmen all busy at their respective trades, the
schools buzzing with the voices of the scholars,
crowds in the streets, and women and children going
about amongst the rest, this way and that, as their
several occasions called them—with never anywhere
an indication of surprise, much less of fear. He looked
everywhere for any visible evidence that a war had
been on foot ; but there was no sign that anything
had been either removed or brought out for the
moment ; everything looked so undisturbed and

omnia constanti tranquilla pace ut eo vix fama
belli perlata videri posset.

XXVI. Victus igitur patientia hostium senatum
eorum vocari iussit. "Soli adhuc" inquit, "Tusculani, vera arma verasque vires quibus ab ira
2 Romanorum vestra tutaremini invenistis. Ite Romam
ad senatum; aestimabunt patres, utrum plus ante
poenae an nunc veniae meriti sitis; non praecipiam
gratiam publici beneficii; deprecandi potestatem a
me habueritis; precibus eventum vestris senatus
quem videbitur dabit."

3 Postquam Romam Tusculani venerunt senatusque
paulo ante fidelium sociorum maestus in vestibulo
curiae est conspectus, moti extemplo patres vocari
eos iam tum hospitaliter magis quam hostiliter
4 iussere. Dictator Tusculanus ita verba fecit: "Quibus bellum indixistis intulistisque, patres conscripti,
sicut nunc videtis nos stantes in vestibulo curiae
vestrae, ita armati paratique obviam imperatoribus
5 legionibusque vestris processimus. Hic noster, hic
plebis nostrae habitus fuit eritque semper, nisi si
quando a vobis proque vobis arma acceperimus.
Gratias agimus et ducibus vestris et exercitibus,
quod oculis magis quam auribus crediderunt, et ubi
6 nihil hostile erat ne ipsi quidem fecerunt. Pacem,
quam nos praestitimus, eam a vobis petimus; bellum

---

[1] For a similar play on words see I. lviii. 8.

peaceful that it seemed scarce credible that so much B.C.
as a rumour of war should have come there. 382-381

XXVI. Overcome therefore by the enemy's submissiveness, he commanded their senate to be called. "Men of Tusculum," he said, "until now you alone have discovered the right weapons and the right resources with which to defend your possessions from the resentment of the Romans. Go to Rome, to the senate; the Fathers will determine whether you have deserved more punishment hitherto or pardon now. I will not forestall them by accepting your gratitude for a favour that must be granted by the state; from me you shall have an opportunity to solicit mercy; the answer to your suit must be such as the senate sees fit to make."

When the Tusculans arrived in Rome, and the senators of a people who before had been faithful allies appeared in the vestibule of the Curia, covered with dejection, the Fathers were straightway moved, and in a spirit that had already more in it of hospitality than hostility [1] bade them be at once admitted. The Tusculan dictator thus addressed them: "Though you declared war on us and invaded our country, Conscript Fathers, we went forth to meet your generals and your legions armed and accoutred exactly as you now behold us standing in the entrance of your senate-house. Such has ever been our garb and the garb of our people—ay, and ever shall be— save at such times as we have been armed by you and for your defence. We give thanks to your commanders and your armies, since they have believed their eyes more than their ears, and where they encountered no hostility, themselves have showed none. The peace we have used towards you, we ask

eo, sicubi est, avertatis precamur ; in nos quid arma
polleant vestra, si patiendo experiundum est, inermes
experiemur. Haec mens nostra est[1]—di immortales

7 faciant—tam felix quam pia. Quod ad crimina
attinet quibus moti bellum indixistis, etsi revicta
rebus verbis confutare nihil attinet, tamen, etiam si
vera sint, vel fateri nobis ea, cum tam evidenter
paenituerit, tutum censemus. Peccetur in vos,

8 dum digni sitis, quibus ita satisfiat." Tantum fere
verborum Tusculanis factum. Pacem in praesentia
nec ita multo post civitatem etiam impetraverunt.
Ab Tusculo legiones reductae.

XXVII. Camillus, consilio et virtute in Volsco
bello, felicitate in Tusculana expeditione, utrobique
singulari adversus collegam patientia et moderatione

2 insignis, magistratu abiit creatis tribunis militaribus
in insequentem annum L. et P. Valeriis—Lucio
quintum, Publio tertium—et C. Sergio tertium L.
Menenio[2] iterum, P. Papirio, Ser. Cornelio Malu-

3 ginense. Censoribus quoque eguit annus maxime
propter incertam famam aeris alieni, adgravantibus
summam etiam invidiae eius[3] tribunis plebis, cum
ab iis elevaretur, quibus fide magis quam fortuna
debentium laborare creditum videri expediebat.

---

[1] nostra est Ω : nostra sit *Karsten (after H. J. Mueller)*.

[2] L. (lucio) Menenio *A Sigonius* : lucinio Menenio *F* : lic (*or*
lit-)inio menenio Ω. *There is great uncertainty regarding
the names, and in view of the reading of* Ω *here and at chap.* 5
§ 7, *and chap.* 31 § 1, *it appears not improbable that Livy
included Licinius in the list.*

[3] invidiae eius Ω *Walters and Conway* : invidiosius *Madvig* :
invidiae causa *Perizonius* : invidiose *Duker*.

---

[1] *i. e.* the honour done you by our confiding in your mercy
should outweigh the injury.

of you in return; direct your war, we beseech you, B.C. 382-381 to that quarter where war, if anywhere, exists; if we must try, by suffering, what your arms can achieve against ourselves, we will try unarmed. Such is our resolution; Heaven send it be not less fortunate than loyal. As to the charges which stirred you to declare a war, though it skills not to disprove with words what facts have already confuted, still, even were they true, we think we might safely plead guilty to them, since our repentance is so evident. Let men wrong you, so long as you continue worthy to receive such amends."[1] To this purport was the speech of the Tusculans. They were granted peace for the present, and not long after were even admitted to be citizens. The legions were withdrawn from Tusculum.

XXVII. Renowned for his strategy and courage B.C. 380 in the Volscian war and his success in the expedition against Tusculum, and for his singular gentleness and generosity on both occasions towards his colleague, Camillus laid down his office, after announcing the election of military tribunes for the ensuing year. The successful candidates were Lucius and Publius Valerius (Lucius for the fifth and Publius for the third time), Gaius Sergius (for the third time), Lucius Menenius (for the second time), Publius Papirius, and Servius Cornelius Maluginensis. There was need also this year of censors, chiefly on account of the uncertain reports which were going about in regard to debt. The tribunes of the plebs even exaggerated the extent of this grievance, whereas it was understated by those who were interested in having it appear that loans were more in danger from the bad faith than the bad fortune of the debtors. The censors

289

4 Creati censores C. Sulpicius Camerinus Sp. Postumius
Regillensis, coeptaque iam res morte Postumi, quia
collegam suffici censori religio erat, interpellata
5 est. Igitur cum Sulpicius abdicasset se magistratu
censores alii vitio creati non gesserunt magistratum ;
tertios creari velut dis non accipientibus in eum
6 annum censuram religiosum fuit. Eam vero ludi-
ficationem plebis tribuni ferendam negabant : fugere
senatum testes tabulas publicas census cuiusque,
quia nolint conspici summam aeris alieni, quae in-
dicatura sit demersam partem a parte civitatis, cum
interim obaeratam plebem obiectari aliis atque aliis
7 hostibus. Passim iam sine ullo discrimine bella
quaeri : ab Antio Satricum, ab Satrico Velitras, inde
Tusculum legiones ductas ; Latinis Hernicis Praenestinis iam intentari arma civium magis quam
hostium odio, ut in armis terant plebem nec respirare
in urbe aut per otium libertatis meminisse sinant aut
consistere in contione, ubi aliquando audiant vocem
tribuniciam de levando fenore et fine[1] aliarum in-
8 iuriarum agentem. Quod si sit animus plebi memor
patrum libertatis, se nec addici quemquam civem
Romanum ob creditam pecuniam passuros neque

---

[1] fine ʓ : finem Ω *Walters and Conway.*

---

[1] *Cf.* v. xxxi. 6.

chosen were Gaius Sulpicius Camerinus and Spurius B.C. 380
Postumius Regillensis, and they had already set about
their task, when it was interrupted by the death of
Postumius; for there were religious scruples against
replacing the colleague of a censor.[1] So then, Sulpicius resigned, and other censors were elected, but,
owing to a defect in the election, did not serve. The
senate could not bring itself to proceed to a third
election, being persuaded that the gods would permit
no censorship that year. But this irresolution the
tribunes characterized as an intolerable mockery of
the plebs. The senate, they said, was seeking to
avoid the evidence of witnesses and public records
regarding the property of every man, because they
were unwilling it should be seen how great was the
volume of debt, which would show that half of
the state had been ruined by the other half, while
the debt-ridden plebs were in the meantime being
exposed to one enemy after another; wars were now
sought indiscriminately, far and wide; from Antium
the legions had been marched to Satricum, from
Satricum to Velitrae, from there to Tusculum; now
it was the Latins, the Hernici and the Praenestini
who were threatened with attack, more out of hatred
of Rome's citizens than of her enemies. The object
was to wear the plebeians out with service and give
them no time to take breath in the City, or leisure to
bethink them of liberty or to stand in the assembly,
where they might sometimes hear the voice of a
tribune urging the reduction of interest and the
removal of their other grievances. But if the plebs
had the spirit to recall their fathers' liberty, they
would allow no Roman citizen to be bound to a
creditor, nor any levy to be held, until the amount of

291

dilectum haberi, donec inspecto aere alieno initaque ratione minuendi eius sciat unus quisque quid sui, quid alieni sit, supersit sibi liberum corpus an id quoque nervo debeatur.[1]

9 Merces seditionis proposita confestim seditionem excitavit. Nam et addicebantur multi, et ad Praenestini famam belli novas legiones scribendas patres censuerant ; quae utraque simul auxilio tribunicio 10 et consensu plebis impediri coepta ; nam neque duci addictos tribuni sinebant neque iuniores nomina dabant. Cum patribus minor in praesens[1] cura creditae pecuniae iuris exsequendi quam dilectus esset—quippe iam a Praeneste profectos hostes in 11 agro Gabino[2] consedisse nuntiabatur—interim tribunos plebis fama ea ipsa inritaverat magis ad susceptum certamen quam deterruerat ; neque aliud ad seditionem exstinguendam in urbe quam prope inlatum moenibus ipsis bellum valuit.

XXVIII. Nam cum esset Praenestinis nuntiatum nullum exercitum conscriptum Romae, nullum ducem certum esse, patres ac plebem in semet ipsos versos, 2 occasionem rati duces eorum raptim agmine acto[3] pervastatis protinus agris ad portam Collinam signa 3 intulere. Ingens in urbe trepidatio fuit. Conclamatum ad arma, concursumque in muros adque[4]

---

[1] in praesens *Stroth* : praesens Ω.
[2] Gabino *Iac. Gronovius* : Sabino Ω.
[3] acto ⊊ *Sigonius* : facto Ω.
[4] adque *Gronovius* : atque Ω. (*but A² or A³ has written* ad *over* in).

---

[1] *i.e.,* to their creditors, to work out their debts.

indebtedness had been examined and a plan for lessening it put into operation, that every man might know what was his own and what another's, and whether his person was still free, or whether even that was owing to the gaol.

The reward held out to sedition soon brought sedition to a head. For many were being bound over,[1] and the senate had voted to enlist new levies on the rumour of hostilities at Praeneste. Both these proceedings began at the same time to be interfered with by the exercise of the tribunician protection and the common action of the plebs; for the tribunes would not allow those who had been bound over to be led away, nor would the young men give in their names. The patricians were for the moment less concerned with enforcing the law of debt than with the levy—not unnaturally, since the enemy were reported as having already set out from Praeneste and encamped in the territory of Gabii— but on the tribunes of the plebs this intelligence had acted more as an incentive to the struggle they had undertaken than as a deterrent, and the only thing that was able to allay the quarrel in the City was the approach of the enemy to its very walls.

XXVIII. For when the Praenestini were informed that no army had been enrolled in Rome, that there was no one definitely in command, that patricians and plebeians had turned against each other, their leaders concluded that their opportunity had come, and quickly putting their troops in motion, they devastated the fields along their line of march and advanced against the Colline Gate. Great was the consternation in the City. The call to arms was given, and men hurried to the walls and gates. They

293

A.U.C.
374

portas est, tandemque ab seditione ad bellum versi
4 dictatorem T. Quinctium Cincinnatum creavere. Is
magistrum equitum A. Sempronium Atratinum dixit.
Quod ubi auditum est—tantus eius magistratus
terror erat,—simul hostes a moenibus recessere
et iuniores Romani ad edictum sine retractatione
convenere.

5 Dum conscribitur Romae exercitus, castra interim
hostium haud procul Allia flumine posita; inde
agrum late populantes fatalem se urbi Romanae
6 locum cepisse inter se iactabant: similem pavorem
inde ac fugam fore ac bello Gallico fuerit; etenim
si diem contactum religione insignemque nomine
eius loci timeant Romani, quanto magis Alliensi die
Alliam ipsam, monumentum tantae cladis, refor-
midaturos? Species profecto iis [1] ibi truces Gallorum
7 sonumque vocis in oculis atque auribus fore. Has
inanium rerum inanes ipsas volventes cogitationes
fortunae loci delegaverant spes suas. Romani
contra, ubicumque esset Latinus hostis, satis scire
eum esse quem ad Regillum lacum devictum centum
8 annorum pace obnoxia [2] tenuerint: locum insignem
memoria cladis inritaturum se potius ad delendam
memoriam dedecoris, quam ut timorem faciat, ne
9 qua terra sit nefasta victoriae suae; quin ipsi sibi
Galli si offerantur illo loco, se ita pugnaturos ut
Romae pugnaverint in repetenda patria ut postero

---

[1] iis *Weissenborn* : hiis *A* : his Ω : hic *D³A³_5̄*.
[2] obnoxia Ω : obnoxium *U Häggström.*

had turned at last from domestic strife to war, and _{B.C. 380} proceeded to make Titus Quinctius Cincinnatus dictator, who named Aulus Sempronius Atratinus master of the horse. No sooner was this known— so great was the terror the dictatorship inspired— than the enemy at once withdrew from before the walls, and the Romans of military age assembled without offering objection, in accordance with the edict.

While the army was being enrolled at Rome, the enemy had gone into camp not far from the Allia. From this centre they pillaged in all directions, and boasted to one another that they had occupied a position that was fraught with fate for the City of Rome; there would be another rout there like the one in the Gallic war; for if the Romans feared a day infected with evil omen and marked it with the name of that place, how much more than the Day of the Allia would they dread the Allia itself, that memorial of their great defeat? They were sure to behold there apparitions of ruthless Gauls, and to have the sound of their voices in their ears. Indulging these idle speculations on idle themes, they had rested their hopes on the fortune of the place. The Romans on the other hand were well assured that wherever their Latin enemy was, he was one whom they had conquered at Lake Regillus and had held in peaceable subjection for a hundred years; a place notorious for the memory of disaster would rather inspire them to wipe out the recollection of the disgrace than cause them to fear that any ground was inauspicious for their victory; nay, if the Gauls themselves should confront them on that spot, they would fight as they had fought at Rome in recovering

295

A.U.C.
374
die ad Gabios, tunc cum effecerint ne quis hostis qui
moenia Romana intrasset nuntium secundae adver-
saeque fortunae domum perferret.

XXIX. His utrimque animis ad Alliam ventum
est. Dictator Romanus, postquam in conspectu
hostes erant instructi intentique, "videsne tu" inquit, "A. Semproni, loci fortuna illos fretos ad
Alliam constitisse ? Nec illis di immortales certioris
quicquam fiduciae maiorisve quod sit auxilii dede-
2 rint. At tu, fretus armis animisque, concitatis equis
invade mediam aciem ; ego cum legionibus in turbatos trepidantesque inferam signa. Adeste, di
testes foederis, et expetite poenas debitas simul
vobis violatis nobisque per vestrum numen deceptis."
Non equitem, non peditem sustinuere Praenestini.
3 Primo impetu ac clamore dissipati ordines sunt ;
dein, postquam nullo loco constabat acies, terga
vertunt consternatique et praeter castra etiam sua
pavore praelati non prius se ab effuso cursu sistunt,
4 quam in conspectu Praeneste fuit. Ibi ex fuga
dissipati [1] locum quem tumultuario opere communirent capiunt ne, si intra moenia se recepissent, extemplo ureretur ager depopulatisque omnibus obsidio
5 urbi inferretur. Sed postquam direptis ad Alliam
castris victor Romanus aderat, id quoque muni-
mentum relictum ; et vix moenia tuta rati oppido
6 se Praeneste includunt. Octo praeterea oppida

---

[1] dissipati Ω : dissipata *Madvig* : dissipata contracti
Walters and Conway (*note*).

their City and on the following day at Gabii, when B.C. 380
they left no enemy who had entered the walls of
Rome, to bear home tidings either of weal or woe.

Such were the feelings on either side when the
Romans arrived at the Allia. As they came within
sight of the enemy, drawn up and eager for the fray,
the dictator addressed Sempronius. " Do you see,"
he said, " how they have made their stand at the Allia,
putting their trust in the fortune of the place? We
shall find the immortal gods have given them no surer
grounds for confidence nor any more substantial
help. But do you confide in arms and valour, and
charge their centre at the gallop; I, with the legions,
will attack them when they are in disorder and confusion. Be with us, gods of the treaty, and exact
the penalties due to you for the injury you have
suffered and to us for the deception put upon us in
your holy name!" The men of Praeneste could
cope with neither horse nor foot. Their ranks were
broken at the first shout and charge; then, as their
line yielded at every point, they turned and fled, and
in their confusion were carried even beyond their
own camp; neither did they check their headlong
flight until they had come within sight of Praeneste.
There the scattered remnants of the rout took up a
position which lent itself to hasty fortification, lest,
if they sought refuge within the walls, they might
immediately find the torch put to their crops, and,
after losing everything, be subjected to a siege. But
no sooner had the victorious Romans appeared, fresh
from plundering the camp on the Allia, than they
abandoned these defences also, and, regarding even
walls as little enough protection, immured themselves in the town of Praeneste. There were eight

LIVY

erant sub dicione Praenestinorum. Ad ea circum-
latum bellum deincepsque haud magno certamine
captis Velitras exercitus ductus. Eae quoque ex-
7 pugnatae. Tum ad caput belli Praeneste ventum.
8 Id non vi, sed per deditionem receptum est. T.
Quinctius semel acie victor, binis castris hostium,
novem oppidis vi captis, Praeneste in deditionem
accepto Romam revertit triumphansque signum
Praeneste devectum Iovis Imperatoris in Capitolium
9 tulit. Dedicatum est inter cellam Iovis ac Minervae
tabulaque sub eo fixa, monumentum rerum gestarum,
his ferme incisa litteris fuit : " Iuppiter atque divi
omnes hoc dederunt, ut T. Quinctius dictator oppida
10 novem caperet." Die vicesimo quam creatus erat
dictatura se abdicavit.

XXX. Comitia inde habita tribunorum militum
consulari potestate, quibus aequatus patriciorum
2 plebeiorumque numerus. Ex patribus creati P. et
C. Manlii[1] cum L. Iulio ; plebes C. Sextilium M.
3 Albinium L. Antistium dedit. Manliis, quod genere
plebeios, gratia Iulium anteibant, Volsci, provincia
sine sorte, sine comparatione extra ordinem data ;
cuius et ipsos postmodo et patres qui dederant
4 paenituit. Inexplorato pabulatum cohortes misere ;
quibus velut circumventis, cum id falso nuntiatum

---

[1] Manlii I^2A^2 : manli *MFBTL* : manlius *OE* : mallius *U* :
manlio (manlio cum *over erasure in* A^1) PA^1 : manlio ūis *H* :
mallii D^3 (*over erasure*).

---

[1] According to Festus (p. 363) the offering was a golden
crown weighing 2⅓ lbs.

other towns which were under the sway of the B.C. 380 Praenestini. Against these the Romans directed their campaign, and having taken them, with no great exertion, one after the other, marched to Velitrae and stormed that place also. Coming then to Praeneste, the fountain-head of the war, they got possession of it not by force but through capitulation. Titus Quinctius had gained one pitched battle, captured two camps, taken nine towns by assault, and received the surrender of Praeneste. He returned to Rome bringing with him from Praeneste the image of Jupiter Imperator. This he bore in triumph to the Capitol, where he dedicated it, between the shrine of Jupiter and that of Minerva. Below it he placed a tablet, in commemoration of his deeds, with an inscription to the following effect: "Jupiter and all the gods granted Titus Quinctius the dictator that he should take nine towns." [1] On the twentieth day after his appointment he resigned the dictatorship.

XXX. In the ensuing election of military tribunes B.C. 379 with consular powers, patricians and plebeians came off alike. Of the patricians Publius and Gaius Manlius were successful, along with Lucius Julius; the plebs returned Gaius Sextilius, Marcus Albinius, and Lucius Antistius. The Manlii were superior in birth to their plebeian colleagues, and in popularity to Julius. To them, therefore, by special enactment, without reference to the lot or to mutual agreement, was given the command against the Volsci—an honour which they rued in the upshot, as did also the senators who had conferred it. Without reconnoitring they sent some troops to forage, and believing them to be cut off, for they had received a false

LIVY

esset, dum praesidio ut essent citati feruntur, ne
auctore quidem adservato qui eos hostis Latinus pro
milite Romano frustratus erat, ipsi in insidias prae-
5 cipitavere. Ibi dum iniquo loco sola virtute militum
restantes caeduntur caeduntque, castra interim Romana iacentia in campo ab altera parte hostes in-
6 invasere. Ab ducibus utrobique proditae temeritate
atque inscitia res; quidquid superfuit fortunae populi Romani, id militum etiam sine rectore stabilis
7 virtus tutata est. Quae ubi Romam sunt relata,
primum dictatorem dici placebat ; deinde, postquam
quietae res ex Volscis adferebantur et apparuit ne-
scire eos victoria et tempore uti, revocati etiam inde
exercitus ac duces, otiumque inde, quantum a Vol-
8 scis, fuit; id[1] modo extremo anno tumultuatum
quod Praenestini concitatis Latinorum populis
rebellarunt.
9   Eodem anno Setiam[2] ipsis querentibus penuriam
hominum novi coloni adscripti. Rebusque haud
prosperis bello domestica quies, quam tribunorum
militum ex plebe gratia maiestasque inter suos
obtinuit, solacium fuit.

XXXI. Insequentis anni principia statim seditione
ingenti arsere tribunis militum consulari potestate
Sp. Furio Q. Servilio iterum L.[3] Menenio tertium

---

[1] fuit ; id ς : fuisset id Ω : fuit seti id *H* (setiae *Harant*).
[2] anno Setiam *Sigonius* : annos etiam *MPT* : anno etiam Ω.
[3] L. *Alschefski* : lucinio *MF* : licinio Ω. (*cf. chap.* xxvii. § 2).

report that such was the case, they hastened to B.C. 379 their assistance, without so much as securing the author of the story—a Latin enemy who had deceived them in the guise of a Roman soldier,—and plunged into an ambuscade. While they were making a stand there on unfavourable ground, by the sheer courage of the men, who were selling their lives dearly, the Roman camp which lay in the plain was attacked by the enemy on the opposite side. In both places victory was thrown away by the rashness and ignorance of the generals. Whatever was left of the good fortune of the Roman People was saved by the pluck of the soldiers, which continued steadfast even when it lacked guidance. On the announcement of these events at Rome, it was at first resolved to appoint a dictator; but later, when word came that things were quiet in the Volscian country, and it appeared that the enemy knew not how to use his victory and opportunity, even the armies and commanders which were there were withdrawn, and thereafter there was no trouble as far as the Volsci were concerned; the only disturbance—towards the close of the year—was a mutiny of the Praenestini, who had stirred the peoples of Latium to revolt.

That same year new colonists were enrolled for Setia, whose inhabitants themselves were complaining of their lack of men. For the ill success of the war there was consolation in the tranquillity at home, which was due to the influence of the plebeian military tribunes and the honour in which their order held them.

XXXI. The following year started off in a blaze B.C. 378 of party strife. The military tribunes with consular powers were Spurius Furius, Quintus Servilius (for

2 P. Cloelio M. Horatio L. Geganio. Erat autem et
materia et causa seditionis aes alienum ; cuius no-
scendi gratia Sp. Servilius Priscus Q. Cloelius Siculus
censores facti, ne rem agerent bello impediti sunt ;
3 namque trepidi nuntii primo, fuga deinde ex agris
legiones Volscorum ingressas fines popularique pas-
4 sim Romanum agrum attulere. In qua trepidatione
tantum afuit ut civilia certamina terror externus
cohiberet, ut contra eo violentior potestas tribunicia
impediendo dilectu esset, donec condiciones impo-
sitae patribus, ne quis, quoad bellatum esset, tri-
5 butum daret aut ius de pecunia credita diceret. Eo
laxamento plebi sumpto mora dilectui non est facta.
Legionibus novis scriptis placuit duos exercitus in
agrum Volscum legionibus divisis duci. Sp. Furius
M. Horatius dextrorsus in[1] maritimam oram atque
Antium, Q. Servilius et L. Geganius[2] laeva ad montes
6 et Ecetram[3] pergunt. Neutra parte hostis obvius
fuit ; populatio itaque non illi vagae similis, quam
Volscus latrocinii more, discordiae hostium fretus et
virtutem metuens, per trepidationem raptim fecerat,
sed ab iusto exercitu iusta ira facta, spatio quoque
7 temporis gravior. Quippe a Volscis timentibus ne
interim exercitus ab Roma exiret incursiones in ex-

---

[1] dextrorsus in *Madvig*: dextrorsus Ω.
[2] L. Geganius ς (*cf.* § 1) : M. Geganius Ω.
[3] et ecetram *Madvig* : et cetram *H* : et etram *B* : ecetram
Ω : ecetra *E?L* (monte se cetra).

the second time), Lucius Menenius (for the third), B.C. 378
Publius Cloelius, Marcus Horatius, and Lucius
Geganius.   Now the subject and reason of the strife
was debt.   But when Spurius Servilius Priscus and
Quintus Cloelius Siculus had been made censors in
order that they might investigate the situation, they
were prevented from doing so by a war; for first
frightened messengers, and then the country-folk
fleeing from the fields, brought word that the
Volscian legions had crossed the border, and were
everywhere devastating Roman territory.   Yet with
all this alarm, the danger from abroad was so far
from restraining dissensions at home, that on the
contrary the tribunes but acted with the greater
violence, in exerting their powers to block the levy;
until the senate submitted to their terms, and agreed
that till the war was finished no one should pay a
war-tax or give judgment in a case of debt.   The
plebs, on obtaining this relief, ceased to obstruct
the levy.   When the new legions had been enrolled,
it was resolved to divide them and form two armies
to invade the country of the Volsci.   Spurius Furius
and Marcus Horatius marched to the right, towards
Antium and the coast; Quintus Servilius and Lucius
Geganius to the left, in the direction of Ecetra and
the mountains.   In neither region did they find the
enemy.   They accordingly laid waste the country,
not in the desultory fashion of the Volsci, who like
bandits, trusting in the discord of their foes but
fearing their courage, had made a hasty foray in fear
and trembling,—but with a regular army, justly provoked, and the more destructive in that they took
more time.   In fact, the Volsci had confined their
pillaging to the borders, because of their fear lest an

trema finium factae erant; Romano contra etiam in
hostico morandi causa erat, ut hostem ad certamen
8 eliceret. Itaque omnibus passim tectis agrorum
vicisque etiam quibusdam exustis, non arbore frugi-
fera, non satis in spem frugum relictis, omni quae
extra moenia fuit hominum pecudumque praeda
abacta Romam utrimque exercitus reducti.

XXXII. Parvo intervallo ad respirandum debi-
toribus dato postquam quietae res ab hostibus erant,
celebrari de integro iuris dictio, et tantum abesse
spes veteris levandi fenoris, ut tributo novum fenus
contraheretur in murum a censoribus locatum saxo
2 quadrato faciundum. Cui succumbere oneri coacta
plebes, quia quem dilectum impedirent non habe-
3 bant tribuni plebis. Tribunos etiam militares
patricios omnes coacta principum opibus fecit: L.
Aemilium P. Valerium quartum C. Veturium Ser.
4 Sulpicium L. et C. Quinctios Cincinnatos. Iisdem
opibus obtinuere, ut adversus Latinos Volscosque,
qui coniunctis legionibus ad Satricum castra habebant, nullo impediente omnibus iunioribus sacra-
5 mento adactis tres exercitus scriberent: unum ad
praesidium urbis: alterum, qui, si qui alibi motus
exstitisset, ad subita belli mitti posset: tertium
longe validissimum P. Valerius et L. Aemilius ad
6 Satricum duxere. Ubi cum aciem instructam hosti-

---

¹ The reference is probably to a section of the city wall,
damaged in the Gallic war.

army might come out from Rome while they were
at it; the Romans, on the contrary, were partly
actuated, in remaining on hostile ground, by the
desire of luring the enemy into a battle. So they
burned all the farm-houses everywhere, and even
certain villages, and leaving not a single fruit-tree
nor the standing corn with its hope of harvest, they
carried off as booty all the men and beasts outside
the towns, and led both armies back to Rome.

XXXII. The debtors had been given a little time
for breathing, but no sooner did hostilities cease
than the courts began once more to be alive with
prosecutions, and not only was there no prospect
of obtaining relief from the old debts, but a tax was
levied to build a wall of hewn stone,[1] which the
censors had contracted for, and new debts were
incurred. To this burden the plebs were forced to
submit, in the absence of any levy which their
tribunes could obstruct. The nobles even possessed
sufficient influence to oblige the plebs to elect all
patricians to the military tribunate; these were
Lucius Aemilius, Publius Valerius (for the fourth
time), Gaius Veturius, Servius Sulpicius, Lucius and
Gaius Quinctius Cincinnatus. The same influence
enabled them to carry through their plans against
the Latins and the Volsci, who had united their
forces and were encamped near Satricum. No one
objected when the men of military age were all
compelled to take the oath, and three armies were
enrolled: one was intended to defend the City;
another was for use in sudden expeditions, if a revolt
should break out anywhere; a third—much the
strongest—marched to Satricum, under Publius
Valerius and Lucius Aemilius. There they found the

305

um loco aequo invenissent, extemplo pugnatum ; et
ut nondum satis claram [1] victoriam, sic prosperae
spei pugnam imber ingentibus procellis fusus diremit.

7 Postero die iterata pugna ; et aliquamdiu aequa virtute fortunaque Latinae maxime legiones, longa
societate militiam Romanam edoctae, restabant.

8 Sed eques immissus ordines turbavit, turbatis signa
peditum inlata, quantumque Romana se invexit
acies, tantum hostes gradu demoti ; et, ut semel
inclinavit pugna, iam intolerabilis Romana vis erat.

9 Fusi hostes cum Satricum, quod duo milia inde
aberat, non castra peterent, ab equite maxime

10 caesi ; castra capta direptaque. Ab Satrico nocte
quae proelio proxima fuit fugae simili agmine petunt
Antium ; et cum Romanus exercitus prope vestigiis
sequeretur, plus tamen timor quam ira celeritatis

11 habuit. Prius itaque moenia intravere hostes quam
Romanus extrema agminis carpere aut morari posset.
Inde aliquot dies vastando agro absumpti nec Romanis satis instructis apparatu bellico ad moenia
adgredienda nec illis ad subeundum pugnae casum.

XXXIII. Seditio tum inter Antiates Latinosque
coorta, cum Antiates victi malis subactique bello in
quo et nati erant et consenuerant deditionem specta-

2 rent,[2] Latinos ex diutina pace nova defectio recenti-
bus adhuc animis ferociores ad perseverandum in

---

[1] claram Ω (cf. Walters and Conway, Class Quart., XII.
(1918) p. 4) : certam Madvig.
[2] spectarent ς : exsp(or exp-)ectarent Ω.

---

[1] These words are really applicable to the Volsci in general,
but not to the Antiates in particular. In § 4 the word
Volscos is used as though equivalent to Antiates.

enemy drawn up in a strong position, and at once attacked them; and though victory was not yet assured, yet the battle was in a hopeful state, when great gusts of wind brought on a heavy downpour of rain and interrupted it. Next day the combat was renewed, and for some little time the enemy— particularly the Latin legions, schooled in Roman discipline by their long alliance—resisted with equal courage and success. But the cavalry were sent against them and threw their ranks into confusion, and before they could recover, the infantry were upon them; in proportion as the Roman line advanced, was the enemy forced out of his position; and when once the tide of battle turned, there was no stopping the onrush of the Romans. The routed enemy made for Satricum, two miles away, instead of their camp, and suffered great slaughter, especially at the hands of the cavalry. Their camp was taken and sacked. The night after the battle they fled rather than marched towards Antium; and though the Roman army followed hard after, fear proved swifter than wrath. So the enemy got within the walls before the Romans could harass or delay their rear. A few days were then consumed in ravaging the land, since the Romans had not enough equipment to attack the walls, nor the enemy to risk a battle.

XXXIII. A quarrel now broke out between the Antiates and the Latins. The men of Antium, overwhelmed by their misfortunes and worn out by a war which had lasted from their birth to their old age,[1] were minded to capitulate: the Latins had but just revolted after a long peace; their spirits were still fresh; and they meant to continue boldly with

307

A.U.C.
377

bello faceret. Finis certaminis fuit postquam utrisque apparuit nihil per alteros stare quo minus
3 incepta persequerentur. Latini profecti ab societate[1] pacis, ut rebantur, inhonestae sese vindicaverunt, Antiates incommodis arbitris salutarium
consiliorum remotis urbem agrosque Romanis de
4 dunt. Ira et rabies Latinorum, quia nec Romanos
bello laedere nec Volscos in armis retinere potuerant,
eo erupit ut Satricum urbem, quae receptaculum
primum eis adversae pugnae fuerat, igni concremarent; nec aliud tectum eius superfuit urbis, cum
faces pariter sacris profanisque inicerent, quam
5 matris Matutae templum; inde eos nec sua religio
nec verecundia deum arcuisse dicitur sed vox horrenda edita templo cum tristibus minis, ni nefandos
6 ignes procul delubris amovissent. Incensos ea rabie
impetus Tusculum tulit ob iram, quod deserto communi concilio Latinorum non in societatem modo
Romanam sed etiam in civitatem se dedissent.
7 Patentibus portis cum improviso incidissent, primo
clamore oppidum praeter arcem captum est. In
arcem oppidani refugere cum coniugibus ac liberis
nuntiosque Romam, qui certiorem de suo casu sena
8 tum facerent, misere. Haud segnius quam fide
populi Romani dignum fuit exercitus Tusculum
ductus; L. Quinctius et Ser. Sulpicius tribuni

---

[1] ab societate D^1 *or* L^2: ad societate D: ad societatem L:
a societate Ω.

---

[1] An ancient Italian deity worshipped by matrons and
having to do with birth, and perhaps with the dawn. She
had a temple in Rome and in Praeneste, and appears to have
been the principal god of Satricum.

the war. The dispute came to an end as soon as
each party saw that the other could not prevent it in
any way from carrying out its policy. The Latins
departed, and freed themselves from all share in
what they considered a degrading peace; the
Antiates, being rid of inconvenient witnesses to
their salutary measures, surrendered their city and
lands to the Romans. The frenzied wrath of the
Latins sought relief—since they could neither do
the Romans any injury in war nor retain the Volsci
under arms—in burning Satricum, the town which
had been their first place of refuge after their defeat.
They applied the torch without discrimination both
to sacred and to secular buildings, and not one
escaped destruction, except the temple of Mater
Matuta;[1] from this they were kept away, according
to the story, neither by their own scruples, nor by
their reverence for the gods, but by an awe-inspiring
voice that issued from the temple and threatened
dire retribution if they did not remove those impious
fires to a distance from the sacred walls. Crazed
and infuriated, a sudden impulse carried them to
Tusculum. They were angry that the Tusculans
had deserted the common council of the Latins and
had yielded themselves to be not only allies but
citizens of Rome. The gates were open, for their
attack was unexpected, and the first shout had not
died away when the town was taken, all except the
citadel. To this the townsfolk fled for safety, with
their wives and children, and sent off messengers to
Rome to let the senate know of their predicament.
With a promptness worthy of the honour of the
Roman People, an army marched to Tusculum, commanded by the military tribunes Lucius Quinctius

LIVY

9 militum duxere. Clausas portas Tusculi Latinosque
simul obsidentium atque obsessorum animo hinc
moenia[1] tueri vident, illinc arcem oppugnare, ter-
10 rere una ac pavere. Adventus Romanorum mutaverat utriusque partis animos: Tusculanos ex ingenti
metu in summam alacritatem, Latinos ex prope certa
fiducia mox capiendae arcis, quoniam oppido poti-
rentur, in exiguam de se ipsis spem verterat.
11 Tollitur ex arce clamor ab Tusculanis; excipit[2]
aliquanto maior ab exercitu Romano. Utrimque
urgentur Latini; nec impetus Tusculanorum de-
currentium ex superiore loco sustinent nec Romanos
subeuntes moenia molientesque obices portarum
12 arcere possunt. Scalis prius moenia capta; inde
effracta claustra portarum; et cum anceps hostis et
a fronte et a tergo urgeret nec ad pugnam ulla vis
nec ad fugam loci quicquam superesset, in medio
caesi ad unum omnes. Reciperato ab hostibus
Tusculo exercitus Romam est reductus.

XXXIV. Quanto magis prosperis eo anno bellis
tranquilla omnia foris erant, tantum[3] in urbe vis
patrum in dies miseriaeque plebis crescebant, cum
eo ipso, quod necesse erat solvi, facultas solvendi
2 impediretur. Itaque cum iam ex re nihil dari
posset, fama et corpore iudicati atque addicti cre-

---

[1] moenia ς: moenia Tusculi Ω.
[2] excipit Alschefski: excipitur Ω.
[3] tantum Madvig (cf. v. x. 5): tanto (wanting in O) Ω.

and Servius Sulpicius. They found the gates of Tusculum closed and the Latins at once besiegers and besieged; on the one hand they were defending the walls of the town, on the other assailing the fortress, and they experienced themselves the same terror they inspired. The arrival of the Romans produced a change in the spirits of both sides: the Tusculans were roused from the depths of despair to the greatest cheerfulness; the Latins, who had felt almost certain that since the town was theirs they would soon possess the citadel, were reduced almost to despair of their own lives. The Tusculans in the citadel gave a cheer and were answered by one much louder from the Roman army. On both sides the Latins were hard pressed: they could neither resist the charges of the townsmen, as they rushed down from above, nor drive back the Romans, who were coming up under the walls and forcing the bars of the gates. The walls were first scaled and captured; then the fastenings of the gates were burst. The Latins were caught between two enemies, who assailed them hotly in front and rear; they had no strength to fight and no room to escape, and were slain where they stood, to the very last man. Having recovered Tusculum from its enemies, the army returned to Rome.

XXXIV. But in proportion as the successful wars of that year had everywhere secured tranquillity abroad, in the City the violence of the patricians and the sufferings of the plebs were increasing from one day to another, since the very fact that payment was compulsory made it more difficult to pay. And so, now that a man could make no compensation with his property, his reputation and his person

ditoribus satisfaciebant, poenaque in vicem fidei
3 cesserat. Adeo ergo obnoxios summiserant animos
non infimi solum sed principes etiam plebis, ut non
modo ad tribunatum militum inter patricios pe-
4 tendum, quod tanta vi ut liceret tetenderant, sed ne
ad plebeios quidem magistratus capessendos peten-
dosque ulli viro acri experientique animus esset,
possessionemque honoris usurpati modo a plebe
per paucos annos reciperasse in perpetuum patres
viderentur.

5 Ne id nimis laetum parti alteri esset, parva, ut
plerumque solet, rem ingentem moliundi causa
intervenit. M. Fabi Ambusti, potentis viri cum
inter sui corporis homines tum etiam ad plebem,
quod haudquaquam inter id genus contemptor eius
habebatur, filiae duae nuptae, Ser. Sulpicio maior,
minor C. Licinio Stoloni erat, illustri quidem viro
tamen plebeio; eaque ipsa adfinitas haud spreta
6 gratiam Fabio ad volgum quaesierat. Forte ita
incidit ut in Ser. Sulpici tribuni militum domo
sorores Fabiae cum inter se, ut fit, sermonibus
tempus tererent, lictor Sulpici, cum is de foro se
domum reciperet, forem, ut mos est, virga percu-
teret. Cum ad id moris eius insueta expavisset
minor Fabia, risui sorori fuit miranti ignorare id
7 sororem; ceterum is risus stimulos parvis mobili

---

[1] Father of the three envoys to the Gauls whose story is
told at v. xxxv. 36.

were made over and assigned to his creditor by way B.C. 377 of satisfaction, and punishment had come to take the place of payment. So abject indeed was the surrender not only of the lowest of the plebs but even of their leaders, that, far from contending with patricians for the military tribuneship—a privilege for which they had striven with such energy—there was not a man of them of sufficient force and enterprise to seek or to administer the plebeian magistracies. The patricians seemed therefore to have regained possession in perpetuity of an office which the plebeians had merely assumed for some few years.

That this state of affairs might not inspire excessive joy in the patricians, a trivial cause—as often happens—set on foot a mighty change. Marcus Fabius Ambustus[1] was very influential, not only amongst his fellows, but with the plebs as well, for the members of that class felt that he was far from looking down upon it. This man had married his two daughters, the elder to Servius Sulpicius, the younger to Gaius Licinius Stolo, a man of mark, albeit a plebeian; and the very fact that he had not rejected such an alliance had won regard for Fabius with the common people. It fell out that the sisters Fabia were together in the house of Servius Sulpicius, then a consular tribune, and were whiling away the time in talk, as women will, when a lictor of Sulpicius, who was returning from the Forum, rapped on the door, in the usual manner, with his rod. At this the younger Fabia, being unused to the custom, went white, which made the elder laugh with surprise at her sister's ignorance. But that laugh rankled in the other's mind, for a woman's feelings

LIVY

rebus animo muliebri subdidit. Frequentia quoque prosequentium rogantiumque num quid vellet credo fortunatum matrimonium ei sororis visum suique ipsam, malo arbitrio quo a proximis quisque mi-
8 nime anteiri volt, paenituisse. Confusam eam ex recenti morsu animi cum pater forte vidisset, percontatus "Satin salvae?"[1] avertentem causam doloris, quippe nec satis piam adversus sororem nec
9 admodum in virum honorificam, elicuit comiter sciscitando ut fateretur eam esse causam doloris, quod iuncta impari esset, nupta in domo quam nec
10 honos nec gratia intrare posset. Consolans inde filiam Ambustus bonum animum habere iussit: eosdem propediem domi visuram honores quos
11 apud sororem videat. Inde consilia inire cum genero coepit adhibito L. Sextio, strenuo adulescente et cuius spei nihil praeter genus patricium deesset.

XXXV. Occasio videbatur rerum novandarum propter ingentem vim aeris alieni, cuius levamen mali plebes nisi suis in summo imperio locatis nullum speraret: accingendum ad eam cogitatio-
2 nem esse; conando agendoque iam eo gradum fecisse plebeios unde, si porro adnitantur, pervenire ad summa et patribus aequari tam honore
3 quam virtute possent. In praesentia tribunos plebis fieri placuit, quo in magistratu sibimet ipsi viam ad
4 ceteros honores aperirent. Creatique tribuni C.

---

[1] Satin salvae *U* : satin salue Ω.

---

[1] Livy has omitted the consuls for A.U.C. 378 = B.C. 376.

are influenced by trifles. I suppose, too, that the B.C. 377
crowd of people who attended the tribune and took
a ceremonious leave of him made her look upon her
sister's marriage as a fortunate one and regret her
own, in that ill-judging spirit which makes us all so
very loath to be outdone by our nearest friends.
She was still suffering from the smart of wounded
pride, when her father, happening to see her, asked
if anything was wrong. She would fain have concealed the reason of her grief, which was too little
consistent with sisterly affection and did no great
honour to her husband; but he brought her by
tender inquiries to confess that she was unhappy in
being mated to one beneath her, having married
into a house where neither dignities nor influence
could enter. Ambustus then comforted his daughter
and bade her be of good cheer: she would see ere
long in her own home the same state she beheld at
her sister's. From that moment he began to make
plans with his son-in-law, taking into their counsels
also Lucius Sextius, a strenuous youth, whose as-
pirations were thwarted only by his lack of patrician
blood.

XXXV. An opportunity for innovation was pre- B.C. 375–
sented by the enormous load of debt, which the 371[1]
plebs could have no hope of lightening but by
placing their representatives in the highest offices.
They therefore argued that they must gird themselves to think of this: with toil and effort the
plebeians had already advanced so far that it was in
their power, if they continued to exert themselves,
to reach the highest ground, and to equal the
patricians in honours as well as in worth. For the
present it was resolved that Gaius Licinius and

A.U.C.
379–383

Licinius et L. Sextius promulgavere leges omnes
adversus opes patriciorum et pro commodis plebis,
unam de aere alieno, ut deducto eo de capite quod
usuris pernumeratum esset, id quod superesset tri-
5 ennio aequis pensionibus [1] persolveretur; alteram de
modo [2] agrorum, ne quis plus quingenta iugera agri
possideret; tertiam ne tribunorum militum comitia
fierent consulumque utique alter ex plebe crearetur;
cuncta ingentia et quae sine certamine maximo obtineri non possent.

6 Omnium igitur simul rerum, quarum immodica
cupido inter mortales est, agri pecuniae honorum,
discrimine proposito, conterriti patres cum trepi-
dassent publicis privatisque consiliis, nullo remedio
alio praeter expertam multis iam ante certaminibus
intercessionem invento collegas adversus tribunicias
7 rogationes comparaverunt.   Qui ubi tribus ad suffragium ineundum citari a Licinio Sextioque viderunt,
stipati patrum praesidiis nec recitari rogationes nec
sollemne quicquam aliud ad sciscendum plebi fieri
8 passi sunt.   Iamque frustra saepe concilio advocato
cum pro antiquatis rogationes essent : " Bene habet "
inquit Sextius ; "quando quidem tantum interces-

---

[1] pensionibus *Cuiacius* (*cf.* VII. xxvii. 3, xxx. xxxvii. 5):
pertionibus *T*: portionibus Ω.
[2] modo *D²A²*: domo Ω: dono *UA²*.

---

[1] This law appears to have had reference only to the public
lands. The reduction of excessive holdings was intended to
make the land accommodate a large number of poorer tenants.
In the year 357 B.C. Licinius was punished for transgressing
his own law (VII. xvi. 9).

Lucius Sextius should be elected tribunes of the
plebs, a magistracy in which they might open for
themselves a way to the other distinctions. Once
elected, they proposed only such measures as abated
the influence of the patricians, while forwarding the
interests of the plebs. One of these had to do
with debt, providing that what had been paid as
interest should be deducted from the original sum,
and the remainder discharged in three annual instalments of equal size. A second set a limit on
lands, prohibiting anyone from holding more than five
hundred *iugera*.[1] A third did away with the election
of military tribunes, and prescribed that of the
consuls one, at any rate, should be chosen from the
plebs. These were all matters of great moment, and
it would not be possible to carry them without a
tremendous struggle.

Now when all the things that men immoderately
covet, lands, money, and promotion, were jeopardized
at once, the patricians became thoroughly alarmed;
and failing, after frightened conference in public
and private gatherings, to devise any other remedy
than that which they had already tried before in
many struggles, provided themselves with friends
amongst the colleagues of the tribunes, to oppose
their measures. These men, seeing Licinius and
Sextius summon the tribes to vote, came up in the
midst of a body-guard of patricians, and refused to
permit the bills to be recited or anything else to be
done that was usual in passing a resolution of the
plebs. And now the assembly had been summoned
repeatedly without avail, and the rogations were as
though they had been voted down, when Sextius
cried out, "So be it! Since it is your pleasure that

LIVY

sionem pollere placet, isto ipso telo tutabimur
9 plebem. Agitedum, comitia indicite, patres, tribunis militum creandis; faxo ne quid iuvet[1] vox
ista 'veto,' qua nunc concinentes collegas nostros
10 tam laeti auditis." Haud inritae cecidere minae:
comitia praeter aedilium tribunorumque plebi nulla
sunt habita. Licinius Sextiusque tribuni plebis refecti nullos curules magistratus creari passi sunt;
eaque solitudo magistratuum et plebe reficiente
duos tribunos et iis comitia tribunorum militum
tollentibus per quinquennium urbem tenuit.

XXXVI. Alia bella opportune quievere: Veliterni
coloni gestientes otio, quod nullus exercitus Romanus
esset, et agrum Romanum aliquotiens incursavere et
2 Tusculum oppugnare adorti sunt; eaque res Tusculanis, veteribus sociis, novis civibus, opem orantibus
verecundia maxime non patres modo sed etiam ple-
3 bem movit. Remittentibus tribunis plebis comitia
per interregem sunt habita, creatique tribuni militum
L. Furius A. Manlius Ser. Sulpicius Ser. Cornelius
P.[2] et C. Valerii. Haudquaquam tam oboedientem
4 in dilectu quam in comitiis plebem habuere; ingentique contentione exercitu scripto profecti non ab
Tusculo modo summovere hostem sed intra suamet
5 ipsum moenia compulere, obsidebanturque haud
paulo vi maiore Velitrae quam Tusculum obsessum

---

[1] ne quid iuvet *Häggström*: ne qd iubet *U*: ne (ni? *M*)
iuuet (*or* iuet *or* iubet) Ω.

[2] P. *Sigonius* (*C.I.L.* i², p. 129): A. Ω: *omitted by U: O
is wanting at this point*.

318

the intercession should be so powerful, we will use that very weapon for the protection of the plebs. Come now, senators, and proclaim an assembly for the choice of military tribunes; I warrant you shall have no joy of that word *veto*, which you now hear with such satisfaction from the chorus of our colleagues." His threats were no idle ones: except for the aediles and tribunes of the plebs, there was not an election held. Licinius and Sextius were chosen again, and suffered no curule magistrates to be elected; and this dearth of magistrates continued in the City for five years, while the plebs continued to re-elect the two men tribunes, and they to prevent the election of military tribunes.

XXXVI. There was fortunately a respite from other wars, but the colonists of Velitrae, growing insolent in time of peace, because they knew that the Romans had no army, not only made several incursions into Roman territory, but went so far as to lay siege to Tusculum. This circumstance affected not only the senators but even the plebeians; that the Tusculans, who had long been their friends and were now their fellow citizens, should be imploring aid filled them with shame. The tribunes of the plebs relaxing their opposition, elections were held by an interrex, which resulted in the choice of the following military tribunes: Lucius Furius, Aulus Manlius, Servius Sulpicius, Servius Cornelius, and Publius and Gaius Valerius. They found the plebs much less submissive to the levy than they had been to the election; but by strenuous efforts they enrolled an army, and, marching out, not only drove the enemy away from Tusculum, but even shut him up within his own walls, and Velitrae was besieged with far

A.U.C.
384-385

fuerat. Nec tamen ab eis a quibus obsideri coeptae

6 erant expugnari potuere; ante novi creati sunt tribuni militum Q. Servilius C. Veturius A. et M.
Cornelii Q. Quinctius M. Fabius. Nihil ne ab his
quidem tribunis ad Velitras memorabile factum.

7   In maiore discrimine domi res vertebantur. Nam
praeter Sextium Liciniumque latores legum, iam
octavum tribunos plebis refectos, Fabius quoque
tribunus militum, Stolonis socer, quarum legum
auctor fuerat, earum suasorem se haud dubium fere-

8 bat; et cum octo ex collegio tribunorum plebi primo
intercessores legum fuissent, quinque soli erant, et,
ut ferme solent qui a suis desciscunt, capti et stu-
pentes animi vocibus alienis id modo quod domi
praeceptum erat intercessioni suae praetendebant:

9 Velitris in exercitu plebis magnam partem abesse;
in adventum militum comitia differri debere, ut
universa plebes de suis commodis suffragium ferret.

10 Sextius Liciniusque cum parte collegarum et uno ex
tribunis militum Fabio, artifices iam tot annorum usu
tractandi animos plebis, primores patrum productos
interrogando de singulis quae ferebantur ad popu-

11 lum, fatigabant: auderentne postulare ut, cum bina
iugera agri plebi dividerentur, ipsis plus quingenta

more vigour than Tusculum had been. Yet those
who had begun the siege were not able to conclude
it before the election of new military tribunes. The
candidates chosen were Quintus Servilius, Gaius
Veturius, Aulus and Marcus Cornelius, Quintus
Quinctius, and Marcus Fabius. Even these tribunes
accomplished nothing memorable at Velitrae.

At home the situation was more dangerous. For
besides Sextius and Licinius, who had proposed the
laws and were now for the eighth time re-elected
tribunes of the plebs, the military tribune Fabius,
Stolo's father-in-law, was openly advocating the
adoption of the measures he had himself suggested.
And whereas there had been at first eight members
of the college of plebeian tribunes who opposed the
bills, there were now but five; and these, puzzled
and confounded, as is apt to be the case with men
who forsake their party, were no more than mouth-
pieces, repeating in justification of their vetoes only
what they had been privately schooled to say, to wit,
that a majority of the plebeians were absent at Velitrae
with the army; and that the assemblies ought to be
put off until the return of the soldiers, so that the
entire body of the plebs might vote on matters that
concerned them. Sextius and Licinius, with some
of their colleagues and one of the military tribunes,
Fabius, being experts now—after so many years of
practice—in the art of playing on the passions of the
commons, would bring the leading senators forward
and ply them with questions about each of the
measures they were laying before the people : Had
they the hardihood to demand that, when land was
being assigned to the plebs in parcels of two *iugera*,
they themselves should be authorized to hold more

321

A.U.C.
384–385

iugera habere liceret, ut singuli prope trecentorum
civium possiderent agros, plebeio homini vix ad tectum necessarium aut locum sepulturae suus pateret
12 ager?   An placeret fenore circumventam plebem,
potius quam sortem [1] solvat, corpus in nervum ac
supplicia dare, et gregatim cottidie de foro addictos
duci et repleri vinctis nobiles domus, et ubicumque
patricius habitet, ibi carcerem privatum esse?

XXXVII. Haec indigna miserandaque auditu cum
apud timentes sibimet ipsos maiore audientium indig-
2 natione quam sua increpuissent, atqui nec agros
occupandi modum nec fenore trucidandi plebem
alium patribus unquam fore, adfirmabant, nisi alterum
ex plebe consulem, custodem suae libertatis, fecissent. [2]
3 Contemni iam tribunos plebis, quippe quae potestas
4 iam suam ipsa [3] vim frangat intercedendo.   Non posse
aequo iure agi ubi imperium penes illos, penes se
auxilium tantum sit; nisi imperio communicato nunquam plebem in parte pari rei publicae fore.   Nec
esse quod quisquam satis putet si plebeiorum ratio
comitiis consularibus habeatur; nisi alterum consulem utique ex plebe fieri necesse sit, neminem
5 fore.   An iam memoria exisse, cum tribunos militum
idcirco potius quam consules creari placuisset, ut et

---

[1] potius quam sortem *Conway*: ni potius quam sortem
creditum Ω (*but U has* sorte, *and O's text is uncertain*).
[2] libertatis fecissent *Walters*: libertatis plebi fecisset
(fecissent *M or* M^3) Ω.
[3] ipsa A^x_{5}: ipsam Ω.

---

[1] *Imperium*, which the tribunes of the plebs did not
possess.

than five hundred *iugera*? Did they desire that single
patricians should possess the allotments of almost
three hundred citizens; and that the plebeian should
have a farm scarce large enough to contain a shelter
for his necessities or a place of burial? Or was it
their wish that the plebs, undone with usury, should
give up their bodies to imprisonment and torture,
instead of paying the principal sums they owed?
Did they mean every day to drag off gangs of condemned debtors from the Forum? to fill with
prisoners the houses of the nobles? to make of
every patrician's dwelling a private gaol?

XXXVII. The shame and pity of these conditions
awoke more indignation in their hearers, who feared
for their own safety, than the speakers had themselves felt in denouncing them. And yet the
patricians—as they proceeded to assert—would never
check their greed for land, nor cease murdering
the plebs with usury, until the commons should
elect one of the two consuls from their own number,
to guard their liberties. Contempt, they argued,
was now become the portion of the plebeian
tribunes, for they used the veto to break down
their own power. There could be no question of
equal rights, where the other side commanded
and they themselves could do nothing but protest.
Until they shared in the authority,[1] the plebs would
never have an equal footing in the state. And let
no one think that it would be sufficient if plebeians
were accepted as candidates at the consular elections:
unless it were required that at least one consul must
be chosen from the commons, none ever would be.
Had they already forgotten, that although the
election of tribunes of the soldiers rather than

323

A.U.C.
385–384

plebeiis pateret summus honos, quattuor et quadraginta annis neminem ex plebe tribunum militum
6 creatum esse ?   Qui crederent duobus nunc [1] in locis
sua voluntate impertituros plebi honorem, qui octona
loca tribunis militum creandis occupare soliti sint, et
ad consulatum viam fieri passuros, qui tribunatum
7 saeptum tam diu habuerint?   Lege obtinendum esse
quod comitiis per gratiam nequeat, et seponendum
extra certamen alterum consulatum, ad quem plebi
sit aditus, quoniam in certamine relictus praemium
8 semper potentioris futurus sit.   Nec iam posse dici id
quod antea iactare soliti sint, non esse in plebeiis
idoneos viros ad curulis magistratus ; numquid enim
socordius aut segnius rem publicam administrari
post [2] P. Licini Calvi tribunatum, qui primus ex
plebe creatus sit, quam per eos annos gesta sit
quibus praeter patricios nemo tribunus militum
fuerit?   Quin contra patricios aliquot damnatos
9 post tribunatum, neminem plebeium.   Quaestores
quoque, sicut tribunos militum, paucis ante annis ex
plebe coeptos creari nec ullius eorum populum Ro-
10 manum paenituisse.   Consulatum superesse plebeiis ;
eam esse arcem libertatis, id columen.   Si eo per-
ventum sit, tum populum Romanum vere exactos ex
urbe reges et stabilem libertatem suam existima-

---

[1] nunc *Iac. Gronovius*: ne (nc *L?*) Ω.
[2] post ⸝: potest post Ω: potens post *H*: potest *D?LA*:
posse post *A^x*.

---

[1] In 400 B.C. (v. xii. 9).

consuls had been resolved upon, expressly in order
that the highest honour might be open even to
plebeians, yet for four and forty years no commoner had been chosen to that office? How could
they suppose, that with two places only now avail-
able, the patricians would of their own volition bestow the office on the plebs, when they had habitually
claimed eight places in electing military tribunes?
Would those men allow the consulship to be
approached, who had blocked so long the road to
the tribuneship? The law must make good for
them what they could not gain by favour at the
elections; one of the two consulships must be set
apart for the undisputed use of the plebs, for if left
in dispute it would always fall a prize to the more
powerful. Neither could it any longer be maintained—as the nobles had been wont to assert—
that among the plebeians were none who were
suitable for curule magistracies. Had the public
administration been a jot more indifferent or slip-
shod since the tribuneship of Publius Licinius
Calvus, who was the first man elected from the
plebs,[1] than it had been during those years in which
none but patricians had been military tribunes?
Nay, on the contrary, several patricians had been
impeached after holding the tribuneship, but not
one plebeian. Quaestors, too, like military tribunes,
had begun a few years before to be elected from
the commons, nor had the Roman People regretted
it in a single case. The consulship remained for
the commons to achieve; this was the citadel of
liberty, this its pillar. If they attained to this, then
would the Roman People hold that the kings had
been really driven from the City, and their freedom

11 turum ; quippe ex illa die in plebem ventura omnia
quibus patricii excellant, imperium atque honorem,
gloriam belli, genus, nobilitatem, magna ipsis fruenda,
maiora liberis relinquenda.

12   Huius generis orationes ubi accipi videre, novam
rogationem promulgant, ut pro duumviris sacris
faciundis decemviri creentur ita ut pars ex plebe,
pars ex patribus fiat ; omniumque earum rogationum
comitia in adventum eius exercitus differunt qui
Velitras obsidebat.

   XXXVIII. Prius circumactus est annus quam a
Velitris reducerentur legiones ; ita suspensa de legibus res ad novos tribunos militum dilata ; nam plebis
tribunos eosdem, duos utique qui [1] legum latores
2 erant, plebes reficiebat.   Tribuni militum creati
T. Quinctius Ser. Cornelius Ser. Sulpicius Sp. Ser-
3 vilius L. Papirius L. Veturius.   Principio statim anni
ad ultimam dimicationem de legibus ventum ; et cum
tribus vocarentur nec intercessio collegarum latoribus
obstaret, trepidi patres ad duo ultima auxilia, summum imperium summumque ad civem decurrunt.
4 Dictatorem dici placet ; dicitur M. Furius Camillus,
qui magistrum equitum L. Aemilium cooptat. Legum
quoque latores adversus tantum apparatum adver-

---

[1] qui ϛ: quia Ω: que *A*.

---

[1] The nobles were those who had held—or whose ancestors
had held—curule chairs. Originally nobility had been confined to the patriciate, with which, indeed—since most
patrician families could point to some office-holding ancestor,
—it had been practically identical. The new nobility comprised plebeians as well as patricians, and owing to the
tendency of the electorate to continue the same families in
office, it became almost as exclusive a body as the old
patriciate.

firmly based; for the commons would thenceforward be partakers in all that made the patricians now surpass them,—authority and honour, martial renown, birth and nobility,[1]—great things for themselves to enjoy, but even greater to bequeath to their children.

Perceiving that speeches of this sort were well received, they introduced a new measure, providing that in place of two men vested with superintendence of the sacred rites, a board of ten should be elected, with a proviso that half the number should be of the plebs, and half patricians; the voting on all these bills they deferred until the return of the army which was besieging Velitrae.

XXXVIII. A year rolled round before the legions could be brought back from Velitrae; consequently the question of the laws remained in abeyance and was put off until the coming in of the new military tribunes; for as to the tribunes of the plebs, the commons chose the same men over again—the two, at any rate, who had brought in the bills. The military tribunes chosen were Titus Quinctius, Servius Cornelius, Servius Sulpicius, Spurius Servilius, Lucius Papirius, and Lucius Veturius. At the very outset of the year came a final struggle over the laws; and when the tribes were summoned to vote, and the proposers of the measures would not yield to the vetoes of their colleagues, the frightened patricians were put to their two last shifts—the greatest office, and the greatest of the citizens. They voted to name a dictator, and appointed Marcus Furius Camillus, who chose Lucius Aemilius for his master of the horse. To meet these formidable preparations of their adversaries, the proposers

sariorum et ipsi causam plebis ingentibus animis
armant concilioque plebis indicto tribus ad suffragium
vocant.

5 Cum dictator, stipatus agmine patriciorum, plenus
irae minarumque consedisset atque ageretur res
solito primum certamine inter se tribunorum plebi
ferentium legem intercedentiumque et, quanto iure
potentior intercessio erat, tantum vinceretur favore
legum ipsarum latorumque et "uti rogas" primae
6 tribus dicerent, tum Camillus "Quando quidem"
inquit, "Quirites, iam vos tribunicia libido, non
potestas regit, et intercessionem secessione quondam
plebis partam vobis eadem vi facitis inritam qua
peperistis, non rei publicae magis universae quam
vestra causa dictator intercessioni adero eversumque
7 vestrum auxilium imperio tutabor. Itaque si C.
Licinius et L. Sextius intercessioni collegarum
cedunt, nihil patricium magistratum inseram concilio
plebis ; si adversus intercessionem tamquam captae
civitati leges imponere tendent, vim tribuniciam a
se ipsa dissolvi non patiar."

8 Adversus ea cum contemptim tribuni plebis rem
nihilo segnius peragerent, tum percitus ira Camillus
lictores qui de medio plebem emoverent misit et
additit minas, si pergerent, sacramento omnes

B.C. 368

of the laws on their side armed the commons with tremendous enthusiasm for the cause, and proclaiming a council of the plebs, called up the tribes to vote.

Attended by a body of patricians, and breathing wrath and menaces, the dictator took his seat, and the affair began with the usual skirmish between the tribunes of the plebs, some of whom urged the passing of the law while others interposed their vetoes. But powerful as the veto was on the legal side, it was being overcome by the popularity of the bills themselves and their proposers, and the tribes which had been summoned first were voting "Ay," when Camillus addressed the people. "Quirites," he said, "since you are now swayed not by the authority of the tribunes but by their lawlessness, and are bringing to naught the right of protest—obtained through the secession of the plebs—with the same violence with which you won it; for your own sake no less than for the sake of the whole republic, I shall, as dictator, sustain the veto, and safeguard with my absolute authority your defence which you are overthrowing. If then Gaius Licinius and Lucius Sextius yield to the protest of their colleagues, I will in no way intrude a patrician magistracy upon a council of the plebs; but if, in defiance of the protest, they try to impose their terms, as though upon a conquered state, I will not permit the tribunician power to work its own undoing."

This warning the tribunes treated with contempt, and were proceeding with unabated energy to carry out their plans, when Camillus, in high dudgeon, sent his lictors to turn the commons out; and threatened, that if they continued in their course, he would

iuniores adacturum exercitumque extemplo ex urbe
9 educturum.   Terrorem ingentem incusserat plebi:
ducibus plebis accendit magis certamine animos
quam minuit.   Sed re neutro inclinata magistratu se
abdicavit, seu quia vitio creatus erat, ut scripsere
quidam, seu quia tribuni plebis tulerunt ad plebem
idque plebs scivit, ut, si M. Furius pro dictatore
10 quid egisset, quingentum milium ei multa esset; sed
auspiciis magis quam novi exempli rogatione deterri-
tum ut potius credam, cum ipsius viri facit ingenium,
tum quod ei suffectus est extemplo P. Manlius dictator—quem quid creari attinebat ad id certamen quo
11 M. Furius victus esset?—et quod eundem M. Furium
dictatorem insequens annus habuit, haud sine pudore
certe fractum priore anno in se imperium repeti-
12 turum; simul quod eo tempore quo promulgatum de
multa eius traditur aut et huic rogationi, qua se in
ordinem cogi videbat, obsistere potuit, aut ne illas
13 quidem propter quas et haec lata erat impedire; et
quod quicquid[1] usque ad memoriam nostram tribuniciis consularibusque certatum viribus est, dictaturae
semper altius fastigium fuit.

XXXIX. Inter priorem dictaturam abdicatam no-
vamque a Manlio initam ab tribunis velut per inter-

----

[1] quod quicquid *Rossbach* (*Berl. Phil. Woch.*, 1920, *col.*
704): quod Ω.

administer the oath to all of military age, and forthwith lead the army out of the City.

The plebs were greatly dismayed; but the courage
of their leaders was rather kindled than damped by
his vehemence. Yet before the matter had been
decided either way, Camillus resigned his office,
whether because there had been a flaw in his election
—as certain writers have held—or because the tribunes proposed to the plebs and the plebs decreed,
that if Marcus Furius should take any action in the
capacity of dictator, he should be fined five hundred
thousand asses. But that the auspices, and not a law
without a precedent, were responsible for his with-
drawal, the very nature of the man inclines me to
believe; also the fact that Publius Manlius was at
once made dictator in his place—for what good
would his appointment do, in a struggle in which
Marcus Furius had been beaten? Besides, Marcus
Furius himself was dictator again in the following
year, and he would surely have been ashamed to
resume an authority which had broken down in his
own hands the year before. Moreover at the time
when the proposal to fine him is said to have been
made, either he had the power to resist this order
—which deprived him, as he could see, of all
authority,—or else he lacked the power to obstruct
even those measures in defence of which this order
had been proposed. Finally, whatever conflicts have
occurred between tribunes and consuls, down to the
times we can ourselves remember, the dictatorship
has always towered above them.

XXXIX. In the interval between the abdication
of the earlier dictator and the entrance upon his
office of the new one, Manlius, the tribunes—as

LIVY

regnum concilio plebis habito apparuit quae ex
promulgatis plebi, quae latoribus gratiora essent.
2 Nam de fenore atque agro rogationes iubebant, de
plebeio consule antiquabant; et perfecta utraque
res esset, ni tribuni se in omnia simul consulere
3 plebem dixissent.   P. Manlius deinde dictator rem
in causam plebis inclinavit C. Licinio, qui tribunus
militum fuerat, magistro equitum de plebe dicto.
4 Id aegre patres passos accipio; dictatorem propinqua cognatione Licini se apud patres excusare solitum, simul negantem magistri equitum maius quam
tribuni consularis imperium esse.
5   Licinius Sextiusque, cum tribunorum plebi crean-
dorum indicta comitia essent, ita se gerere ut
negando iam sibi velle continuari honorem acerrime
accenderent ad id quod dissimulando petebant ple-
6 bem: nonum se annum iam velut in acie [1] adversus
optimates maximo privatim periculo, nullo publice
emolumento stare. Consenuisse iam secum et rogationes promulgatas et vim omnem tribuniciae potesta-
7 tis. Primo intercessione collegarum in leges suas
pugnatum esse, deinde ablegatione iuventutis ad
Veliternum bellum, postremo dictatorium fulmen in

---

[1] in acie *UD*[3] *Gronovius* (1665): in aciem Ω.

---

[1] *i. e.* the consular tribunes counted for nothing, and the
tribunes of the plebs could proceed without let or hindrance.
[2] Not the tribune of the plebs, but possibly his father.
Livy perhaps included him among the consular tribunes for
378 B.C. (*cf.* chap. xxi. § 1; where the text is uncertain) or
should have included him among those for the year 376 B.C.,
but has omitted the entire list (chap. xxxiv). *Diod.* xv. 57,
gives Gaius Licinius as one of four consular tribunes for the
year 378 B.C.

though there were an interregnum [1]—held a council B.C. 368
of the plebs, and it became evident which of the
measures proposed were more acceptable to the
plebeians, and which to their introducers. For
the tribes were on the point of passing the bills
relating to interest and land, and of rejecting the
one about the plebeian consul, and both policies
would have been finally disposed of, if the tribunes
had not said that they were putting all these
questions to the plebs collectively. Then Publius
Manlius, becoming dictator, gave the affair a turn
in favour of the plebs by naming Gaius Licinius,[2]
who had been military tribune and was a commoner,
his master of the horse. I find that the patricians
took offence at this, but that the dictator was wont
to excuse himself to them by alleging his close
relationship to Licinius, and asserting that a master
of the horse possessed no greater authority than a
consular tribune.

Licinius and Sextius, when an assembly had been
proclaimed for the election of plebeian tribunes, so
bore themselves that while professing an unwilling-
ness to be re-elected, they furnished the plebs with
the strongest incentives to give them what they
pretended not to covet. They said it was now nine
years that they had stood embattled, as it were,
against the optimates, with the greatest danger to
themselves and no advantage to the public. The
measures they had proposed and the whole power
of the tribunate had, like themselves, grown old and
useless. First the intercession of their colleagues
had been employed to attack their laws; then the
young men had been banished to the seat of war at
Velitrae; finally they had themselves been menaced

8 se intentatum. Iam nec collegas nec bellum nec
dictatorem obstare, quippe qui etiam omen plebeio
consuli magistro[1] equitum ex plebe dicendo dederit:
9 se ipsam plebe et commoda morari sua. Liberam
urbem ac forum a creditoribus, liberos agros ab
iniustis possessoribus extemplo, si velit, habere posse.
10 Quae munera quando tandem satis grato animo
aestimaturos, si inter accipiendas de suis commodis
rogationes spem honoris latoribus earum incidant?
Non esse modestiae populi Romani id postulare ut
ipse fenore levetur et in agrum iniuria possessum a
potentibus inducatur, per quos ea consecutus sit
senes tribunicios non sine honore tantum sed etiam
11 sine spe honoris relinquat. Proinde ipsi primum
statuerent apud animos quid vellent deinde comitiis
tribuniciis declararent voluntatem. Si coniuncte[2]
ferre ab se promulgatas rogationes vellent, esse
quod eosdem reficerent tribunos plebis; perlaturos
12 enim quae promulgaverint; sin quod cuique privatim
opus sit id modo accipi velint, opus esse nihil invi-
diosa continuatione honoris; nec se tribunatum nec
illos ea quae promulgata sint habituros.

XL. Adversus tam obstinatam orationem tribunorum cum prae indignitate rerum stupor silentiumque

---

[1] magistro Ω: magistrum *U Häggström*.
[2] coniuncte (*or* -tae) Ω: coniuxte *HTDLA?*: coniunctim ς
D akenborch.

with the thunderbolt of the dictatorship. At present B.C. 368
they were thwarted neither by their colleagues, nor
by war, nor even by the dictator, for he had actually
given them a presage of plebeian consuls by appointing a plebeian master of the horse : no, it was the
plebs themselves who stood in the way of their own
advancement. A City and a Forum rid of creditors,
and lands delivered from unlawful occupation, were
things they might enjoy at once, if they would.
When, pray, did they expect to weigh these blessings
and be duly grateful, if at the very moment of
entertaining measures for their own advantage they
cut off all hope of office from the men who introduced them ? It was not like the reasonableness
of the Roman People to ask to be relieved themselves of usury and settled on lands which the nobles
had unjustly held, while leaving the men to whom
they owed these advantages to grow old as tri-
bunicians—not only without honours, but even without the hope of them. So let them first make up
their minds what it was they wished ; and then
declare their wishes at the election of the tribunes.
If they desired to enact together the measures which
the tribunes had brought forward, there was some
reason for re-electing them ; for they would carry
through what they had advocated ; but if every man
cared only for the adoption of such clauses as concerned him personally, there was no use in an
invidious prolongation of their term ; they would
do without the tribuneship, and the people would
do without the proposed reforms.

XL. On hearing the tribunes make this stubborn
speech, though the other senators were dazed and
dumbfounded by such outrageous arguments, they

A.U.C.
386

2 inde ceteros patrum defixisset, Ap. Claudius Crassus, nepos decemviri, dicitur odio magis iraque quam spe ad dissuadendum processisse et locutus in hanc fere

3 sententiam esse : " Neque novum neque inopinatum mihi sit, Quirites, si, quod unum familiae nostrae semper obiectum est ab seditiosis tribunis, id nunc ego quoque audiam, Claudiae gentis[1] iam inde ab initio nihil antiquius in re publica patrum maiestate fuisse, semper plebis commodis adversatos esse.

4 Quorum alterum neque nego neque infitias eo, nos, ex quo adsciti sumus simul in civitatem et patres, enixe operam dedisse ut per nos aucta potius quam imminuta maiestas earum gentium inter quas nos esse

5 voluistis dici vere posset: illud alterum pro me maioribusque meis contendere ausim, Quirites, nisi quae pro universa re publica fiant ea plebi tamquam aliam incolenti urbem adversa quis putet, nihil nos neque privatos neque in magistratibus quod incommodum plebi esset scientes fecisse nec ullum factum dictumve nostrum contra utilitatem vestram, etsi quaedam

6 contra voluntatem fuerint, vere referri posse. An hoc, si Claudiae familiae non sim nec ex patricio sanguine ortus sed unus Quiritium quilibet, qui modo me duobus ingenuis ortum et vivere in libera civitate

7 sciam, reticere possim, L. illum Sextium et C. Licinium, perpetuos, si dis placet, tribunos, tantum licen-

---

[1] Claudiae gentis Ω (*cf. Walters and Conway ad loc.*): claudiae genti ς.

---

[1] See II. xvi. 4–5.

say that Appius Claudius Crassus, the decemvir's grandson, moved more by hate and resentment than by hope, came forward to oppose them, and spoke to the following purpose: " It would be no strange or surprising thing to me, Quirites, if on this occasion I, too, should be taunted with the one reproach that rebellious tribunes have ever directed at our family, to wit, that the Claudian gens from its very origin has regarded no feature of our public life as more important than the majesty of the senate and has always opposed the interests of the plebs. The former of these charges I neither deny nor seek to refute—namely, that we have striven with all our might, from the day we were first called to be citizens and senators,[1] that, so far as in us lay, the dignity of those families with which you proposed to rank us might truthfully be said to have rather gained than lost ; as to the other charge, I would venture to maintain, Quirites, speaking for myself and for my forefathers, that unless one should assume that what is done for the good of the whole nation is opposed to the welfare of the plebs,—as though they inhabited another city,—we have never wittingly done anything, whether as private citizens or magistrates, disadvantageous to the plebs ; and that no word or act of ours can be truthfully alleged as being against your interests, though some there may have been which ran counter to your wishes. But were I not a Claudius, nor sprung from a patrician line, but were merely any one of the Quirites, assuming only that I knew my parents had both been born to freedom and that I lived in a free state, could I pass this by in silence ? Are L. Sextius yonder and Gaius Licinius, our perpetual tribunes—

337

tiae novem annis quibus regnant sumpsisse ut vobis
negent potestatem liberam suffragii non in comitiis,
non in legibus iubendis, se permissuros esse?

8   "'Sub condicione' inquit, 'nos reficietis decimum
tribunos.' Quid est aliud dicere 'quod petunt alii
nos adeo fastidimus ut sine mercede magna non

9 accipiamus'? Sed quae tandem ista merces est qua
vos semper tribunos plebis habeamus? 'Ut rogationes' inquit 'nostras, seu placent seu displicent,
seu utiles seu inutiles sunt, omnes coniunctim acci-

10 piatis.' Obsecro vos, Tarquinii tribuni plebis, putate
me ex media contione unum civem succlamare, 'bona
venia vestra liceat ex his rogationibus legere quas

11 salubres nobis censemus esse, antiquare alias.' 'Non'
inquit 'licebit tu[1] de fenore atque agris quod ad vos
omnes pertinet iubeas, et hoc portenti non fiat in
urbe Romana uti L. Sextium atque hunc C. Licinium
consules, quod indignaris, quod abominaris, videas;

12 aut omnia accipe, aut nihil fero'; ut si quis ei quem
urgeat fames venenum ponat cum cibo et aut absti-
nere eo quod vitale sit iubeat aut mortiferum vitali
admisceat. Ergo si esset libera haec civitas, non
tibi frequentes succlamassent, 'abi hinc cum tribunatibus ac rogationibus tuis!' Quid? Si tu non
tuleris quod commodum est populo accipere, nemo

13 erit qui ferat? Illud si quis patricius, si quis—quod
illi volunt invidiosius esse—Claudius diceret, 'aut

---

¹ licebit tu (tum *O*) Ω : licebit ut *Madvig*: licebit. Tu *H. J.
Mueller, Luterbacher*: licebit. Tu—— videas? *Alschefski*:
licebit ut et tu *Conway*.

---

¹ *i.e.*, tribunes as tyrannical as the Tarquin kings.

save the mark !—grown so presumptuous in the nine B.C. 3€
years of their reign, as to threaten that they will
leave you free to exercise your right of suffrage
neither in elections nor in enacting laws?

" ' On a certain condition,' says one of them, ' you
shall elect us tribunes for the tenth time ' ; as though
he were to say, ' What others sue for we are so surfeited
withal that we will not accept it without a great
reward.' But what in short is that reward by the
grant of which we may always have you for tribunes
of the plebs? ' That you adopt,' says he, ' all our
rogations in a lump, whether you like them or detest
them,—be they good or bad.' I beseech you,
Tarquin tribunes of the plebs,[1] imagine me a simple
citizen calling out from the midst of the assembly,
' By your good leave, suffer us to choose from these
proposals those we regard as wholesome for us, and
to reject the rest.' ' No,' he answers, ' you shall
not have leave to enact the measures that concern
you all, touching interest and lands, unless you will
put up with the monstrous sight in Rome of Lucius
Sextius and Gaius Licinius here as consuls—an idea
you loathe and abominate ;—accept everything, or I
offer nothing.' As though a man were starving, and
one should serve poison to him with his food, and
command him either to abstain from what would give
him life, or mix the deadly with the life-giving. Well
then ! If this state were free, would not the people
have cried out to you in full assembly, ' Begone,
with your tribuneships and your rogations !' Come !
If you will not propose what is profitable to the
people to accept, shall there be none to do it?
Suppose that some patrician, or—what those fellows
would make out to be still more hateful—some

339

LIVY

omnia accipite, aut nihil fero,' quis vestrum, Quirites,

14 ferret? Numquamne vos res potius quam auctores
spectabitis sed omnia semper quae magistratus ille
dicet secundis auribus, quae ab nostrum quo dicentur
adversis accipietis?

15 "At hercule sermo est minime civilis. Quid? Rogatio qualis est, quam a vobis antiquatam indignan-
tur? Sermoni, Quirites, simillima. 'Consules'

16 inquit, 'rogo ne vobis quos velitis facere liceat.'
An aliter rogat qui utique alterum ex plebe fieri
consulem iubet nec duos patricios creandi potestatem

17 vobis permittit? Si hodie bella sint, quale Etruscum
fuit cum Porsinna [1] Ianiculum insedit, quale Gallicum modo, cum praeter Capitolium atque arcem
omnia haec hostium erant, et consulatum cum hoc
M. Furio et quolibet alio ex patribus L. ille Sextius
peteret, possetisne ferre Sextium haud pro dubio

18 consule [2] esse, Camillum de repulsa dimicare? Hocine est in commune honores vocare, ut duos plebeios
fieri consules liceat, duos patricios non liceat? Et
alterum ex plebe creari necesse sit, utrumque ex
patribus praeterire liceat? Quaenam ista societas,
quaenam consortio est? Parum est, si, cuius pars
tua nulla adhuc fuit, in partem eius venis, nisi

19 partem petendo totum traxeris? 'Timeo' inquit,
'ne, si duos licebit creari patricios, neminem creetis

[1] *The form* Porsinna *is used throughout this edition, though*
Ω *here read* Porsenna (persona *B*). *Cf. Conway and Walters*
on II. ix. 1.
[2] consule *Madvig*: consulem Ω.

Claudius, should say, 'Either take all or I will propose nothing,' which of you, Quirites, would endure it? Will you never choose rather to look at facts than at advocates, but always lend ready ears to the utterances of that noble magistrate, and refuse to hear what is said by any of us?

"His *language*, you will admit, is far from appropriate in a free state; well, what of his *rogation*, which they resent your refusal to accept? Quirites, it is all of a piece with his words. 'I propose,' he says, 'that it shall not be permitted you to choose such consuls as you will.' For can aught else be his meaning, when he commands that in any case one consul be chosen from the plebs, and deprives you of the power to name two patricians? If wars should arise in these days, like the Etruscan war, when Porsinna held Janiculum, or like the Gallic war a little while ago, when all this City—except the Capitol and the Citadel—was in the hands of your enemies; and if Lucius Sextius were standing for the consulship, along with Marcus Furius here, and any other patrician whomsoever; could you endure that Lucius Sextius should be certain of election, while Camillus had to risk defeat? Is it thus they would equalize the opportunities of office? Would they authorize the election of two plebeian consuls, and forbid the choice of two patricians? Must we perforce take one plebeian, while for both places we may pass the patricians by? What sort of fellowship, of partnership, is this? Are you not satisfied to get a part of that in which you had no part before, unless in reaching for the part you can seize the whole? 'I fear' he replies, 'lest if it be permitted to choose two patricians, you may

plebeium.' Quid est dicere aliud 'quia indignos
vestra voluntate creaturi non estis, necessitatem
20 vobis creandi quos non voltis, imponam'? Quid
sequitur, nisi ut ne beneficium quidem debeat populo, si cum duobus patriciis unus petierit plebeius et
lege se, non suffragio, creatum dicat?

XLI. "Quomodo   extorqueant,   non   quomodo
petant honores, quaerunt; et ita maxima sunt adep-
turi, ut nihil ne pro minimis quidem debeant; et
occasionibus potius quam virtute petere honores
2 malunt.   Est aliquis, qui se inspici, aestimari fasti-
diat, qui certos sibi uni honores inter dimicantes
competitores aequum censeat esse, qui se arbitrio
vestro eximat, qui vestra necessaria suffragia pro
3 voluntariis et serva pro liberis faciat.   Omitto Licinium Sextiumque, quorum annos in perpetua potestate tamquam regum in Capitolio numeratis: quis
est hodie in civitate tam humilis cui non via ad consulatum facilior per istius legis occasionem quam
nobis ac liberis nostris fiat?   Si quidem nos ne cum
volueritis quidem creare interdum poteritis, istos
etiam si nolueritis necesse sit.

4   " De indignitate satis dictum est.   At enim[1] digni-
tas ad homines pertinet.   Quid de religionibus
atque auspiciis, quae propria deorum immortalium
contemptio atque iniuria est, loquar?   Auspiciis
hanc urbem conditam esse, auspiciis bello ac pace

[1] at enim *Madvig*: etenim Ω.

---

[1] Statues of the kings were set up on the Capitol, and on
their bases were recorded the years they had reigned.   But
this had not yet been done in 368 B.C.

342

choose no one from the plebs.' His meaning is: B.C. 368
'Since of your own accord you will never choose
unworthy men, I will make it obligatory on you to
elect those whom you do not wish.' What follows?
Why, a man would not owe the people so much as
thanks, if he were the sole plebeian candidate along
with two patricians: he would say that he had been
elected not by your suffrages, but by the statute.

XLI. "They would force us, not invite us, to
grant them office; and thus they mean to win the
very highest honours without incurring even such
obligations as would be imposed by the least important. They would make their canvass not on
worth but on opportunity. There is many a man who
resents being investigated and appraised, who thinks
it right that he alone should be certain of success,
while his competitors are struggling for office;
who would withdraw himself from your judgment;
who would have you vote for him from compulsion,
not from choice—not as freemen, but as slaves. I
say nothing of Licinius and Sextius, whose years of
continuous power you reckon like those of the kings
on the Capitol: [1] who is there in the state to-day so
lowly that the opportunities afforded by that law
would not make access to the consulship easier for
him than for us and for our children? To elect us will
sometimes be beyond your power, even though you
wish it; but those persons you would be compelled
to elect, even against your inclinations.

"Of the indignity of the thing I have said enough.
But dignity after all is concerned with men: what
of religious observances and auspices—for the immortal gods are involved in insult and disrespect to
these? That this City was founded under auspices;

LIVY

domi militiaeque omnia geri, quis est qui ignoret?
5 Penes quos igitur sunt auspicia more maiorum?
Nempe penes patres; nam plebeius quidem magis-
6 tratus nullus auspicato creatur; nobis adeo propria
sunt auspicia ut non solum quos populus creat
patricios magistratus non aliter quam auspicato
creet, sed nos quoque ipsi sine suffragio populi
auspicato interregem prodamus et privatim[1] auspicia
habeamus, quae isti ne in magistratibus quidem
7 habent. Quid igitur aliud quam tollit ex civitate
auspicia qui plebeios consules creando a patribus,
8 qui soli ea habere possunt, aufert? Eludant nunc
licet religiones, 'quid enim esse, si pulli non pascantur,[2] si ex cavea tardius exierint, si occecinerit[3]
avis?' Parva sunt haec; sed parva ista non con-
temnendo maiores vestri maximam hanc rem fece-
9 runt; nunc nos, tamquam iam nihil pace deorum
opus sit, omnes caerimonias polluimus. Volgo ergo
pontifices augures sacrificuli reges creentur; cuili-
bet apicem Dialem, dummodo homo sit, imponamus;
tradamus ancilia, penetralia, deos deorumque curam

---

[1] privatim Ω: privati *Crévier.*
[2] esse—pascantur *Madvig*: est—pascentur Ω.
[3] si occecinerit *PFBTL*: si occinerit *U*: si occecinerint
H: si hoc cecinerit *DA*: hoc cecinerit *O*: *omitted by M*
(*which has* exierit auis).

---

[1] The speaker alludes to two kinds of omens: (1) the
general took with him to the field a coop of chickens, and
if these, on being offered corn, came out and devoured it
with avidity, the presage was favourable; this kind of
divination was called *ex tripudiis*, from the way the corns
danced upon the ground as they fell from the beaks of the
greedy fowls; (2) the flight of certain birds was observed and
any noise—such as the cry of a bird—was held to vitiate the
auspice.

344

that all measures, warlike and peaceful, at home and B.C. 368
in the field, are carried out with auspices, who does
not know ? Who then control the auspices, by the
tradition of our fathers? The patricians, to be sure ;
for no plebeian magistrate is elected under auspices ;
the auspices belong so exclusively to us, that not
only are the patrician magistrates whom the people
elect no otherwise elected than with auspices, but
we ourselves even—without the people's suffrage—
take auspices and nominate an interrex ; and have,
as private citizens, the right of taking them, which
you plebeians have not even in your magistracies.
He therefore deprives the state outright of auspices,
who by electing plebeian consuls deprives the
patricians of them—for they alone can take them.
They may jeer now, if they like, at religious scruples.
'After all,' they will say, 'what difference does
it make if the sacred chickens [1] will not feed ; if they
are slow to come out from the coop ; if a bird utters
an ill-omened cry ? ' These are trivial things ; but
because they did not scorn these trivial things, your
fathers were able to build this great republic ; and
now we, as though we had no further use for
Heaven's favour, are polluting all the ceremonies.
Let pontiffs then, augurs, and kings of the sacrifices,
be chosen from the vulgar herd ; let us set the mitre
of the Flamen Dialis on anybody's head, so he but
be a man ; let us make over the sacred shields, the
inner shrine,[2] the gods and the service of the gods,
to those whom we may not without sin intrust with
them ; let laws be proposed and magistrates elected

[2] In the Atrium of Vesta, where among other relics was
preserved the Palladium.

A.U.C
386 .10 quibus nefas est; non leges auspicato ferantur, non
magistratus creentur, nec centuriatis nec curiatis
comitiis patres auctores fiant; Sextius et Licinius
tamquam Romulus ac Tatius in urbe Romana reg-
nent, quia pecunias alienas, quia agros dono dant.
11 Tanta dulcedo est ex alienis fortunis praedandi, nec
in mentem venit altera lege solitudines vastas in
agris fieri pellendo finibus dominos, altera fidem
abrogari cum qua omnis humana societas tollitur?
12 Omnium rerum causa vobis antiquandas censeo istas
rogationes. Quod faxitis deos velim fortunare.[1]"

A.U.C.
387 XLII. Oratio Appi ad id modo valuit ut tempus
2 rogationum iubendarum proferretur. Refecti de-
cumum iidem [2] tribuni, Sextius et Licinius, de decemviris sacrorum ex parte de plebe creandis legem
pertulere. Creat quinque patrum, quinque plebis;
graduque eo iam via facta ad consulatum videbatur.
3 Hac victoria contenta plebes cessit patribus ut in
praesentia consulum mentione omissa tribuni militum
crearentur. Creati A. et M. Cornelii iterum M.
Geganius P. Manlius L. Veturius P. Valerius sextum.
4 Cum praeter Velitrarum obsidionem, tardi magis
rem exitus quam dubii, quietae externae res Romanis
essent, fama repens belli Gallici allata perpulit
civitatem ut M. Furius dictator quintum diceretur.
Is T. Quinctium Poenum magistrum equitum dixit.

---

[1] velim fortunare ς: uel infortunare Ω: velinfortunare
PFT.
[2] iidem ς: idem Ω: id est P.

---

without the approval of the auspices; neither to B.C. 368
centuriate nor curiate comitia let the patricians give
their sanction; let Sextius and Licinius bear sway
in Rome, like Romulus and Tatius—because they
give away the moneys and the lands of others. Is
it so sweet to plunder others of their fortunes?
Does it not occur to them that one of their laws will
make vast deserts in the country-side, by driving
the landlords out from their demesnes, while the
other will wipe out credit, and with it all human
intercourse? Upon every account I urge you to
reject these bills; and may Heaven prosper what
you do!"

XLII. The speech of Appius availed no further B.C. 367
than to put off the passing of the measures. Returned for the tenth time to office, the tribunes
Sextius and Licinius obtained the enactment of a
law requiring that half the board of ten who had
charge of sacred rites should be plebeians.[1] Having
elected five patricians and five plebeians, the people
felt that they had set a precedent for the consulship.
Satisfied with their victory, the plebs gave way to
the patricians, and relinquishing for the moment
discussion about the consuls, permitted the election
of military tribunes. Those chosen were Aulus and
Marcus Cornelius (for their second terms), Marcus
Geganius, Publius Manlius, Lucius Veturius, and
(for the sixth time) Publius Valerius.

Rome's foreign relations were now peaceful everywhere except for the siege of Velitrae—the result
of which, though delayed, was scarce in doubt—
when a sudden rumour of a Gallic war drove the
state to appoint Marcus Furius to his fifth dictatorship. He nominated Titus Quinctius Poenus to be

347

LIVY

5 Bellatum cum Gallis eo anno circa Anienem flumen
auctor est Claudius inclitamque in ponte pugnam,
qua T. Manlius Gallum, cum quo provocatus manus
conseruit, in conspectu duorum exercituum caesum
6 torque spoliavit, tum pugnatam.[1] Pluribus auctoribus magis adducor ut credam decem haud minus
post annos ea acta, hoc autem anno in Albano agro
7 cum Gallis dictatore M. Furio signa conlata. Nec
dubia nec difficilis Romanis, quamquam ingentem
Galli terrorem memoria pristinae cladis attulerant,
victoria fuit. Multa milia barbarorum in acie, multa
8 captis castris caesa; palati alii Apuliam maxime
petentes cum fuga se longinqua, tum quod passim
eos simul pavor errorque[2] distulerant, ab hoste[3]
tutati sunt. Dictatori consensu patrum plebisque
triumphus decretus.

9   Vixdum perfunctum eum bello atrocior domi
seditio excepit, et per ingentia certamina dictator
senatusque victus, ut rogationes tribuniciae accipe-
rentur; et comitia consulum adversa nobilitate
habita, quibus L. Sextius de plebe primus consul
10 factus. Et ne is[4] quidem finis certaminum fuit.
Quia patricii se auctores futuros negabant, prope

---

[1] pugnatam ς: pugnatum Ω.
[2] errorque *Harant*: terrorque Ω.
[3] ab hoste *Crévier*: ab hoste sese Ω.
[4] ne is ς: in his (*or* hiis *or* is) Ω.

---

[1] Quintus Claudius Quadrigarius, the annalist, *cf.* Vol. I.,
introd., p. xxx, and note 2.

[2] Livy himself narrates the episode as having occurred *six*
years later ; cf. Book VII. chapters ix–x. (361 B.C.).

348

master of the horse. Claudius [1] relates that the
battle with the Gauls took place that year near the
river Anio; and that this was the occasion of
the famous duel on the bridge in which Titus
Manlius slew a Gaul who had challenged him to
combat, and despoiled him of his chain, while the
two armies looked on. But I am more inclined to
believe, with the majority of our authorities, that
this exploit took place no less than ten years later,[2]
and that in the year of which I am now writing, the
dictator, Marcus Furius, fought a battle against the
Gauls on Alban soil. Notwithstanding the great
terror occasioned by the invasion of the Gauls and
the recollection of their old defeat, the Romans
gained a victory that was neither difficult nor uncertain. Many thousands of barbarians fell in battle,
and many after the camp was taken. The others
roamed about, making mostly towards Apulia, and
owed their escape from the Romans to their distant
flight and the dispersion which resulted from their
panic and their straggling. The dictator was
awarded a triumph with the consent of both senate
and plebs.

Hardly had Camillus brought the war to an end,
when he was confronted with a fiercer opposition
in the City. After desperate struggles the senate
and the dictator were beaten, and the measures
advocated by the tribunes were adopted. An
election of consuls was held, against the wishes of
the nobles, and resulted in the choice of Lucius
Sextius, the first of the plebeians to attain that
honour. Even this did not end their disputes.
The patricians declared that they would not ratify
the election, and the affair had almost led to a

LIVY

secessionem plebis res terribilesque alias minas
11 civilium certaminum venit, cum tandem[1] per dictatorem condicionibus sedatae discordiae sunt, con-
cessumque ab nobilitate plebi de consule plebeio, a
plebe nobilitati de praetore uno, qui ius in urbe
12 diceret, ex patribus creando.   Ita ab diutina ira
tandem in concordiam redactis ordinibus, cum dignam
eam rem senatus censeret esse meritoque id, si
quando unquam alias, deum immortalium fore[2] ut
ludi maximi fierent et dies unus ad triduum adice-
13 retur, recusantibus id munus aedilibus plebis, conclamatum a patriciis est iuvenibus se id honoris
14 deum immortalium causa libenter facturos.[3]   Quibus
cum ab universis gratiae actae essent, factum senatus
consultum ut duumviros aediles ex patribus dictator
populum rogaret, patres auctores omnibus eius anni
comitiis fierent.

[1] tandem *Perizonius* : tamen Ω : tum tamen ς *Gruter.*
[2] fore *Madvig* : causa libenter facturos fore Ω.
[3] facturos *Alschefski* : acturos Ω (*and after that the words*
ut aediles fierent, *which Conway brackets* (*Class. Quart.* XII.
(1918) *p.* 5).

secession of the plebs and threatened other terrible B.C. 367
embroilments, when the dictator finally proposed a
compromise which allayed the discord; the nobles
gave way to the plebs in regard to the plebeian
consul, and the plebs conceded to the nobles that
they might elect from the patricians one praetor to
administer justice in the City.[1] Thus after their
long quarrel the orders were reconciled at last.
The senate decided that this was a fitting occasion
to honour the immortal gods—who deserved it then,
if ever at any time—by celebrating the Great Games,
and voted that one day should be added to the
customary three; this burden the aediles of the
plebs refused to shoulder, whereupon the young
patricians called out that they would willingly do it
for the sake of honouring the gods. The entire
people united in thanks to them, and the senate
decreed that the dictator should hold a popular
election of two aediles[2] to be chosen from the
patricians, and that the Fathers should ratify all
the elections of that year.

[1] This step was made necessary by the growth of the City
and the increasing burden laid upon the consuls ; but, as
Livy intimates, it also served as partial compensation to the
patricians for the privileges they were now forced to share
with the plebs—until, in 337 B.C. (cf. VIII. xv. 9), the praetorship, too, was thrown open to the plebs.

[2] Later known as *aediles curules*. The provision that only
patricians might be chosen was modified in the following
year (cf. VII. i.).

LIBRI VI PERIOCHA

Res adversus Vulscos et Aequos et Praenestinos prospere
gestas continet.   Quattuor tribus adiectae sunt, Stellatina
Tromentina [1] Sabatina Arniensis.   M. Manlius, qui
Capitolium a Gallis defenderat, cum obstrictos aere alieno
liberaret, nexos exsolveret, crimine adfectati regni damnatus de saxo deiectus est ; in cuius notam S.C. factum
est, ne cui de Manlia gente Marco nomen [2] esset.   C.
Licinius et L. Sextius tribuni pl. legem promulgaverunt
ut consules ex plebe fierent, qui ex patribus creabantur,
eamque cum magna contentione repugnantibus patribus,
cum idem tribuni pl. per quinquennium soli magistratus
fuissent, pertulerunt ; et primus ex plebe consul L. Sextius
creatus est.   Lata est et altera lex, ne cui plus quingentis
iugeribus agri liceret possidere.

[1] Tromentina *edd.* : promentina *MSS.*
[2] Marco nomen *Sigonius* : manli cognomen *or* manlia cogn.
or marco cogn. *MSS.*

SUMMARY OF BOOK VI

THE book contains the victorious campaigns against the
Volsci, the Aequi, and the Praenestini. Four tribes were
added, the Stellatina, the Tromentina, the Sabatina,
and the Arniensis. Marcus Manlius, who had defended
the Capitol against the Gauls, after liberating the debtors
and releasing those whose persons had been seized, was
found guilty of aiming at sovereignty, and was flung from
the Rock ; to stigmatize him the senate decreed that none
of the Manlian family should bear the name of Marcus.[1]
Gaius Licinius and Lucius Sextius, tribunes of the plebs,
proposed a law that the consuls, who were formerly chosen
from the patricians, might be elected from the plebs, and
in a strenuous struggle against the opposition of the
patricians, carried their point, after these same tribunes
of the plebs had for five years been the only magistrates,[2]
and Lucius Sextius was the first plebeian to be elected
consul. Another law was also passed, that none might
hold above five hundred *iugera* of land.

[1] Livy himself ascribes the decree to the Manlian *gens*
(chap. xx. § 14).
[2] *Cf.* Livy chap. xxxv. § 10.

BOOK VII

LIBER VII

I. Annus hic erit insignis novi hominis consulatu,
insignis novis duobus magistratibus, praetura et curuli
aedilitate. Hos sibi patricii quaesivere honores pro
concesso plebi altero consulatu. Plebes consulatum
2 L. Sextio, cuius lege partus erat, dedit: patres
praeturam Sp. Furio M. f. Camillo, aedilitatem Cn.
Quinctio Capitolino et P. Cornelio Scipioni, suarum
gentium viris, gratia campestri ceperunt. L. Sextio
collega ex patribus datus L. Aemilius Mamercus.[1]
3 Principio anni et de Gallis, quos primo palatos per
Apuliam congregari iam fama erat, et de Hernicorum
4 defectione agitata mentio. Cum de industria omnia,
ne quid per plebeium consulem ageretur, profer-
rentur, silentium omnium rerum ac iustitio simile
5 otium fuit, nisi quod non patientibus tacitum tribunis,
quod pro consule uno plebeio tres patricios magistratus curulibus sellis praetextatos tamquam consules

---

[1] Mamercus Ω *Diod.* xv. lxxxii, i, *Cassiod.*: Mamercinus
Pighius (*C.I.L.* 1², p. 126).

---

[1] Where the voting took place.

BOOK VII

I. This year will stand out as the one in which a "new man" held the consulship, and also for the establishment of two new magistracies, the praetorship and the curule aedileship. These dignities the patricians had devised for themselves, to compensate them for the second consulship, which they had granted to the commons. The plebs bestowed their consulship on Lucius Sextius, by whose law it had been won. The patricians, through their influence in the Campus Martius,[1] obtained the praetorship for Spurius Furius Camillus, the son of Marcus, and the aedileship for Gnaeus Quintius Capitolinus and Publius Cornelius Scipio, who belonged to their own houses. Lucius Aemilius Mamercus was chosen from the patricians as colleague of Lucius Sextius. Early in the year there was some talk about the Gauls—who having at first scattered through Apulia were now rumoured to be gathering—and about a defection on the part of the Hernici. The patricians purposely deferred all action, in order that the plebeian consul might have no hand in anything; it seemed from the general hush and lack of bustle as though a cessation of the courts had been proclaimed; save that the tribunes would not suffer it to pass in silence that the nobles, in return for one plebeian consul, had got three patrician magistrates for themselves, who wore the purple-bordered toga and sat, like consuls,

357

6 sedentes nobilitas sibi sumpsisset, praetorem quidem
etiam iura reddentem et collegam consulibus atque
iisdem auspiciis creatum, verecundia inde imposita
est senatui ex patribus iubendi aediles curules creari.
Primo ut alternis annis ex plebe fierent convenerat :
postea promiscuum fuit.

7   Inde L. Genucio et Q. Servilio consulibus et ab
seditione et a bello quietis rebus, ne quando a metu
8 ac periculis vacarent, pestilentia ingens orta. Cen-
sorem, aedilem curulem, tres tribunos plebis mortuos
ferunt, pro portione et ex multitudine alia multa
funera fuisse ; maximeque eam pestilentiam insignem
9 mors quam matura, tam acerba M. Furi fecit. Fuit
enim vere vir unicus in omni fortuna, princeps pace
belloque, priusquam exsulatum iret, clarior in exsilio,
vel desiderio civitatis, quae capta absentis imploravit
opem, vel felicitate qua restitutus in patriam secum [1]
10 patriam ipsam restituit ; par deinde per quinque et
viginti annos—tot enim postea vixit—titulo tantae
gloriae fuit dignusque habitus quem secundum a
Romulo conditorem urbis Romanae ferrent.

    II. Et hoc et insequenti anno C.[2] Sulpicio Petico
2 C. Licinio Stolone consulibus pestilentia fuit. Eo
nihil dignum memoria actum, nisi quod pacis deum

---

[1] restitutus in patriam secum Ω : restitutus secum O :
restitutus H.
[2] C. Glareanus, Sigonius (Diod. xv. xcv. 1 and Cassiod., cf.
C.I.L: 1², p. 126 and chap. xvii. § 13): T. Ω : L. L? : omitted
by A.

B.C.
366–365

in curule chairs, while the praetor even dealt out justice—having been elected as a colleague to the consuls and under the same auspices. In consequence of this criticism the senate was ashamed to order that the curule aediles be chosen from the patricians. At first it was arranged to take them from the plebs in alternate years : later the election was thrown open without distinction.

Then came the consulship of Lucius Genucius and Quintus Servilius. There was neither party strife nor war to disturb the peace, but lest there should ever be freedom from fear and danger, a great pestilence broke out. It is stated that a censor, a curule aedile, and three plebeian tribunes died, with a correspondingly large number from the rest of the population. But what chiefly made this pestilence noteworthy was the death of Marcus Furius, who, though ripe in years, was bitterly regretted. For he was truly a man of singular excellence whether in good or evil fortune ; foremost in peace and in war before his banishment, and in exile even more distinguished, whether one thinks of the yearning of his countrymen who called on him in his absence to save their captured City, or of the success with which on being restored to his country he restored the country itself at the same time ; after this for five and twenty years—for he survived so long—he maintained his glorious reputation, and was deemed worthy of being named next after Romulus, as Rome's second Founder.

II. The pestilence lasted during both this and the B.C. 364 following year, the consulship of Gaius Sulpicius Peticus and Gaius Licinius Stolo. In the latter year nothing memorable occurred, except that with the

exposcendae causa tertio tum post conditam urbem
3 lectisternium fuit. Et cum vis morbi nec humanis
consiliis nec ope divina levaretur, victis superstitione
animis ludi quoque scenici, nova res bellicoso
populo—nam circi modo spectaculum fuerat,—inter
alia caelestis irae placamina instituti dicuntur;
4 ceterum parva quoque,[1] ut ferme principia omnia,
et ea ipsa peregrina res fuit. Sine carmine ullo,
sine imitandorum carminum actu, ludiones ex Etruria
acciti ad tibicinis modos saltantes haud indecoros
5 motus more Tusco dabant. Imitari deinde eos
iuventus, simul inconditis inter se iocularia fundentes
versibus, coepere; nec absoni a voce motus erant.
6 Accepta itaque res saepiusque usurpando excitata.
Vernaculis artificibus, quia ister Tusco verbo ludio
vocabatur, nomen histrionibus inditum; qui non,
7 sicut ante, Fescennino versu similem incompositum [2]
temere ac rudem alternis iaciebant, sed impletas
modis saturas descripto iam ad tibicinem cantu
motuque congruenti peragebant.

---

[1] parva quoque Ω: parua haec quoque *Eussner*: parva ea
quoque *Madvig* (*which would require—as Walters and Conway
note—the deletion of* ea *before* ipsa)**.**
[2] incompositum Ω: compositum *Sigonius, Karsten*.

---

[1] The first lectisternium was in 399 B.C., and is described at
v. xiii. 5 sq. The second is not mentioned by Livy. It
may have occurred in 392 (v. xxxi. 5).
[2] Livy distinguishes five stages in the development of
scenic entertainments : (1) dances, accompanied by the flute ;
(2) improvisation of rude verses in addition to the music and
dancing ; (3) medleys, of a musical character, accompanied
by flute and dance ; (4) the comedy with a regular plot,
special singers for the lyric parts, etc. ; (5) the addition of
an after-play, *exodium* or *Atellana*. With this account,
Horace, *Epistles* II. i. 139 ff. should be compared.

object of appeasing the divine displeasure they made B.C. 364
a *lectisternium*, or banquet to the gods, being the
third in the history of the City;[1] and when neither
human wisdom nor the help of Heaven was found to
mitigate the scourge, men gave way to superstitious
fears, and, amongst other efforts to disarm the wrath
of the gods, are said also to have instituted scenic
entertainments. This was a new departure for a
warlike people, whose only exhibitions had been
those of the circus; but indeed it began in a small
way, as most things do, and even so was imported
from abroad.[2] Without any singing, without imitating
the action of singers, players who had been brought in
from Etruria danced to the strains of the flautist and
performed not ungraceful evolutions in the Tuscan
fashion. Next the young Romans began to imi-
tate them, at the same time exchanging jests in
uncouth verses, and bringing their movements into a
certain harmony with the words. And so the
amusement was adopted, and frequent use kept it
alive. The native professional actors were called
histriones, from *ister*, the Tuscan word for player;
they no longer—as before—alternately threw off
rude lines hastily improvised, like the Fescennines,[3]
but performed medleys, full of musical measures,
to melodies which were now written out to go with
the flute, and with appropriate gesticulation.

[3] The name was derived by the ancients either from
Fescennia, a place in Etruria, or from *fascinum*, a phallic
symbol.

LIVY

8   Livius post aliquot annis, qui ab saturis ausus [1] est
primus argumento fabulam serere, idem scilicet—id
quod omnes tum erant—suorum carminum actor,
9 dicitur, cum saepius revocatus vocem obtudisset,
venia petita puerum ad canendum ante tibicinem
cum statuisset, canticum egisse aliquanto magis
vigente motu, quia nihil vocis usus impediebat.
10 Inde ad manum cantari histrionibus coeptum, diver-
11 biaque [2] tantum ipsorum voci relicta. Postquam
lege hac fabularum ab risu ac soluto ioco res avoca-
batur et ludus in artem paulatim verterat, iuventus
histrionibus fabellarum actu relicto ipsa inter se
more antiquo ridicula intexta versibus iactitare
coepit; unde exorta quae exodia [3] postea appellata
12 consertaque fabellis potissimum Atellanis sunt; quod
genus ludorum ab Oscis acceptum tenuit iuventus
nec ab histrionibus pollui passa est; eo institutum
manet ut actores Atellanarum nec tribu moveantur
et stipendia, tamquam expertes artis ludicrae, faciant.
13 Inter aliarum parva principia rerum ludorum quoque
prima origo ponenda visa est, ut appareret quam ab

---

[1] ausus Ω : aversus ausus *Cornelissen*.
[2] diverbiaque ϛ : deuerbiaque (deuerbia quae *M* : deuerbi
atque *B*) Ω.
[3] unde exorta quae exodia *Alschefski* : unde exodia quae
(*or* que) exordia *MA²*ϛ : quae (*or* que) exordia *HTDLAR* :
quae (*or* que) unde exodia *PBO?* : quae inde exodia *F*ϛ : quae
exodia *T¹* (*or* *T²*) *D³* : unde exodia *Conway*.

---

[1] Livius Andronicus, a Greek captured at Tarentum, produced the first translation of a Greek play into Latin, in
240 B.C.
[2] Atella was a little town in Campania. *Atellanae* were
coarse farces presenting certain stock characters, Maccus.
Pappus, Bucco, and Dossenus. The Oscans were a branch
of the Samnites and lived in Campania.

Livius [1] was the first, some years later, to abandon B.C. 364
saturae and compose a play with a plot. Like
everyone else in those days, he acted his own pieces;
and the story goes that when his voice, owing to the
frequent demands made upon it, had lost its fresh-
ness, he asked and obtained the indulgence to let
a boy stand before the flautist to sing the monody,
while he acted it himself, with a vivacity of gesture
that gained considerably from his not having to use
his voice. From that time on actors began to use
singers to accompany their gesticulation, reserving
only the dialogue parts for their own delivery.
When this type of performance had begun to wean
the drama from laughter and informal jest, and the
play had gradually developed into art, the young
men abandoned the acting of comedies to pro-
fessionals and revived the ancient practice of
fashioning their nonsense into verses and letting fly
with them at one another; this was the source of
the after-plays which came later to be called *exodia*,
and were usually combined with Atellan farces. The
Atellan was a species of comedy acquired from the
Oscans,[2] and the young men kept it for themselves
and would not allow it to be polluted by the professional actors; that is why it is a fixed tradition
that performers of Atellan plays are not disfranchised,
but serve in the army as though they had no connexion with the stage.[3] Amongst the humble
origins of other institutions it has seemed worth
while to set down the early history of the play, that
it might be seen how sober were the beginnings of

[3] Actors were regularly reckoned in the *aerarii* or lowest
class of citizens, who were not permitted to serve in the
army.

LIVY

sano initio res in hanc vix opulentis regnis tolerabilem
insaniam venerit.

III. Nec tamen ludorum primum initium pro-
curandis religionibus datum aut religione animos
2 aut corpora morbis levavit; quin etiam, cum medios
forte ludos circus Tiberi superfuso inrigatus im-
pedisset, id vero, velut aversis iam dis aspernanti-
busque placamina irae, terrorem ingentem fecit.
3 Itaque Cn.[1] Genucio L. Aemilio Mamerco[2] iterum
consulibus, cum piaculorum magis conquisitio animos
quam corpora morbi adficerent, repetitum ex seniorum
memoria dicitur pestilentiam quondam clavo ab dic-
4 tatore fixo sedatam. Ea religione adductus senatus
dictatorem clavi figendi causa dici iussit; dictus
L. Manlius Imperiosus L. Pinarium magistrum
equitum dixit.
5 Lex vetusta est, priscis litteris verbisque scripta,
ut qui praetor maximus sit idibus Septembribus
clavum pangat; fixa fuit dextro lateri aedis Iovis
optimi maximi, qua parte[3] Minervae templum est.
6 Eum clavum, quia rarae per ea tempora litterae
erant, notam numeri annorum fuisse ferunt eoque
Minervae templo dicatam legem quia numerus

---

[1] Cn. *Sigonius* (*cf Diod.* XVI. ii. 1, *C.I.L.* i², *p.* 126): C
Ω : Claudio *O*.
[2] Mamerco Ω (*cf. chap.* i. § 2): Mamercino *Pighius* (*Diod.*
omits the cognomen here).
[3] qua parte (*Walters in his note*): .ea. qua parte *H* : ea qua
parte Ω : ea parte qua *U* : ex qua parte *Gronovius*.

an art that has nowadays reached a point where B.C. 364 opulent kingdoms could hardly support its mad extravagance.

III. However, the plays thus for the first time B.C. 363 introduced by way of expiation neither freed men's minds of religious fears nor their bodies of disease. Indeed, it fell out quite otherwise; for the games were in full swing when an inundation of the Tiber flooded the circus and put a stop to them, an accident which—as though the gods had already turned away, rejecting the proffered appeasement of their anger—filled the people with fear. And so when Gnaeus Genucius and Lucius Aemilius Mamercus (for the second time) were consuls, and men's minds were more troubled by the search for means of propitiation than were their bodies by disease, it is said that the elders recollected that a pestilence had once been allayed by the dictator's driving a nail.[1] Induced thereto by this superstition, the senate ordered the appointment of a dictator to drive the nail. Lucius Manlius Imperiosus was appointed, and named Lucius Pinarius master of the horse.

There is an ancient law, recorded in archaic words and letters, that the chief magistrate shall on the thirteenth of September drive a nail; the tablet was formerly affixed to the right side of the temple of Jupiter Optimus Maximus, where Minerva's chapel is. This nail served, they say, in those days of little writing, to mark the number of years, and the law was confided to the chapel of Minerva, for the reason

[1] The instance here referred to may have occurred in 435 B.C., when Quintus Servilius Priscus was dictator (iv. xxi. 6–9).

LIVY

7 Minervae inventum sit.—Volsiniis quoque clavos
indices numeri annorum fixos in templo Nortiae,
Etruscae deae, comparere diligens talium monu-
8 mentorum auctor Cincius adfirmat.—M. Horatius
consul ea lege templum [1] Iovis optimi maximi dedicavit anno post reges exactos; a consulibus postea
ad dictatores, quia maius imperium erat, sollemne
clavi figendi translatum est. Intermisso deinde
more digna etiam per se visa res propter quam
9 dictator crearetur. Qua de causa creatus L. Manlius,
perinde ac rei gerendae ac non solvendae religionis
gratia creatus esset, bellum Hernicum adfectans
dilectu acerbo iuventutem agitavit; tandemque
omnibus in eum tribunis plebis coortis seu vi seu
verecundia victus dictatura abiit.

IV. Neque eo minus principio insequentis anni,
Q. Servilio Ahala L. Genucio consulibus, dies Manlio
2 dicitur a M. Pomponio tribuno plebis. Acerbitas in
dilectu non damno modo civium sed etiam laceratione
corporum lata,[2] partim virgis caesis qui ad nomina
non respondissent, partim in vincula ductis, invisa
3 erat, et ante omnia invisum ipsum ingenium atrox
cognomenque Imperiosi; grave liberae civitati, ab
ostentatione saevitiae adscitum, quam non magis in

---

[1] ea lege templum *H. J. Mueller, Luterbacher (C.I.L.* iii.
1933) : ex lege templum Ω : et legem et templum *Madvig.*
[2] lata Ω *(wanting in O)*: inlata *van der Vliet*: laeta
Madvig : cumulata *M. Mueller.*

---

[1] We do not know whether Livy alludes to a book or to
an oral communication. It has been suggested that Cincius—
not otherwise known—may have been an antiquary of Livy's
own time.
[2] A goddess of Fortune.
[3] The text here is uncertain, but Livy seems to mean that
Horatius in dedicating the temple also drove the first nail.

that number was an invention of that goddess. B.C. 363
(Cincius, a careful student of such memorials,
asserts [1] that at Volsinii, too, nails may be seen in
the temple of Nortia,[2] an Etruscan goddess, driven
in to indicate the number of years.) Marcus Horatius
the consul dedicated the temple of Jupiter Optimus
Maximus in accordance with this law, in the year
after the expulsion of the kings ; [3] later the ceremony
of driving the nail was transferred from consuls to
dictators, because theirs was the higher authority.
Then, after the custom had been allowed to lapse, it
was thought to be of sufficient importance to warrant
the appointment of a dictator for that very purpose.
It was for this reason that Manlius was designated,
who, however, as though appointed to wage war
and not to discharge a religious obligation, aspired
to conduct the war with the Hernici, and hunted
down the men of military age in a rigorous levy ;
but in the upshot, opposed by the united efforts of
all the tribunes of the plebs, he yielded either to
force or to a sense of shame, and resigned his
dictatorship.

IV. Nevertheless, at the beginning of the ensuing B.C. 362
year—the consulship of Quintus Servilius Ahala and
Lucius Genucius—Manlius was put upon his trial by
Marcus Pomponius, a tribune of the plebs. The
people hated him for the severity of his levy, in
which they had endured not only fines but bodily
distress, some having suffered stripes for failure to
respond to their names and others having been
dragged off to prison ; but more than all else they
hated the man's cruel disposition and his surname,
Imperiosus, which offended a free state and had
been assumed in ostentation of the truculence which

alienis quam in proximis ac sanguine ipse[1] suo
4 exerceret. Criminique ei tribunus inter cetera dabat
quod filium iuvenem, nullius probri compertum, extorrem urbe domo penatibus, foro luce congressu aequa-
lium prohibitum, in opus servile, prope in carcerem
5 atque in ergastulum dederit, ubi summo loco natus
dictatorius iuvenis cotidiana miseria disceret vere
imperioso patre se natum esse. At quam ob noxam?
6 Quia infacundior sit et lingua impromptus; quod
naturae damnum utrum nutriendum patri, si quicquam in eo humani esset, an castigandum ac vexatione
insigne faciendum fuisse? Ne mutas quidem bestias
minus alere ac fovere si quid ex progenie sua parum
7 prosperum sit; at hercule L. Manlium malum malo
augere filii et tarditatem ingenii insuper premere, et,
si quid in eo exiguum naturalis vigoris sit, id ex-
stinguere vita agresti et rustico cultu inter pecudes
habendo.

V. Omnium potius his criminationibus quam
ipsius iuvenis inritatus est animus; quin contra se
quoque parenti causam invidiae atque criminum
2 esse aegre passus, ut omnes di hominesque scirent
se parenti opem latam quam inimicis eius malle,
capit consilium rudis quidem atque agrestis animi
et[2] quamquam non civilis exempli, tamen pietate

----

[1] ipse *ς*: ipso Ω.   [2] et Ω: sed *Wesenberg*.

he used as freely with his nearest friends and his
own family as with strangers. Amongst other
charges the tribune cited the man's behaviour to
his son : the youth, he said, had been found guilty
of no misconduct, yet Manlius had excluded him from
the City, from his home and household gods, from
the Forum, the light of day, and the fellowship of
his young friends, consigning him to slavish drudgery
in a kind of gaol or work-house, where a youth of
distinguished birth and the son of a dictator might
learn by his daily wretchedness how truly "im-
perious" was the father that had begot him. Yes,
but what was the young man's fault ? Why, he had
been a little slow of speech—unready with his
tongue ! But ought not his father to have healed
and mended this infirmity of nature—if he had a
particle of humanity about him—instead of chastising
it and by persecution making it conspicuous ? Why
even the dumb brutes, if one of their young is un-
fortunate, do none the less cherish it and foster it.
But Lucius Manlius was aggravating his son's evil
plight by evil treatment, and was doubling the burden
on his heavy wits ; and any spark of native talent that
might be there he was quenching in the rustic life
and clownish bringing up amongst the dumb brutes
where he kept him.

V. Everyone was incensed by these charges, except
the young man himself. He, on the contrary, was
vexed to be the cause of additional dislike and
accusation of his father ; and that all gods and men
might know that he had rather help his father than
his father's enemies, he conceived a plan, in keeping
to be sure with his rude and uncouth spirit, which,
though it set no pattern of civic conduct, was yet

369

3 laudabile. Inscientibus cunctis cultro succinctus mane in urbem atque a porta domum confestim ad M. Pomponium tribunum pergit; ianitori opus esse sibi domino eius convento extemplo ait; nuntiaret 4 T. Manlium L. filium esse. Mox introductus—etenim percitum ira in patrem spes erat aut criminis aliquid novi aut consilii ad rem agendam deferre—salute accepta redditaque esse ait quae cum eo agere 5 arbitris remotis velit. Procul inde omnibus abire iussis cultrum stringit et super lectum stans ferro intento, nisi in quae ipse concepisset verba iuraret se patris eius accusandi causa concilium plebis nunquam habiturum, se eum extemplo transfixurum 6 minatur. Pavidus tribunus, quippe qui ferrum ante oculos micare, se solum inermem, illum praevalidum iuvenem, et, quod haud minus timendum erat, stolide ferocem viribus suis cerneret, adiurat in quae adactus est verba; et, prae se deinde tulit ea vi subactum se 7 incepto destitisse. Nec perinde ut maluisset plebes sibi suffragii ferendi de tam crudeli et superbo reo potestatem fieri, ita aegre habuit filium id pro parente ausum; eoque id laudabilius erat quod animum eius tanta acerbitas patria nihil a pietate 8 avertisset. Itaque non patri modo remissa causae

370

praiseworthy for its filial piety.   Without anybody's B.C. 362
knowledge, he girded himself with a knife in the
early morning, and coming to the City, made his
way at once from the gate to the house of Marcus
Pomponius, the tribune.   There he told the porter
that he must see his master instantly, and bade him
say that it was Titus Manlius, the son of Lucius.
Being presently admitted—for it seemed likely that
he was moved with wrath against his father, or was
bringing some fresh charge or plan of action—he
received and returned the salutation of his host, and
then announced that there were matters of which
he wished to speak to him without witnesses.   When
they had all been sent away, he drew his knife, and
standing over the tribune's couch with his weapon
ready, he threatened that unless the man should
swear, in the terms he himself should dictate, never
to hold a council of the plebs for the purpose of
accusing his father, he would immediately stab him.
The frightened tribune, seeing the blade flash in his
face, and perceiving himself to be alone and unarmed,
and the other to be a stalwart youth, and, what was
no less terrifying, foolhardy by reason of his strength,
took the oath that was required of him, and afterwards publicly declared that he had been compelled
by force to relinquish his undertaking.   And the
plebs, however much they would have liked to be
given the opportunity to cast their votes in the case
of so cruel and insolent a defendant, were yet not
displeased that a son had dared such a deed in
defence of his parent ; and they praised it all the
more, because the father's shocking harshness had
made no difference in the son's filial devotion.   And
so not only was the arraignment of the father dis-

371

dictio est, sed ipsi etiam adulescenti ea res honori
9 fuit, et cum eo anno primum placuisset tribunos
militum ad legiones suffragio fieri—nam antea,[1]
sicut nunc quos Rufulos vocant, imperatores ipsi
faciebant,—secundum in sex locis tenuit, nullis
domi militiaeque ad conciliandam gratiam meritis,
ut qui rure et procul coetu hominum iuventam
egisset.

VI. Eodem anno, seu motu terrae seu qua vi alia,
forum medium ferme specu vasto conlapsum in im-
mensam altitudinem dicitur; neque eam voraginem
2 coniectu terrae, cum [2] pro se quisque gereret, expleri [3]
potuisse, priusquam deum monitu quaeri coeptum
3 quo plurimum populus Romanus posset; id enim
illi loco dicandum vates canebant, si rem publicam
Romanam perpetuam esse vellent. Tum M. Curtium,
iuvenem bello egregium, castigasse ferunt dubitantes
an ullum magis Romanum bonum quam arma virtus-
4 que esset, et [4] silentio facto templa deorum immortalium, quae foro imminent, Capitoliumque intuentem
et manus nunc in caelum nunc in patentes terrae
hiatus ad deos manes porrigentem se devovisse;
5 equo deinde quam poterat maxime exornato insidentem armatum se in specum immisisse, donaque
ac fruges super eum a multitudine virorum ac
mulierum congestas, lacumque Curtium non ab

[1] nam antea *Duker*: nam et antea Ω.
[2] cum Ω : quam *Gronovius*. [3] expleri $L^3\varsigma$: explere Ω.
[4] esset, et *Madvig*: esset Ω.

[1] Pseudo-Asconius, on Cic. *Act* 1 *in Verr.* 30 says: "There
are two kinds of military tribunes, the first consisting of
those called *Rufuli;* these are ordinarily appointed in the
army; the others are the *comitiati*, who are designated at
the comitia in Rome."

missed, but the youth himself gained distinction from
the affair; for in the election of military tribunes for
the legions, which had that year for the first time
been resolved upon—until then the generals themselves had nominated them, as they do to-day those
who are known as *Rufuli* [1]—he was chosen second
of the six, though neither at home nor in the field
had he done aught to merit popularity, and no
wonder, since his youth had been passed in the
country, remote from the gatherings of men.

VI. That same year, whether owing to an earth-
quake or to some other violent force, it is said that
the ground gave way, at about the middle of the
Forum, and, sinking to an immeasurable depth, left a
prodigious chasm. This gulf could not be filled with
the earth which everyone brought and cast into it,
until admonished by the gods, they began to inquire
what it was that constituted the chief strength of the
Roman People; for this the soothsayers declared
that they must offer up, as a sacrifice to that spot, if
they wished the Roman Republic to endure. Thereupon Marcus Curtius, a young soldier of great
prowess, rebuked them, so the story runs, for
questioning whether any blessing were more Roman
than arms and valour. A hush ensued, as he
turned to the temples of the immortal gods which
rise above the Forum, and to the Capitol, and
stretching forth his hands, now to heaven, and now
to the yawning chasm and to the gods below, devoted
himself to death. After which, mounted on a horse
caparisoned with all possible splendour, he plunged
fully armed into the gulf; and crowds of men and
women threw offerings and fruits in after him. It
was he, they say, and not Curtius Mettius, the soldier

LIVY

antiquo illo T. Tati milite Curtio Mettio sed ab
6 hoc appellatum. Cura non deesset, si qua ad verum
via inquirentem ferret; nunc fama rerum standum
est, ubi certam derogat vetustas fidem; et lacus
nomen ab hac recentiore insignitius fabula est.

7 Post tanti prodigii procurationem eodem anno de
Hernicis consultus senatus cum fetiales ad res repetendas nequiquam misisset, primo quoque die feren-
dum ad populum de bello indicendo Hernicis censuit,
populusque id bellum frequens iussit. L. Genucio
8 consuli ea provincia sorte evenit. In exspectatione
civitas erat, quod primus ille de plebe consul bellum
suis auspiciis gesturus esset, perinde ut evenisset
res ita communicatos honores pro bene aut secus
9 consulto habitura. Forte ita tulit casus ut Genucius
ad hostes magno conatu profectus in insidias praecipitaret et [1] legionibus necopinato pavore fusis consul
circumventus ab insciis quem intercepissent [2] occi-
10 deretur. Quod ubi est Romam nuntiatum, nequaquam tantum publica calamitate maesti patres
quantum feroces infelici consulis plebeii ductu,
fremunt omnibus locis: irent crearent consules ex
11 plebe, transferrent auspicia quo nefas esset; potuisse
patres plebi scito pelli honoribus suis: num etiam
in deos immortales inauspicatam legem valuisse?

---

[1] praecipitaret et *Duker*: praecipitaret *M*: praecipi-
taretur Ω.
[2] intercepissent *Madvig*: interfecissent Ω.

---

[1] See I. xii. 10 and xiii. 5, with note.
[2] The law had been passed in the *comitia tributa* presided
over by a tribune, who had not the right to take auspices.

of Titus Tatius in days of old, who gave his name to B.C. 362
the Curtian Lake.[1] Diligence would not be wanting,
were there any path which could lead the inquirer to
the truth ; as it is, one must hold by the tradition,
where antiquity will not allow us to be certain ; and
the name of the pool is better known from this more
recent legend.

After the expiation of this great portent, the
senate dealt in the same year with the question of
the Hernici, and having dispatched fetials to demand
reparations, without avail, resolved to submit to the
people for their approval, at the earliest possible day,
a declaration of war against that nation. In a
crowded assembly the people voted for war, and the
consul Lucius Genucius was by lot intrusted with the
conduct of it. The citizens were in a fever of suspense,
since he would be the first plebeian consul to conduct
a war under his own auspices, and they would judge
by the sequel whether they had done well or ill to
throw these honours open. It so happened that
Genucius, marching in great force against the enemy,
plunged into an ambuscade. The legions, in a sudden
panic, were put to flight, and the consul was
surrounded and slain by men who knew not whom
they had taken. When the news reached Rome, the
patricians, by no means so cast down by the general
disaster as elated at the unlucky generalship of the
plebeian consul, filled the City with their taunts.
Let them go and choose consuls from the plebs !
Let them transfer the auspices to those who might
not have them without sin ! They had been able by
a plebiscite to expel the patricians from their rightful honours : had their unsanctioned [2] law prevailed
also against the immortal gods ? The gods them-

375

A.U.C.
392
Vindicasse ipsos suum numen, sua auspicia, quae ut
primum contacta sint ab eo a quo nec ius nec fas
fuerit, deletum cum duce exercitum documento
fuisse ne deinde turbato gentium iure comitia
12 haberentur. His vocibus curia et forum personat.
Ap. Claudium, quia dissuaserat legem, maiore nunc
auctoritate eventum reprehensi ab se consilii incu-
santem, dictatorem consensu patriciorum Servilius
consul dicit, dilectusque et iustitium indictum.

VII. Priusquam dictator legionesque novae in
Hernicos venirent, ductu C. Sulpici legati res per
2 occasionem gesta egregie est. In Hernicos, morte
consulis contemptim ad castra Romana cum haud
dubia expugnandi spe succedentes, hortante legato
et plenis irae atque indignitatis militum animis
eruptio est facta. Multum ab spe adeundi valli
res Hernicis afuit; adeo turbatis inde ordinibus
3 abscessere. Dictatoris deinde adventu novus veteri
exercitus iungitur et copiae duplicantur; et pro
contione dictator laudibus legati militumque, quorum
virtute castra defensa erant, simul audientibus laudes
meritas tollit animos, simul ceteros ad aemulandas
4 virtutes acuit. Neque segnius ad hostes bellum
apparatur, qui et parti ante decoris memores neque

376

selves had vindicated their divine authority and their B.C. 362
auspices; for these had no sooner been touched by
one who had no legal or religious warranty for so
doing, than the army and its general had been
annihilated, as a lesson never again to overturn the
rights of the patrician families in conducting an
election. Such words as these resounded through
the Curia and the Forum. Appius Claudius had urged
the rejection of the law, and this now gave his words
the greater weight, as he denounced the outcome of
a policy which he himself had censured. Him, therefore, the consul Servilius, with the approval of the
patricians, appointed dictator. An enrolment was
proclaimed, and the courts were suspended.

VII. But before the dictator and his new levies
were got to the country of the Hernici, the lieutenant
Gaius Sulpicius, profiting by a favourable opportunity,
had fought a brilliant engagement. The Hernici,
whom the consul's death had made contemptuous,
approached the Roman camp with every expectation
of taking it by storm; but the soldiers, heartened by
their general and bursting with anger and resentment,
made a sortie, and so far were the Hernici from
attacking the stockade, as they had hoped to do,
that they actually fell back in confusion from the
ground. Then came the dictator, and the new army
was joined to the old and the forces doubled. Calling
the men together, Appius lauded the lieutenant and
his soldiers, by whose bravery the camp had been
defended; thus at the same stroke he encouraged
those who heard themselves deservedly commended,
and stimulated the others to emulation of their conduct. Nor were the enemy less energetic in making
ready for the war; mindful of the glory they had won

ignari auctarum virium hostis[1] suas quoque vires
augent. Omne Hernicum nomen, omnis militaris
aetas excitur; quadringenariae octo cohortes, lecta
5 robora virorum, scribuntur. Hunc eximium florem
iuventutis eo etiam quod ut duplex acciperent
stipendium decreverant, spei animorumque im-
plevere; immunes quoque operum militarium erant,
ut in unum pugnae laborem reservati plus sibi quam
6 pro virili parte adnitendum scirent; extra ordinem
etiam in acie locati quo conspectior virtus esset.

Duum milium planities castra Romana ab Hernicis
7 dirimebat; ibi pari ferme utrimque spatio in medio
pugnatum est. Primo stetit ambigua spe pugna
nequiquam saepe conatis equitibus Romanis impetu
8 turbare hostium aciem. Postquam equestris pugna
effectu quam conatibus vanior erat, consulto prius
dictatore equites, permissu deinde eius relictis equis,
clamore ingenti provolant ante signa et novam inte-
9 grant pugnam. Neque sustineri poterant, ni extra-
ordinariae cohortes pari corporum animorumque
robore se obiecissent.

VIII. Tunc inter primores duorum populorum res
geritur; quidquid hinc aut illinc communis Mars
belli[2] aufert, multiplex quam pro numero damnum
est. Volgus aliud armatorum, velut delegata
primoribus pugna, eventum suum in virtute aliena

---

[1] hostis Ω : hosti *Gronovius*.
[2] belli *Sigonius* : bello Ω.

before, and aware that the forces of their adversaries had been augmented, they also strengthened theirs. All who bore the name of Hernici and were of military age were called upon, and eight cohorts were formed, each numbering four hundred of their best men. This choice flower of their manhood they inspired with additional hope and courage by a decree which allowed them double pay. They were exempted, also, from military tasks, in order that, being reserved for the one labour of fighting, they might be sensible of an obligation to exert themselves beyond the capacity of ordinary men. Finally, they were assigned a post in the battle outside the line, to make their bravery the more conspicuous.

A plain extending for two miles separated the Roman camp from the Hernici. In the middle of this plain, at a spot almost equidistant from both camps, the battle was fought. At first the event of the struggle was in doubt and nothing came of the oft-repeated attempts of the Roman horse to break the enemy's line. Finding their charges ineffectual, despite their efforts, they consulted the dictator and with his permission left their horses, and, rushing to the front with a mighty cheer, inaugurated a new kind of fighting. There would have been no stopping them, had it not been for the special cohorts, who flung themselves across their path with a vigour and gallantry equal to their own.

VIII. The struggle then lay between the best men of both nations, and whatever losses the chance of war inflicted on either side were serious out of all proportion to their number. The common herd of soldiers, as though they had made over the battle to their betters, rested their future on the bravery of

ponit. Multi utrimque cadunt, plures volnera
2 accipiunt; tandem equites alius alium increpantes,
quid deinde restaret quaerendo, si neque ex equis
pepulissent hostem neque pedites quicquam momenti
facerent? Quam tertiam exspectarent pugnam?
Quid ante signa feroces prosiluissent et alieno pug-
3 narent loco?—his inter se vocibus concitati clamore
renovato inferunt pedem et primum gradu moverunt
hostem, deinde pepulerunt, postremo iam haud
4 dubie avertunt; neque, tam vires pares quae supera-
verit res facile dictu est, nisi quod perpetua fortuna
utriusque populi et extollere animos et minuere
5 potuit. Usque ad castra fugientes Hernicos Romanus sequitur: castrorum oppugnatione, quia serum
erat diei, abstinuere;—diu non perlitatum tenuerat
dictatorem, ne ante meridiem signum dare posset;
6 eo in noctem tractum erat certamen.—Postero die
deserta fuga castra Hernicorum et saucii relicti
quidam inventi, agmenque fugientium ab Signinis,[1]
cum praeter moenia eorum infrequentia conspecta
signa essent, fusum ac per agros trepida fuga palatum
7 est. Nec Romanis incruenta victoria fuit: quarta
pars militum amissa, et ubi haud minus iacturae fuit,
aliquot equites Romani cecidere.

IX. Insequenti anno cum C. Sulpicius[2] et C.
Licinius Calvus consules in Hernicos exercitum

---

[1] Signinis *Crévier*: signis Ω.
[2] C. Sulpicius *Sigonius* (*Diod.* XVI. vi. 1, *C.I L.* i², p. 126)
l. sulpicius Ω.

others. Many on both sides were slain and more B.C. 362
were wounded. At length the knights began to rail
at one another. What else, they asked, was there to
do, if they had neither beaten the enemy when
mounted, nor were able to accomplish anything on
foot? What third kind of battle were they waiting
for? What good had they done by dashing boldly
out in front of the line and fighting in a place that
belonged to others? Stirred by these mutual
reproaches, they advanced with renewed cheering,
and first they made the enemy yield, then forced
them back, and finally routed them in no uncertain
fashion. What it was that turned the scale, where
forces were so evenly matched, would be hard to say,
unless the fortune regularly attendant on each nation
had the power to quicken or to daunt their resolution. The Romans chased the fleeing Hernici clear
to their camp, which, owing to the lateness of the
hour, they refrained from attacking;—the dictator
had been unable to give the battle-signal before noon,
having failed for a long time to obtain favourable
omens, for which reason the struggle had been protracted until night.—On the following day the camp
was discovered to have been deserted by the fleeing
Hernici, and a few of their wounded were found,
whom they had left behind. The column of fugitives
was passing the walls of Signia, when the townsfolk
espied their thinly attended ensigns, and falling upon
them, scattered them in headlong flight across the
country. Yet the Romans got no bloodless victory:
they lost a fourth part of their foot, and a number of
Roman horsemen fell, which was no less grave a loss.

IX. Next year the consuls Gaius Sulpicius and B.C. 361
Gaius Licinius Calvus led an army against the

duxissent neque inventis in agro hostibus Ferentinum urbem eorum vi cepissent, revertentibus inde
2 eis Tiburtes portas clausere. Ea ultima fuit causa,
cum multae ante querimoniae ultro citroque iactatae
essent, cur per fetiales rebus repetitis bellum Tiburti
populo indiceretur,

3   Dictatorem T. Quinctium Poenum eo anno fuisse
satis constat et magistrum equitum Ser. Cornelium
4 Maluginensem.   Macer Licinius comitiorum haben-
dorum causa et ab Licinio consule dictum scribit,
quia collega comitia bello praeferre festinante ut
continuaret consulatum, obviam eundum pravae
5 cupiditati fuerit. Quaesita ea propriae[1] familiae
laus leviorem auctorem Licinium facit. Cum
mentionem eius rei in vetustioribus annalibus
nullam inveniam, magis ut belli Gallici causa
6 dictatorem creatum arbitrer inclinat animus. Eo
certe anno Galli ad tertium lapidem Salaria via
trans pontem Anienis castra habuere.

Dictator cum tumultus Gallici causa iustitium
edixisset, omnes iuniores sacramento adegit ingentique exercitu ab urbe profectus in citeriore ripa
7 Anienis castra posuit. Pons in medio erat, neutris
eum rumpentibus, ne timoris indicium esset. Proelia
de occupando ponte crebra erant, nec qui poterentur

---

[1] propriae *A𝟝* : propria Ω.

---

[1] Tribune of the plebs in 73 B.C. and author of annals
written from the democratic standpoint (Introd. p. xxix).

Hernici, and not finding the enemy abroad, captured B.C. 361 their city of Ferentinum by assault. As they were returning thence, the men of Tibur closed their gates against them. Many complaints had before this been bandied back and forth between the two peoples, but this new offence made the Romans finally determine that after sending the fetials to demand redress they would declare war on the Tiburtine people.

It is well established that Titus Quinctius Poenus was dictator that year and that Servius Cornelius Maluginensis was master of the horse. Licinius Macer[1] states that the appointment was for the purpose of holding an election and was made by Licinius the consul, who, because his colleague was in haste to hold the election before the campaign, so that he might succeed himself in the consulship, felt obliged to thwart his evil designs. But the praise which he seeks to bestow on his own family makes the testimony of Licinius less weighty, and since I find no mention of the circumstance in the older annals, I am more disposed to think that it was a Gallic war which occasioned the appointment of a dictator. In any case, this was the year in which the Gauls encamped at the third milestone on the Salarian road, beyond the bridge over the Anio.

The dictator having, by reason of the Gallic rising, proclaimed a suspension of the courts, administered the oath to all of military age. Then marching out of the City with a great army he pitched his camp on the hither bank of the stream. The bridge lay between, and neither side would break it down, lest it be regarded as a sign of fear. There were frequent skirmishes for the possession of the bridge, and yet, so evenly matched were their forces, it could not be

383

LIVY

8 incertis viribus satis discerni poterat. Tum eximia
corporis magnitudine in vacuum pontem Gallus
processit et quantum maxima voce potuit, "Quem
nunc" inquit "Roma virum fortissimum habet,
procedat agedum ad pugnam, ut noster duorum
eventus ostendat utra gens bello sit melior."

X. Diu inter primores iuvenum Romanorum
silentium fuit, cum et abnuere certamen vererentur
2 et praecipuam sortem periculi petere nollent; tum
T. Manlius L. filius, qui patrem a vexatione tribunicia
vindicaverat, ex statione ad dictatorem pergit.
"Iniussu tuo" inquit, "imperator, extra ordinem
nunquam pugnaverim, non si certam victoriam
3 videam; si tu permittis, volo ego illi beluae
ostendere, quando adeo ferox praesultat hostium
signis, me ex ea familia ortum quae Gallorum
4 agmen ex rupe Tarpeia deiecit." Tum dictator
"Macte virtute" inquit "ac pietate in patrem
patriamque, T. Manli, esto. Perge et nomen
5 Romanum invictum iuvantibus dis praesta." Armant
inde iuvenem aequales; pedestre scutum capit,
Hispano cingitur gladio ad propiorem habili pugnam;
armatum adornatumque adversus Gallum stolide
laetum et—quoniam id quoque memoria dignum
antiquis visum est—linguam etiam ab inrisu exseren-
6 tem producunt. Recipiunt inde se ad stationem,
et duo in medio armati spectaculi magis more quam
lege belli destituuntur, nequaquam visu ac specie
7 aestimantibus pares. Corpus alteri magnitudine

---

[1] The Spanish sword was short and pointed, and a sword
of this type—required by the story—is what Livy means.
The *name* for it is anachronistic here.

determined who were masters of it. Then a Gaul <small>B.C. 361</small> of extraordinary size advanced upon the empty bridge, and making his voice as loud as possible, cried out, " Let him whom Rome now reckons her bravest man come out and fight, that we two may show by the outcome which people is the superior in war."

X. The young Roman nobles were for a long time silent. Ashamed to decline the challenge, they were loath to volunteer for a service of transcendent peril. Then Titus Manlius, the son of Lucius, who had rescued his father from the persecution of the tribune, left his station and went to the dictator. " Without your orders, General," he said, " I would fain never leave my place to fight, not though I saw that victory was assured; but if you permit me, I would show that beast who dances out so boldly before the standards of the enemy, that I come of the family that hurled the column of Gauls from the Tarpeian Rock." To whom the dictator made answer, " Success attend your valour, Titus Manlius, and your loyalty to father and to country! Go, and with Heaven's help make good the unconquerable Roman name." The young man's friends then armed him; he assumed the shield of a foot-soldier, and to his side he buckled a Spanish sword, convenient for close fighting.[1] Armed and accoutred, they led him forth to the Gaul, who in his stupid glee—for the ancients have thought even this worth mentioning—thrust his tongue out in derision. They then retired to their station, and the two armed men were left by themselves in the midst, like gladiators more than soldiers, and by no means evenly matched, to judge from outward show. One

A.U.C.
393

eximium, versicolori veste pictisque et auro caelatis
refulgens armis : media in altero militaris statura
modicaque in armis habilibus magis quam decoris
8 species. Non cantus, non exsultatio armorumque
agitatio vana, sed pectus animorum iraeque tacitae
plenum ; omnem ferociam in discrimen ipsum certa-
9 minis distulerat. Ubi constitere inter duas acies,
tot circa mortalium animis spe metuque pendentibus,
Gallus velut moles superne imminens proiecto laeva
scuto in advenientis arma hostis vanum caesim cum
10 ingenti sonitu ensem deiecit; Romanus mucrone
subrecto,[1] cum scuto scutum imum perculisset toto-
que corpore interior periculo volneris factus insinu-
asset se inter corpus armaque, uno alteroque subinde
ictu ventrem atque inguina hausit et in spatium
11 ingens ruentem porrexit hostem. Iacentis inde
corpus ab omni alia vexatione intactum uno torque
spoliavit, quem respersum cruore collo circumdedit
12 suo. Defixerat pavor cum admiratione Gallos :
Romani alacres ab statione obviam militi suo progressi,[2] gratulantes laudantesque ad dictatorem
13 perducunt. Inter carminum prope in modum[3] in-
condita quaedam militariter ioculantes Torquati

---

[1] subrecto (sur- D^3) Ω : *Walters and Conway suggest*
suberecto (*cf.* VIII. viii. 10).
[2] progressi D^2 (*or* D^3) A^2 (*or* A^1): praegressi (*or* p̄-) Ω.
[3] in modum *Madvig* : modum Ω : modo *Conway* (*cf.* IV.
xx. 2).

---

[1] *i.e.* the man with a chain, or necklace.

had a body extraordinary for its size, and resplendent B.C. 361
in a coat of shifting hues and armour painted and
chased with gold: the other was of a middling
stature for a soldier, and his arms were but indifferent to look at, being suitable but not ornate.
He neither sang nor danced about with idle flourishes
of his weapons, but his bosom swelled with courage
and silent wrath, and all his ferocity was reserved for
the crisis of the combat. When they had taken
their ground between the two embattled armies,
while the hearts of the surrounding multitude were
suspended betwixt hope and fear, the Gaul, whose
huge bulk towered above the other, advanced his
shield with the left arm, to parry the attack of his
oncoming enemy, and delivered a slashing stroke
with his sword, that made a mighty clatter but did
no harm. The Roman, with the point of his weapon
raised, struck up his adversary's shield with a blow
from his own against its lower edge; and slipping in
between the man's sword and his body, so close that
no part of his own person was exposed, he gave one
thrust and then immediately another, and gashing
the groin and belly of his enemy brought him
headlong to the ground, where he lay stretched out
over a monstrous space. To the body of his fallen
foe he offered no other indignity than to despoil it
of one thing—a chain which, spattered with blood,
he cast round his own neck. The Gauls were
transfixed with fear and wonder, while the Romans,
quitting their station, ran eagerly to meet their
champion and brought him with praise and gratula-
tion to the dictator. Amidst the rude banter
thrown out by the soldiers in a kind of verse, was
heard the appellation of Torquatus,[1] and thereafter

A.U.C.
393
cognomen auditum; celebratum deinde posteris
14 etiam familiaeque honori fuit. Dictator coronam
auream addidit donum mirisque pro contione eam
pugnam laudibus tulit.

A.U.C.
394
XI. Et hercule tanti ea ad unversi belli eventum
momenti dimicatio fuit ut Gallorum exercitus
proxima nocte relictis trepide castris in Tiburtem
agrum atque inde societate belli facta commeatuque
benigne ab Tiburtibus adiutus mox in Campaniam
2 transierit. Ea fuit causa cur proximo anno C.
Poetelius[1] Balbus consul, cum collegae eius M.
Fabio Ambusto Hernici provincia evenisset, adversus
3 Tiburtes iussu populi exercitum duceret. Ad quorum
auxilium cum Galli ex Campania redissent, foedae
populationes in Labicano Tusculanoque et Albano
agro haud dubie Tiburtibus ducibus sunt factae;
4 et cum adversus Tiburtem hostem duce consule
contenta res publica esset, Gallicus tumultus dictatorem creari coegit. Creatus Q. Servilius Ahala T.
Quinctium magistrum equitum dixit et ex auctoritate
patrum, si prospere id bellum evenisset, ludos
5 magnos vovit. Dictator, ad continendos proprio
bello Tiburtes consulari exercitu iusso manere,
omnes iuniores nullo detractante militiam sacra-
6 mento adegit. Pugnatum haud procul porta Collina

---

[1] Poetelius *Sigonius* (*C.I.L.* i², *pp.* 126, 130): poetilius Ω:
petelius *B*: petilius *B*¹*L*: poetious (?) *D*: poetibus *D*² (*or D*¹):
poetilib' *A*: potilius *A*². *Similar corruptions in* §§ 7, 9, 10.

this was given currency as an honoured surname, B.C. 361
used even by descendants of the family. The
dictator gave him, besides, a golden chaplet, and
loudly extolled that fight of his in a public speech.

XI. And in fact the combat was of so great B.C. 360
consequence to the issue of the whole war, that
the army of the Gauls withdrew in trepidation
from their camp on the succeeding night and
crossed over into the territory of Tibur. There
they formed a military alliance with the Tiburtes,
and having been liberally assisted by them with
provisions, they soon departed and went into Campania. This was the reason why in the following
year the consul Gaius Poetelius Balbus, when
his colleague Marcus Fabius Ambustus had been
appointed to the campaign with the Hernici, was
commanded by the people to march against the
men of Tibur. To aid their allies, the Gauls returned from Campania, and the cruel devastations
which ensued in the districts of Labici, Tusculum,
and Alba were clearly instigated and directed by the
Tiburtes. Against the Tiburtine foe the state was
satisfied to be commanded by a consul; but the
Gallic invasion required the appointment of a
dictator. The choice fell on Quintus Servilius
Ahala, who designated Titus Quinctius master of
the horse, and, instructed by the senate, made a
vow to celebrate the Great Games, in the event of
a successful termination of the war. Directing the
consular army to remain where they were, in order
to confine the Tiburtes to their own field of action,
the dictator administered the oath to all the young
men, none of whom endeavoured to avoid the service.
The battle was fought not far from the Colline

389

est totius viribus urbis in conspectu parentum coniu-
gumque ac liberorum quae magna etiam absentibus
hortamenta animi tum subiecta oculis simul vere-
7 cundia misericordiaque militem accendebant. Magna
utrimque edita caede avertitur tandem acies Gallorum. Fuga Tibur sicut arcem belli Gallici petunt ;
palati a consule Poetelio haud procul Tibure excepti,
egressis ad opem ferendam Tiburtibus simul cum iis
8 intra portas compelluntur. Egregie cum ab dictatore
tum ab consule res gesta est. Et consul alter Fabius
proeliis primum parvis, postremo una insigni pugna,
cum hostes totis adorti copiis essent, Hernicos
9 devincit. Dictator consulibus in senatu et apud
populum magnifice conlaudatis et suarum quoque
rerum illis remisso honore dictatura se abdicavit.
Poetelius de Gallis Tiburtibusque geminum triumphum egit : Fabio satis visum ut ovans urbem
iniret.

10 Inridere Poeteli triumphum Tiburtes : ubi enim
eum secum acie conflixisse ? Spectatores paucos
fugae trepidationisque Gallorum extra portas
egressos, postquam in se quoque fieri impetum
viderint et sine discrimine obvios caedi, recepisse
11 se intra urbem : eam rem triumpho dignam visam
Romanis. Ne nimis mirum magnumque censerent

Gate. The Romans put forth all their strength B.C. 360 in full sight of their parents and their wives and children. These are powerful incentives to courage even when unseen, but being then in full view, set the soldiers on fire with a sense of honour and compassion. The slaughter was great on both sides, but at last the Gallic army was driven off. In their flight they turned towards Tibur, as though it had been the stronghold of the Gallic war; as they straggled on, they encountered the consul Poetelius, not far from the town, and when the Tiburtes came out to their assistance they were beaten back through the gates along with the Gauls. The affair was admirably handled by the consul as well as by the dictator. And the other consul Fabius defeated the Hernici—at first in little skirmishes, but ultimately in one remarkable battle, in which the enemy attacked with all their forces. The dictator, having handsomely lauded the consuls in the senate and before the people, even giving them the credit for his own achievements, resigned his office. Poetelius celebrated a double triumph over the Gauls and the Tiburtes: it was thought enough for Fabius that he should enter the City in an ovation.

The Tiburtes ridiculed the triumph of Poetelius. Where was it, they asked, that he had fought a battle with them? A handful of people had gone outside the gates to look on at the flight and panic of the Gauls, and finding that they too were attacked and that all who came in the way of the Romans were cut down without discrimination, had retired within their walls; this was the great achievement that the Romans had deemed worthy of a triumph! That they might not regard it as too wonderful and

A.U.C.
394
tumultum exciere in hostium portis, maiorem ipsos
trepidationem ante moenia sua visuros. ·

A.U.C.
395-396
XII. Itaque insequenti anno M. Popilio[1] Laenate
Cn. Manlio consulibus primo silentio noctis ab
Tibure agmine infesto profecti ad urbem Romam
2 venerunt.   Terrorem repente ex somno excitatis
subita res et nocturnus pavor praebuit, ad hoc
multorum inscitia, qui aut unde hostes advenissent;
3 conclamatum tamen celeriter ad arma est et portae
stationibus murique praesidiis firmati; et ubi prima
lux mediocrem multitudinem ante moenia neque
alium quam Tiburtem hostem ostendit, duabus portis
egressi consules utrimque aciem subeuntium iam
4 muros adgrediuntur, apparuitque occasione magis
quam virtute fretos venisse: adeo vix primum impetum Romanorum sustinuere.   Quin etiam bono
fuisse Romanis adventum eorum constabat orientem-
que iam seditionem inter patres et plebem metu tam
propinqui belli compressam.

5   Alius adventus hostium fuit[2] agris terribilior[3]:
6 populabundi Tarquinienses fines Romanos, maxime
qua ex parte Etruriam adiacent, peragravere rebusque nequiquam repetitis novi consules iis C. Fabius
et C. Plautius iussu populi bellum indixere; Fabio-
que ea provincia, Plautio Hernici evenere.

---

[1] Popilio (*or* Popillio) *Sigonius* (*cf. Diod.* XVI. xv. 1 *and
chap.* xxiii. § 1): pŏpilio *H* : ponpilio *B* : pompilio Ω.
[2] fuit *Madvig* : fuit proximo bello Ω.
[3] terribilior ς, *Walters* : quam terribilior urbi Ω : quam
urbi terribilior *D*² (*or D*³) *R*²,

great a thing to cause a flurry at their enemy's B.C. 360
gates, they should themselves behold a greater panic
in front of their own walls.

XII. Accordingly, in the following year, when B.C.
Marcus Popilius Laenas and Gnaeus Manlius were 359–358
consuls, a hostile expedition set out from Tibur and
arrived in the first silence of the night, at the walls
of Rome. It was terrifying to be suddenly waked
out of sleep by a surprise and a night alarm; moreover many of the people knew not who their enemies
were nor whence they had come; nevertheless the
call to arms was quickly given, and watches were set
at the gates and the walls were manned. And
when the first light showed the enemy before the
City to be in no great force, and only the men of
Tibur, the consuls sallied out at two gates and
assailed them on both flanks as they were now
drawing near the walls. It was evident that in
coming they had relied more on opportunity than
on courage, for they scarcely withstood the first
shock of the Roman onset. In fact their expedition
was confessedly a good thing for the Romans, and
the fear occasioned by so near an enemy repressed
a quarrel that was already in the air, between the
patricians and the plebs.

Another hostile incursion was more terrifying to
the countryside. The Tarquinienses, bent on
plundering, ranged over the Roman territory, particularly that part which adjoins Etruria; and demands for reparation proving futile, the new consuls,
Gaius Fabius and Gaius Plautius, declared war
against them, as commanded by the people. This
campaign fell to Fabius, that against the Hernici to
Plautius.

LIVY

7 Gallici quoque belli fama increbrescebat. Sed inter multos terrores solacio fuit pax Latinis petentibus data, et magna vis militum ab iis[1] ex foedere vetusto, quod multis intermiserant annis, accepta. 8 Quo praesidio cum fulta res Romana esset, levius fuit quod Gallos mox Praeneste venisse atque inde 9 circa Pedum consedisse auditum est. Dictatorem dici C. Sulpicium placuit; consul ad id accitus C. Plautius dixit; magister equitum dictatori additus M. Valerius. Hi robora militum ex duobus consularibus exercitibus electa adversus Gallos duxerunt.

10 Lentius id aliquanto bellum, quam parti utrique placebat, fuit. Cum primo Galli tantum avidi certaminis fuissent, deinde Romanus miles ruendo in arma ac dimicationem aliquantum Gallicam ferociam 11 vinceret, dictatori neutiquam placebat, quando nulla cogeret res, fortunae se committere adversus hostem, quem tempus deteriorem in dies faceret, locis alienis[2] sine praeparato commeatu, sine firmo munimento morantem, ad hoc iis[3] corporibus animisque, quorum omnis in impetu vis esset, parva eadem languesceret mora.

12 His consiliis dictator bellum trahebat gravemque edixerat poenam, si quis iniussu in hostem pugnasset. Milites aegre id patientes primo in stationibus vigiliisque inter se dictatorem sermonibus carpere, in-

---

[1] iis ⸲ : hiis *A* : his Ω.
[2] faceret locis alienis *Madvig* : et locis alienis faceret Ω : et locus alienus faceret ⸲ *Gelenius, Gebhard*.
[3] iis ⸲ : is *D* : hiis *A* : his Ω.

Rumours of a Gallic war began also to be rife. B.C.
359-358
But with many perils, there was this consolation, that
they had granted peace to the Latins, at their
desire, and had received a large force of soldiers
from them, under the terms of an ancient treaty
which the Latins had for many years disregarded.
Thus strengthened, the Romans heard soon after
with small concern that the Gauls had come to
Praeneste and had then pitched their camp in the
vicinity of Pedum. They resolved on making Gaius
Sulpicius dictator, and sent for Gaius Plautius the
consul to appoint him; Marcus Valerius was named
as his master of the horse. These two marched
against the Gauls, with the choicest troops from
both the consular armies.

The war was considerably more protracted than
was pleasing to either side. At first only the Gauls
had been eager for battle; but later the Romans far
exceeded the Gauls in the ardour with which they
would run to arm themselves and fight. Yet the
dictator was by no means willing, being under no
compulsion, to hazard his fortune against an enemy
whom each day made less formidable, as he lingered
on in an unfriendly country, without a magazine of
food, and without adequate defences—an enemy,
too, whose strength and courage lay wholly in
attacking, and languished as soon as there came a
slight delay.

Upon these considerations the dictator spun out
the war and threatened to punish anyone severely
who should fight the enemy without his orders.
The soldiers were mortified at this. At first they
grumbled among themselves about the dictator,
when on picket-duty or watching in the night, and

terdum patres communiter increpare, quod non
13 iussissent per consules geri bellum : electum esse
eximium imperatorem, unicum ducem, qui nihil
agenti sibi de caelo devolaturam in sinum victoriam
censeat. Eadem deinde haec interdiu propalam ac
ferociora his iactare : se iniussu imperatoris aut dimi-
14 caturos aut agmine Romam ituros. Immiscerique
militibus centuriones, nec in circulis modo fremere
sed iam in principiis ac praetorio in unum sermones
confundi atque in contionis magnitudinem crescere
turba et vociferari ex omnibus locis ut extemplo ad
dictatorem iretur ; verba pro exercitu faceret Sex.
Tullius, ut virtute eius dignum esset.

XIII. Septimum primum pilum iam Tullius ducebat, neque erat in exercitu, qui quidem pedestria
2 stipendia fecisset, vir factis nobilior. Is praecedens
militum agmen ad tribunal pergit mirantique Sulpicio
non turbam magis quam turbae principem Tullium,
3 imperiis oboedientissimum militem, "Si licet, dictator," inquit "condemnatum se universus exercitus
a te ignaviae ratus et prope ignominiae causa desti-
tutum sine armis oravit me ut suam causam apud te
4 agerem. Equidem, sicubi loco cessum, si terga data
hosti, si signa foede amissa obici nobis possent, tamen

sometimes railed at the senators collectively for not
having given the consuls charge of the war ; a fine
general they had chosen, a unique commander, who
thought that without his lifting a finger victory
would fly down from heaven into his lap ! But they
presently began to utter these same sentiments
quite openly and in the light of day, and even
bolder things than these : they would not wait,
they declared, for the general's orders, but would
either fight or go in a body to Rome. The centurions
began to mingle with the soldiers ; the murmuring
was not confined to little knots of men, but in the
main street and before the commander's tent there
was now one general clamour ; the throng increased
to the bigness of an assembly, and on every side
shouts were heard that they should go instantly to
the dictator, and that Sextus Tullius should be
spokesman for the army, as became his courage.

XIII. It was now the seventh campaign in which
Tullius had served as first centurion, nor was there
anyone in the army, at least among the foot-soldiers,
more distinguished for his services. At the head of
the men, who followed in a body, he approached
the platform, where the amazement of Sulpicius on
seeing the mob was not greater than at seeing it
led by Tullius, a soldier most obedient to authority.
" By your leave, Dictator," he began, " the entire
army, deeming itself condemned in your mind for
cowardice and almost deprived of its arms by way
of humiliation, has asked me to plead its cause
with you. For my part, even if we could be taunted
with anywhere quitting a post, with turning our
backs on the foe, with shamefully losing our
standards, I should still think you ought to hearken

397

LIVY

hoc a te impetrari aequum censerem ut nos virtute
culpam nostram corrigere et abolere flagitii memoriam
5 nova gloria patereris. Etiam ad Alliam fusae legiones
eandem quam per pavorem amiserant patriam pro-
fectae postea a Veiis[1] virtute reciperavere. Nobis
deum benignitate, felicitate tua populique Romani,
6 et res et gloria est integra. Quamquam de gloria
vix dicere ausim, si nos et hostes haud secus quam
feminas abditos intra vallum omnibus contumeliis
eludunt, et tu imperator noster—quod aegrius pa-
timur—exercitum tuum sine animis, sine armis, sine
manibus iudicas esse, et, priusquam expertus nos
esses, de nobis ita desperasti ut te mancorum ac
7 debilium ducem iudicares esse. Quid enim aliud
esse causae credamus, cur veteranus dux, fortissimus
bello, compressis, quod aiunt, manibus sedeas? Ut-
cumque enim se habet res, te de nostra virtute
8 dubitasse videri quam nos de tua verius est. Sin
autem non tuum istuc sed publicum est consilium,
et consensus aliqui patrum, non Gallicum bellum,
nos ab urbe a penatibus nostris ablegatos tenet,
quaeso ut ea quae dicam non a militibus imperatori
dicta censeas sed a plebe patribus,—quae si, ut[2]
vos vestra habeatis consilia, sic se sua habituram
9 dicat, quis tandem succenseat?—milites nos esse, non
servos vestros, ad bellum, non in exsilium missos;
si quis det signum, in aciem educat, ut viris ac

---

[1] a Veiis *Alschefski* (*cf.* IV. xxxi. 9): ab Veis D^2 (*or* D^3):
ab Veiis ς: ab eis Ω: ab eius *T*.

[2] si, ut *Madvig*: sicut Ω: sīc *FB*: sic ut *D*: sit ut *L*.

to our entreaty that we be permitted to redeem our
fault with valour, and by winning new renown blot
out the memory of our disgrace. Even the legions
that were routed at the Allia afterwards set out
from Veii and by manful conduct won back the
very City their cowardice had lost. In our case,
thanks to the kindness of the gods and to your good
fortune and that of the Roman People, both our
cause and our glory are unimpaired. Yet I hardly
dare to mention glory, since the enemy flout us with
every species of insult, as though we were women
cowering behind our rampart; and since you, our
general—a thing far harder to bear—regard us as
an army without spirit, without swords, and without
hands, and ere you have given us a trial, have so
despaired of us as to reckon yourself a commander
of cripples and weaklings. For how else can we
account for it, that you, an experienced and fearless
general, should, as they say, be sitting down with
folded hands? Indeed, however this may be, it is
more reasonable that you should seem to distrust our
bravery, than that we should seem to distrust yours.
But if this is not your own but public policy, and if
some agreement amongst the senators, and not the
Gallic war, keeps us in exile from the City and from
our homes, then I beg you to hear what I have to
say, as though it were spoken not by his soldiers to
a general but by the plebs to the patricians—for if
the plebs, even as you have your policies, should
assert that they proposed likewise to have theirs,
who, pray, could be angry with them? I say, then,
we are your soldiers, not your slaves; you have sent
us to war, not into banishment; if anyone would
give us the signal and lead us into battle, we are

LIVY

Romanis dignum sit, pugnaturos ; si nihil armis opus
sit, otium Romae potius quam in castris acturos.
10 Haec dicta sint patribus. Te, imperator, milites tui
oramus ut nobis pugnandi copiam facias.   Cum
vincere cupimus, tum te duce vincere, tibi lauream
insignem deferre, tecum triumphantes urbem inire,
tuum sequentes currum Iovis optimi maximi templum
11 gratantes ovantesque adire." Orationem Tulli ex-
ceperunt preces multitudinis, et undique ut signum
daret, ut capere arma iuberet, clamabant.

XIV. Dictator quamquam rem bonam exemplo
haud probabili actam censebat, tamen facturum
quod milites vellent in se [1] recepit, Tulliumque
secreto quaenam haec res sit aut quo acta more
2 percontatur. Tullius magno opere a dictatore petere
ne se oblitum disciplinae militaris, ne sui neve
imperatoriae maiestatis crederet : multitudini con-
citatae, quae ferme auctoribus similis esset, non
subtraxisse se ducem ne quis alius, quales mota
3 creare multitudo soleret, exsisteret ; nam se quidem
nihil non arbitrio imperatoris acturum.   Illi quoque
tamen videndum magno opere esse ut exercitum in
potestate haberet ; differri non posse adeo concitatos
animos ; ipsos sibi locum ac tempus pugnandi sump-
4 turos, si ab imperatore non detur. Dum haec loquun-

---

[1] in se *Weissenborn* : se Ω.

B.C. 359-358

ready to quit us in the fight like men and Romans: but if there be no occasion for our arms, we had rather spend our leisure in Rome than in a camp. Thus much we would say to the patricians. But of you, our general, we, your soldiers, beg that you give us an opportunity of fighting. We are eager not only to conquer, but to conquer under your leadership; to win for you the glorious laurel; to enter the City with you in the march of triumph; and following your chariot, to approach the throne of Jupiter Optimus Maximus with gratulations and rejoicings." The speech of Tullius was supported by the entreaties of the crowd, who on all sides clamoured for the signal and the command to arm.

XIV. Though the dictator felt that a good thing had been carried out in a way to set a bad example, yet he undertook to do as the soldiers wished. In private he questioned Tullius what this proceeding meant and on what precedent he had acted. Tullius earnestly besought the dictator not to believe that he had forgotten the training of a soldier, nor forgotten himself and the honour due to his commander: the crowd, he said, had become excited; crowds were generally like their leaders, and he had not refused to lead it, for fear that some other might come forward, of the sort that an unruly mob was likely to choose; for his own part he would do nothing without the approval of his general. But Sulpicius, he continued, must none the less be very wary himself, to keep the army in hand; postponement would not do, where feelings were so exasperated; the men would choose for themselves a time and place for fighting, if their general did not provide them. While they were talking thus,

401

LIVY

tur, iumenta forte pascentia extra vallum Gallo
abigenti duo milites Romani ademerunt. In eos
saxa coniecta a Gallis; deinde ab Romana statione
5 clamor ortus ac procursum utrimque est. Iamque
haud procul iusto proelio res erat,[1] ni celeriter di-
remptum certamen per centuriones esset; adfirmata
certe eo casu Tulli apud dictatorem fides est; nec
recipiente iam dilationem re in posterum diem edicitur
acie pugnaturos.

6 Dictator tamen, ut qui magis animis quam viribus
fretus ad certamen descenderet, omnia circumspicere
atque agitare coepit ut arte aliqua terrorem hostibus
incuteret. Sollerti animo rem novam excogitat, qua
deinde multi nostri atque externi imperatores, nostra
7 quoque quidam aetate, usi sunt. Mulis strata detrahi
iubet binisque tantum centunculis relictis agasones
partim captivis partim aegrorum armis ornatos im-
8 ponit. His fere mille effectis centum admiscet
equites et nocte super castra in montes evadere ac
silvis se occultare iubet neque inde ante movere
9 quam ab se acceperint[2] signum. Ipse, ubi inluxit,
in radicibus montium extendere aciem coepit sedulo,
10 ut adversus montes consisteret hostis instructos[3]
vani terroris apparatu, qui quidem terror plus paene

---

[1] erat ς: erant Ω.
[2] acceperint *Frag. Haverk.*: acceperent *PFB*: ac|caeperent
M: acciperent Ω.
[3] instructos *Foster* (*adopting the punct. of Walters and
Conway, instead of* hostis. Instructo—profuit, primo *of
previous edd.*): instructo Ω.

---

[1] *e. g.* C. Marius at Aquae Sextiae (Frontinus, II. iv. 6),
and Julius Caesar at Gergovia (Bell. Gall. VII. xlv. 2).
Bannockburn has been cited as a modern instance.

B.C.
359–358

it chanced that a Gaul attempted to drive off certain
sumpter animals that were grazing outside of the
stockade, and two Roman soldiers took them away
from him. These men were stoned by the Gauls.
Whereupon a shout arose in the Roman outpost, and
men ran forward on both sides. And now the mellay
was likely to end in a regular battle, had not the
centurions speedily parted the combatants. Sulpicius
was assured by this incident that Tullius spoke
truth, and, the situation admitting of no delay, he
announced a general engagement for the morrow.

Yet the dictator was entering a struggle in which
he relied more on the spirit of his troops than on
their strength. He began therefore to cast about
and every way to consider how he might strike
terror into the enemy by some stratagem. His
cleverness produced a new expedient, which many
generals both of our own and foreign countries—
some even in the present age—have since employed.[1]
Commanding the muleteers to remove the pack-
saddles from the mules, leaving only a pair of
saddle-cloths on each, and arming them, partly with
captured weapons, partly with those belonging to
the sick, he mounted them. Having in this way
made out near a thousand, he mixed a hundred
cavalrymen with them and ordered them to go up
by night on to the mountains above the camp and
conceal themselves in the woods, and not to stir from
thence until they received a signal from him. The
dictator himself, as soon as it was light, began to
deploy his front along the lower slopes, on purpose
to make the enemy take their stand facing the
mountains where the preparations had been made
for inspiring them with a fear which, groundless

403

A.U.C.
395-396

veris viribus profuit. Primo credere duces Gallorum
non descensuros in aequum Romanos; deinde, ubi
degressos repente viderunt, et ipsi avidi certaminis
in proelium ruunt, priusque pugna coepit quam
signum ab ducibus daretur.

XV. Acrius invasere Galli dextro[1] cornu; neque
sustineri potuissent, ni forte eo loco dictator fuisset,
2 Sex. Tullium nomine increpans rogitansque sicine
pugnaturos milites spopondisset? Ubi illi clamores
sint arma poscentium, ubi minae iniussu imperatoris
proelium inituros? En ipsum imperatorem clara voce
vocare ad proelium et ire armatum ante prima signa;
ecquis sequeretur eorum qui modo ducturi fuerint,
3 in castris feroces, in acie pavidi? Vera audiebant;
itaque tantos pudor stimulos admovit, ut ruerent in
hostium tela alienatis a memoria periculi animis.
Hic primo impetus prope vecors turbavit hostes,
4 eques deinde emissus turbatos avertit. Ipse dictator,
post quam labantem una parte vidit aciem, signa in
laevum cornu confert, quo turbam hostium congregari
cernebat, et iis qui in monte erant signum quod
5 convenerat dedit. Ubi inde quoque novus clamor

---

[1] dextro *Drakenborch* (*cf.* §§ 4 *and* 6): dextrum Ω.

though it was, yet served the Romans almost better B.C.
259–358 than actual strength. At first the Gallic leaders supposed that the Romans would not come down into the plain; then, when they saw that they had suddenly begun to descend, they also, being themselves eager for the combat, rushed into battle, and the fighting began before the signal could be given by the generals.

XV. The right wing of the Gauls attacked fiercely, and it would have been impossible to stop them, if the dictator had not happened to be there. Calling out to Sextius Tullius by name, he chid him and asked if this was the kind of fighting he had promised that the men should do. Where were those shouts with which they had called for arms? Where were their threats that they would begin the battle without the general's orders? Here was their general himself, who with a loud voice summoned them to fight, and advanced, sword in hand, in the very van! Of those who but now were ready to lead, was there none to follow? They might swagger in camp; in the field they were arrant cowards. What he said was the truth, and so stung them with shame that they rushed on the weapons of the enemy in utter forgetfulness of danger. This well-nigh frenzied onset first threw their enemies into disarray, and before they could recover their confusion the cavalry charged and routed them. The dictator himself, as soon as he saw that a part of their line was wavering, turned the infantry attack against their left, where he descried a throng of the enemy gathering, and made the appointed signal to those on the mountain. And when they too raised a shout and were seen to

A.U.C.
395–396

ortus est[1] et tendere obliquo monte ad castra Gallorum visi sunt, tum metu ne excluderentur omissa pugna est cursuque effuso ad castra ferebantur.

6 Ubi cum occurrisset eis M. Valerius magister equitum, qui profligato dextro[2] cornu obequitabat hostium

7 munimentis, ad montes silvasque vertunt fugam plurimique ibi a fallaci equitum specie agasonibusque excepti sunt; et eorum quos pavor pertulerat[3] in silvas atrox caedes post sedatum proelium fuit.

8 Nec alius post M. Furium quam C. Sulpicius iustiorem de Gallis egit triumphum. Auri quoque ex Gallicis spoliis satis magnum pondus saxo quadrato saeptum in Capitolio sacravit.

9 Eodem anno et a consulibus vario eventu bellatum; nam Hernici a C. Plautio devicti subactique sunt. Fabius collega eius incaute atque inconsulte adversus

10 Tarquinienses pugnavit. Nec in acie tantum ibi cladis acceptum quam quod trecentos septem milites Romanos captos Tarquinienses immolarunt, qua foeditate supplicii aliquanto ignominia populi Romani

11 insignitior fuit. Accessit ad eam cladem et vastatio Romani agri, quam Privernates, Veliterni deinde, incursione repentina fecerunt.

12 Eodem anno duae tribus, Pomptina et Publilia,

---

[1] ortus est *Luterbacher* : ortus (hort' *H*) Ω.
[2] dextro Ω : sinistro *Glareanus*.
[3] pertulerat *D³ς* : perculerat Ω.

---

[1] Bringing up the total number at this time to twenty-seven.

be moving obliquely down the mountain in the direction of the Gallic camp, the enemy, fearing to be shut out, ceased fighting and rushed pell-mell for their entrenchments. There however they were met by Marcus Valerius, the master of the horse, who, having scattered the enemy's right wing, was then riding up to their works; whereupon they turned and fled towards the mountains and the woods, where very many of them were intercepted by the muleteers masquerading as cavalry; and those whose fright had carried them into the woods were pitilessly slaughtered, after the battle had died down. Not since the time of Marcus Furius has anyone celebrated a Gallic triumph that was better deserved than that of Gaius Sulpicius. He also collected from the spoils a considerable weight of gold, which he walled up with hewn stone in the Capitol, and so dedicated.

In the same year the consuls, too, waged war with varying success. Gaius Plautius defeated the Hernici and reduced them to subjection; his colleague Fabius showed neither prudence nor skill in his battle with the Tarquinienses. And yet the disaster experienced on the field was overshadowed by the fact that the Tarquinienses slew three hundred and seven captured Roman soldiers as a sacrifice—an act of savage cruelty that greatly emphasized the humiliation of the Roman People. In addition to this defeat, the Romans suffered the devastation of their fields in sudden incursions made by the Privernates, and afterwards by the Veliterni.

In the same year two tribes were added;[1] the Pomptine and the Publilian; the votive games,

LIVY

additae; ludi votivi, quos M. Furius dictator voverat,
facti; et de ambitu ab C. Poetelio[1] tribuno plebis
auctoribus patribus tum primum ad populum latum
13 est; eaque rogatione novorum maxime hominum
ambitionem, qui nundinas et conciliabula obire soliti
erant, compressam credebant.

XVI. Haud aeque laeta patribus insequenti anno
C. Marcio Cn. Manlio consulibus de unciario fenore
a M. Duillio[2] L. Menenio tribunis plebis rogatio est
perlata; et plebs aliquanto eam cupidius scivit.[3]
2 Ad bella nova priore anno destinata Falisci quoque
hostes exorti duplici crimine, quod et cum Tarquiniensibus iuventus eorum militaverat et eos qui Falerios
perfugerant cum male pugnatum est, repetentibus
3 fetialibus Romanis non reddiderant. Ea provincia
Cn. Manlio obvenit. Marcius exercitum in agrum
Privernatem, integrum pace longinqua, induxit mili-
temque praeda implevit. Ad copiam rerum addidit
munificentiam, quod nihil in publicum secernendo
4 augenti[4] rem privatam militi favit. Privernates
cum ante moenia sua castris permunitis consedissent,
vocatis ad contionem militibus "Castra nunc" inquit
"vobis hostium urbemque praedae do, si mihi polli-

[1] Poetelio *C.I.L.* i², *pp.* 126, 130: poetilio (*or* petilio) Ω.
[2] Duillio *edd.*: duilio (*and other corruptions*) Ω.
[3] scivit *Weissenborn and Madvig*: sciuit accepit *M*: sciuit
accepitque (*or* accepi- *or* accepti-) Ω.
[4] augenti ⌐: augendi (*wanting in O*) Ω.

---

[1] Tacitus tells us (*Annals* VI. xvi.) that the twelve Tables
had forbidden a higher rate of interest. If so, the tribunes
were merely reviving an obsolete enactment. *Unciarium
fenus*—interest at the rate of $\frac{1}{12}$ of 1 for each 100 of the
principal sum, calculated monthly, hence 1 per cent. annually.

which Marcus Furius had vowed as dictator, were B.C. 359–358 given; and a statute against bribery was then for the first time laid before the people by Gaius Poetelius, tribune of the plebs, with the approbation of the senate. By this measure they thought to have suppressed corrupt practices, particularly on the part of men risen from the people, who were wont to haunt the country fairs and gathering-places.

XVI. Less agreeable to the senate was a measure B.C. 357 which came up in the following year, in the consulship of Gaius Marcius and Gnaeus Manlius. It fixed the rate of interest at one per cent., and was carried through by Marcus Duillius and Lucius Menenius, tribunes of the plebs. The commons ratified it much more eagerly than they had done the other law.[1]

Besides the new wars determined on in the previous year, the Faliscans also rose up as enemies. They were charged with two offences: their youth had fought on the side of the Tarquinienses; and they had refused the demand of the fetials that they should give up the Romans who had taken refuge in Falerii, after the defeat. This command was assigned to Gnaeus Manlius. Marcius led an army into the territory of Privernum, unravaged during a long period of peace, and loaded his troops with booty. This abundance he administered bountifully, and sequestering nothing to the public treasury, encouraged the men to augment their private fortunes. The Privernates having encamped in front of their town, within strong intrenchments, Marcius called his soldiers together and thus addressed them: "I give you now for booty the camp and city of our enemies, if you promise me

LIVY

cemini vos fortiter in acie operam navaturos nec
5 praedae magis quam pugnae paratos esse." Signum
poscunt ingenti clamore celsique et spe haud dubia
feroces in proelium vadunt. Ibi ante signa Sex.
Tullius, de quo ante dictum est, exclamat "Aspice,
imperator" inquit, "quemadmodum exercitus tuus
tibi promissa praestet," piloque posito stricto gladio
6 in hostem impetum facit. Sequuntur Tullium ante-
signani omnes primoque impetu avertere hostem;
fusum inde ad oppidum persecuti, cum iam scalas
moenibus admoverent, in deditionem urbem acce-
perunt. Triumphus de Privernatibus actus.
7 Ab altero consule nihil memorabile gestum, nisi
quod legem novo exemplo ad Sutrium in castris
tributim de vicensima eorum qui manumitterentur
tulit. Patres, quia ea lege haud parvum vectigal
8 inopi aerario additum esset, auctores fuerunt; ceterum
tribuni plebis, non tam lege quam exemplo moti, ne
quis postea populum sevocaret, capite sanxerunt;
nihil enim non per milites iuratos in consulis verba,
quamvis perniciosum populo, si id liceret, ferri
posse.
9 Eodem anno C. Licinius Stolo a M. Popilio Laenate
sua lege decem milibus aeris est damnatus, quod
mille iugerum agri cum filio possideret emancu-
pandoque filium fraudem legi fecisset.

---

[1] Within a distance of one mile from the walls a citizen
might appeal from the decision of a consul, but beyond that
point the consul's authority was absolute.
[2] From his paternal authority.
[3] By the Licinio-Sextian legislation of 377 it had been
forbidden that anybody should hold more than 500 *iugera*.
cf. VI. XXXV. 5.

that in the battle you will play the part of men,
and be not more ready to plunder than to fight."
They clamoured loudly for the signal and entered
the battle with spirit, emboldened by no uncertain
expectations. There in the fore-front Sextus Tullius,
who has been mentioned before, cried out, "Look,
general, and see how your army keeps the promises it
gave you!" Then, laying down his javelin, he drew
his sword and charged the foe. All of the front line
followed Tullius, and putting the enemy to flight at
the first shock, pursued them to the town, where
the Romans were already bringing up their scaling
ladders to the wall, when the place surrendered.
A triumph was celebrated over the Privernates.

The other consul accomplished nothing worth
recording, except that without precedent he got a
law passed in his camp before Sutrium—the men
voting by tribes—which levied a tax of one-twentieth
on manumissions. The Fathers ratified this law,
since it brought in no small revenue to the empty
treasury; but the tribunes of the plebs, troubled
less by the law than by the precedent established,
had it made a capital offence for anyone thereafter
to summon the people to the comitia away from
Rome. If this should be permitted, there was
nothing, they argued, however baneful to the
people, which could not be carried through by the
votes of soldiers sworn to obey their consul.[1]

In the same year Gaius Licinius Stolo was prosecuted under his own statute by Marcus Popilius
Laenas, and condemned to pay a fine of ten thousand
asses, on the charge that he held with his son a
thousand *iugera* of land, and by emancipating his
son[2] had evaded the law.[3]

A.U.C.
398–399

XVII. Novi consules inde, M. Fabius Ambustus
2 iterum et M. Popilius Laenas iterum, duo bella
habuere, facile alterum cum Tiburtibus, quod Laenas
gessit, qui hoste in urbem compulso agros vastavit;
Falisci Tarquiniensesque alterum consulem prima
3 pugna fuderunt. Inde terror maximus fuit quod
sacerdotes eorum facibus ardentibus anguibusque
praelatis incessu furiali militem Romanum insueta
turbaverunt specie. Et tum quidem velut lymphati
et attoniti munimentis suis trepido agmine inci-
4 derunt; deinde, ubi consul legatique ac tribuni
puerorum ritu vana miracula paventes inridebant
increpabantque, vertit animos repente pudor, et in
5 ea ipsa quae fugerant velut caeci ruebant. Discusso
itaque vano apparatu hostium cum in ipsos armatos
se intulissent, averterunt totam aciem; castrisque
etiam eo die potiti praeda ingenti parta victores
reverterunt, militaribus iocis cum apparatum hostium
6 tum suum increpantes pavorem. Concitatur deinde
omne nomen Etruscum, et Tarquiniensibus Faliscisque
ducibus ad Salinas perveniunt. Adversus eum terrorem dictator C. Marcius Rutulus[1] primus de plebe
dictus magistrum equitum item de plebe C. Plau-
7 tium dixit. Id vero patribus indignum videri, etiam
dictaturam iam in promiscuo esse; omnique ope

---

[1] Rutulus *Conway* (*cf. chap.* xxxviii. § 8 *and Conway's note
at* iii. vii. 6): rutilius *UHA*[2]: utilius (*omitted by O*) Ω.

B.C.
356-355

XVII. New consuls now came in, Marcus Fabius
Ambustus and Marcus Popilius Laenas, each for the
second time. They had two wars. One of these
was easy; it was waged by Laenas against the
Tiburtes, and he shut up the enemy within their
city and pillaged their fields. The other consul was
routed by the Faliscans and Tarquinienses in his
first engagement. The panic was chiefly due to
this, that their priests, bearing serpents and blazing
torches before them, came rushing on like Furies,
and utterly dismayed the Roman soldiers with the
extraordinary sight. At first they were like men
frantic and distraught, and flung themselves in a
disordered mob into their own works. Then when
the consul, the lieutenants and the tribunes laughed
at them and upbraided them for being scared like
children at idle tricks, shame caused a sudden
revulsion in their feelings, and they rushed, as if
blinded, on the very objects from which they had
fled. In this spirit they brushed aside the enemy's
vain paraphernalia, and hurling themselves on his
real fighting men, they routed the whole army, and
even captured the camp that day. As they returned
victorious with the rich plunder they had won, they
jested in soldier-fashion and scoffed not only at the
enemy's devices but at their own fright as well.
All who bore the Etruscan name then rose in arms,
and led by the men of Tarquinii and Falerii,
advanced as far as Salinae. To meet this fearful
danger Gaius Marcius Rutulus was made dictator,
the first that was ever appointed from the plebs, and
he named a plebeian also, Gaius Plautius, to be
master of the horse. But the patricians thought
it shameful that even the dictatorship should now

413

impediebant ne quid dictatori ad id bellum decerneretur parareturve.   Eo promptius cuncta ferente
8 dictatore populus iussit.   Profectus ab urbe utraque
parte Tiberis, ratibus exercitu, quocumque fama
hostium ducebat, traiecto multos populatores agrorum
9 vagos palantes oppressit; castra quoque necopinato
adgressus cepit et octo milibus hostium captis, ceteris
aut caesis aut ex agro Romano fugatis sine auctoritate
patrum populi iussu triumphavit.

10   Quia nec per dictatorem plebeium nec per consulem comitia consularia haberi volebant et alter
consul Fabius bello retinebatur, res ad interregnum
11 redit.   Interreges deinceps Q. Servilius Ahala M.
Fabius Cn. Manlius C. Fabius C. Sulpicius L. Aemi-
12 lius Q. Servilius M. Fabius Ambustus.   In secundo
interregno orta contentio est, quod duo patricii consules creabantur, intercedentibusque tribunis interrex
Fabius aiebat in duodecim tabulis legem esse ut
quodcumque postremum populus iussisset, id ius
ratumque esset; iussum populi et suffragia esse.
13 Cum intercedendo tribuni nihil aliud quam ut differ-
rent comitia valuissent, duo patricii consules creati
sunt, C. Sulpicius Peticus tertium M. Valerius Publicola, eodemque die magistratum inierunt, (XVIII.)

---

[1] Compare the story of Valerius and Horatius at III.
lxiii. 11.

[2] Perhaps identical with the M. Fabius Ambustus of VI.
xxii., xxxiv., xxxvi. ; perhaps with the M. Fabius Dorsuo of
VII. xxviii.

B.C.
356-355

be common; and they exerted all their influence to prevent anything being decreed or made ready for the dictator, to carry on that war. For which reason the people voted the more promptly everything that the dictator proposed. Marching out from the City and setting his army across the Tiber by means of rafts, wherever a rumour of the enemy called him, he surprised many straggling pillagers as they roamed about the fields, on both sides of the river; he also captured their camp in a surprise attack, and with it eight thousand soldiers; and having slain the rest, or driven them out of Roman territory, was granted a triumph by the people, but without the authorization of the senate.[1]

The patricians were not willing that a consular election should be held by a plebeian, whether dictator or consul, and the other consul being detained by the war, the state relapsed into an interregnum. The office of interrex was held successively by Quintus Servilius Ahala, Marcus Fabius,[2] Gnaeus Manlius, Gaius Fabius, Gaius Sulpicius, Lucius Aemilius, Quintus Servilius, and Marcus Fabius Ambustus. In the second interregnum a controversy arose because two patricians were on the point of being named as consuls; and when the tribunes sought to veto the announcement, the interrex Fabius declared that the Twelve Tables enacted that whatsoever the people decreed last should have the binding force of law, and their votes were also a decree. The tribunes gained nothing more by their intervention than a postponement of the comitia, and two patrician consuls were elected, namely Gaius Sulpicius Peticus (for the third time) and Marcus Valerius Publicola. They entered office that very day. (XVIII.)

B.C. 354

LIVY

quadringentesimo anno quam urbs Romana condita
erat, quinto tricesimo quam a Gallis reciperata,
ablato post undecimum [1] annum a plebe consulatu. [2]

2 Empulum [3] eo anno ex Tiburtibus haud memorando
certamine captum, sive duorum consulum auspicio
bellum ibi gestum est, ut scripsere quidam, seu per
idem tempus Tarquiniensium quoque sunt vastati
agri ab Sulpicio consule, quo Valerius adversus
Tiburtes legiones duxit.

3 Domi maius certamen consulibus cum plebe ac
tribunis erat. Fidei iam suae non solum virtutis
ducebant esse, ut accepissent duo patricii consu-
4 latum, ita ambobus patriciis mandare : quin aut toto
cedendum esse, ut [4] plebeius iam magistratus consulatus fiat, aut totum possidendum quam possessionem
5 integram a patribus accepissent.   Plebes contra
fremit : quid se vivere, quid in parte civium censeri,
si, quod duorum hominum virtute, L. Sexti ac C.
Licini, partum sit, id obtinere universi non possint ?
6 Vel reges vel decemviros vel si quod tristius sit
imperii nomen patiendum esse potius, quam ambos
7 patricios consules videant, nec in vicem pareatur
atque imperetur, sed pars altera in aeterno imperio
locata plebem nusquam alio natam quam ad servi-
8 endum putet. Non desunt tribuni auctores turbarum,
sed inter concitatos per se omnes vix duces eminent.

---

[1] undecimum *Sigonius and Glareanus* : nonum (*or some
corruption of* nonum) Ω.
[2] consulatu *Walters and Conway* : consulatu patricii consules ambo ex interregno magistratum iniere, C. Sulpicius
Peticus tertium M. Valerius Publicola Ω.
[3] Empulum ς : emaepulum (*and other corruptions*) Ω.
[4] esse ut *Madvig* : esset si (est si *DL*) Ω.

in the four hundredth year from the founding of Rome B.C. 354
and the thirty-fifth from its recovery from the Gauls,
depriving the plebs of the consulship they had
enjoyed for ten years. Empulum was won that year
from the Tiburtes without any memorable battle
being fought; whether, as some writers state, the
campaign was conducted there under the auspices of
the two consuls; or whether the lands belonging to
Tarquinii were ravaged by the consul Sulpicius at
the same time that Valerius led his legions against
the Tiburtes.

The consuls had a harder struggle at home, with the
plebs and the tribunes. They held that honour as
well as courage required of them that, even as two
patricians had received the consulship, so they should
hand it over to successors who were both patricians:
indeed they ought rather to withdraw from the consulship altogether, that it might at once become a
plebeian magistracy, or else retain undivided that
control which they had inherited entire from their
fathers. On the other side, the plebeians were asking
angrily why they lived, why they were counted a part
of the state, if they were unable by their collective
efforts to maintain what the courage of two men,
Lucius Sextius and Gaius Licinius, had won for them.
It were better to put up with kings or decemvirs, or
—if possible—a more stern type of government than
theirs, rather than see the consuls both patricians and
have no turns at obeying and commanding, while a
part of the people thought themselves established
forever in authority and the commons born for no
other end than servitude. There was no lack of
tribunes to promote disturbances, but where all were
so excited, to begin with, the leaders were hardly to

417

LIVY

A.U.C.
400

9 Aliquotiens frustra in campum descensum cum esset multique per seditiones acti comitiales dies, postremo vicit [1] perseverantia consulum : plebis eo dolor erupit ut tribunos actum esse de libertate vociferantes relinquendumque non campum iam solum sed etiam urbem captam atque oppressam regno patriciorum

10 maesta [2] sequeretur. Consules relicti a parte populi per infrequentiam comitia nihilo segnius perficiunt. Creati consules ambo patricii, M. Fabius Ambustus tertium T. Quinctius. In quibusdam annalibus pro T. Quinctio M. Popilium consulem invenio.

A.U.C.
401

XIX. Duo bella eo anno prospere gesta. Cum Tarquiniensibus Tiburtibusque [3] ad deditionem pugnatum. Sassula ex his urbs capta ; ceteraque oppida eandem fortunam habuissent, ni universa gens positis

2 armis in fidem consulis venisset. Triumphatum de Tiburtibus ; alioquin mitis victoria fuit. In Tarquinienses acerbe saevitum ; multis mortalibus in acie caesis ex ingenti captivorum numero trecenti quinquaginta octo delecti, nobilissimus quisque, qui Romam

3 mitterentur ; volgus aliud trucidatum. Nec populus in eos qui missi Romam erant mitior fuit : medio in foro omnes virgis caesi ac securi percussi. Id pro immolatis in foro Tarquiniensium Romanis poenae

---

[1] vicit *Conway* : uicta (victa *O*) Ω : uictae ς.
[2] maesta ς (*Alschefski*) : maesta plebs Ω.
[3] Tarquiniensibus Tiburtibusque *Walters* : Tarquiniensibus Tiburtibusque cum Tiburtibus *A*ˣ : Tarquiniensibus Tiburtibusque cum Tiburtibus usque *Frag. Haverk.* : Tarquiniensibus Tiburtibusque usque *cod. Gaertn.* : Tiburtibus usque *Madvig* : Tiburtibusque Ω.

---

[1] Where the voting took place.

be discerned. After the people had several times
gone down to the Campus Martius ¹ to no purpose,
and many meeting days had been spent in rioting,
the persistence of the consuls finally prevailed. The
plebs, thereupon, in a burst of resentment, followed
their tribunes, who cried out that liberty was lost
and that they ought now to leave not only the voting-
field but the City, too, which was taken captive and
enslaved by the tyranny of the patricians. The consuls, being deserted by half the people, nevertheless,
despite the paucity of voters, completed the election.
The successful candidates were both patricians,
Marcus Fabius Ambustus (for the third time) and
Titus Quinctius. In certain annals I find Marcus
Popilius given as consul instead of Titus Quinctius.

XIX. Two wars were successfully prosecuted this
year, and the Tarquinienses and Tiburtes were
forced to make submission. From the latter their
city of Sassula was taken, and the rest of their towns
would have met with the same fortune, had the
whole nation not laid down their arms and cast
themselves upon the mercy of the consul. A
triumph was celebrated over them, but in all other
respects the victory was used with clemency. The
men of Tarquinii were shown no ruth ; many were
slain in the field of battle, and out of the vast
number taken prisoners three hundred and fifty-eight
were selected—the noblest of them all—to be sent
to Rome, and the rest of the populace were put to
the sword. Neither were the People less stern
towards those who had been sent to Rome, but
scourged them all with rods in the middle of the Forum
and struck off their heads. Such was the vengeance
they exacted of their enemies for the Romans sacrificed

419

4 hostibus redditum. Res bello bene gestae ut Samnites quoque amicitiam peterent effecerunt. Legatis
eorum comiter ab senatu responsum; foedere in
societatem accepti.

5 Non eadem domi quae militiae fortuna erat plebi
Romanae. Nam etsi unciario fenore facto levata
usura erat, sorte ipsa obruebantur inopes nexumque
inibant; eo nec patricios ambo consules neque comitiorum curam publicave studia prae privatis incom-
6 modis plebs ad animum admittebat. Consulatus
uterque apud patricios manet; consules creati C.
Sulpicius Peticus quartum M. Valerius Publicola
iterum.

In bellum Etruscum intentam civitatem, quia Cae-
ritem populum misericordia consanguinitatis Tarquiniensibus adiunctum fama ferebatur, legati Latini
ad Volscos convertere, nuntiantes exercitum conscriptum armatumque iam suis finibus imminere;
inde populabundos in agrum Romanum venturos
7 esse. Censuit igitur senatus neutram neglegendam
rem esse; utroque legiones scribi consulesque sortiri
8 provincias iussit. Inclinavit deinde pars maior curae
in Etruscum bellum, postquam litteris Sulpici con-

---

[1] Chap. xv. § 10.

in the market-place of Tarquinii.[1]   Their success in
war induced the Samnites also to apply for their
friendship.   The senate made a courteous answer to
their ambassadors, and granted them a treaty of
alliance.

The Roman commons were not so fortunate at home
as in the field.   For notwithstanding they had been
relieved of usury by the adoption of a one per cent.
rate, the very poor found even the principal
sum a crushing burden, and were being bound over
to their creditors.   Hence it was that neither the
incumbency of two patrician consuls, nor concern for
the elections or affairs of state, could divert the
thoughts of the plebeians from their personal dis-
tresses.   Accordingly both consulships continued in
the hands of the patricians; Gaius Sulpicius Peticus
was elected for the fourth time, and Marcus Valerius
Publicola for the second.

While the citizens were occupied with thoughts
of an Etruscan war—for it was rumoured that the
people of Caere, out of compassion for their kinsmen
of Tarquinii, had made common cause with them—
came envoys from the Latins and turned their
thoughts upon the Volsci, with a report that they
had mustered and equipped an army, which was
even then descending upon Latium, from whence it
would invade and devastate the territory of the
Romans.   The senate therefore resolved that neither
threat must be neglected ; and ordered that legions
should be enrolled for both campaigns, and that the
consuls should decide the commands by lot.   But
the Etruscan war afterwards came to be their chief
concern, on the receipt of a dispatch from the
consul Sulpicius, who had received the assignment

LIVY

sulis, cui Tarquinii provincia evenerat, cognitum est
depopulatum agrum circa Romanas salinas praedaeque
partem in Caeritum fines avectam et haud dubie
iuventutem eius populi inter praedatores fuisse.
9 Itaque Valerium consulem, Volscis oppositum castraque ad finem Tusculanum habentem, revocatum
inde senatus dictatorem dicere iussit. T. Manlium
10 L. filium dixit. Is cum sibi magistrum equitum A.
Cornelium Cossum dixisset, consulari exercitu contentus ex auctoritate patrum ac populi iussu Caeritibus bellum indixit.

XX. Tum primum Caerites, tamquam in verbis
hostium vis maior ad bellum significandum quam in
suis factis, qui per populationem Romanos lacessi-
erant, esset, verus belli terror invasit, et quam non
2 suarum virium ea dimicatio esset cernebant; paenite-
batque populationis et Tarquinienses exsecrabantur
defectionis auctores; nec arma aut bellum quisquam
apparare, sed pro se quisque legatos mitti iubebat
3 ad petendam erroris veniam. Legati senatum cum
adissent, ab senatu reiecti ad populum deos rogave-
runt, quorum sacra bello Gallico accepta rite pro-
curassent, ut Romanos florentes ea sui misericordia
caperet quae se rebus adfectis quondam populi
4 Romani cepisset; conversique ad delubra Vestae
hospitium flaminum Vestaliumque ab se caste ac

---

[1] sc. Torquatus. See chap. v. § 3 and chap. x. § 13.
[2] See v. xl. 7 and l. 3.

to Tarquinii, with the news that the countryside
lying near the Roman salt-works had been pillaged,
and a part of the booty carried into the borders of
the Caerites, whose soldiers had, without question,
been amongst the depredators. And so the senate
recalled Valerius the consul, who was opposing the
Volsci and had his camp close to the Tuscan frontier,
and ordered him to nominate a dictator. His choice
fell upon Titus Manlius,[1] the son of Lucius, who
appointed as master of the horse Aulus Cornelius
Cossus. Asking for no more than the consular army,
the dictator, by the senate's authority, and at the
bidding of the people, proclaimed war on the
Caerites.

XX. It was then that the Caerites realized for the
first time the full danger of war, as if the words of
their enemies conveyed a more emphatic hint of it
than their own acts, though they had pillaged the
Romans and harried them. Beginning then to
perceive how inadequate was their strength to such
a quarrel, they repented of their raid, and cursed
the Tarquinienses, who had encouraged them to fall
away. Nobody made ready his arms and prepared
for war, but one and all bade dispatch ambassadors
to Rome, to beg forgiveness for their error. The
envoys, having approached the senate, were sent by
them to be dealt with by the people. Calling on
the gods whose sacred emblems they had received and
religiously protected in the Gallic war, they besought
them to inspire the Romans in their prosperity with
such compassion for the men of Caere as they themselves had formerly shown for Rome in her time of
tribulation.[2] Then, turning to the shrine of Vesta,
they invoked the flamens and Vestals whom they had

LIVY

5 religiose cultum invocabant: eane meritos crederet
quisquam hostes repente sine causa factos? aut, si
quid hostiliter fecissent, consilio id magis quam
furore lapsos fecisse, ut sua vetera beneficia, locata
praesertim apud tam gratos, novis corrumperent
maleficiis, florentemque populum Romanum ac feli-
cissimum bello sibi desumerent hostem, cuius adflicti
amicitiam petissent?[1] Ne appellarent consilium quae
6 vis ac necessitas appellanda esset. Transeuntes[2]
agmine infesto per agrum suum Tarquinienses, cum
praeter viam nihil petissent, traxisse quosdam agrestium populationis eius, quae sibi crimini detur,
7 comites. Eos seu dedi placeat, dedere se paratos
esse, seu supplicio adfici, daturos poenas. Caere,
sacrarium populi Romani, deversorium sacerdotum
ac receptaculum Romanorum sacrorum, intactum in-
violatumque crimine belli hospitio Vestalium cultisque
8 dis darent. Movit populum non tam causa praesens
quam vetus meritum, ut maleficii quam beneficii
potius immemores essent. Itaque pax populo Caeriti
data, indutiasque in centum annos factas in aes[3]

---

[1] petissent M: cepissent Ω: coepissent HTD: . . pis-
sent O.
[2] transeuntes A[1] or A[2]: tanseuntes H: transeuntis
PFTDLA: transeundis M: wanting in O.
[3] aes Madvig: senatus consultum (sc̄) Ω.

424

entertained with a pure and scrupulous hospitality. B.C. 353
Could anyone, they asked, believe that those who
had deserved so well of the Romans had suddenly
turned enemies without reason? or that if they
had in fact committed an act of hostility, it had
been deliberately planned, and had not rather been
owing to a fit of madness? Would they undo their
own kindness of old, especially kindness to such
grateful friends, with new misdeeds; and choose to
be enemies of the Roman People in their flourishing
state and at the height of their success in war, when
they had sought their friendship in the hour of their
adversity? Let them not give the name of "purpose"
to what should properly be called "force" and
"necessity." The Tarquinienses, marching in hostile
array through their territories, had sought nothing of
them save permission to pass, but had drawn certain
rustics after them in their train, who had borne a
part in the pillaging with which the people of Caere
were now taxed. If it pleased the Romans that
these men should be surrendered, they would
surrender them; if they would have them punished,
they should be made to suffer. But Caere, the
sanctuary of the Roman People, the hostel of its
priests and refuge of the Roman religion, let them
preserve intact and unstained by the imputation of
making war, for the sake of the hospitality it had
shown their Vestals and the reverence it had paid
their gods. The people were moved, not so much
by their present claims as by their ancient merits,
and chose rather to forget an injury than a kindness.
So peace was granted to the people of Caere, and it
was resolved that a truce of a hundred years be
made, and recorded on a table of bronze. The

A.U.C.
401

9 referri placuit. In Faliscos eodem noxios crimine vis belli conversa est; sed hostes nusquam inventi. Cum populatione peragrati fines essent, ab oppugnatione urbium temperatum; legionibusque Romam reductis reliquum anni muris turribusque reficiendis consumptum et aedis Apollinis dedicata est.

A.U.C.
402

XXI. Extremo anno comitia consularia certamen patrum ac plebis diremit, tribunis negantibus passuros comitia haberi ni secundum Liciniam legem haberentur, dictatore obstinato tollere potius totum e re publica consulatum quam promiscuum patribus 2 ac plebi facere. Prolatandis igitur comitiis cum dictator magistratu abisset, res ad interregnum rediit. Infestam inde patribus plebem interreges cum accepissent, ad undecimum interregem seditioni- 3 bus certatum est. Legis Liciniae patrocinium tribuni iactabant; propior dolor plebi fenoris ingravescentis erat, curaeque privatae in certaminibus publicis 4 erumpebant. Quorum [1] taedio patres L. Cornelium Scipionem interregem concordiae causa observare legem Liciniam comitiis consularibus iussere. P. Valerio Publicolae datus e plebe collega C. Marcius 5 Rutulus. [2] Inclinatis semel in concordiam animis novi consules fenebrem quoque rem, quae distinere

---

[1] quorum O𝟓: quarum Ω.
[2] Rutulus *Conway*: rutilius Ω.

---

[1] Brother of the Marcus Valerius of chap. xxiii. § 3.

brunt of the war was turned against the Faliscans, B.C. 353 who lay under the same accusation; but the enemy were nowhere encountered. Having ranged over their lands and laid them waste, the Romans refrained from attacking their cities, and led their legions home. The rest of the year was consumed in repairing the walls and towers, and a temple was dedicated to Apollo.

XXI. In the latter part of the year the consular B.C. 352 election was broken off by a quarrel between the patricians and the plebs: the tribunes refused to permit the assembly to be held unless it were held agreeably to the Licinian law, and the dictator was obstinately determined rather to remove the consulship root and branch out of the state than to throw it open to patricians and plebs without distinction. The assembly was therefore repeatedly adjourned, until the dictator's term had expired, and the state reverted to an interregnum. The interreges found the commons hostile to the patricians, and the factional struggle continued until there had been eleven interreges. The tribunes continually vaunted their backing of the Licinian law: the plebs were more concerned with the distress they suffered from the increasing weight of usury, and their private worries broke out into public quarrels. Worn out with these, the senate ordered Lucius Cornelius Scipio, the interrex, for harmony's sake to observe the Licinian law at the consular election. Publius Valerius Publicola[1] was elected, with a plebeian colleague named Gaius Marcius Rutulus. Now that the minds of men were once inclined to concord, the new consuls set themselves to obtain relief in the matter of usury also, which appeared to be the sole

LIVY

una animos [1] videbatur, levare adgressi solutionem
alieni aeris in publicam curam verterunt quinqueviris
creatis quos mensarios ab dispensatione pecuniae
6 appellarunt.   Meriti aequitate curaque sunt, ut per
omnium annalium monumenta celebres nominibus
essent; fuere autem C. Duillius [2] P. Decius Mus
7 M. Papirius Q. Publilius [3] et T. Aemilius.   Qui rem
difficillimam tractatu et plerumque parti utrique,
semper certe alteri gravem cum alia moderatione
tum impendio magis publico quam iactura sustinue-
8 runt.   Tarda enim nomina et impeditiora inertia
debitorum quam facultatibus aut aerarium mensis
cum aere in foro positis dissolvit, ut populo prius
caveretur, aut aestimatio aequis rerum pretiis libera-
vit, ut non modo sine iniuria sed etiam sine queri-
moniis partis utriusque exhausta vis ingens aeris
alieni sit.

9   Terror inde vanus belli Etrusci, cum coniurasse
duodecim populos fama esset, dictatorem dici coegit.
Dictus in castris—eo enim ad consules missum
senatus consultum est—C. Iulius, cui magister
equitum adiectus L. Aemilius.   Ceterum foris tran-

quilla omnia fuere: (XXII.) temptatum domi per
dictatorem ut ambo patricii consules crearentur rem
2 ad interregnum perduxit.   Duo interreges C. Sulpi-

---

[1] una animos ς Jenicke: unanimos Ω: in animos D?A.
[2] Duillius A^x: duellius Ω.
[3] Publilius Glareanus: publius Ω.

obstacle to harmony. They made the discharge of B.C. 352
debts a concern of the state, appointing five commissioners, whom they called bankers, from their
having the disposition of the money. These men
by their impartiality and diligence fairly earned the
distinction which attaches, in all the histories, to
the names of Gaius Duillius, Publius Decius Mus,
Marcus Papirius, Quintus Publilius, and Titus
Aemilius. In the discharge of a very difficult duty,
involving always a hardship for one of the parties,
and in most instances for both, they managed
matters wisely in other respects, and, in particular,
they expended without throwing away the public
funds. For with long-standing accounts, embarrassed
more by the debtors' neglect than by their lack of
means, they dealt in one of the following ways: either
they paid them out of the treasury—taking security
for the people first—at the banking tables they had
set up in the Forum; or they settled them upon a
valuation, at fair prices, of the debtor's effects. And
so, not only without injustice, but even without
complaint from either side, a vast amount of
indebtedness was cleared off.

A groundless fear of war with Etruria, on a report
that the twelve nations had conspired, compelled
the appointment of a dictator. The appointment
was made in camp—for thither had the resolution of
the senate been sent to the consuls—and Gaius
Julius became dictator, with Lucius Aemilius for
master of the horse. But abroad all was serene,
(XXII.) while at home an attempt, made through the B.C. 351
dictator, to obtain the return of patricians to both
consulships, brought the state to an interregnum.
The two interreges who were put in, Gaius Sulpicius

cius et M. Fabius interpositi obtinuere, quod dictator
frustra tetenderat, mitiore iam plebe ob recens
meritum levati aeris alieni, ut ambo patricii consules
3 crearentur. Creati ipse C. Sulpicius Peticus, qui
prior interregno abiit, et T. Quinctius Poenus;
quidam Caesonem, alii Gaium praenomen [1] Quinctio
4 adiciunt. Ad bellum ambo profecti, Faliscum Quinctius, Sulpicius Tarquiniense, nusquam acie congresso
hoste cum agris magis quam cum hominibus urendo
5 populandoque gesserunt bella; cuius lentae velut
tabis senio victa utriusque pertinacia populi est, ut
primum a consulibus, dein permissu eorum ab senatu
6 indutias peterent. In quadraginta annos impetraverunt.

Ita posita duorum bellorum quae imminebant
cura, dum aliqua ab armis quies esset, quia solutio
aeris alieni multarum rerum mutaverat dominos,
7 censum agi placuit. Ceterum cum censoribus creandis
indicta comitia essent, professus censuram se petere
C. Marcius Rutulus,[2] qui primus dictator de plebe
8 fuerat, concordiam ordinum turbavit; quod videbatur quidem tempore alieno fecisse, quia ambo tum
forte patricii consules erant, qui rationem eius se
9 habituros negabant; sed et ipse constantia inceptum
obtinuit et tribuni omni vi, ut reciperaturi [3] ius con-

---

[1] Gaium praenomen (*i. e.* c̄p̄nomen) *Walters:* cognomen Ω:
c. cognomen *Gelenius* ("*vetus lectio*"): C. nomen *Sigonius*
(*Diod.* XVI. liii. 1, *has* Γάϊos).

[2] Rutulus *Conway:* rutilius Ω.

[3] vi ut reciperaturi *Conway:* vi reciperaturi *Weissenborn:*
ui reciperantur *M:* ui recuperandos *O:* ui reci (*or* -cu-) perando
Ω: ui recuperatū *A²:* vi ut reciperaretur *Alschefski.*

and Marcus Fabius, brought to pass what the
dictator had vainly striven for; and the plebs being
now grown more tractable, thanks to the help lately
granted them in the relief of debt, both men
elected consuls were patricians. These were that
very Gaius Sulpicius Peticus, who was the earlier of
the two interreges, and Titus Quinctius Poenus.
(Some give Caeso, others Gaius, as the praenomen
of Quinctius.) Both marched out to fight, Quinctius
against the Faliscans, Sulpicius against the Tarquinienses; but nowhere encountering their enemies
in battle, they warred rather with the land, which
they burnt and pillaged, than with men; until the
obstinacy of both peoples was overcome, as by the
wasting of a lingering illness, and they requested a
truce, first of the consuls, and later, by their permission, of the senate. They were granted one for
forty years.

The anxiety arising from two threatening wars
being thus allayed, it was resolved that while there
was some rest from arms they would take the
census; for the settlement of debts had brought
about the change of ownership in many properties.
But when notice had been given of an assembly for
the election of censors, an announcement that he
should be a candidate on the part of Gaius
Marcius Rutulus, who had been the first plebeian
dictator, played havoc with the harmony of the
orders; for he seemed to have taken this step at
an untoward time, since both the consuls, as it
fell out, were then patricians, who declared that
they would receive no votes for him; but Rutulus
himself held firmly to his purpose, and the tribunes
aided him with all their power, in the hope of re-

sularibus comitiis amissum, adiuverunt, et cum ipsius
viri maiestas nullius honoris fastigium non aequabat,
tum per eundem qui ad dictaturam aperuisset viam
censuram quoque in partem vocari plebes volebat.
10 Nec variatum comitiis est, quin cum Manlio Naevio
censor Marcius [1] crearetur.

Dictatorem quoque hic annus habuit M. Fabium
nullo terrore belli, sed ne Licinia lex comitiis consularibus observaretur. Magister equitum dictatori
11 additus Q. Servilius. Nec tamen dictatura poten-
tiorem eum consensum [2] patrum consularibus comitiis

fecit, quam censoriis [3] fuerat. XXIII. M. Popilius
Laenas a plebe consul, a patribus L. Cornelius Scipio
datus.

Fortuna quoque inlustriorem plebeium consulem
2 fecit; nam cum ingentem Gallorum exercitum in
agro Latino castra posuisse nuntiatum esset, Scipione
gravi morbo implicito Gallicum bellum Popilio extra
3 ordinem datum. Is impigre exercitu scripto, cum
omnes extra portam Capenam ad Martis aedem convenire armatos iuniores iussisset signaque eodem
quaestores ex aerario deferre, quattuor expletis
legionibus quod superfuit militum P. Valerio Publi-
4 colae praetori tradidit, auctor [4] patribus scribendi

---

[1] Naevio (*or* neuio *or* ne uio *or* le uio *or* naebio *or* cnaebio)
Ω. *The names are evidently corrupted: Walters thinks
Livy wrote* cum Cn. Manlio T. f. C. Marcius crearetur.
[2] consensum ς : consensu Ω : *wanting in O.*

covering what they had lost in the election of B.C. 351 consuls; and not only was the man's own greatness equal to any honour, however lofty, but the plebs desired that they might be called to share the censorship by the same man who had opened up for them a path to the dictatorship. There was no dissenting opinion shown at the assembly, and Marcius was elected, along with Manlius Naevius.

There was a dictator in this year also, namely, Marcus Fabius, not because of any threatened war, but to prevent the observance of the Licinian law in the consular election. Quintus Servilius was assigned to the dictator as master of the horse. But the dictatorship made the unanimity of the patricians no more potent in the election of consuls than it had been in the election of censors. XXIII. B.C. 350 Marcus Popilius Laenas was chosen from the plebs, Lucius Cornelius Scipio from the patricians.

Fortune even made the plebeian consul the more illustrious, for the news that a huge army of Gauls had encamped in Latium found Scipio afflicted with a grave disorder, and the conduct of the war was entrusted by special arrangement to Popilius. He levied troops with energy, and ordered all the young men to assemble under arms outside the Porta Capena, at the temple of Mars, commanding the quaestors to convey the standards thither, from the treasury. After filling up four legions, he turned over the supernumeraries to the praetor, Publius Valerius Publicola, urging the senators to enroll

---

³ censoriis ⸀: censor·is *HT*: censor·is Ω: *wanting in O.*
⁴ auctor Ω: auctori ⸀ *Alschefski*: auctoribus ⸀.

A.U.C.
404

alterius exercitus, quod ad incertos belli eventus
5 subsidium rei publicae esset. Ipse iam satis omnibus
instructis comparatisque ad hostem pergit. Cuius ut
prius nosceret vires quam periculo ultimo temptaret,
in tumulo quem proximum castris Gallorum capere
6 potuit vallum ducere coepit. Gens ferox et ingenii
avidi ad pugnam cum procul visis Romanorum signis
ut extemplo proelium initura explicuisset aciem,
postquam neque in aequum demitti [1] agmen vidit et
cum loci altitudine tum vallo etiam tegi Romanos,
perculsos pavore rata, simul opportuniores quód intenti tum maxime operi essent, truci clamore ad-
7 greditur. Ab Romanis nec opus intermissum—triarii
erant qui muniebant—et ab hastatis principibusque,
qui pro munitoribus intenti armatique steterant,[2]
8 proelium initum. Praeter virtutem locus quoque
superior adiuvit, ut pila omnia hastaeque non tamquam ex aequo missa vana, quod plerumque fit,
caderent, sed omnia librata ponderibus figerentur;
9 oneratique telis Galli, quibus aut corpora transfixa
aut praegravata inhaerentibus gerebant scuta, cum
cursu paene in adversum subissent, primo incerti
10 restitere; dein, cum ipsa cunctatio et his anĭmos
minuisset et auxisset hosti, impulsi retro ruere alii

---

[1] demitti *Sigonius*: dimitti Ω.
[2] steterant ⊊: steterunt Ω: steterit *H.*

a second army as a national reserve against the
uncertain emergencies of war.   Having at length
concluded all the necessary preparations, he himself
marched against the enemy; and that he might
first learn their strength before putting it to the
test of a decisive battle, he seized and began to
fortify an eminence as close as he could find to the
camp of the Gauls.   These, being a fierce people
and by nature eager for the combat, on beholding
the Roman ensigns in the distance, at once drew
out their line, as if for instant battle.   But perceiving that the Romans did not descend into the
plain, but sought to protect themselves not only by
their position but even with a rampart, they supposed them to be panic-stricken and at the same
time the more open to attack for being just then
taken up with their task.   They advanced, therefore,
with hideous yells.   The Romans without a pause
in their work, on which the reserves were engaged, began the action with their troops of the
first and second lines, who had been standing alert
and armed in front of the working party.   Besides
their valour, they had an advantage from the
elevation, for their javelins and spears, instead of
falling without effect, as they mostly do when
thrown on a level field, were steadied by their own
weight and all struck home.   The Gauls were
burdened with the missiles which had either transfixed their bodies, or, sticking in their shields, had
made them very heavy; their dash had carried them
almost up the slope, but first they halted, uncertain
what to do, and then—for the mere delay had
abated their ardour and increased that of their foes
—they were thrown back, and falling one upon

435

A.U.C.
404
super alios stragemque inter se caede ipsa foediorem
dare; adeo praecipiti turba obtriti plures quam
ferro necati.

A.U.C.
405
XXIV. Necdum certa Romanis victoria erat; alia
2 in campum degressis supererat moles; namque
multitudo Gallorum, sensum omnem talis damni
exsuperans, velut nova rursus exoriente acie integrum
3 militem adversus victorem hostem ciebat; stetitque
suppresso impetu Romanus, et quia iterum fessis
subeunda dimicatio erat, et quod consul, dum inter
primores incautus agitat, laevo umero matari prope
4 traiecto cesserat parumper ex acie. Iamque omissa
cunctando victoria erat, cum consul volnere alligato
revectus ad prima signa " Quid stas, miles ? " inquit;
" non cum Latino Sabinoque hoste res est, quem
5 victum armis socium ex hoste facias; in beluas
strinximus ferrum; hauriendus aut dandus est
sanguis. Propulistis a castris, supina valle praecipites
egistis, stratis corporibus hostium superstatis; complete eadem strage campos qua montes replestis.
6 Nolite exspectare, dum stantes vos fugiant; inferenda
7 sunt signa et vadendum in hostem." His adhortationibus iterum coorti pellunt loco primos manipulos
Gallorum; cuneis deinde in medium agmen perrum-

436

another wrought greater carnage than even their B.C. 350 enemies had done; for so headlong was the rout, that more were trodden under foot than slain with the sword.

XXIV. But the Romans were not yet sure of B.C. 349 victory; on descending into the plain they found another fight awaiting them. For the Gallic host, superior to any feeling for such losses, sprang up like a new army, and urged their fresh troops against the victorious foe. The Romans, slowing down, came to a halt, for they were confronted, weary as they were, with a second struggle, and the consul, rashly exposing himself in the van, had received a javelin in his left shoulder that had like to have gone clean through it, and had withdrawn for a brief space from the fight. And now the delay had almost lost them the victory, when the consul, whose wound had been dressed, rode up again to the front. "Why are you standing there, my men?" he exclaimed. "You have no Latin or Sabine foe to deal with, whom you may overcome in fight and transform from an enemy into an ally; we have drawn the sword against wild beasts, and we must have their blood or yield them ours. You have repulsed them from your camp, you have driven them headlong down a sloping valley, you stand on heaps of your slain enemies; cover the plain with the same carnage you have spread upon the mountains. Do not wait for the enemy to flee from you, while you stand still; you must move forward and attack them." Roused once more to action by these exhortations, they drove back the foremost of the Gallic maniples, and then, forming in wedges, burst through into the midst of the main

A U.O.
405
8 punt. Inde barbari dissipati, quibus nec certa
imperia nec duces essent, vertunt impetum in suos ;
fusique per campos et praeter castra etiam sua fuga
praelati, quod editissimum inter aequales tumulos
9 occurrebat oculis, arcem Albanam petunt. Consul
non ultra castra insecutus, quia et volnus degravabat
et subicere exercitum tumulis ab hoste occupatis
nolebat, praeda omni castrorum militi data victorem
exercitum opulentumque Gallicis spoliis Romam
10 reduxit. Moram triumpho volnus consulis attulit
eademque causa dictatoris desiderium senatui fecit,
ut esset qui aegris consulibus comitia haberet.
11 Dictator L. Furius Camillus dictus, addito magistro
equitum P. Cornelio Scipione, reddidit patribus possessionem pristinam consulatus. Ipse ob id meritum
ingenti patrum studio creatus consul collegam Ap.
Claudium Crassum dixit.

A.U.O.
406
XXV. Prius quam inirent novi consules magistratum, triumphus a Popilio de Gallis actus magno
favore plebis ; mussantesque inter se rogitabant
2 num quem plebeii consulis paeniteret ; simul dictatorem increpabant, qui legis Liciniae spretae mercedem[1] privata cupiditate quam publica iniuria foediorem
cepisset, ut se ipse consulem dictator crearet.

---

[1] mercedem *Doering* : mercedem (*or* mercede) consulatum
Ω.

---

[1] Livy seems to have in mind the summit now called
Monte Cavo, though it is strangely described as *editissimum
inter aequales tumulos.*

[2] Probably, at this time, on the 1st of July.

array; whereat the barbarians were thrown into con- B.C. 349
fusion, having no definite orders nor commanders,
and, turning, charged upon their fellows; and so,
dispersed about the fields, and even carried past
their own camp in the rout, they made for the
highest point in the range of hills that met their
eyes, namely, the Alban Citadel.[1] The consul did
not pursue them beyond their camp, for his wound
was troubling him, and he was unwilling to send
his troops against the hills which the enemy had
occupied. Giving over to his soldiers the entire
booty of the camp, he led back his army, flushed
with victory and enriched with the Gallic spoils, to
Rome. The consul's triumph was delayed by reason
of his wound, which also made the senate wish for
a dictator, that there might be someone—in the
illness of the consuls—who could hold the election.
Lucius Furius Camillus was appointed to that office,
and Publius Cornelius Scipio was made his master
of the horse. Camillus restored to the patricians
their ancient possession of the consulship, and in
recognition of this service was himself, with their
warm support, elected consul, and announced the
election of Appius Claudius Crassus as his colleague.

XXV. Before the new consuls entered office,[2] B.C. 348
Popilius celebrated his triumph over the Gauls, with
great enthusiasm on the part of the plebeians, who,
muttering low, would often ask each other if anyone
regretted the choice of a plebeian consul. At the
same time they railed against Camillus, who by
declaring himself elected consul, when he was
dictator, had got a reward, they said, for his contempt
of the Licinian law more disgraceful for his personal
cupidity than for the injury done the commonwealth.

LIVY

A.U.C.
406

3 Annus multis variisque motibus fuit insignis:
Galli ex Albanis montibus, quia hiemis vim pati
nequiverant, per campos maritimaque loca vagi
4 populabantur; mare infestum classibus Graecorum
erat oraque litoris Antiatis Laurensque tractus et
Tiberis ostia, ut praedones maritimi cum terrestribus
congressi ancipiti semel proelio decertarint [1] dubii-
que discesserint in castra Galli, Graeci retro ad
5 naves, victos se an victores putarent. Inter hos
longe maximus exstitit terror concilia populorum
Latinorum ad lucum Ferentinae habita responsum-
que haud ambiguum imperantibus milites Romanis
datum, absisterent imperare iis,[2] quorum auxilio
6 egerent: Latinos pro sua libertate potius quam pro
7 alieno imperio laturos arma. Inter duo simul bella
externa defectione etiam sociorum senatus anxius,
cum cerneret metu tenendos quos fides non tenuisset,
extendere omnes imperii vires consules dilectu
habendo iussit: civili quippe standum exercitu esse,
8 quando socialis coetus desereret. Undique, non
urbana tantum sed etiam agresti iuventute, decem
legiones scriptae dicuntur quaternum milium et
9 ducenorum [3] peditum equitumque trecenorum,[4] quem
nunc novum exercitum, si qua externa vis ingruat,

---

[1] decertarint ς: decertarent Ω.
[2] iis ς: is *MDL*: hiis *A*; his Ω.
[3] ducenorum ς: ducentorum Ω.
[4] trecenorum ς: c c c Ω.

existing resources of the Roman People, though B.C. 348
the world hardly contains them; so strictly has
our growth been limited to the only things for
which we strive,—wealth and luxury.

Among the untoward occurrences of this year was
the death of one of the consuls, Appius Claudius,
in the midst of the preparations for war. The
administration of the state passed to Camillus, over
whom, as sole consul,—whether owing to his general
high standing, which deserved not to be subordinated
to the dictatorship, or to the happy omen, in a
Gallic rising, of his surname,[1]—the Fathers concluded it not meet to set a dictator. The consul
appointed two legions to defend the City, and
divided the other eight with Lucius Pinarius the
praetor. Having a lively recollection of his father's
prowess, he took upon himself, without drawing
lots, the conduct of the Gallic war, and commanded
the praetor to secure the seaboard and prevent the
Greeks from landing. Then, marching down into
the Pomptine district, he chose a suitable site for
a permanent camp; for he had no mind to meet
the enemy in the field, unless compelled to do so,
believing that he should effectually subdue them
if he kept them from making raids, since they
subsisted necessarily on plunder.

XXVI. While they were there quietly passing
the time in guard-duty, a Gaul came out to them,
remarkable for his great stature and his armour,
and, smiting his spear against his shield and thereby
obtaining silence, challenged the Romans, through
an interpreter, to send a man to fight with him.
There was a young tribune of the soldiers, named
Marcus Valerius, who, regarding himself as no less

443

A.U.C.
406

se quam T. Manlium ratus, prius sciscitatus consulis
3 voluntatem in medium armatus processit. Minus
insigne certamen humanum numine interposito
deorum factum; namque conserenti iam manum
Romano corvus repente in galea consedit, in hostem
4 versus. Quod primo ut augurium caelo missum
laetus accepit tribunus, precatus deinde, si divus si
diva esset qui sibi praepetem misisset, volens pro-
5 pitius adesset. Dictu mirabile, tenuit non solum
ales captam semel sedem, sed quotienscumque certamen initum est, levans se alis os oculosque hostis
rostro et unguibus appetit, donec territum prodigii
talis visu oculisque simul ac mente turbatum Valerius
obtruncat; corvus ex conspectu elatus orientem petit.
6 Hactenus quietae utrimque stationes fuere; postquam spoliare corpus caesi hostis tribunus coepit,
nec Galli se statione tenuerunt et Romanorum cursus
ad victorem etiam ocior fuit. Ibi circa iacentis
Galli corpus contracto certamine pugna atrox con-
7 citatur. Iam non manipulis proximarum stationum
sed legionibus utrimque effusis res geritur. Camillus
laetum militem victoria tribuni, laetum tam praesentibus ac secundis dis ire in proelium iubet; osten-
tansque insignem spoliis tribunum, "hunc imitare,
miles" aiebat, "et circa iacentem ducem sterne
8 Gallorum catervas." Di hominesque illi adfuere

worthy of that honour than Titus Manlius had been, B.C. 348
first ascertained the consul's wishes, and then armed
himself and advanced into the midst. But the
human interest of the combat was eclipsed by the
intervention of the gods; for the Roman was in
the very act of engaging, when suddenly a raven
alighted on his helmet, facing his adversary. This
the Roman first received with joy, as a heaven-
sent augury, and then prayed that whosoever, be it
god or goddess, had sent the auspicious bird might
attend him with favour and protection. Marvellous
to relate, the bird not only held to the place it had
once chosen, but as often as the combatants closed,
it rose on its wings and attacked the enemy's face
and eyes with beak and talons, till he was terror-
struck with the sight of such a portent, and
bewildered at once in his vision and his mind, was
dispatched by Valerius,—whereupon the raven flew
off towards the east and was lost to sight. Hitherto the outguards on either side had stood quietly
by; but when the tribune began to despoil the
corpse of his fallen foe, the Gauls remained no
longer at their station, and the Romans ran up
even more swiftly to the victor. There a scuffle,
arising over the body of the prostrate Gaul, led to
a desperate fight that was not long confined to the
maniples of the nearest outposts, for the legions,
rushing out on both sides, carried on the battle.
Camillus ordered his soldiers to fall on, elated as
they were by the tribune's victory, elated too by
the present assistance of the gods; and pointing
to the tribune, decked out in his spoils, he cried,
"Here is your pattern, soldiers! Bring down the
Gauls in troops around their prostrate leader!"

pugnae, depugnatumque haudquaquam certamine
ambiguo cum Gallis est; adeo duorum militum eventum, inter quos pugnatum erat, utraque acies animis
9 praeceperat.   Inter primos,[1] quorum concursus alios
exciverat, atrox proelium fuit; alia multitudo, priusquam ad coniectum teli veniret, terga vertit.   Primo
per Volscos Falernumque agrum dissipati sunt; inde
Apuliam ac mare inferum [2] petierunt.

10   Consul contione advocata laudatum tribunum decem bubus aureaque corona donat; ipse iussus ab
11 senatu bellum maritimum curare cum praetore iunxit
castra.   Ibi quia res trahi segnitia Graecorum non
committentium se in aciem videbantur,[3] dictatorem
comitiorum causa T. Manlium Torquatum ex aucto-
12 ritate senatus dixit.   Dictator magistro equitum A.
Cornelio Cosso dicto comitia consularia habuit aemu-
lumque decoris sui absentem M. Valerium Corvum—
id enim illi deinde cognominis fuit—summo favore
populi, tres et viginti natum annos, consulem renun
13 tiavit.   Collega Corvo de plebe M. Popilius Laenas,
quartum consul futurus, datus est.   Cum Graecis
a Camillo nulla memorabilis gesta res; nec illi terra
14 nec Romanus mari bellator erat. Postremo cum
litoribus arcerentur, aqua etiam praeter cetera neces-

---

[1] inter primos Ω : in primos *Harant.*
[2] inferum Ω : superum ⲋ.
[3] videbantur Ω : uidebatur *H.*

Both gods and men helped in that battle, and they B.C. 348 fought it out with the Gauls to a conclusion that was never doubtful, so clearly had each side foreseen the result implicit in the outcome of the single combat. Between those who began the fray, and by their conflict drew in the others, there was a bitter struggle; but the rest of the Gallic host turned tail ere they came within the cast of a javelin. At first they scattered among the Volsci and through the Falernian countryside; from there they made their way into Apulia or to the Tuscan Sea.

The consul assembled his soldiers, and having eulogized the tribune, bestowed on him ten oxen and a golden coronet; Camillus himself was commanded by the senate to take charge of the operations on the coast, and accordingly joined forces with the praetor. The campaign there seemed likely to be long drawn out, for the Greeks were poltroons and refused to risk an engagement. He therefore, on the authorization of the senate, appointed Titus Manlius Torquatus to be dictator, that an election might be held. The dictator, after naming Aulus Cornelius Cossus master of the horse, presided over a consular election, and announced, amid great popular rejoicings, that the choice had fallen—in his absence—upon a youth of twenty-three, the Marcus Valerius Corvus—for this was his surname from that time—who had rivalled Manlius's own glorious achievement. As colleague of Corvus they elected the plebeian Marcus Popilius Laenas to be for the fourth time consul. With the Greeks, Camillus fought no memorable action; they were no warriors on land, nor were the Romans on the sea. In the end, being kept off shore, and their

447

LIVY

A.U.C. 15 saria usui deficiente Italiam reliquere. Cuius populi
406 ea cuiusque gentis classis fuerit nihil certi est.
Maxime Siciliae fuisse tyrannos crediderim; nam
ulterior Graecia ea tempestate intestino fessa bello
iam Macedonum opes horrebat.

A.U.C. 407-408 XXVII. Exercitibus dimissis cum et foris pax et
domi concordia ordinum otium esset, ne nimis laetae
res essent pestilentia civitatem adorta coegit senatum
imperare decemviris ut libros Sibyllinos inspicerent;
2 eorumque monitu lectisternium fuit. Eodem anno
Satricum ab Antiatibus colonia deducta restitutaque
urbs quam Latini diruerant. Et cum Carthaginien-
sibus legatis Romae foedus ictum, cum amicitiam ac
societatem petentes venissent.

3 Idem otium domi forisque mansit T. Manlio Torquato [1] C. Plautio consulibus. Semunciarium tantum
ex unciario fenus factum, et in pensiones aequas
triennii, ita ut quarta praesens esset, solutio aeris
4 alieni dispensata est; et sic quoque parte plebis
adfecta fides tamen publica privatis difficultatibus
potior ad curam senatui fuit. Levatae maxime res,
quia tributo ac dilectu supersessum.

5 Tertio anno post Satricum restitutum a Volscis
M. Valerius Corvus [2] iterum consul cum C. Poetelio
factus, cum ex Latio nuntiatum esset legatos ab

---

[1] T. Manlio Torquato ç : T. Manlio Torquato, (·ii·) Ω.
(*Walters thinks this a corruption of* l. f., *i. e.* Luci filio.)
[2] Corvus Ω : coruinus U.

---

[1] For these commissioners see VI. xlii. 2.
[2] See v. xiii. 2 and note there.
[3] This is the first mention in Livy of a treaty with the
Carthaginians, and Diodorus (XVI. lxix.) also speaks of it as
the first, but Polybius (III. xxii.) tells of a treaty between
Rome and Carthage made in the first year of the Republic
(509 B.C.).
[4] *cf.* chap. xvi. § 1 and note.

448

water giving out, as well as other necessaries, they B.C. 348
abandoned Italy. To what people or race their
fleet belonged is uncertain. I am most inclined to
think that they were Sicilian tyrants; for Greece
proper was at that time exhausted with civil wars and
trembled, even then, at the power of the Macedonians.

XXVII. When the armies had been disbanded, B.C.
and there was peace with other nations, and—thanks 347–346
to the goodwill betwixt the orders—quietness at
home, that the happiness of the citizens might not
pass all bounds, a pestilence attacked them and the
senate was compelled to order the ten commissioners[1]
to consult the Sibylline Books. By their direction
a lectisternium[2] was held. In the same year a colony
was sent out to Satricum by the Antiates, and that
city, which had been destroyed by the Latins, was
rebuilt. Further, a treaty was entered into at Rome
with envoys of the Carthaginians, who had come
seeking friendship and an alliance.[3]

The same peaceful conditions continued at home
and abroad during the consulship of Titus Manlius
Torquatus and Gaius Plautius. But the rate of
interest was reduced from one to one-half per cent.,[4]
and debts were made payable, one-fourth down and
the remainder in three annual instalments; even so
some of the plebeians were distressed, but the public
credit was of greater concern to the senate than
were the hardships of single persons. What did the
most to lighten the burden was the omission of the
war-tax and the levy.

In the second year after the rebuilding of Satricum
by the Volsci, Marcus Valerius Corvus became consul
for the second time, with Gaius Poetelius. A report
having come out of Latium that emissaries of the

449

A.U.C.
407–408

Antio circumire populos Latinorum ad concitandum
6 bellum, priusquam plus hostium fieret Volscis arma
inferre iussus, ad Satricum exercitu infesto pergit.
Quo cum Antiates aliique Volsci praeparatis iam
ante, si quid ab Roma moveretur, copiis occurrissent,
nulla mora inter infensos diutino odio dimicandi
7 facta est. Volsci, ferocior ad rebellandum quam ad
bellandum gens, certamine victi fuga effusa Satrici
moenia petunt. Et ne in muris quidem satis firma
spe cum corona militum cincta iam scalis caperetur
urbs, ad quattuor milia militum [1] praeter multitudi-
8 nem imbellem sese dedidere. Oppidum dirutum
atque incensum : ab aede tantum matris Matutae
abstinuere ignem. Praeda omnis militi data. Extra
praedam quattuor milia deditorum habita ; eos vinctos
consul ante currum triumphans egit ; venditis deinde
9 magnam pecuniam in aerarium redegit. Sunt qui
hanc multitudinem captivam servorum fuisse scribant,
idque magis veri simile est quam deditos venisse.

A.U.C.
409–411

XXVIII. Hos consules secuti sunt M. Fabius
Dorsuo Ser. Sulpicius Camerinus. Auruncum inde
2 bellum ab repentina populatione coeptum ; metuque
ne id factum populi unius consilium omnis nominis
Latini esset, dictator—velut adversus [2] armatum iam

---

[1] ad $\overline{\text{IIII}}$ (or IIII milia) militum (militum *omitted by*
OHLA) Ω.
[2] adversus ⸑ : aduersum Ω.

---

[1] An Italian goddess associated with birth and the dawn,
and widely worshipped ; in Satricum apparently the chief
deity. *cf.* Warde Fowler, *Festivals*, p. 155.

Antiates were circulating amongst the Latin peoples with a view to stir up war, Valerius was ordered to deal with the Volsci before more enemies should arise, and marched to the attack of Satricum. There he was opposed by the Antiates and the other Volsci, with forces which they had levied in advance, in case any measures should be taken by the Romans; and both sides being actuated by inveterate hatred, the battle was joined without delay. The Volsci, a race more spirited in beginning than in prosecuting war, were defeated in the struggle and fled in disorder to the walls of Satricum. Indeed, they put no great reliance even in their walls, for when the city had been encircled with troops and was on the point of being escaladed, they surrendered, being in number about four thousand soldiers, besides the unarmed populace. The town was dismantled and burnt; only the temple of Mater Matuta[1] was saved from the flames. All the booty was given to the soldiers. The four thousand who had surrendered were not reckoned a part of the spoils; these the consul sent in chains before his chariot when he triumphed, and they were subsequently sold, and brought in a great sum to the treasury. Some think that this multitude of captives consisted of slaves, and this is more likely than that surrendered men were sold.

XXVIII. These consuls were succeeded by Marcus Fabius Dorsuo and Servius Sulpicius Camerinus. War then broke out with the Aurunci, in consequence of a raid which they unexpectedly executed. It was feared that this act of a single nation might be the joint design of all of the Latin name, and a dictator was appointed—as though to

Latium—L. Furius creatus magistrum equitum Cn.
3 Manlium Capitolinum dixit; et cum—quod per
magnos tumultus fieri solitum erat—iustitio indicto
dilectus sine vacationibus habitus esset, legiones
quantum maturari potuit in Auruncos ductae. Ibi
praedonum magis quam hostium animi inventi;
4 prima itaque acie debellatum est. Dictator tamen,
quia et ultro bellum intulerant et sine detractatione
se certamini offerebant, deorum quoque opes adhi-
bendas ratus inter ipsam dimicationem aedem Iunoni
Monetae vovit; cuius damnatus voti cum victor
5 Romam revertisset, dictatura se abdicavit. Senatus
duumviros ad eam aedem pro amplitudine populi
Romani faciendam creari iussit; locus in arce de-
stinatus, quae area aedium M. Manli Capitolini fuerat.
6 Consules dictatoris exercitu ad bellum Volscum usi
Soram ex hostibus, incautos adorti, ceperunt.

Anno postquam vota erat aedes Monetae dedicatur C. Marcio Rutulo [1] tertium T. Manlio Torquato
7 iterum consulibus. Prodigium extemplo dedicationem secutum, simile vetusto montis Albani prodigio; namque et lapidibus pluit et nox interdiu
visa intendi; librisque inspectis cum plena religione

---

[1] Rutulo *Conway*: rutilo Ω: rutilio *UO*.

---

[1] I. xxxi. 1.
[2] *i.e.* the Sibylline Books.

B.C.
345-343

oppose a Latium already up in arms—in the person of Lucius Furius. After naming Gnaeus Manlius Capitolinus to be his master of the horse, he suspended the courts, and having levied troops without exemptions—as was customary in great emergencies—he led them with all possible speed against the Aurunci. These he discovered to possess the spirit of freebooters rather than of enemies, and so brought the war to a conclusion in the first engagement. Howbeit the dictator, considering that they had been the aggressors in the war and were accepting battle without shrinking, saw fit to summon even the gods to help him, and in the heat of the encounter vowed a temple to Juno Moneta. This vow the result made binding, and the dictator having returned to Rome victorious, resigned his authority. The senate ordered that two commissioners should be designated to erect the temple in a style becoming to the grandeur of the Roman People, and a site was appointed for it in the Citadel, where once had stood the house of Marcus Manlius Capitolinus. The consuls, employing the dictator's army for the Volscian war, made a surprise attack upon the enemy and captured Sora.

The temple of Moneta was dedicated the next year after it was vowed, when Gaius Marcius Rutulus was consul for the third time and Titus Manlius Torquatus for the second. The dedication was immediately followed by a prodigy like the one which had happened long before on the Alban Mount;[1] for a shower of stones fell, and a curtain of night seemed to stretch across the sky; and when the Books[2] had been consulted and the City was filled with forebodings of divine displeasure, the

LIVY

civitas esset, senatui placuit dictatorem feriarum
8 constituendarum causa dici. Dictus P. Valerius
Publicola; magister equitum ei Q. Fabius Ambustus
datus est.   Non tribus tantum supplicatum ire placuit
sed finitimos etiam populos, ordoque iis, quo quisque
9 die supplicarent, statutus.   Iudicia eo anno populi
tristia in feneratores facta, quibus ab aedilibus dicta
dies esset, traduntur.   Et res haud ulla insigni ad
10 memoriam causa ad interregnum redit; ex interregno, ut id actum videri posset, ambo patricii
consules creati sunt, M. Valerius Corvus tertium
A. Cornelius Cossus.

XXIX. Maiora iam hinc bella et viribus hostium et vel longinquitate regionum vel temporum
spatio¹ quibus bellatum est dicentur.   Namque eo
anno adversus Samnites, gentem opibus armisque
2 validam, mota arma; Samnitium bellum ancipiti
Marte gestum Pyrrhus hostis, Pyrrhum Poeni secuti.
Quanta rerum moles! Quotiens in extrema pericu-
lorum ventum, ut in hanc magnitudinem quae vix
3 sustinetur erigi imperium posset! Belli autem causa
cum Samnitibus Romanis, cum societate amicitiaque
iuncti essent, extrinsecus venit, non orta inter ipsos
4 est.   Samnites Sidicinis iniusta arma, quia viribus
plus poterant, cum intulissent, coacti inopes ad opu-

---

¹ et vel longinquitate regionum vel temporum spatio
Cornelissen: et longinquitate uel regionum uel temporum
spatio Ω (*but U transposes* regionum *and* temporum: *L has*
religionum uel templorum: *HTD have* religionum).

454

senate resolved on the appointment of a dictator, to establish days of worship. The choice fell on Publius Valerius Publicola, who was given Quintus Fabius Ambustus as master of the horse. They determined that not only the Roman tribes but the neighbouring peoples also should offer supplications; and they appointed an order for them, on what day each should make entreaty. It is handed down that during this year the people rendered severe judgments against usurers, who had been brought to trial by the aediles. The state—for no specially memorable reason—reverted to an interregnum, which was followed—so that this might appear to have been intended—by the election to both consulships of patricians, namely Marcus Valerius Corvus, for the third time, and Aulus Cornelius Cossus.

XXIX. Wars of greater magnitude, in respect both of the forces of our enemies and of the remoteness of their countries and the long periods of time involved, now fall to be related. For in that year the sword was drawn against the Samnites, a people powerful in arms and in resources; and hard upon the Samnite war, which was waged with varying success, came war with Pyrrhus, and after that with the Carthaginians. How vast a series of events! How many times the extremity of danger was incurred, in order that our empire might be exalted to its present greatness, hardly to be maintained! Now the cause of the war between the Romans and the Samnites, who had been united in friendship and alliance, was of external origin and not owing to themselves. The Samnites had unjustly attacked the Sidicini, because they happened to be more powerful than they, and the Sidicini, driven in their

lentiorum auxilium confugere Campanis sese coniun-
5 gunt.   Campani magis nomen ad praesidium sociorum
quam vires cum attulissent, fluentes luxu ab duratis
usu armorum, in Sidicino pulsi agro in se deinde
6 molem omnem belli verterunt.   Namque Samnites,
omissis Sidicinis ipsam arcem finitimorum Campanos
adorti, unde aeque facilis victoria, praedae atque
gloriae plus esset, Tifata, imminentes Capuae colles,
cum praesidio firmo occupassent, descendunt inde
quadrato agmine in planitiem quae Capuam Tifataque
7 interiacet.   Ibi rursus acie dimicatum ; adversoque
proelio Campani intra moenia compulsi, cum robore
iuventutis suae acciso nulla propinqua spes esset,
coacti sunt ab Romanis petere auxilium.

XXX. Legati introducti in senatum maxime in
hanc sententiam locuti sunt.   "Populus nos Campanus
legatos ad vos, patres conscripti, misit amicitiam in
perpetuum, auxilium praesens a vobis petitum.
2 Quam si secundis rebus nostris petissemus, sicut
coepta celerius ita infirmiore vinculo contracta esset ;
tunc enim, ut qui ex aequo nos venisse in amicitiam
meminissemus, amici forsitan pariter ac nunc, subiecti
3 atque obnoxii vobis minus essemus ; nunc, miseri-

B.C.
345-343

need to fly for succour to a more wealthy nation, had attached themselves to the Campanians. The Campanians had brought reputation rather than real strength to the defence of their allies; enervated by luxury, they had encountered a people made hardy by the use of arms, and being defeated in the territory of the Sidicini, had then drawn down the full force of the war upon themselves. For the Samnites, disregarding the Sidicini and attacking the Campanians—the very stronghold of their neighbours,—from whom they would gain full as easy a victory and more plunder and renown, had seized and with a strong force occupied Tifata— a range of hills looking down on Capua—and thence had descended in battle-order into the plain that lies between. There a second battle had been fought, and the Campanians, being worsted, had been shut up within their walls; and having, after the loss of their choicest troops, no prospect of relief at hand, had been driven to seek assistance of the Romans.

XXX. Their ambassadors, on being introduced into the senate, spoke substantially as follows: "The Campanian people has sent us to you as ambassadors, Conscript Fathers, to solicit your lasting friendship and present help. Had we sought this amity when our affairs were prosperous, though it had been begun more quickly, yet had it been contracted with a weaker bond; for in that case, as those who remembered that they had joined with you in friendship on an equal footing, though perhaps as much your friends as now, we should have been less subject and beholden to you; as it is, attached to you by your compassion

457

LIVY

cordia vestra conciliati auxilioque in dubiis rebus
defensi, beneficium quoque acceptum colamus oportet,
ne ingrati atque omni ope divina humanaque indigni
4 videamur. Neque hercule, quod Samnites priores
amici sociique vobis facti sunt, ad id valere arbitror
ne nos in amicitiam accipiamur, sed ut ii[1] vetustate
et gradu honoris nos praestent; neque enim foedere
Samnitium, ne qua nova iungeretis foedera, cautum
est.

5 "Fuit quidem apud vos semper satis iusta causa
amicitiae velle eum vobis amicum esse qui vos appe-
6 teret: Campani, etsi fortuna praesens magnifice
loqui prohibet, non urbis amplitudine, non agri uber-
tate ulli populo praeterquam vobis cedentes, haud
parva, ut arbitror, accessio bonis rebus vestris in
7 amicitiam venimus vestram. Aequis Volscisque,
aeternis hostibus huius urbis, quandocumque se
moverint, ab tergo erimus; et quod vos pro salute
nostra priores feceritis, id nos pro imperio vestro et
8 gloria semper faciemus. Subactis his gentibus quae
inter nos vosque sunt, quod propediem futurum
spondet et virtus et fortuna vestra, continens im-
9 perium usque ad nos habebitis. Acerbum ac miserum
est, quod fateri nos fortuna nostra cogit: eo ventum
est, patres conscripti, ut aut amicorum aut inimicorum
10 Campani simus. Si defenditis, vestri, si deseritis,
Samnitium erimus; Capuam ergo et Campaniam

---

[1] ut ii *Walters*: ut hi *U*: ut Ω.

and defended in our time of trouble by your aid, we must lovingly remember the benefit also, lest we appear as ingrates and undeserving of any help, divine or human. Nor do I think, in sober truth, that the circumstance of the Samnites having become your allies and friends before ourselves should make against our being received into your friendship, though it entitle them to an advantage over us in respect of priority and rank; and indeed there was no stipulation in your treaty with the Samnites that you should make no further treaties.

"It has ever been with you a sufficiently just cause for friendship that he who sought you desired to be friends with you. We Campanians, though our present plight will not suffer us to boast, are inferior neither in the splendour of our city, nor yet in the fertility of our soil, to any people but yourselves; and in associating ourselves with you we bring, as I think, no small accession to your prosperity. As often as the Aequi and the Volsci—perpetual enemies of this city—shall stir abroad, we shall be upon their backs, and what you will have done first for our preservation, that we will ever do for your empire and your glory. When once you have subdued these nations that lie between our boundaries and your own—a thing which your valour and good fortune guarantee will speedily come to pass—your rule will extend unbroken all the way to our frontier. Grievous and pitiful is the confession that our misfortune obliges us to make: to that pass, Conscript Fathers, are we Campanians come that we must be the chattels either of our friends or of our enemies. Defend us, and we are yours; desert us, and the Samnites will possess us. Consider there-

A.U.C.
409–411 omnem vestris an Samnitium viribus accedere malitis, deliberate.

11 "Omnibus quidem, Romani, vestram misericordiam
vestrumque auxilium aequum est patere, iis[1] tamen
maxime, qui, ea[2] implorantibus aliis[3] dum supra
vires suas praestant, ante omnes[4] ipsi in hanc
12 necessitatem venerunt. Quamquam pugnavimus
verbo pro Sidicinis re pro nobis, cum videremus
finitimum populum nefario latrocinio Samnitium peti
et, ubi conflagrassent Sidicini, ad nos traiecturum
13 illud incendium esse. Nec enim nunc quia dolent
iniuriam acceptam Samnites, sed quia gaudent obla-
14 tam sibi esse causam, oppugnatum nos veniunt. An,
si ultio irae haec et non occasio cupiditatis explendae
esset, parum fuit quod semel in Sidicino agro iterum
15 in Campania ipsa legiones nostras cecidere? Quae
est ista tam infesta ira quam per duas acies fusus
sanguis explere non potuerit? Adde huc populationem agrorum, praedas hominum atque pecudum
actas, incendia villarum ac ruinas, omnia ferro ignique
16 vastata. Hiscine ira expleri non potuit? Sed cupiditas explenda est. Ea ad oppugnandam Capuam
rapit; aut delere urbem pulcherrimam aut ipsi pos-
17 sidere volunt. Sed vos potius, Romani, beneficio
vestro occupate eam quam illos habere per maleficium
sinatis. Non loquor apud recusantem iusta bella

----

[1] iis ς: hiis *A* : his Ω.
[2] ea *Madvig* : eam Ω : etiam *UOς*.
[3] aliis *Madvig* : aliis auxilium (*wanting in O*) Ω.
[4] ante omnes *Buettner* : omnes Ω.

fore whether it be your preference that Capua and _{B.C.}
all Campania augment Rome's power, or that of ^{345–343}
Samnium.

" It is meet that your compassion, Romans, and
your succour should be open to all mankind, but
especially to those who in endeavouring beyond
their strength to grant these blessings to the
prayers of others, have come themselves to require
them most of all. And yet we fought but ostensibly
for the Sidicini, in reality for ourselves, since we saw
that a people on our borders was being cruelly despoiled by the brigand Samnites, and that, once that
conflagration had consumed the Sidicini, it would
spread to us. Nor at this very moment are the
Samnites come to attack us out of resentment for any
injury received, but rejoicing rather that a pretext
has been afforded them. Otherwise, if this were the
satisfaction of revenge and not an opportunity to
appease their greed, was it not enough that first in
the territory of Sidicinum, and again in Campania
itself, they made slaughter of our legions ? What
wrath is this, that is so implacable that the blood
two armies have poured out cannot appease it ? Add
to this the devastation of our lands and the booty
they have driven off, both men and cattle ; add the
burning and destruction of our farm-houses and the
general havoc fire and sword have wrought. Could
not all this placate their wrath ? Nay, but their
greed must be appeased. It is this that hurries
them to the siege of Capua ; they must needs either
destroy the fairest of cities, or themselves become
its masters. But do you, Romans, sooner gain it by
your generosity than suffer them to have it by their
malice. I am not speaking before a people that

LIVY

populum; sed tamen, si ostenderitis auxilia vestra,
18 ne bello quidem arbitror vobis opus fore.   Usque ad
nos contemptus Samnitium pervenit, supra non
ascendit; itaque umbra vestri auxilii, Romani, tegi
possumus, quidquid deinde habuerimus, quidquid
19 ipsi fuerimus,[1] vestrum id omne existimaturi.   Vobis
arabitur ager Campanus, vobis Capua urbs frequenta-
bitur; conditorum, parentium, deorum immortalium
numero nobis eritis; nulla colonia vestra erit, quae
nos obsequio erga vos fideque superet.

20   "Adnuite, patres conscripti, nutum numenque[2]
vestrum invictum Campanis et iubete sperare incolu-
21 mem Capuam futuram.   Qua frequentia omnium[3]
generum multitudinis prosequente creditis nos illinc
profectos?   Quam omnia votorum lacrimarumque
plena reliquisse?   In qua nunc exspectatione senatum
populumque Campanum, coniuges liberosque nostros
22 esse?   Stare omnem multitudinem ad portas viam
hinc ferentem prospectantes certum habeo.   Quid
illis nos, patres conscripti, sollicitis ac pendentibus
23 animi[4] renuntiare iubetis?[5]   Alterum responsum
salutem victoriam lucem ac libertatem; alterum—
ominari horreo quae ferat.   Proinde ut aut de vestris
futuris sociis atque amicis aut nusquam ullis futuris
nobis consulite."

XXXI. Summotis deinde legatis cum consultus
senatus esset, etsi magnae parti urbs maxima opulen-
tissimaque Italiae, uberrimus ager marique propin-

---

[1] quidquid ipsi fuerimus A^2 (or A^1)$_5$: quidquid id ipsi
fuerimus (but M omits the whole phrase and H everything
between quidquid and arabitur) Ω.
[2] numenque Ω: nomenque M_5.
[3] omnium M^3A^x: ominum D^x: hominum Ω.
[4] animi Florebellus: animis Ω: wanting in O.
[5] iubetis? Madvig: iubeatis Ω.

refuses righteous wars ; still, if you make but a show
of helping us, you will have, I think, no need of
going to war. As far as to ourselves does the scorn
of the Samnites reach, it mounts not higher ; accordingly the shadow of your help is able, Romans, to
protect us, and whatever thereafter we shall have,
whatever we ourselves shall be, we shall consider
wholly yours. For you shall be ploughed the Campanian plain, for you shall the city of Capua be
crowded ; you shall be to us as founders, parents,
and immortal gods ; you shall have no colony that
surpasses us in obedience and loyalty.

"Grant the favour of your countenance, Conscript
Fathers, and of your unconquered might, to the
Campanians, and bid them hope that Capua will
be saved. With what thronging crowds of every
sort were we accompanied, think you, at our setting
out? How did we leave on every hand prayers and
tears ! In what suspense are now the senate and
the people of Campania, our wives and our children !
Well I know that all the people are standing at
the gates, their eyes fixed on the northern road.
What message, Conscript Fathers, do you bid us
carry back to their perplexed and troubled spirits?
One answer would bring salvation, victory, light,
and liberty ; the other—I shrink from the ominous
prediction ! Do you therefore deliberate regarding us, as regarding those who shall either be
your allies and friends, or else have no being
anywhere."

XXXI. The ambassadors were then made to withdraw while the senate considered their request. It
was evident to many that the largest and wealthiest
city of Italy, with a very fertile territory near the

A.U.C.
409–411

quus ad varietates annonae horreum populi Romani
fore videbatur, tamen tanta utilitate fides antiquior
fuit, responditque ita ex auctoritate senatus consul.
2 "Auxilio vos, Campani, dignos censet senatus; sed
ita vobiscum amicitiam institui par est, ne qua
vetustior amicitia ac societas violetur. Samnites
nobiscum foedere iuncti sunt; itaque arma, deos
prius quam homines violatura, adversus Samnites
vobis negamus; legatos, sicut fas iusque est, ad
socios atque amicos precatum mittemus, ne qua vobis
3 vis fiat." Ad ea princeps legationis—sic enim domo
mandatum attulerant—"Quando quidem" inquit,
"nostra tueri adversus vim atque iniuriam iusta vi
4 non voltis, vestra certe defendetis; itaque populum
Campanum urbemque Capuam, agros, delubra deum,
divina humanaque omnia in vestram, patres conscripti, populique Romani dicionem dedimus, quidquid deinde patiemur, dediticii vestri passuri."
5 Sub haec dicta omnes, manus ad consules ten-
dentes, pleni lacrimarum in vestibulo curiae
6 procubuerunt. Commoti patres vice fortunarum
humanarum, si ille praepotens opibus populus, luxuria
superbiaque clarus, a quo paulo ante auxilium finitimi

---

¹ *i. e.* the gods who were witnesses and guardians of the
treaty.

sea, would in times of scarcity be a store-house for the Roman People. Yet this great advantage was of less moment with them than their honour, and the consul, being so instructed by the senate, returned the following answer to the ambassadors: "Men of Campania, the senate holds you worthy of assistance; but on such terms only can we become your friends as shall not violate an older friendship and alliance. The Samnites and we are united by a covenant; we must therefore refuse to make war in your behalf upon the Samnites, for this would be to wrong first gods,[1] and then men; we will, however, dispatch envoys, as is right and just, to entreat our allies and friends to do you no violence." To this the leader of the delegation answered—in accordance with instructions they had brought with them:—"Since you decline to use a righteous violence to protect from violence and injustice what belongs to us, you will at least defend your own; to your sovereignty, therefore, Conscript Fathers, and to the sovereignty of the Roman People, we surrender the people of Campania and the city of Capua, with our lands, the shrines of our gods, and all things else, whether sacred or profane; whatever we endure henceforth, we shall endure as your surrendered subjects."

When these words had been pronounced, they all stretched forth their hands in supplication to the consul, and weeping bitterly, threw themselves face downwards on the floor of the entrance to the Curia. The Fathers were profoundly moved by the vicissitudes of human fortune, considering how that great and opulent people, famed for its luxury and pride, of whom a little while before its neighbours

LIVY

409-4117 petissent adeo infractos gereret animos ut se ipse
suaque omnia potestatis alienae faceret. Tum iam
fides agi visa deditos non prodi ; nec facturum aequa
Samnitium populum censebant, si agrum urbemque
per deditionem factam populi Romani oppugnarent.

8 Legatos itaque extemplo mitti ad Samnites placuit.
Data mandata ut preces Campanorum, responsum
senatus amicitiae Samnitium memor, deditionem
9 postremo factam Samnitibus exponerent; peterent
pro societate amicitiaque, ut dediticiis suis parcerent
neque in eum agrum qui populi Romani factus esset
10 hostilia arma inferrent; si leniter agendo parum
proficerent, denuntiarent Samnitibus, populi Romani
senatusque verbis, ut Capua urbe Campanoque agro
11 abstinerent. Haec legatis agentibus in concilio
Samnitium adeo est ferociter responsum ut non
solum gesturos se esse dicerent id bellum, sed
magistratus eorum e curia egressi stantibus[1] legatis
praefectos cohortium vocarent iisque clara voce
12 imperarent ut praedatum in agrum Campanum
extemplo proficiscerentur.

XXXII. Hac legatione Romam relata positis
omnium aliarum rerum curis patres fetialibus ad res
repetendas missis belloque, quia non redderentur,
sollemni more indicto decreverunt ut primo quoque

[1] stantibus Ω: astantibus *unknown scholar in marg. ed.
Curionis.*

---

[1] The Samnites were a loose federation comprising the
following tribes : the Hirpini, the Caudini, the Pentri, the
Caraceni, and perhaps the Frentani (Weissenborn).

[2] For the fetials and their procedure in declaring war,
see I. xxiv. 4 and xxxii. 5, with notes.

466

B.C. 345–343

had sought assistance, was become so broken in spirit as to yield itself up with all its possessions to the dominion of another. They now held it to be a point of honour not to betray those who were become their subjects; neither did they think that the Samnite people would deal justly, if they attacked a country and a city, which, by surrendering, had become the property of the Roman People. The senate accordingly voted to dispatch ambassadors to the Samnites, without loss of time. Their instructions were to inform the Samnites what the Campanians had asked, how the senate, mindful of the friendship of the Samnites, had replied to them, and lastly how they had surrendered; they were then to request that the Samnites, out of regard for the friendship and alliance of the Romans, would spare their subjects, and make no hostile incursion into a territory which belonged now to the Roman People; if soft words proved ineffectual, they were to warn the Samnites, in the name of the Roman People and the senate, not to meddle with the city of Capua or the Campanian domain. But the Samnites, when these things were represented to them in their council [1] by the envoys, behaved so insolently as not only to declare that they meant to carry on the war, but their magistrates stepping out of the senate-house—while the envoys stood by— summoned the commanders of their cohorts, and with a loud voice gave them orders to proceed at once to make a raid upon Campania.

XXXII. When the news of this embassy reached Rome, the Fathers, putting aside all other business, sent fetials to demand redress, and failing to obtain it, declared war after the customary fashion.[2] They

467

LIVY

2 tempore de ea re ad populum ferretur; iussuque
populi consules ambo cum duobus exercitibus [1]
profecti, Valerius in Campaniam Cornelius in Samnium, ille ad montem Gaurum [2] hic ad Saticulam [3]
3 castra ponunt.   Priori Valerio Samnitium legiones—
eo namque omnem belli molem inclinaturam censebant—occurrunt; simul in Campanos stimulabat ira
tam promptos nunc ad ferenda nunc ad accersenda
4 adversus se auxilia.   Ut vero castra Romana viderunt, ferociter pro se quisque signum duces poscere;
adfirmare eadem fortuna Romanum Campano laturum
opem qua Campanus Sidicino tulerit.

5   Valerius levibus certaminibus temptandi hostis
causa haud ita multos moratus dies signum pugnae
6 proposuit, paucis suos adhortatus ne novum bellum
eos novusque hostis terreret: quidquid ab urbe
longius proferrent arma, magis magisque in imbelles
7 gentes eos prodire.   Ne Sidicinorum Campanorum-
que cladibus Samnitium aestimarent virtutem; qualescumque inter se certaverint, necesse fuisse alteram
partem vinci.   Campanos quidem haud dubie magis
nimio luxu fluentibus rebus mollitiaque sua quam vi
8 hostium victos esse.   Quid autem esse duo prospera
in tot saeculis bella Samnitium adversus tot decora

---

[1] exercitibus ᵴ *Walters and Conway*: ab urbe exercitibus
Ω: exercitibus ab urbe M̅ᵴ: *wanting in* O.
[2] Gaurum D⁴A² *Frag. Haverk.* ᵴ: caurum UHT²A: c.
aurum MTDL: caubrum P: claurum F: *illegible in* O.
[3] Saticulam *Sigonius*: satriculam Ω: satriaculam T:
satriculum A.

468

B.C.
345-343

then voted that the people be asked to ratify this action at the earliest possible moment; and being commanded so to do, both consuls took the field; and Valerius marching into Campania and Cornelius into Samnium, the one encamped at the foot of Mount Gaurus, the other near Saticula. It was Valerius whom the Samnite levies encountered first —for that was the direction which they expected the invasion to take. The Campanians moreover had incurred their sharp resentment, having been so ready now to render aid against them, now to invoke it. But when they beheld the Roman camp, they began, every man for himself, to call loudly on their leaders for the battle-signal, affirming that the Romans would have no better fortune in helping the Campanians than these had experienced in helping the Sidicini.

Valerius, having delayed not many days for the purpose of testing the enemy in small skirmishes, hung out the signal for a battle. But first he spoke a few words of encouragement to his soldiers, bidding them have no fear of a strange war and a strange enemy. With every advance of their arms from Rome, he said, they came to nations that were more and more unwarlike. They must not judge of the courage of the Samnites by the defeats they had administered to the Sidicini and Campanians. Whatever their respective qualities, it was inevitable that when they fought together, one side should be vanquished. As for the Campanians, there was no question they had been beaten rather by the enervation resulting from excessive luxury and by their own effeminacy, than by the strength of their enemies. Furthermore, what were the Samnites' two successful wars in so many ages, as

469

LIVY

populi Romani, qui triumphos paene plures quam
annos ab urbe condita numeret; qui omnia circa se,
9 Sabinos Etruriam Latinos Hernicos Aequos Volscos
Auruncos, domita armis habeat[1] qui Gallos tot proeliis caesos postremo in mare ac naves fuga com-
10 pulerit? Cum gloria belli ac virtute sua quemque
fretos ire in aciem debere, tum etiam intueri cuius
ductu auspicioque ineunda pugna sit, utrum qui,
11 audiendus dumtaxat, magnificus adhortator sit, verbis
tantum ferox, operum militarium expers, an qui et
ipse tela tractare, procedere ante signa, versari media
12 in mole pugnae sciat. "Facta mea, non dicta vos,
milites" inquit, "sequi volo, nec disciplinam modo
sed exemplum etiam a me petere. Non factionibus[2]
nec per coitiones[3] usitatas nobilibus, sed hac dextra
mihi tres consulatus summamque laudem peperi.
13 Fuit cum hoc dici poterat: "Patricius enim eras et
a liberatoribus patriae ortus, et eodem anno familia
ista consulatum quo urbs haec consulem habuit":
14 nunc iam nobis patribus vobisque plebei promiscuus
consulatus patet nec generis, ut ante, sed virtutis
est praemium. Proinde summum quodque spectate,
15 milites, decus. Non, si mihi novum hoc Corvini

---

[1] habeat A^2: habeant Ω: habebant (habebat D^3) D.
[2] factiones *Glareanus*: factionibus modo Ω.
[3] coitiones ς: ctiones (*or* cciones, *or* conciones) Ω.

---

[1] This, the later form of the name, is found here and in
chap. xl. § 3, though in other places Livy gives the earlier
form, Corvus.

against the many glorious achievements of the
Roman People, who could count almost more
triumphs than the years since their City had been
founded; who had subjugated by their arms all
the nations round about them, the Sabines, Etruria,
the Latins, the Hernici, the Aequi, the Volsci,
and the Aurunci; who after beating the Gauls time
after time in battle, had ended by compelling them
to flee to the sea-board and their ships? He said
that they ought, as they went into action, not only
to rely every man on his own courage and martial
glory, but also to consider under whose command
and auspices they would have to fight; whether he
were one who only merited a hearing as a brilliant
orator, warlike only in his words, and ignorant of
military operations, or one who knew himself how
to handle weapons, to advance before the standards,
and to play his part in the press and turmoil of a
battle. "Soldiers," he cried, "it is my deeds and
not my words I would have you follow, and look to
me not only for instruction but for example. Not
with factions, nor with the intrigues common amongst
the nobles, but with this right hand, have I won
for myself three consulships and the highest praise.
Time was when it might have been said: 'Ah, but
you were a patrician and sprung from the liberators
of your country, and your family held the consulship
in the very year that saw the institution of that
office.' But now the consulship lies open on equal
terms to us, the nobles, and to you plebeians, nor is
it any longer a reward of birth, but of merit. Have
regard, therefore, soldiers, in every instance, to great
honours. Though you men have given me, with
Heaven's sanction, my surname of Corvinus,[1] I have

cognomen dis auctoribus homines dedistis, Publico-
larum vetustum familiae nostrae cognomen memoria
16 excessit ; semper ego plebem Romanam militiae
domique, privatus, in magistratibus parvis magnisque,
aeque tribunus ac consul, eodem tenore per omnes
17 deinceps consulatus colo atque colui. Nunc, quod
instat, dis bene iuvantibus novum atque integrum de
Samnitibus triumphum mecum petite."

XXXIII. Non alias militi familiarior dux fuit omnia
inter infimos militum haud gravate munia obeundo.
2 In ludo praeterea militari, cum velocitatis viriumque
inter se aequales certamina ineunt, comiter facilis ;
vincere ac vinci voltu eodem, nec quemquam asper-
3 nari parem qui se offerret ; factis benignus pro re,
dictis haud minus libertatis alienae quam suae digni-
tatis memor ; et, quo nihil popularius est, quibus
4 artibus petierat magistratus iisdem gerebat. Itaque
universus exercitus incredibili alacritate adhorta-
tionem prosecutus ducis castris egreditur.

5   Proelium, ut quod maxime unquam, pari spe
utrimque, aequis viribus, cum fiducia sui sine con-
6 temptu hostium commissum est. Samnitibus ferociam augebant novae res gestae et paucos ante dies
geminata victoria, Romanis contra quadringentorum
annorum decora et conditae urbi aequalis victoria ;

---

[1] *i. e.* "Friends of the People." See II. viii. 1.

B.C.
345–343

not forgot the ancient surname of our family—the
Publicolae :[1] at home and in the field, as a private
citizen, in little magistracies and in great ones, as
consul no less than as tribune, and with the same
undeviating course through all my successive consulships, have I cherished, and cherish still, the Roman
plebs. Now, with Heaven's good help, to the work
we have in hand ! Seek with me a novel triumph
never yet won from the Samnites !"

XXXIII. There was never a commander who
more endeared himself to his men by cheerfully
sharing all their duties with the meanest of the
soldiers. At the military sports, too, in which those
of a like age contend with one another in strength
and swiftness, he was easy-going and good-natured ;
he would win or lose without changing countenance,
nor did he scorn to match himself with anyone who
challenged him ; in his acts his kindness was suited
to the circumstances, in his speech he had regard
to the liberty of others no less than to his own
dignity ; finally—and nothing can be more popular
than this—he was the same in office that he had
been while a candidate. It was therefore with
incredible eagerness that the whole army, after
listening to the general's speech, marched out of
camp.

The battle began, if ever battle did, with like
hopes on both sides and equal strength, and a
self-confidence which yet was not mixed with
contempt for the enemy. The Samnites were emboldened by their recent exploits and by their
double victory of a few days before, the Romans
on their part by the glories of four centuries and
a victorious career that dated from the founding of

473

LIVY

7 utrisque tamen novus hostis curam addebat. Pugna
indicio fuit quos gesserint animos; namque ita con-
flixerunt ut aliquamdiu in neutram partem inclina-
8 rent acies. Tum consul trepidationem iniciendam
ratus, quando vi pelli non poterant, equitibus im-
9 missis turbare prima signa hostium conatur. Quos
ubi nequiquam tumultuantes in spatio exiguo volvere
turmas vidit nec posse aperire in hostes viam, revectus
ad antesignanos legionum cum desiluisset ex equo,
10 "Nostrum" inquit "peditum illud, milites, est opus;
agitedum, ut me videritis, quacumque [1] incessero in
aciem hostium, ferro viam facientem, sic pro se
quisque obvios sternite; illa omnia, qua nunc erectae
11 micant hastae, patefacta strage vasta cernetis." Vix
haec [2] dicta dederat, cum equites consulis iussu discurrunt in cornua legionibusque in mediam aciem
aperiunt viam. Primus omnium consul invadit
hostem et cum quo forte contulit gradum obtruncat.
12 Hoc spectaculo accensi dextra laevaque ante se
quisque memorandum proelium cient [3]; stant obnixi
Samnites, quamquam plura accipiunt quam inferunt
vulnera.

13 Aliquamdiu iam pugnatum erat, atrox caedes circa
signa Samnitium, fuga ab nulladum parte erat: adeo
14 morte sola vinci destinaverant animis. Itaque

---

[1] quacumque $F^3A^3\varsigma$: quacū ; MFO : quacum Ω : quāecū H.
[2] vix haec *Luchs*: haec Ω.
[3] cient ς *Gronov.* (L^3?): ciet Ω.

the City; each side nevertheless experienced some anxiety at meeting an untried foe. The engagement testified how resolute they were, for they so fought that for some time neither battle-line gave ground. Then the consul, thinking that he must inspire his enemies with fear, since he could not drive them back by force, attempted by sending in the cavalry to throw their front ranks into disorder. But when he saw that nothing came of the confused fighting of the squadrons, as they tried to manœuvre in a narrow space, and that they could not break the enemy's line, he rode back to the front ranks of his legions, and, dismounting from his horse, exclaimed, "Soldiers, it is for us, the infantry, to accomplish yonder task! Come, as you shall see me making a path for myself with my sword wherever I advance against the enemy's line, so do you every man strike down whom you encounter; all that array where now uplifted spears are glancing you shall see laid open with great carnage." No sooner had he said these words, than the horsemen, by the consul's order, drew off towards the wings and left the legions room to attack the centre. The consul was the very foremost in the charge, and slew the man he chanced to meet with. Kindled by this sight, the Romans on the right and on the left pushed forward, every man of them, and fought a memorable combat; the Samnites stood manfully at bay, but they took more strokes than they delivered.

The battle had now lasted a considerable time; there was dreadful slaughter about the standards of the Samnites, but as yet no retreating anywhere, so determined were they to be overcome by naught but death. And so the Romans, who saw that their

Romani cum et fluere iam lassitudine vires sentirent
et diei haud multum superesse, accensi ira concitant
15 se in hostem. Tum primum referri pedem atque
inclinari rem in fugam apparuit; tum capi, occidi
Samnis; nec superfuissent multi, ni nox victoriam
16 magis quam proelium diremisset. Et Romani fatebantur nunquam cum pertinaciore hoste conflictum,
et Samnites, cum quaereretur quaenam prima causa
17 tam obstinatos movisset in fugam, oculos sibi Romanorum ardere visos aiebant vesanosque voltus et
furentia ora; inde plus quam ex alia ulla re terroris
ortum. Quem terrorem non pugnae solum eventu
18 sed nocturna profectione confessi sunt. Postero die
vacuis hostium castris Romanus potitur, quo se omnis
Campanorum multitudo gratulabunda effudit.

XXXIV. Ceterum hoc gaudium magna prope clade
in Samnio foedatum est. Nam ab Saticula[1] profectus
Cornelius consul exercitum incaute in saltum cava
valle pervium circaque insessum ab hoste induxit
2 nec prius quam recipi tuto signa non poterant im-
3 minentem capiti hostem vidit. Dum id morae Samnitibus est, quoad totum in vallem infimam demit-
teret agmen, P. Decius tribunus militum conspicit
unum editum in saltu collem, imminentem hostium

---

[1] Saticula *Sigonius* (*cf. chap.* xxxii. § 2) : satricula Ω.

B.C.
345-343

strength was fast ebbing away in weariness and that little daylight yet remained, were filled with rage, and hurled themselves against the enemy. Then for the first time were there signs of giving way and the beginning of a rout; then were the Samnites captured or slain; nor would many have survived, if night had not ended what was now a victory rather than a battle. The Romans admitted that never had they fought with a more stubborn adversary; and the Samnites, on being asked what it was that first had turned them, resolute as they were, to flight, replied that it was the eyes of the Romans, which had seemed to blaze, and their frenzied expression and infuriated looks; this it was more than anything else that had caused their panic. And this panic stood confessed not alone in the outcome of the fight but in the night-retreat that followed. On the morrow the Romans took possession of the deserted camp, and thither the whole population of Capua streamed out to congratulate them.

XXXIV. But this rejoicing came near to being marred by a great reverse in Samnium. For the consul Cornelius, marching from Saticula, had unwarily led his army into a forest which was penetrated by a deep defile, and was there beset on either hand by the enemy; nor, until it was too late to withdraw with safety, did he perceive that they were posted on the heights above him. While the Samnites were only holding back till he should send down the whole column into the bottom of the valley, Publius Decius, a tribune of the soldiers, espied a solitary hill, which rising above the pass, commanded the enemy's camp, and though arduous

A.U.C.
409–411

castris, aditu arduum impedito agmini, expeditis haud
4 difficilem. Itaque consuli territo animi "Videsne tu"
inquit, "A. Corneli, cacumen illud supra hostem?
Arx illa est spei salutisque nostrae, si eam, quoniam
5 caeci reliquere Samnites, impigre capimus. Ne tu
mihi plus quam unius legionis principes hastatosque
dederis; cum quibus ubi evasero in summum, perge
hinc omni liber metu, teque et exercitum serva;
neque enim moveri hostis, subiectus nobis ad omnes
6 ictus, sine sua pernicie poterit. Nos deinde aut
fortuna populi Romani aut nostra virtus expediet."
7 Conlaudatus ab consule accepto praesidio vadit occul-
tus per saltum; nec prius ab hoste est visus quam loco
8 quem petebat appropinquavit. Inde admiratione
paventibus cunctis cum omnium in se vertisset
oculos, et spatium consuli dedit ad subducendum
agmen in aequiorem locum et ipse in summo con-
9 stitit vertice. Samnites dum huc illuc signa vertunt
utriusque rei amissa occasione neque insequi consulem nisi per eandem vallem, in qua paulo ante
subiectum eum telis suis habuerant, possunt, nec
erigere agmen in captum super se ab Decio tumu-
10 lum; sed cum ira in hos magis, qui fortunam gerendae
rei eripuerant, tum propinquitas loci atque ipsa

---

[1] The legion was drawn up in three lines; in the first were
the *hastati*, in the second the *principes*, and behind these the
triarii.

478

of access to an army encumbered with baggage, was B.C. 345–343 not difficult for men in light marching order. He accordingly said to the consul, who was much perturbed: "Do you see, Aulus Cornelius, that summit that rises above the enemy? It is the fortress of our hope and safety, if we are prompt to seize it, since the Samnites have been so blind as to neglect it. Give me no more than the first and second lines of a single legion;[1] when with these I have mounted to the top, do you go forward fearlessly and save yourself and the army; for the enemy, exposed to all our missiles, will not be able to stir without bringing destruction on themselves. As for us, thereafter the fortune of the Roman People or our own manhood will extricate us." Being commended by the consul and receiving his detachment, he advanced under cover through the wood, nor did the enemy perceive him till he had nearly reached the place which he wished to gain. They were then all overcome with astonishment and dread, and while they turned, every man of them, and gazed at him, the consul was given time to withdraw his army to more favourable ground, and Decius himself took his post on the top of the hill. The Samnites, turning their standards now this way and now that, threw away both opportunities; they could not pursue the consul, except through the same defile where a little before they had held him at the mercy of their javelins, nor could they charge up the hill which Decius had captured over their heads. But not only did their resentment urge them rather against those who had snatched victory from their grasp, but so also did the nearness of the place and the fewness of its

11 paucitas incitat; et nunc circumdare undique collem
armatis volunt, ut a consule Decium intercludant,
nunc viam patefacere, ut degressos in vallem ado-
riantur. Incertos quid agerent nox oppressit.

12 Decium primum [1] spes tenuit cum subeuntibus in
adversum collem ex superiore loco se pugnaturum;
deinde admiratio incessit quod nec pugnam inirent
nec, si ab eo consilio iniquitate loci deterrerentur,

13 opere se valloque circumdarent. Tum centurionibus
ad se vocatis: "Quaenam illa inscitia belli ac pigritia
est, aut quonam modo isti ex Sidicinis Campanisque
victoriam pepererunt? Huc atque illuc signa moveri ac modo in unum conferri modo educi [2] videtis;
opus quidem incipit nemo, cum iam circumdati vallo

14 potuerimus esse. Tum vero nos similes istorum
simus, si diutius hic moremur quam commodum sit.
Agitedum, ite mecum ut, dum lucis aliquid superest,
quibus locis praesidia ponant, qua pateat hinc exitus,

15 exploremus." Haec omnia sagulo gregali amictus
centurionibus item manipularium militum habitu
ductis,[3] ne ducem circumire hostes notarent, perlu-
stravit.

XXXV. Vigiliis deinde dispositis ceteris omnibus
tesseram dari iubet, ubi secundae vigiliae bucina da-
2 tum signum esset, armati cum silentio ad se conveni-

---

[1] primum (wanting in O) Ω: primo Häggström "dubitanter."
[2] educi Ω: diduci Weissenborn.
[3] ductis (ductus OL) Ω: secum ductis M. Mueller.

B.C.
345-343

defenders; and first they would be for surrounding
the hill with troops, so as to cut Decius off from
the consul, and next for leaving his road open, so
that they might attack him when he was got down
into the valley. Before they had made up their
minds, night overtook them.

Decius at first had hopes of fighting from the
higher ground, as they mounted the hill; then he
marvelled that they neither began to attack, nor,
if they were deterred from that design by the
difficulty of the ground, attempted to shut him
in with trench and rampart. Then, calling the
centurions to him, he said: "What want of military
skill, what slothfulness can that be? How did those
people conquer the Sidicini and Campanians? You
see their standards moving now this way, now that,
first closing in together, then deploying, while no
man falls to work, though we might ere this have
been fenced in with a palisade. Then in truth
should we be no better than they, were we to tarry
here longer than suits our interest. Come on then
and follow me, so that while there is yet a little
light we may find out where they post their guards,
and where the way out from this place lies open."
Wrapped in a common soldier's cloak and accompanied by his centurions, who were also dressed
like privates, lest the enemy should notice that the
general was on his rounds, he investigated all these
matters.

XXXV. Next, having disposed the sentries, he
commanded that the word be passed to everybody,
that on hearing the trumpet sound for the second
watch they should silently arm and present themselves before him. When they had assembled there

481

A.U.C.
409–411

rent. Quo ubi, sicut edictumerat, taciti convenerunt,
" Hoc silentium, milites," inquit, " omisso militari adsensu in me audiendo servandum est. Ubi sententiam
meam vobis peregero, tum quibus eadem placebunt
in dextram partem taciti transibitis; quae pars
3 maior erit, eo stabitur consilio. Nunc quae mente
agitem audite.   Non fuga delatos nec inertia relic-
tos hic vos circumvenit hostis : virtute cepistis
4 locum, virtute hinc oportet evadatis. Veniendo
huc exercitum egregium populo Romano servastis :
erumpendo hinc vosmet ipsos servate; digni estis
qui pauci pluribus opem tuleritis, ipsi nullius auxilio
5 egueritis.   Cum eo hoste res est qui hesterno die
delendi omnis exercitus fortuna per socordiam usus
non sit, hunc tam opportunum collem imminentem
capiti suo non ante viderit quam captum a nobis,
6 nos tam paucos tot ipse[1] milibus hominum nec
ascensu arcuerit[2] nec tenentes locum, cum diei
tantum superesset, vallo circumdederit. Quem vi-
dentem ac vigilantem sic eluseritis, sopitum oportet
7 fallatis, immo necesse est; in eo enim loco res sunt
nostrae, ut vobis ego magis necessitatis vestrae
8 index quam consilii auctor sim. Neque enim maneatis an abeatis hinc deliberari potest, cum praeter
arma et animos armorum memores nihil vobis fortuna reliqui fecerit fameque et siti moriendum sit,

---

[1] ipse ς : ipsi (*corrected by A from* ipsis) Ω.
[2] arcuerit ς : arcuerint A^2 : arguerit *PFU* : arguerint Ω.

without a word, as he had ordered, he thus began: B.C. 345-343
"You must preserve this silence, soldiers, as you
listen to me, omitting all soldier-like acclaim.
When I have finished explaining my plan, then
those of you who find it good will quietly pass over
to the right; on whichever side the majority shall
be, we will abide by their decision. Hear now
what I have in mind. The enemy has not invested
you here as men who ran away or were left behind
through laziness: it was by valour that you took the
place, and by valour you must escape from it. By
coming hither you saved a splendid army for the
Roman People; save yourselves by breaking out.
You are worthy to have carried help, though few, to
greater numbers, and to have needed no man's help
yourselves. You have an enemy to deal with who
neglected yesterday through indolence an opportunity of destroying our whole army; who failed to
see the importance of this hill by which he is
commanded, until we had taken it; who, though
we were so few and his own thousands so many,
neither kept us from gaining the ascent, nor,
when the place was ours and much daylight still
remained, surrounded us with entrenchments. An
enemy whom you thus eluded while he was wide
awake and watching, you ought to baffle when
he is overcome with sleep. Indeed it is necessary
that you do so, for our situation is such that
I am rather pointing out your necessity to you
than advocating a plan. Nor truly can it be a
debatable question whether you should stay or go
away from here, since Fortune has left you nothing
but your arms and the spirit to employ them, and
we must die of hunger and thirst, if we dread the

si plus quam viros ac Romanos decet ferrum time-
9 amus. Ergo una est salus erumpere hinc atque
abire; id aut interdiu aut nocte faciamus oportet.
10 Ecce autem aliud minus dubium; quippe si lux
exspectetur, quae spes est non vallo perpetuo fossaque nos saepturum hostem, qui nunc corporibus
suis subiectis undique cinxerit, ut videtis, collem?
Atqui si nox opportuna est eruptioni, sicut est,
11 haec profecto noctis aptissima hora est. Signo
secundae vigiliae convenistis, quod tempus mortales
somno altissimo premit; per corpora sopita vadetis
vel silentio incautos fallentes vel sentientibus clamore
12 subito pavorem iniecturi. Me modo sequimini, quem
secuti estis; ego eandem quae duxit huc sequar
fortunam. Quibus haec salutaria videntur, agitedum,
in dextram partem pedibus transite."

XXXVI. Omnes transierunt, vadentemque per
2 intermissa custodiis loca Decium secuti sunt. Iam
evaserant media castra, cum superscandens vigilum
strata somno corpora miles offenso scuto praebuit
sonitum; quo excitatus vigil cum proximum movisset
erectique alios concitarent, ignari cives an hostes
essent, praesidium erumperet an consul castra
3 cepisset, Decius, quoniam non fallerent, clamorem

sword's point more than it is fitting men and Romans B.C. 345–343 should. Our one way of safety, then, is to break through and get away. We must do this either in the day-time or at night. But this, look you, is a question that is even less in doubt, for if we should wait for dawn, what hope is there that the enemy would not hem us in with a continuous trench and rampart, who has now, as you see, encompassed the hill on every hand with the bodies of his men lying below us. And yet, if night is favourable for our sally, as it is, this is surely the fittest hour of the night. You have come together on the signal of the second watch, when sleep lies heaviest on mortals: you will make your way among drowsy forms, either eluding them unsuspected in your silence, or ready, if they should perceive you, to affright them with a sudden shout. Do but follow me, whom you have followed hitherto; I will follow that same Fortune that has led us hither. Now then let those who approve my plan step over to the right."

XXXVI. They all crossed over. Decius then made his way through the spaces left unguarded, and they followed him. They had already got half way through the camp, when a soldier in stepping over the bodies of some sleeping sentries struck his shield and made a sound. A sentry was awakened by this, and having shaken his neighbour, they stood up and began to rouse the rest, not knowing whether they had to do with friends or foes, whether the party on the hill were escaping, or the consul had captured the camp. Decius, seeing that they were discovered, gave the order to his men, and they set up such a shout that the Samnites,

LIVY

tollere iussis militibus torpidos somno insuper pavore
exanimat, quo praepediti nec arma impigre capere
4 nec obsistere nec insequi poterant. Inter trepidationem tumultumque Samnitium praesidium Romanum obviis custodibus caesis ad castra consulis
pervadit.

5   Aliquantum supererat noctis iamque in tuto videbantur esse, cum Decius " Macte virtute " inquit,
" milites Romani, este ; [1] vestrum iter ac reditum
6 omnia saecula laudibus ferent ; sed ad conspiciendam
tantam virtutem luce ac die opus est, nec vos digni estis
quos cum tanta gloria in castra reduces silentium ac nox
7 tegat ; hic lucem quieti opperiamur." Dictis obtem-
peratum ; atque ubi primum inluxit, praemisso nun-
tio ad consulem castra ingenti gaudio concitantur et
tessera data incolumes reverti, qui sua corpora pro
salute omnium haud dubio periculo obiecissent, pro
se quisque obviam effusi laudant, gratulantur, singulos universos servatores suos vocant, dis laudes
8 gratesque agunt, Decium in caelum ferunt. Hic
Deci castrensis triumphus fuit incedentis per media
castra cum armato praesidio coniectis in eum omnium
oculis et omni honore tribunum consuli aequantibus.
9 Ubi ad praetorium ventum est, consul classico ad
contionem convocat orsusque meritas Deci laudes
10 interfante ipso Decio distulit contionem ; qui auctor

----

[1] Romani, este *A²* : r̄ (*or* r.) este *M²* or *M¹* (r este *M*)
PFOT² : recte *HTDLA*.

486

who had been stupefied with sleep, were now in addition breathless with terror, which prevented them from either arming promptly or making a stand against the Romans or pursuing them. During the fright and confusion amongst the Samnites, the Romans cut down such guards as they came across, and proceeded towards the consul's camp.

It wanted yet some time till daylight, and they now appeared to be in safety, when Decius said, " All honour to your courage, Roman soldiers! Your expedition and return shall be renowned through all the ages. But the light of day is needed to set off such gallantry, nor do you merit that your glorious return to camp should be accomplished in silence and under cover of night. Let us wait here quietly until the dawn." They did as he said. With the first rays of light they sent forward a courier to the consul, and the camp was woke with loud rejoicings. When word was sent round that those were returning safe and sound, who in behalf of the general safety, had exposed their bodies to no uncertain peril, they all poured out to meet them, and, each for himself, praised and congratulated them, calling them their saviours, one and all. To the gods they offered praise and thanks, and Decius they extolled to the skies. Now followed a triumph for Decius in the camp, as he marched through the midst with his battalion under arms. All eyes were directed towards him, and paid the tribune equal homage with the consul. When they reached headquarters, the consul bade the trumpet sound an assembly, and fell to lauding Decius, as he deserved. But Decius, interrupting him, induced him to defer his speech;

omnia posthabendi dum occasio in manibus esset,
perpulit consulem ut hostes et nocturno pavore
attonitos et circa collem castellatim dissipatos ad-
grederetur : credere etiam aliquos ad se sequendum
11 emissos per saltum vagari. Iussae legiones arma
capere egressaeque castris, cum per exploratores
notior iam saltus esset, via patentiore ad hostem
12 ducuntur ; quem incautum improviso adortae, cum
palati passim Samnitium milites, plerique inermes,
nec coire in unum nec arma capere nec recipere
intra vallum se possent, paventem primum in castra
compellunt, deinde castra ipsa turbatis stationibus
13 capiunt. Perfertur circa collem clamor fugatque ex
suis quemque praesidiis. Ita magna pars absenti
hosti cessit : quos intra vallum egerat pavor — fuere
autem ad triginta milia [1] — omnes caesi, castra
direpta.

XXXVII. Ita rebus gestis consul advocata contione P. Deci non coeptas solum ante sed cumulatas
nova virtute laudes peragit et praeter militaria alia
dona aurea corona eum et centum bubus eximioque
2 uno albo opimo auratis cornibus donat. Milites qui

---

[1] triginta milia Ω : tria milia *conj. Walters, assuming that*
∞ ∞ ∞ *was corrupted to* xxx *or* xxx *mil.*

then, urging that all other considerations should be postponed whilst they had such an opportunity at hand, he persuaded him to attack the enemy. They were now, he said, bewildered by the night alarm and dispersed about the hill in separate detachments, and he doubted not that a party would have been sent out after him and would be wandering through the forest. The troops were commanded to arm, and marching out of camp, were led by a more open route—for, thanks to their scouts, the forest was now better known to them—in the direction of the enemy. These they caught quite off their guard by a surprise attack, for the Samnite soldiers were scattered far and wide, and most of them were without their weapons. Unable either to assemble or to arm or to regain their works, they were first driven headlong into their camp, and then the outposts were routed and the camp itself was taken. The shouting was heard all round the hill and sent the detachments flying from their several stations. Thus a great part of the Samnites fled without coming into contact with the enemy. Those whom panic had driven within the enclosure—to the number of some thirty thousand —were all put to the sword, and the camp was spoiled.

XXXVII. The battle having sped thus, the consul called an assembly, and pronounced a panegyric upon Decius, in which he rehearsed, in addition to his former services, the fresh glories which his bravery had achieved. Besides other military gifts, he bestowed on him a golden chaplet and a hundred oxen, and one choice white one, fat, and with gilded horns. The soldiers who had been on the

LIVY

in praesidio simul fuerant duplici frumento in perpetuum, in praesentia bubus privis binisque tunicis[1]
donati. Secundum consulis donationem legiones
gramineam coronam obsidialem, clamore donum
approbantes, Decio imponunt ; altera corona, eiusdem honoris index, a praesidio suo imposita est.
3 His decoratus insignibus bovem eximium Marti
immolavit, centum boves militibus dono dedit qui
secum in expeditione fuerant. Iisdem militibus
legiones libras farris et sextarios vini contulerunt ;
omniaque ea ingenti alacritate per clamorem militarem, indicem omnium adsensus, gerebantur.
4   Tertia pugna ad Suessulam commissa est, quia
fugatus a M. Valerio Samnitium exercitus omni
robore iuventutis domo accito certamine ultimo for-
5 tunam experiri statuit.   Ab Suessula nuntii trepidi
Capuam, inde equites citati ad Valerium consulem
6 opem oratum veniunt.   Confestim signa mota relic-
tisque impedimentis castrorum cum[2] valido praesidio
raptim agitur agmen ; nec procul ab hoste locum
perexiguum, ut quibus praeter equos ceterorum
iumentorum calonumque turba abesset, castris cepit.
7   Samnitium exercitus, velut haud ulla mora pugnae
futura esset, aciem instruit ; deinde, postquam nemo
obvius ibat, infestis signis ad castra hostium succedit.
8 Ibi ut militem in vallo vidit missique ab omni parte

---

[1] bubus privis binisque tunicis *Weissenborn*: singulis
bobus binisque priuis O_5: singulis b. priuisque binisque
(bonisque *T*) HT^1DLAR: singulis b. binisque $MPFUT^2$
(or T^1) A^2 (or A^3) R^2 (but P^1 has priuisque *in marg.*).
[2] castrorum cum $_5$: cum castrorum *Madvig*: ac castrorum
Weissenborn: castrorum Ω: castrorumque *Klock*.

---

[1] This decoration was next in importance to the *corona
aurea* or *triumphalis*. It was made of green grass plucked
from the place which had been beleaguered.

B.C.
345–343

hill with him were rewarded with a double ration
in perpetuity, and for the present an ox apiece and
two tunics. Following the consul's award, the
legions placed on Decius's head a wreath of grass,[1]
to signify his rescuing them from a siege; and his
own detachment crowned him with a second wreath,
indicative of the same honour. Adorned with these
insignia, he sacrificed the choice ox to Mars, and
presented the hundred others to the soldiers who
had served with him on the expedition. To these
same soldiers the legions contributed a pound of
spelt and a pint of wine for each man. All these
awards were carried out amid the greatest cheerfulness, the shouts of the soldiers testifying to the
general approval.

A third engagement was fought at Suessula,
for the Samnites, after the rout inflicted on them
by Marcus Valerius, had called out all the men
they had of military age, determined to try
their fortune in a final encounter. From Suessula
the alarming news was carried to Capua, whence
gallopers were dispatched to Valerius the consul, to
implore assistance. The troops were immediately
set in motion, and leaving behind the baggage and
a strong garrison for the camp, made a rapid march,
and being got within a short distance of the enemy,
encamped in a very small compass, for they had
only their horses with them and neither beasts of
burden nor a crowd of camp-followers.

The Samnites, assuming that the battle would
not be delayed, formed up in line; then, as no
one came out to meet them, they advanced against
the enemy's camp. When they saw the soldiers on
the rampart, and when the scouts whom they had

LIVY

exploratum quam [1] in exiguum orbem contracta
castra essent — paucitatem inde hostium colligentes

9 — rettulerunt, fremere omnis acies complendas esse
fossas scindendumque vallum et in castra inrum-
pendum ; transactumque ea temeritate bellum foret,

10 ni duces continuissent impetum militum. Ceterum,
quia multitudo sua commeatibus gravis et prius
sedendo ad Suessulam et tum certaminis mora haud
procul ab rerum omnium inopia esset, placuit, dum
inclusus paveret hostis, frumentatum per agros

11 militem duci : interim quieto [2] Romano, qui expedi-
tus quantum umeris inter arma geri posset frumenti
secum attulisset, defutura omnia.

12   Consul palatos per agros cum vidisset hostes,
stationes infrequentes relictas, paucis milites adhor-

13 tatus ad castra oppugnanda ducit. Quae cum primo
clamore atque impetu cepisset, pluribus hostium
in tentoriis suis quam in portis valloque caesis,
signa captiva in unum locum conferri iussit relic-
tisque duabus legionibus custodiae et praesidii causa
gravi edicto monitis ut, donec ipse revertisset,

14 praeda abstinerent, profectus agmine instructo, cum
praemissus eques velut indagine dissipatos Samnites

15 ageret, caedem ingentem fecit. Nam neque quo

---

[1] quam ς : quamquam $\Omega^{.}_{.}$: quia F^3 : postquam quam
Alschefski.

[2] quieto A^2 or $A^1\varsigma$: quia et Ω : quia M : et A ; *deleted by*
Madvig.

dispatched to spy out the camp on every hand B.C.
345-343 reported how straitened its dimensions were, inferring thence the paucity of their foes, the whole army began to murmur that they ought to fill up the trenches, breach the rampart, and burst into the enclosure; and their rashness would have brought the war to a conclusion, had not the commanders restrained the ardour of their men. But since their numbers were a burden on the commissariat, and since, owing first to their sitting down before Suessula and afterwards to the delay in fighting, they were almost reduced to want for everything, they decided that while the enemy were cowering within their works, they would send their soldiers over the country-side to forage: meantime the Romans, remaining inactive, would be reduced to destitution, for they had come in light marching order, with only so much corn as they could carry, along with their armour, on their shoulders.

Seeing the Samnites dispersed about the fields, and their stations thinly manned, the consul addressed a few words of encouragement to his soldiers and led them to the assault of the enemy's camp. Having taken it at the first shout and rush, and slain more men in their tents than at the gates and on the breastworks, he ordered the captured standards to be collected in one spot. Then, leaving two legions to guard them and defend the place,— with strict injunctions to refrain from spoiling until he himself returned,—he marched out in serried column, and sending the cavalry on before to surround the scattered Samnites, as with a cordon of hunters, and so drive them in, he made a prodigious slaughter of them. For in their terror they were

LIVY

signo coirent [1] inter se neque utrum castra peterent
an longiorem intenderent fugam, territis constare
16 poterat; tantumque fugae ac formidinis fuit ut ad
quadraginta milia scutorum — nequaquam tot caesis
— et signa militaria cum iis [2] quae in castris capta
erant ad centum septuaginta ad consulem defer-
17 rentur. Tum in castra hostium reditum ibique
omnis praeda militi data.

XXXVIII. Huius certaminis fortuna et Faliscos,
cum in indutiis essent, foedus petere ab senatu
coegit et Latinos iam exercitibus comparatis ab
2 Romano in Paelignum vertit bellum. Neque ita
rei gestae fama Italiae se finibus tenuit, sed Car-
thaginienses quoque legatos gratulatum Romam
misere cum coronae aureae dono, quae in Capitolio
in Iovis cella poneretur; fuit pondo viginti quinque.
3 Consules ambo de Samnitibus triumpharunt sequente
Decio insigni cum laude donisque, cum incondito
militari ioco haud minus tribuni celebre nomen
quam consulum esset.
4 Campanorum deinde Suessulanorumque [3] auditae
legationes, precantibusque datum ut praesidium eo
in hiberna mitteretur, quo Samnitium excursiones
arcerentur.
5 Iam tum minime salubris militari disciplinae
Capua instrumento omnium voluptatium delenitos

---

[1] coirent $T^2A^3\overline{\jmath}$: coire Ω.
[2] cum iis M?: cum is M^1 or M^2 (*over erasure*): cum hiis A^2
(*over erasure*): cum his $PFOT^2$: cunctis $HTDL$.
[3] Suessulanorumque A^3 *Sigonius*: Suessanorumq. (*illegible
in O*) Ω.

494

unable to agree either under what standard they should rally, or whether they should make for their camp or direct their flight towards some more remote place; and so great was their discomfiture and panic, that the Romans brought in to the consul no less than forty thousand shields—though not near so many men were slain—and of military standards, including those which had been captured in the camp, no fewer than a hundred and seventy. The victors then returned to the enemy's camp and there the plunder was all given to the soldiers.

B.C.
345–343

XXXVIII. The fortunate outcome of this war not only impelled the Faliscans, with whom there was a truce, to ask the senate for a treaty, but caused the Latins, whose armies were ready to take the field, to transfer their attack from Rome to the Paeligni. Nor was the fame of this success confined to Italy; even the Carthaginians sent their envoys to Rome, with congratulations and the gift of a golden crown, weighing five and twenty pounds, to be placed in the shrine of Jupiter on the Capitol. Both consuls triumphed over the Samnites, and after them came Decius, conspicuous in his decorations and so renowned, that the soldiers in their rude jests named the tribune no less often than the consuls.

B.C. 342

The deputations of the Campanians and the Suessulani were then heard, and a favourable reply was made to their petition that a garrison should be dispatched, to remain through the winter with them and protect them against inroads by the Samnites.

Capua was even then a far from wholesome place for military discipline, and with its means for grati-

LIVY

militum animos avertit a memoria patriae inibantur-
que consilia in hibernis eodem scelere adimendae
Campanis Capuae per quod illi eam antiquis cul-
6 toribus ademissent : neque immerito suum ipsorum
exemplum in eos versurum. Cur autem potius
Campani agrum Italiae uberrimum, dignam agro
urbem, qui nec se nec sua tutari possent, quam
victor exercitus haberet qui suo sudore ac sanguine
7 inde Samnites depulisset? An aequum esse dediticios
suos illa fertilitate atque amoenitate perfrui, se
militando fessos in pestilenti atque arido circa urbem
solo luctari aut in urbe insidentem labem[1] crescentis
in dies fenoris pati?

8   Haec. agitata occultis coniurationibus necdum
volgata in omnes consilia invenit novus consul C.
Marcius Rutulus,[2] cui Campania sorte provincia even-
9 erat, Q. Servilio collega ad urbem relicto. Itaque
cum omnia ea, sicut gesta erant, per tribunos com-
perta haberet et aetate[3] et usu doctus, quippe qui
iam quartum consul esset dictatorque et censor
fuisset, optimum ratus differendo spem quandocumque vellent consilii exsequendi militarem impetum frustrari,[4] rumorem dissipat in iisdem oppidis

---

[1] labem Ω : tabem $P^2 T^2_5$.
[2] Rutulus H : rutilius Ω : rutilius F.
[3] haberet et aetate $H^1 T^1 A^2$ (or A^3) $_5$: et aetate haberet
Ω : et aetate *omitted by* $D^2 A$.
[4] frustrari $T^2 D^3$: frustrare Ω : frustrarem omnem A^2
(frustrare A ?) : frustare U.

---

[1] *i. e.* the Etruscans, see IV. xxxvii. 2.

fying every pleasure proved so fascinating to the
soldiers that they forgot their native land, and
formed a project, while in winter quarters, for
taking the city away from the Campanians by the
same wicked practice by which the Campanians had
taken it from its ancient inhabitants.[1] There would
be a certain justice, they argued, in turning their
own example against them. Besides, why should the
most fertile land in Italy, and a city worthy of the
land, belong to the Campanians, who were incapable
of defending either themselves or their possessions?
Why, rather, should it not belong to the conquering
army, which had toiled and bled to drive the
Samnites out of it? Was it fair that their surrendered subjects should enjoy that fertile and
agreeable tract, while they, exhausted with campaigning, wrestled with the arid and noxious soil
in the neighbourhood of Rome, or endured the
ruinous usury that had fastened on the City and
was increasing from one day to the next?

These schemes, discussed in secret cabals and not
yet communicated to all the troops, were discovered
by the new consul, Gaius Marcius Rutulus, to whom
the lot had assigned Campania for his province,
leaving Quintus Servilius, his colleague, in charge
at Rome. And so having found out through his
tribunes exactly what had taken place, Rutulus,
who was of ripe years and experience,—for the
present consulship was his fourth and he had been
both dictator and censor—thought that his best
course would be to frustrate the men's impetuosity,
by encouraging the hope that they would be able
at any time they chose to carry out their plan. He
accordingly set on foot a rumour that the garrisons

497

10 et anno post praesidia hibernatura — divisa enim
erant per Campaniae urbes, manaverantque a Capua
consilia in exercitum omnem. Eo laxamento cogi-
tationibus dato quievit in praesentia seditio.

XXXIX. Consul educto in aestiva milite, dum
quietos Samnites habebat, exercitum purgare mis-
sionibus turbulentorum hominum instituit, aliis
emerita dicendo stipendia esse, alios graves iam
2 aetate aut viribus parum validos. Quidam in commeatus mittebantur, singuli primo, deinde et cohortes
quaedam, quia procul ab domo ac rebus suis hibernassent; per speciem etiam militarium usuum, cum
3 alii alio mitterentur, magna pars ablegati. Quam
multitudinem consul alter Romae praetorque alias
4 ex aliis fingendo moras retinebat. Et primo quidem
ignari ludificationis minime inviti domos revisebant;
postquam neque reverti ad signa primos nec ferme
alium quam qui in Campania hibernassent praeci-
pueque ex his seditionis auctores mitti viderunt,
primum admiratio, deinde haud dubius timor incessit
5 animos consilia sua emanasse: iam quaestiones, iam
indicia, iam occulta singulorum supplicia impo-
tensque et crudele consulum ac patrum in se regnum
6 passuros. Haec qui in castris erant occultis sermoni-

498

would winter in the same towns in the following
year also,—for they had been distributed among
the cities of Campania and from Capua their designs
had spread to the entire army,—and the conspirators
being thus afforded time for breathing, the sedition
subsided for the present.

XXXIX. The consul having led out his troops to
the summer encampment, and finding the Samnites
quiet, resolved to purge the army of its trouble-
makers by discharging them. Of some of them he
said that they had served out their time ; of others,
that they were now too old or deficient in sturdiness.
To some he granted furlough, singling out individuals at first, but later dismissing certain cohorts,
on the ground that they had passed the winter far
from their homes and their affairs. Many, too, were
sent off on some pretext of military employment,
some one way, some another. All these the other
consul and the praetor detained at Rome, alleging a
variety of reasons. And at first, not suspecting a
trick, they were far from sorry to visit their homes
again. Later on, when they saw that the first to go
failed to rejoin the colours, and that practically none
were dismissed but those who had wintered in
Campania, and particularly such of these as had
encouraged the conspiracy, they marvelled at first,
and presently began to entertain very definite fears
that their designs had come to light : soon there
would be investigations, soon informations would
be lodged, they would soon be punished in secret,
one by one, and would be made to feel the un-
restrained and cruel despotism with which the
consuls and the senate governed them. Such were
the fears that were secretly put about by the soldiers

499

LIVY

A.U.C.
412
bus serunt, nervos coniurationis electos [1] arte consulis
cernentes.

7 Cohors una, cum haud procul Anxure [2] esset, ad
Lautulas saltu angusto inter mare ac montes consedit
ad excipiendos quos consul aliis atque aliis, ut ante
8 dictum est, causis mittebat. Iam valida admodum
numero manus erat nec quicquam ad iusti exercitus
formam praeter ducem deerat. Incompositi itaque
praedantes in agrum Albanum perveniunt et sub
9 iugo Albae Longae castra vallo cingunt. Perfecto
inde opere reliquum diei de imperatore sumendo
sententiis decertant, nulli ex praesentibus satis
10 fidentes: quem autem ab Roma posse exciri? quem
patrum aut plebis esse qui aut se tanto periculo
sciens offerat aut cui ex iniuria insanientis exercitus
11 causa recte committatur? Postero die cum eadem
deliberatio teneret, ex praedatoribus vagis quidam
compertum attulerunt T. Quinctium in Tusculano
12 agrum colere, urbis honorumque immemorem. Patriciae hic vir gentis erat, cui cum militiae magna
cum gloria actae finem pes alter ex volnere claudus
fecisset, ruri agere vitam procul ambitione ac foro
13 constituit. Nomine audito extemplo agnovere virum
et, quod bene verteret, acciri iusserunt. Sed parum

---

[1] electos *Gebhard* : eiectos Ω *Frag. Haverk.* ϛ : exsectos
Claud Dupuy.
[2] Anxure ϛ: anxur ϛ: anxyr Ω.

---

[1] Later called Tarracina.
[2] As Livy has mentioned no particular grievance, it is
supposed that he refers to the oppressive usury.

B.C. 342

in the camp, for they saw that the sinews of their plot had been plucked out by the consul's artifice.

One cohort which was stationed not far from Anxur[1] went into camp near Lautulae, in the narrow pass between the sea and the mountains, where they could intercept those whom the consul continued to dismiss, on one pretext or another, as has been said before. They were soon a very numerous body, and lacked no essential element of an army except a general. And so, without order, and pillaging as they went, they proceeded as far as the Alban country, and under the ridge of Alba Longa encamped and threw up a rampart. Having finished the work, they employed the remainder of the day in wrangling over the choice of a general, for they had no great confidence in any-one there present. But whom could they summon from Rome? What patrician or plebeian was there who would wittingly expose himself to so great a danger, or to whom the cause of the army, maddened by its wrongs,[2] could fitly be committed? On the following day, while they were debating the same question, certain of their roving foragers reported having learned that Titus Quinctius was living on a farm near Tusculum, with no thoughts of the City or its honours. This man, who belonged to a noble family, had won great distinction in the wars, but a lameness in one of his feet, resulting from a wound, had put an end to his campaigning, and had determined him to take up his residence in the country, far from the Forum and from politics. On hearing his name they remembered the man at once, and bade send for him, invoking a blessing on this step. But there being little prospect that

A.U.C.
412 spei erat voluntate quicquam facturum ; vim adhiberi
14 ac metum placuit. Itaque silentio noctis cum tectum
villae qui ad id missi erant intrassent, somno gravem
Quinctium oppressum, nihil medium aut imperium
atque honorem aut ubi restitaret mortem ni seque-
15 retur denuntiantes, in castra pertraxerunt. Imperator extemplo adveniens appellatus, insigniaque
honoris exterrito subitae rei miraculo deferunt et
16 ad urbem ducere iubent. Suo magis inde impetu
quam consilio ducis convolsis signis infesto agmine
ad lapidem octavum viae quae nunc Appia est
17 perveniunt; issentque confestim ad urbem, ni venire
contra exercitum dictatoremque adversus se M.
Valerium Corvum dictum audissent et magistrum
equitum L. Aemilium Mamercum.

XL. Ubi primum in conspectum ventum est et [1]
arma signaque agnovere, extemplo omnibus memoria
2 patriae iras permulsit. Nondum erant tam fortes ad
sanguinem civilem nec praeter externa noverant
bella, ultimaque rabies secessio ab suis habebatur ;
itaque iam duces, iam milites utrimque congressus
3 quaerere ac conloquia;—Quinctius, quem armorum
etiam pro patria satietas teneret, nedum adversus

---

[1] est et *Duker* : est (*wanting in O*) Ω.

he would voluntarily assist them, they resolved on B.C. 342
employing threats and violence. Coming therefore
to his farm-house in the silence of the night, those
who had been dispatched upon this errand caught
Quinctius sound asleep, and offering him no choice
but authority and rank, or death,—with which, when
he held back, they threatened him, unless he would
go along with them—they carried him off to the
camp. Once there they immediately hailed him
General, and dazed as he was by the astounding
suddenness of it all, conferred on him the insignia
of that office and bade him lead them to the City.
Then, more on their own impulse than by the
counsel of their general, they pulled up their
standards and marched in warlike array as far as
the eighth milestone, on what is now the Appian
Way; whence they would at once have gone on
to the City, had they not learned that an army was
coming to oppose them, under Marcus Valerius
Corvus, who had been created dictator for that
purpose, with Lucius Aemilius Mamercus as master
of the horse.

XL. As soon as they came within sight of one
another and recognized one another's arms and ensigns, all were at once reminded of their fatherland,
and their anger cooled. Men were not yet so hardy
in shedding the blood of countrymen; they knew
no wars but those with outside nations, and thought
that frenzy could go no further than secession from
their people. And so on either side both the
leaders and their men began to seek for ways
to meet and confer together. For Quinctius
was sated with war, even war in behalf of his
country, to say nothing of fighting against it;

LIVY

patriam, Corvinus omnes caritate cives, praecipue milites, et ante alios suum exercitum, complexus. 4 Is ad[1] conloquium processit. Cognito ei extemplo haud minore[2] ab adversariis verecundia quam ab suis silentium datum.

"Deos" inquit "immortales, milites, vestros[3] meosque ab urbe proficiscens ita adoravi veniamque supplex poposci ut mihi de vobis concordiae partae 5 gloriam non victoriam darent. Satis fuit eritque unde belli decus pariatur: hinc pax petenda est. Quod deos immortales inter nuncupanda vota exposci, eius me compotem voti vos facere potestis, 6 si meminisse voltis non vos in Samnio nec in Volscis, sed in Romano solo castra habere, si illos colles quos cernitis patriae vestrae esse, si hunc exercitum civium vestrorum, si me consulem vestrum, cuius ductu auspicioque priore anno bis legiones Sam-7 nitium fudistis, bis castra vi cepistis. Ego sum M. Valerius Corvus, milites, cuius vos nobilitatem beneficiis erga vos, non iniuriis, sensistis, nullius superbae in vos legis, nullius crudelis senatus consulti auctor, in omnibus meis imperiis in me severior quam in 8 vos. Ac si cui genus, si cui sua virtus, si cui etiam maiestas, si cui honores subdere spiritus potuerunt, iis[4] eram natus, id specimen mei dederam, ea aetate consulatum adeptus eram, ut potuerim tres et viginti

---

[1] is ad *Madvig*: ad Ω.
[2] minore *Perizonius*: minor Ω: minor eius L.
[3] vestros *H. J. Mueller*: uestros publicos Ω.
[4] iis ς: his U: is Ω.

and the affection of Corvinus embraced all his B.C. 342
fellow-citizens, particularly the soldiers, and above
all others, his own army. He now came forward to
parley, and being recognized, was instantly accorded
a silent attention, in which his opponents showed as
great respect for him as did his followers.

"Soldiers," he began, "as I was setting forth
from the City, I adored your gods and mine, and
humbly besought them of their goodness to vouch-
safe to me the glory of reconciling, not of conquering you. There have been wars in plenty,
and will be others, where men may win renown : in
this crisis we must seek for peace. The petition
which I made to the immortal gods, as I offered
up my prayer, you are able of yourselves to grant
me, if you are willing to reflect that your camp is
pitched not in Samnium nor among the Volsci, but
on Roman soil; that those hills which you see
are in your native land; that this army is made
up of your fellow-citizens; that I am your consul,
under whose command and auspices you twice
last year defeated the Samnite legions, and twice
stormed their camp. I am Marcus Valerius Corvus,
soldiers, whose patrician blood has declared itself in
kindnesses done you, not in injuries ; I have urged
no insolent law against you, no cruel senatorial
resolution ; in every position of authority I have
been sterner to myself than to you. And in truth
if any man's family, if any man's own worth, if any
man's dignities and honours have been able to inspire pride in him, my birth was such, l had given
such proof of my capacity, and had achieved so
young the highest magistracy, that I might easily,
on becoming consul at the age of three and twenty,

LIVY

annos natus consul patribus quoque ferox esse non
9 solum plebi. Quod meum factum dictumve consulis
gravius quam tribuni audistis? Eodem tenore duo
insequentes consulatus gessi, eodem haec imperiosa
dictatura geretur; ut neque[1] in hos meos et patriae
meae milites sim mitior[2] quam in vos — horreo
10 dicere — hostes. Ergo vos prius in me strinxeritis
ferrum quam in vos ego; istinc signa canent, istinc
clamor prius incipiet atque impetus, si dimicandum
11 est. Inducite in animum quod non induxerunt
patres avique vestri, non illi qui in Sacrum montem
secesserunt, non hi qui postea Aventinum insederunt.
12 Exspectate, dum vobis singulis, ut olim Coriolano,
matres coniugesque crinibus passis obviae ab urbe
veniant! Tum Volscorum legiones, quia Romanum
habebant ducem, quieverunt: vos, Romanus exer-
13 citus, ne destiteritis impio bello? T. Quincti, quocumque istic loco seu volens seu invitus constitisti,
si dimicandum erit, tum tu in novissimos te recipito;
fugeris etiam honestius tergumque civi dederis quam
14 pugnaveris contra patriam. Nunc ad pacificandum
bene atque honeste inter primos stabis et conloquii
huius salutaris interpres fueris. Postulate aequa et
ferte; quamquam vel iniquis standum est potius
quam impias inter nos conseramus manus.''

---

[1] ut neque Ω : neque *Heusinger.*
[2] sim mitior *Walters and Conway* : mitior sim $A^2\varsigma$: mitior
Ω : militio *H.*

---

[1] See II. xxxii and III. l.   [2] See II. xl.

B.C. 342

have been overbearing even towards the nobles, not merely towards the plebs. But what have you heard that I said or did, when consul, more tyrannical than my words and deeds as tribune? In that same spirit I administered two subsequent consulships; in that same spirit shall this dictatorship with its dread power be administered; so that I shall be no gentler to these my soldiers and the soldiers of my country, than to you—I shudder to say the word,—our enemies. You shall therefore sooner draw sword on me than I on you. It is on your side that the trumpets will sound, on your side that the battle-cry will be raised and the attack begin, if fight we must. Steel your hearts to do that which neither your fathers nor yet your grand-fathers could resolve upon—neither those who seceded to the Sacred Mount, nor those who later encamped upon the Aventine.[1] Wait until to each of you—as once to Coriolanus [2]—your mothers and wives come forth from the City with dishevelled hair. On that day the legions of the Volsci ceased fighting, because they had a Roman leader : will you, an army of Romans, not relinquish this impious war? Titus Quinctius, whatever be your position over there—whether you have taken it voluntarily or against your will,—if we must do battle, do you retire to the rear; you will even flee with less discredit, turning your back upon your fellow-citizens, than you will incur in fighting against your country. Now, however, to make peace you will stand with honour and credit amongst the foremost, and will be a salutary mediator at this conference. Let your men ask what is reasonable, and receive it ; yet must we rather put up with what is not, than join together in impious strife."

A.U.C.
412 15 T. Quinctius plenus lacrimarum ad suos versus
"Me quoque" inquit, "milites, si quis usus mei
16 est, meliorem pacis quam belli habetis ducem. Non
enim illa modo Volscus aut Samnis sed Romanus
verba fecit, vester consul, vester imperator, milites,
cuius auspicia pro vobis experti nolite adversus vos
17 velle experiri. Qui pugnarent vobiscum infestius,
et alios duces senatus habuit: qui maxime vobis,
suis militibus, parceret, cui plurimum vos, imperatori
18 vestro, crederetis, eum elegit. Pacem etiam qui
vincere possunt volunt; quid nos velle oportet?
19 Quin omissis ira et spe, fallacibus auctoribus, nos
ipsos nostraque omnia cognitae permittimus fidei?"

XLI. Approbantibus clamore cunctis T. Quinctius
ante signa progressus in potestate dictatoris milites
fore dixit; oravit ut causam miserorum civium
susciperet susceptamque eadem fide qua rem publi-
2 cam administrare solitus esset tueretur: sibi se
privatim nihil cavere; nolle alibi quam in innocentia
spem habere; militibus cavendum, quod apud patres
semel plebi iterum legionibus cautum sit ne fraudi
secessio esset.

3 Quinctio conlaudato, ceteris bonum animum habere
iussis, dictator equo citato ad urbem revectus auctori-

---

[1] Livy said nothing of such a stipulation at the time of the
first reconciliation; for the circumstances attending the
second, see II. liv.

Titus Quinctius turned with streaming eyes and B.C. 342 addressed his people: "I, too, soldiers, if I am of any use to you, can better lead you to peace than into war. For it was no Volscian or Samnite that just spoke those words, but a Roman. It was your consul, your general, soldiers. You have proved his auspices in your own behalf; seek not to prove their worth against you. The senate had other leaders who would have made more ruthless war on you; but they have chosen him who would deal most mercifully with you, his men; one in whom, as in your general, you might place the most utter confidence. Peace is the goal desired even by those who are able to conquer: what then ought our desire to be? Nay, let us abandon wrath and hope—deceitful counsellors—and commit ourselves and all our cause to a man of known fidelity!"

XLI. A shout of approval burst from every throat, and Titus Quinctius, advancing in front of the standards, announced that the soldiers would submit to the dictator's authority. He begged him to undertake the cause of his wretched fellow-citizens, and having done so to forward it with the same fidelity with which he had been used to deal with the interests of the state. For himself privately, he said, he demanded no assurance, he had no wish to found a hope on aught but innocence. But the soldiers must be assured, as in their fathers' day the plebs had been, and, on a second occasion, the legions, that they should not be punished for secession.[1]

After praising Quinctius and bidding the rest be of good cheer, the dictator galloped back to the City, and having secured the authority of the

LIVY

bus patribus tulit ad populum in luco Petelino,[1] ne
cui militum fraudi secessio esset. Oravit etiam
bona venia Quirites ne quis eam rem ioco seriove
4 cuiquam exprobraret. Lex quoque sacrata militaris
lata est ne cuius militis scripti nomen nisi ipso
volente deleretur; additumque legi ne quis, ubi
tribunus militum fuisset, postea ordinum ductor
5 esset. Id propter P. Salonium postulatum est ab
coniuratis, qui alternis prope annis et tribunus militum et primus centurio erat, quem nunc primi pili
6 appellant. Huic infensi milites erant, quod semper
adversatus novis consiliis fuisset et, ne particeps
7 eorum esset, ab Lautulis fugisset.[2] Itaque cum hoc
unum propter Salonium ab senatu non impetraretur,
tum Salonius obtestatus patres conscriptos ne suum
honorem pluris quam concordiam civitatis aesti-
8 marent, perpulit ut id quoque ferretur. Aeque impotens postulatum fuit ut de stipendio equitum
— merebant autem triplex ea tempestate — aera
demerentur, quod adversati coniurationi fuissent.

XLII. Praeter haec invenio apud quosdam L.
Genucium tribunum plebis tulisse ad plebem ne

---

[1] Petelino ς: petillini Ω: petelini U: pollutum O.
[2] fugisset *Rubenius*: fugissent (*with* qui *before* ab Lautulis)
Ω: *nothing after* qui *in* O.

---

[1] *cf.* VI. xx. 11 and note there.
[2] Whoever broke a *lex sacrata* was *ipso facto* consecrated to
the lower gods, and became an outlaw.
[3] The law protected insolvent debtors, whose goods might
not be seized so long as they were in the service, and also
assured the soldier of his rightful share of such emoluments
as the campaign might produce. With regard to the addition, the commentators are doubtful what its object was;
perhaps it was felt as unfair to the rest that one who had
enjoyed the (elective) tribuneship should next year be

Fathers, got the people to enact a law, in the B.C. 342
Peteline Wood,[1] that none of the soldiers should
be held to answer for the secession. He begged
them also, as citizens, to grant him the favour that
none would make the incident a matter of reproach
to any, either in jest or in earnest. There was also
passed a military law, under penalty of devotion,[2]
to the effect that the name of no one enrolled as
a soldier might be struck off the list, except with
his own consent. To this a provision was added
that no one might later command a century in the
legion where he had been a military tribune.[3]
This clause was demanded by the conspirators on
account of Publius Salonius, who in almost regular
alternation was tribune of the soldiers one year, and
chief centurion—whom they now call " centurion of
the first javelin "—the next. The men were incensed at Salonius because he had always opposed
their mutinous schemes, and had fled from Lautulae
that he might not share in them. And so, when
this one provision would have failed of enactment
by the senate, out of consideration for Salonius, he
himself besought the Fathers not to think more
highly of his distinction than of harmony in the
state, and induced them to pass this also. An
equally shameless demand was made that the pay
of the cavalry should be reduced—they served at
that time for treble pay—on the ground that they
had opposed the conspiracy.

XLII. In addition to these transactions, I find in
certain writers that Lucius Genucius, a tribune of
the plebs, proposed to the plebs that it should be

appointed to the but slightly less desirable post of first
centurion.

A.U.C.
412

2 fenerare liceret; item aliis plebi scitis cautum ne
quis eundem magistratum intra decem annos caperet
neu duos magistratus uno anno gereret utique liceret
consules ambos plebeios creari. Quae si omnia
concessa sunt plebi, apparet haud parvas vires de-
3 fectionem habuisse. Aliis annalibus proditum est
neque dictatorem Valerium dictum sed per consules
omnem rem actam, neque antequam Romam veniretur sed Romae eam multitudinem coniuratorum
4 ad arma consternatam esse nec in T. Quincti villam
sed in aedes C. Manli[1] nocte impetum factum
eumque a coniuratis comprehensum ut dux fieret;
inde ad quartum lapidem profectos loco munito
5 consedisse; nec ab ducibus mentionem concordiae
ortam sed repente, cum in aciem armati exercitus
6 processissent, salutationem factam et permixtos
dextras iungere ac complecti inter se lacrimantes
milites coepisse coactosque consules, cum viderent
aversos a dimicatione militum animos, rettulisse
7 ad patres de concordia reconcilianda. Adeo nihil
praeterquam seditionem fuisse eamque compositam
inter antiquos rerum auctores constat.

8   Et huius fama seditionis et susceptum cum Samnitibus grave bellum aliquot populos ab Romana
societate avertit, et praeter Latinorum infidum iam
diu foedus Privernates etiam Norbam[2] atque Setiam, finitimas colonias Romanas, incursione subita
depopulati sunt.

---

[1] Manli ς: manili Ω: manilii U^2O: mallii U: malli D^3.
[2] Norbam A^2 (or A^4) ς: norbē F^3: norbę $MPOT$: norbae
U: orbe LA.

unlawful to lend at interest. Also that it was B.C. 342
provided in other plebiscites that no one might hold
the same office twice within ten years, nor two
offices in one year; and that it should be legal
for both consuls to be chosen from the plebs. If all
these concessions were made to the commons, it is
evident that the revolt possessed no little strength.
Other annalists have recorded that Valerius was not
made dictator, but that the whole affair was managed
through the consuls, and that it was not before they
came to Rome, but in Rome, that this great company
of conspirators was dismayed into arming; further,
that the night attack was made, not on the farm of
Titus Quinctius, but on the town house of Gaius
Manlius, and that it was he whom the conspirators
seized and made their leader. Thence they proceeded
—according to this account—to the fourth milestone,
where they entrenched a camp. Nor was it the
leaders who suggested a reconciliation, but suddenly,
when the two armies had marched out in battle array,
salutations were exchanged, and the soldiers, mingling
together, began tearfully to clasp hands and embrace
each other, so that the consuls, seeing the men to be
in no mood for fighting, had been compelled to lay
proposals before the senate for the re-establishment of
harmony. Thus in no single instance do the ancient
authorities agree, except that there was a sedition,
and that it was composed.

The report of this sedition, in conjunction with the
dangerous war entered upon with the Samnites, caused
several nations to forsake their alliance with the
Romans, and not only were the Latins unfaithful to
the treaty—as they had been for some time—but the
Privernates even, in a sudden raid, laid waste the
neighbouring Roman colonies of Norba and Setia.

LIBRI VII PERIOCHA

Duo novi magistratus adiecti sunt, praetura et curulis aedilitas. Pestilentia civitas laboravit, eamque insignem fecit mors Furi Camilli. Cuius remedium et finis cum per novas religiones quaereretur, ludi scaenici tunc primum facti sunt. Cum dies L. Manlio dicta esset a M. Pomponio tribuno pl. propter dilectum acerbe actum et T. Manlium filium rus relegatum sine ullo crimine, adulescens ipse cuius relegatio patri obiciebatur venit in cubiculum tribuni strictoque gladio coegit eum in verba sua iurare se non perseveraturum in accusatione. Tunc omnia pretiosa missa sunt in praealtam voraginem urbis Romanae. In eam Curtius armatus sedens equo praecipitavit; ita expleta.[1] T. Manlius adulescens, qui patrem a tribunicia vexatione vindicaverat, contra Gallum provocantem aliquem ex militibus Romanis in singulare certamen descendit[2] eique occiso torquem aureum detraxit, quem ipse postea tulit et ex eo Torquatus vocatus est. Duae tribus adiectae, Pomptina et Publilia. Licinius Stolo lege lata damnatus est, quod plus quingentis iugeribus agri possideret. M. Valerius tribunus militum Gallum a quo provocatus erat, insidente galeae corvo et unguibus rostroque hostem infestante, occidit et ex eo Corvi nomen accepit consulque proximo anno, cum annos xxiii habe-

---

[1] ita expleta *Weissenborn*: ex plet *or* expletat *or* expleta. t. *or* exiit *MSS.*

[2] descendit *omitted by all the MSS. but one* (*r*): processit *coni.* Rossbach (*Liv.* VII. xxvi. 2).

514

SUMMARY OF BOOK VII

Two new magistracies were added, the praetorship and the curule aedileship. The citizens were afflicted with a pestilence, and this the death of Furius Camillus rendered memorable. While a remedy for stopping it was being sought in new religious observances, scenic exhibitions were given for the first time. Lucius Manlius having been cited by Marcus Pomponius, tribune of the plebs, to answer for his ruthless conduct of the levy and for having relegated his son to the country without making any charge against him, the young man himself whose relegation was being used against his father entered the bed-room of the tribune, and drawing his sword, compelled him to swear, after a form which he dictated to him, that he would not go on with the prosecution. At this time all sorts of precious things were cast into a chasm which had opened to a great depth in Rome. Into it leaped Curtius, fully armed and bestriding his horse; and so it was closed over. Titus Manlius, the youth who had saved his father from the persecution of the tribune, went down to confront a Gaul who had challenged any Roman soldier to single combat; and, having slain him, took from him a golden necklace, which he afterwards wore himself and from it was given the name of Torquatus. Two tribes were added, the Pomptina and the Publilia. Licinius Stolo was condemned, under a statute that had been enacted, because he possessed more than five hundred *iugera* of land. Marcus Valerius, a tribune of the soldiers, killed a Gaul by whom he had been challenged, while a raven perched on the Roman's crest and with beak and talons attacked his enemy; from this circumstance he received the name of Corvus, and the next year was, for his bravery, elected

515

ret, ob virtutem creatus est. Amicitia cum Carthagini-
ensibus iuncta est. Campani cum a Samnitibus bello
urgerentur, auxilio adversus eos a senatu petito, cum id
non inpetrarent, urbem et agros populo R. dediderunt.
Ob quam causam ea quae populi Romani facta essent,
defendi bello adversus Samnites placuit. Cum ab Aulo
Cornelio cos. exercitus in locum inicum deductus in magno
discrimine esset, P. Deci Muris[1] tribuni militum opera
servatus est, qui occupato colle super id iugum in quo
Samnites consederant occasionem consuli in aequiorem
locum evadendi dedit; ipse ab hostibus circumsessus
erupit.[2] Cum milites Romani qui Capuae in praesidio
relicti erant de occupanda ea urbe conspirassent et detecto
consilio metu supplici a populo R. defecissent, per M.
Valerium Corvum dictatorem, qui consilio suo eos a furore
revocaverat, patriae restituti sunt. Res praeterea contra
Hernicos et Gallos et Tiburtes et Privernates et Tarquinienses et Samnites et Vulscos prospere gestas continet.

[1] P. Deci Muris *Sigonius* (*ex vet. libro*): Deci Muris *MSS.*
[2] erupit *edd.*: eripuit *MSS.*

SUMMARY OF BOOK VII

consul, at the age of twenty-three. Friendship was made with the Carthaginians. The Campanians, when hard pressed in war by the Samnites, asked aid against them from the senate, and, failing to obtain it, surrendered their city and territory to the Roman People. In view of this action, the Roman People voted to go to war with the Samnites, to defend these their possessions. The army was led by Aulus Cornelius, the consul, into a difficult position, and was in great danger, but was saved by the act of Publius Decius Mus, a tribune of the soldiers, who by occupying a hill which commanded the ridge on which the Samnites had encamped, afforded the consul an opportunity of withdrawing to more favourable ground; after which, though encircled by the enemy, Decius himself broke through. The Roman soldiers who had been left in garrison at Capua conspired to seize the city, and fearful of punishment, on the detection of their crime, revolted from the Roman People, but were restored to their country through the influence of the dictator, Marcus Valerius Corvus, who by his counsel had recalled them from their madness. The book also comprises victorious campaigns against the Hernici, Gauls, Tiburtes, Privernates, Tarquinienses, Samnites, and Volsci.

INDEX OF NAMES

(The References are to Pages.)

519

INDEX OF NAMES

INDEX OF NAMES

INDEX OF NAMES

INDEX OF NAMES

INDEX OF NAMES

INDEX OF NAMES

Made and Printed in Great Britain.
Richard Clay & Sons, Limited,
Printers, Bungay, Suffolk.

THE LOEB CLASSICAL LIBRARY.

VOLUMES ALREADY PUBLISHED

Latin Authors.

AENEAS TACTICUS, ASCLEPIODOTUS AND ONASANDER.
Trans. by The Illinois Club.

APULEIUS. The Golden Ass (Metamorphoses). Trans. by W. Adlington
(1566). Revised by S. Gaselee. (*2nd Impression.*)

AUSONIUS. Trans. by H. G. Evelyn White. 2 Vols.

BOETHIUS: TRACTS AND DE CONSOLATIONE PHILOSO-
PHIAE. Trans. by Rev. H. F. Stewart and E. K. Rand.

CAESAR: CIVIL WARS. Trans. by A. G. Peskett. (*2nd Impression.*)

CAESAR: GALLIC WAR. Trans. by H. J. Edwards. (*3rd Impression.*)

CATULLUS. Trans. by F. W. Cornish; TIBULLUS. Trans. by J. P.
Postgate; and PERVIGILIUM VENERIS. Trans. by J. W. Mackail.
(*5th Impression.*)

CICERO: DE FINIBUS. Trans. by H. Rackham. (*2nd Impression.*)

CICERO: DE OFFICIIS. Trans. by Walter Miller. (*2nd Impression.*)

CICERO: DE SENECTUTE, DE AMICITIA, DE DIVINATIONE.
Trans. by W. A. Falconer.

CICERO: LETTERS TO ATTICUS. Trans. by E. O. Winstedt.
3 Vols. (Vol. I *3rd Impression.* Vol. II *2nd Impression.*)

CICERO: PRO ARCHIA POETA, POST REDITUM IN SENATU,
POST REDITUM AD QUIRITES, DE DOMO SUA, DE HARUS-
PICUM RESPONSIS, PRO PLANCIO. Trans. by N. H. Watts.

CLAUDIAN. Trans. by M. Platnauer. 2 Vols.

CONFESSIONS OF ST. AUGUSTINE. Trans. by W. Watts (1631).
2 Vols. (*2nd Impression.*)

FRONTO: CORRESPONDENCE. Trans. by C. R. Haines. 2 Vols.

HORACE: ODES AND EPODES. Trans. by C. E. Bennett. (*5th Imp.*)

JUVENAL AND PERSIUS. Trans. by G. G. Ramsay. (*2nd Impression.*)

LIVY. Trans. by B. O. Foster. 13 Vols. Vols. I, II and III.

MARTIAL. Trans. by W. C. Ker. 2 Vols.

OVID: HEROIDES AND AMORES. Trans. by Grant Showerman.
(*2nd Impression.*)

OVID: METAMORPHOSES. Trans. by F. J. Miller. 2 Vols.
(*2nd Edition.*)

PETRONIUS. Trans. by M. Heseltine; SENECA: APOCOLO-
CYNTOSIS. Trans. by W. H. D. Rouse. (*4th Impression.*)

PLAUTUS. Trans. by Paul Nixon. 5 Vols. Vols. I and II. (Vol. I *2nd
Impression.*)

PLINY: LETTERS. Melmoth's Translation revised by W. M. L.
Hutchinson. 2 Vols. (*2nd Impression.*)

PROPERTIUS. Trans. by H. E. Butler. (*3rd Impression.*)

QUINTILIAN. Trans. by H. E. Butler. 4 Vols.

SALLUST. Trans. by J. C. Rolfe.

SCRIPTORES HISTORIAE AUGUSTAE. Trans. by D. Magie.
4 Vols. Vol. I.

SENECA: EPISTULAE MORALES. Trans. by R. M. Gummere.
3 Vols. Vols. I and II.

SENECA: TRAGEDIES. Trans. by F. J. Miller. 2 Vols.

SUETONIUS. Trans. by J. C. Rolfe. 2 Vols. (*2nd Impression.*)

TACITUS: DIALOGUS. Trans. by Sir Wm. Peterson: and AGRICOLA
AND GERMANIA. Trans. by Maurice Hutton. (*2nd Impression.*)

TERENCE. Trans. by John Sargeaunt. 2 Vols. (*3rd Impression.*)

VIRGIL. Trans. by H. R. Fairclough. 2 Vols. (Vol. I *3rd Impression.*
Vol. II *2nd Impression.*)

Greek Authors.

ACHILLES TATIUS. Trans. by S. Gaselee.
AESCHINES. Trans. by C. D. Adams.
AESCHYLUS. Trans. by H. Weir Smyth. 2 Vols. Vol. I.
APOLLODORUS. Trans. by Sir James G. Frazer. 2 Vols.
APOLLONIUS RHODIUS. Trans. by R. C. Seaton. (*2nd Impression.*)
THE APOSTOLIC FATHERS. Trans. by Kirsopp Lake. 2 Vols. (*3rd Impression.*)
APPIAN'S ROMAN HISTORY. Trans. by Horace White. 4 Vols.
CALLIMACHUS AND LYCOPHRON, trans. by A. W. Mair, and ARATUS, trans. by G. R. Mair.
CLEMENT OF ALEXANDRIA. Trans. by Rev. G. W. Butterworth.
DAPHNIS AND CHLOE. Thornley's Translation revised by J. M. Edmonds; and PARTHENIUS. Trans. by S. Gaselee.
DIO CASSIUS: ROMAN HISTORY. Trans. by E. Cary. 9 Vols. Vols. I to VI.
EURIPIDES. Trans. by A. S. Way. 4 Vols. (Vols. I, II and IV *3rd Impression.* Vol. III *2nd Impression.*)
GALEN: ON THE NATURAL FACULTIES. Trans. by A. J. Brock.
THE GREEK ANTHOLOGY. Trans. by W. R. Paton. 5 Vols. (Vols. I and II *2nd Impression.*)
THE GREEK BUCOLIC POETS (THEOCRITUS, BION, MOSCHUS). Trans. by J. M. Edmonds. (*4th Impression.*)
HERODOTUS. Trans. by A. D. Godley. 4 Vols. Vols. I to III.
HESIOD AND THE HOMERIC HYMNS. Trans. by H. G. Evelyn White. (*2nd Impression.*)
HIPPOCRATES. Trans. by W. H. S. Jones. 4 Vols. Vols. I and II.
HOMER: ODYSSEY. Trans. by A. T. Murray 2 Vols. (Vol. I. *2nd Imp.*)
JULIAN. Trans. by Wilmer Cave Wright. 3 Vols.
LUCIAN. Trans. by A. M. Harmon. 8 Vols. Vols. I to III. (Vols. I and II *2nd Impression.*)
LYRA GRAECA. Trans. by J. M. Edmonds. 3 Vols. Vol. I.
MARCUS AURELIUS. Trans. by C. R. Haines. (*2nd Impression.*)
MENANDER. Trans. by F. G. Allinson.
PAUSANIAS: DESCRIPTION OF GREECE. Trans. by W. H. S. Jones. 5 Vols. and Companion Vol. Vol. I.
PHILOSTRATUS: THE LIFE OF APOLLONIUS OF TYANA. Trans. by F. C. Conybeare. 2 Vols. (*2nd Impression.*)
PHILOSTRATUS AND EUNAPIUS, LIVES OF THE SOPHISTS. Trans. by Wilmer Cave Wright.
PINDAR. Trans. by Sir J. E. Sandys. (*3rd Impression.*)
PLATO: EUTHYPHRO, APOLOGY, CRITO, PHAEDO, PHAEDRUS. Trans. by H. N. Fowler (*3rd Impression.*)
PLATO: THEAETETUS AND SOPHIST. Trans. by H. N. Fowler.
PLUTARCH: THE PARALLEL LIVES. Trans. by B. Perrin. 11 Vols. Vols. I to X.
POLYBIUS. Trans. by W. R. Paton. 6 Vols. Vols. I to III.
PROCOPIUS: HISTORY OF THE WARS. Trans. by H. B. Dewing. 7 Vols. Vols. I to III.
QUINTUS SMYRNAEUS. Trans. by A. S. Way.
SOPHOCLES. Trans. by F. Storr. 2 Vols. (Vol. I *5th Impression.* Vol. II *2nd Impression.*)
ST. JOHN DAMASCENE: BARLAAM AND IOASAPH. Trans. by the Rev. G. R. Woodward and Harold Mattingly.
STRABO: GEOGRAPHY. Trans. by Horace L. Jones. 8 Vols. Vols. I and II.
THEOPHRASTUS: ENQUIRY INTO PLANTS. Trans. by Sir Arthur Hort, Bart. 2 Vols.
THUCYDIDES. Trans. by C. F. Smith. 4 Vols.
XENOPHON: CYROPAEDIA. Trans. by Walter Miller. 2 Vols.
XENOPHON: HELLENICA, ANABASIS, APOLOGY, AND SYMPOSIUM. Trans. by C. L. Brownson and O. J. Todd. 3 Vols.
XENOPHON: MEMORABILIA AND OECONOMICUS. Trans. by E. C. Marchant.